YOUTH

IN CONFLICT WITH THE LAW

FOURTH EDITION

YOUTH
IN CONFLICT WITH THE LAW

DENISE WHITEHEAD
and MARK D. HUNTER

CANADIAN
SCHOLARS

Toronto | Vancouver

Youth in Conflict with the Law, Fourth Edition
Denise Whitehead and Mark D. Hunter

First published in 2018 by
Canadian Scholars, an imprint of CSP Books Inc.
425 Adelaide Street West, Suite 200
Toronto, Ontario
M5V 3C1

www.canadianscholars.ca

Library and Archives Canada Cataloguing in Publication

Whitehead, Denise L. (Denise Louise), 1967-, author
      Youth in conflict with the law / Denise Whitehead and Mark Hunter. – Fourth edition.

Includes bibliographical references and index.
Includes text of Youth Criminal Justice Act.
Previous editions written by Paul Maxim and Paul Whitehead.
Includes bibliographical references and index.
Issued in print and electronic formats.
ISBN 978-1-77338-043-8 (softcover).--ISBN 978-1-77338-044-5 (PDF).--
ISBN 978-1-77338-045-2 (EPUB)

      1. Canada. Youth Criminal Justice Act. 2. Juvenile justice, Administration of--Canada--Textbooks. 3. Youth--Legal status, laws, etc.--Canada--Textbooks. 4. Juvenile delinquency--Canada--Textbooks. 5. Textbooks. I. Hunter, Mark, 1963-, author II. Maxim, Paul S., 1950- . Youth in conflict with the law. III. Canada. Youth Criminal Justice Act. IV. Title.

KE9445.W45 2018   345.71'03   C2018-901945-X
KF9780.ZA2W45 2018   C2018-901946-8

Cover and type design by Elisabeth Springate

Printed and bound in Ontario, Canada

Contents

Foreword

Bryan M. Larkin
Chief of Police
Waterloo Regional Police Service

Choosing a career in policing is done with the knowledge that you are choosing a career like no other. It is a decision that will change a person's life forever. The job is a demanding one. It's a dangerous one. It is one that can be routine and unpredictable, traumatizing and heartwarming. But, what makes this job worthwhile, at the end of every single day, is that it is also an extremely rewarding one.

Policing takes you into the lives of people you likely would never meet in any other career and, as such, requires officers to be compassionate and understanding. They must have a passion for helping others while maintaining the safety and wellness of the community.

Throughout my years in policing, I can attest to the fact that there is nothing more gratifying than helping someone turn his or her life around and become a positive contributor to the community. Few tasks, that we take on, in our policing career can compare to that feeling, especially when it involves youth who find themselves in conflict with the law.

Understandably, the justice system is different for youths than it is for adults. The *Youth Criminal Justice Act* recognizes that youth between the ages of 12 and 17 have different needs than adults and, therefore, requires a different approach. This approach is one that aims to deter youth from reoffending and that puts supports in place to help young people take responsibility for their actions, make better choices, and contribute in a positive way to society.

Responses can vary from an officer issuing a warning, a referral being made to a community program or, in more serious cases, seeing a youth charged and sent to a court of law. Sometimes, a form of restorative justice may be recommended where the youth works with the victim and community to decide the proper action to correct whatever crime was committed. This could result in an apology to the victim, restitution, or community service. Whatever the response, the goal is the same—to rehabilitate youth while, at the same time, maintaining public safety in the community.

Because police officers generally have families and children of their own, they have an understanding of the obstacles and challenges faced by parents and youth. In our profession, it is vital that we use our personal experience, coupled with a dedication to community safety, to make the proper decisions when a response to crime is required. After all, policing isn't just about criminalizing bad behaviour. It's about helping those who need help. To do that, it is important that we look at *why* youth are committing crime in the first place and look at ways to deter them from recommitting.

There are several risk factors that have been used to identify at-risk youth and, as police services, it is important that we try to understand the root of these factors to determine the true reason a young person has committed a crime. Sometimes, a sense of alienation or a feeling that they are not accepted by anyone is enough to lead a young person down the wrong path. Low self-esteem, lack of hope, and hanging out with the wrong group of people are also factors that should be considered. This is not to say that everyone who associates with these characteristics will commit a crime. In fact, many times they will not. However, it's up to us—all of us as a community—to work together to help prevent those who may turn to a life of crime and attempt to stop them from recommitting.

While it may be difficult to comprehend, it's important to note that when youth commit crime, they are generally scared, angry, and at their most vulnerable. Instead of labelling them as a "criminal," we should work together to help them. We must help them feel included and valued because, in the end, we know that youth who feel connected to society and who feel a sense of value are the ones who will succeed in life.

This book provides an in-depth look into youth in conflict with the law and how police services work together to ensure the best responses for the safety and well-being of all involved. This edition has been updated to reflect the most up-to-date legislation with, among other informative information, chapters outlining the relationship between young people and the police and the role of restorative justice in our legal system. After reading this book, I have no doubt you will look at youth in conflict in a much different, clearer, more informed way.

Preface

It can feel like an indomitable task to assume the updating and caretaking of a book that has already had three editions. It is even more unnerving when you take over the book from your father (and for Mark, your father-in-law). We are very mindful that we are building this fourth edition on the already well-established and knowledgeable foundation created by Dr. Paul Whitehead and Dr. Paul Maxim. We are indebted to them for their faith and trust in allowing us to be the stewards of this new edition and carry forward their years of teaching, research, and writing on youth and crime.

Some of the changes to this fourth edition include the following:

- Substantial updating on statistics related to youth offending (Chapter 4, "Youth Crime: How Big a Problem?"
- Incorporation of the new *Child, Youth and Family Services Act*. Ontario introduced new legislation in 2017 that resulted in major changes in the acknowledgement of children's rights and a substantial revamping in the applicable section numbers.
- Extensive inclusion of The United Nations Convention on the Rights of the Child. This is now mentioned throughout the text to reflect the importance of this legal document, to which Canada is a signatory.
- An enhanced section on interactions with police with inclusion of the topics of race and ethnicity, carding, and mental health.

TIPS FOR STUDENT LEARNING

Each chapter of the book contains a series of questions designed to test your knowledge through a variety of approaches: definitions, true/false, multiple choice, and short answer. Using these practice questions to review the material is one of the best ways to ascertain whether you have learned and accurately retained the information. I have learned—both as a professor and even more years as a student—that it can be tempting to simply use a highlighter and vigorously mark up various passages in the book. Research, however, has shown that this is one of the *least* effective learning strategies. As Brown, Roediger, and McDaniel discuss in their book *Make It Stick: The Science of Successful Learning* (2014), highlighting and rereading the text are not the most productive strategies for learning. What is effective is *retrieval practice*—recalling facts or concepts or events from memory. Flash cards and practice questions are great examples of this type of practice. In fact, a "quiz" (much like you will find at the end of each chapter) has been shown to result in better learning than rereading the text or even your lecture notes. Simply rereading tends to just leave you with the illusion of knowing rather than giving you true feedback as to whether the knowledge has in fact stuck in your brain. Our advice—actually do the questions—you will do better on the tests and exams!

POLICING AND YOUTH IN CONFLICT WITH THE LAW

Many police officers do not view dealing with young offenders as a very glamorous aspect of policing. From a social point of view, however, dealing with young people who come into conflict with the law is one of the most important parts of policing. Young persons, particularly those who are 16–17 years old, proportionally commit more crimes than any other age group. Criminologists have determined that most serious adult offenders start their criminal careers as young offenders. On the other hand, criminologists know that most young offenders do not go on to become adult criminals.

Despite all of the resources we put in to provide youth with school counsellors, social workers, and child care workers, it is the police who most often meet young people at a time of crisis. It is the police who are called to intervene in domestic disputes between parents, and between parents and their children. The police may be called to intervene when a minor ruckus breaks out on the school grounds or when some young people are being an annoyance in the neighbourhood or at a local shopping mall. They are certainly called when a young person commits a serious infraction of criminal law.

Handling this range of problems is one of the greatest challenges police officers can face. Successful intervention with an angry or misguided young person, or one who comes from a highly dysfunctional family, can be a rewarding experience for the police officer and a benefit for the society. Such interventions do not generate newspaper headlines the way a solved murder or significant fraud case does, but then again, most police officers rarely get to crack a really "big case."

Most police officers do have families, though, and most officers appreciate how difficult it is to raise children. Most are also aware of how difficult growing up can be. These experiences contribute to the good judgment that needs to be exercised in dealing with young people in a wide array of circumstances.

One example of a Toronto police officer generating news headlines happened during the writing of this book. In August 2017, Officer Niran Jeyanesan was called to the local Wal-Mart, where a young 18-year-old man was stealing a shirt, tie, and socks for a job interview. The officer chose to not charge the young man and instead purchased the items that the young man had tried to steal. Technically, at age 18, this person no longer falls under the jurisdiction of the *Youth Criminal Justice Act*, but the officer took the same approach that is used under the *YCJA*—try to understand the action of the individual and form a response that meets the need. In this case, the young man had no money to make the purchases that could benefit him by giving him a second chance if he could get a job. As reported, this officer "exercised his discretion, definitely showed some humanity in dealing with this particular individual." The happy ending as reported: the young man got the job!

There are many ways of writing about young people and the law, even for a targeted audience. In this instance, we have chosen not to deal with legislation in its entirety. Instead, we have chosen to focus on how the *Youth Criminal Justice Act (YCJA)* requires the police to handle young persons in ways different from handling adults.

Terminology

As a final point, both the *YCJA* and the *Criminal Code of Canada* make reference to law enforcement personnel as "peace officers." The term *peace officer*, as defined by the *Criminal Code of Canada*, covers a range of individuals from mayors, to justices of the peace, to police officers, to (in some circumstances) aircraft pilots. Keep this in mind as you read this book and the corresponding legislation.

INSTRUCTORS' MANUAL/TEST BANK

The Instructors' Manual/Test Bank includes the following features that have been requested by professors who used the previous editions:

1. Answers to the definitions, true/false, and multiple choice questions that appear in the text.
2. Additional true/false and multiple choice items, clearly distinguished from the ones that appear in the text that can be used for the purpose of creating examinations; and
3. Supplementary cases for the "You Be the Judge" exercises.

The Instructors' Manual is available in both print and electronic copy. Please contact your local sales representative.

Acknowledgements

From beginning to end this book has benefitted from the guidance and expertise of the wonderful team at Canadian Scholars—Emma Melnyk, Karri Yano, the sharp editorial eye of Wendy Yano, and many others. This book is better for their labours and efforts. We are grateful for their collaborative approach as they steered us through the process.

We are appreciative that Bryan Larkin, Chief of Police of the Waterloo Regional Police Service, was so willing to write the foreword for this book. His narrative and years of police experience help capture the critical role that police serve when dealing with youth who are in conflict with the law. His foreword is a tribute to the critical and positive role that police can play in the lives of citizens, especially our youngest and most vulnerable.

As parents, we are mindful that time spent on a book is less time for our children. Fortunately they are now young adults who need us far less, but nevertheless they are probably tired of hearing about "the book." We are grateful to Laura and Sarah for their patience and understanding as we brought this volume to publication. Such an endeavour is always a family team effort.

D.L.W.
M.D.H.
Kitchener, Ontario
2018

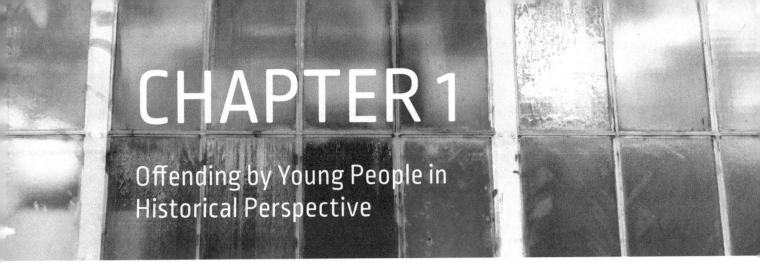

CHAPTER 1

Offending by Young People in Historical Perspective

LEARNING OUTCOMES

Students who have mastered this chapter will have the ability to do the following:

- Identify what *mens rea* and *actus reus* have to do with the notion of offences by young people and adults.
- Explain the view of young people in British common law.
- Know the legal roots of Canadian criminal law.
- Explain how the manner in which children were viewed affected how they were treated and punished.
- Describe the impact of the Industrial Revolution on the legal rights of young people.
- Explain why juvenile criminality became linked to concerns for the social welfare of children.
- Distinguish between "prisons" and "houses of refuge."
- Explain the doctrine of *parens patriae* and its relation to the "child-saving" movement.
- Distinguish between reformatories and how young people were previously jailed.
- Understand the North American roots of the juvenile court.

INTRODUCTION

The study of youth in conflict with the law is a worthy endeavour if for no other reason than that most western countries have separate legal systems to deal with young persons who violate their laws. This is certainly true of the Canadian experience. We have accepted the notion that young people have developmental differences that make them distinct from adults and thus present opportunities or challenges that require separate treatment. This book is an examination of how the Canadian legal system deals with youth who have offended. To understand why we treat youth separately and why we have arrived at our current legislative framework, it is helpful to start with a brief look at how adults are treated.

Adults and the Law

Despite the ruminations of criminologists, explaining how adults run afoul of the criminal justice system is relatively straightforward. Violate the law and, if you are discovered, apprehended, and convicted, you will be sanctioned. Some exceptions exist: for example, the mentally "incompetent" are generally excused. Overall, however, the criminal justice system is a relatively focused instrument of social control when applied to adults.

Actus Reus and Mens Rea: The Elements of a Crime

In examining whether or not an accused committed the offence, the common law, from which our criminal law arose, determined two necessary elements to a crime. The first is the **actus reus**, a Latin phrase that refers to the physical action of committing an offence. The second is **mens rea**, another Latin phrase roughly meaning, "guilty mind." To convict at common law, an accused had to have both committed the act and intended to commit the act. It is on the basis of an absence of *mens rea* that we make allowances for the mentally incompetent. In other words, if a person cannot form the required intent, they ought not to be sanctioned. The *Criminal Code of Canada* carries that tradition forward for some offences (but excludes it from others). To understand the history leading to the decision to treat youth differently from adult offenders, it is sufficient to know that the act and the intention were considered as separate.

Youth and the Law

Young people have been viewed differently from adults in the legal system primarily over issues related to intent. For most of our history, it has been accepted that, at some age, young people are incapable or have diminished capacity to form criminal intent.

Determination of Youth Status

The notion that young people have limited capacities compared to adults has been an underlying constant in our history. The issue for debate has generally revolved around the age at which a young person acquires the intellectual capacities of adulthood. Attempts to measure mental capacity objectively have only achieved some recent success with the growth of developmental psychology. Historically, age was and continues to remain the main indication of intellectual development.

Youth under Seven Years Old

Under English common law—still the basis of the Canadian legal system—young people were not held criminally responsible until they reached the age of seven years. Children less than seven years of age were considered **legal infants** and were assumed not capable of appreciating fully the moral aspects of the law. Both society and the legal system expected, however, that when these children did break the law, their parents would deal with them. Corporal punishment, typically a serious beating with a cane or a belt, was the general practice in these instances.

Youth Seven to Fourteen Years Old

Between the ages of seven and fourteen years, young people were held to limited legal responsibility. In theory, at least, the Crown was obliged to make the case that a young offender within this age range was legally mature and could appreciate the nature of the law and the consequences of their behaviour. All too often, however, little was required for the Crown to convince a presiding magistrate to treat the youth as an adult.

Youth Fourteen to Twenty-One Years Old

Beyond the age of 14 years and up to 21 years, young people were typically treated as adults. They could, however, argue that they suffered from diminished mental capacity. In such an instance, it would be maintained that the young person was "slow" and could not form the intent—the *mens rea*—expected of adults. While rarely leading to complete acquittal, this defence sometimes led to a far lighter sentence. At the age of 21 years, however, a person reached the age of majority and was considered a legal adult.

As we will see in later chapters, those age boundaries have been and continue to be matters of considerable debate. We now tend to consider age 18 as signifying adulthood and age 12 as the separation of legal infancy from childhood.

Treatment of Youth in the Criminal Justice System

When dealing with young persons, the criminal justice system is expected to be both a much broader and a much more subtle instrument of control than is the case with adults. Some statutory prohibitions apply only to young people and not to adults. Young people, for example, are prohibited from purchasing and consuming liquor and cigarettes. On the other hand, some adult prohibitions, such as engaging in underage sex, are not applied to young persons. For adults, the criminal justice system adheres to the fairly narrow roles of detection, apprehension, and sanctioning. For young persons, we often expect the criminal justice system to take on a broader set of tasks. Thus, at times, we expect the police and the courts to act also as teachers, mentors, and social welfare agents.

Later, we will focus on the current statutory prohibitions that apply to young persons and how the police, in particular, are involved in enforcing those prohibitions. What we need to keep in mind, however, is that laws and statutes are evolving entities that reflect current norms and values. They also contain residues of past thinking on the matter as well as future aspirations. Laws and law enforcement agencies are attempts to deal with social problems; hence, they reflect the problems of the day. They also reflect past successes and failures of dealing with similar problems. As such, why we do what we do, and what we think we ought to be doing, is largely conditioned by both our recollections and our failures to recollect past conditions. Many of the apparent contradictory goals of the criminal justice system are consequences of both conflicting philosophies on how to maintain social control and changing social circumstances.

Punishment Versus Rehabilitation

Historically, for both youths and adults, the criminal justice system has needed to address two competing perspectives or approaches. The first might be called the punishment or "just desserts" model, based on the moral underpinnings of natural justice. Simply stated, this perspective argues that those who commit sins or break rules deserve to be punished. This approach posits that crime can be prevented by creating a punishment of sufficient strength to deter people from violating the law. The second approach has tended to focus on rehabilitation. This involves the recognition that criminal acts have "causes" associated with one's social location and that by addressing the causes, one can influence the likelihood of criminal behaviour occurring.

These approaches represent two ends on a spectrum. Seldom have we taken a pure "just desserts" approach or a pure rehabilitation approach. Even for offences where the focus leans toward a just desserts framework, the acknowledgement that a criminal act might be the logical outcome of unfortunate circumstances may serve to modify or mitigate the punishment. Over time, the relative emphasis on those two approaches changes. One model appears to gain ascendancy only to reach a state where it seems to achieve an unacceptable extreme. At that point, critics argue for greater balance and the pendulum starts to swing back. This dynamic can be traced in how we respond to adult crime; it is amplified when we focus on young people.

Youth Crime as a Social Problem

Historically, within Anglo-American culture, the lot of a youth had not been an easy one. The law rarely made much distinction between the legal responsibilities of young persons and those of adults. On the other hand, children (and women, for that matter) have usually been denied many legal rights granted to adult males. Women and children were often viewed as subservient to, and sometimes the property of, their fathers, guardians, or, in the case of women, their husbands.

Pre-Confederation (Pre-1867)

In early colonial times, life was harsh in Canada (although, as this was pre-Confederation, "Canada" didn't yet exist). Most people lived in small towns and rural areas and depended upon farming and resource extraction for their livelihoods. Mechanization was limited, and the physical labour of people and beasts was the primary source of production. The lack of effective birth control, a constant need for manual labour, high infant mortality rates, and short life expectancies meant that many women had a dozen or more children. In a real sense, very young children were an unproductive liability to the family unit. As they aged, children increased in value to the family as they took on the physical, productive burdens of adults.

Young children were often raised by their older siblings, and a "spare the rod and spoil the child" philosophy of child rearing was common among parents. While a good thrashing was a typical way of keeping most young persons in line, military service was an option for dealing with older miscreants. In much of Canada, particularly in colonial times, the military was also the first and last line of law enforcement.

If the legal rights of young persons did not improve with the Industrial Revolution, their social conditions certainly deteriorated, since the age of mechanization and mass production drew heavily upon the labour of women and children. The excesses of industrialism spurred reformers in the 19th century to reassess the social and legal statuses of children. The development of large cities with their high population densities displayed human misery much more intensely than was seen in the agrarian (agricultural) sectors. Canada has always been an immigrant country with newcomers appearing in waves usually due to issues in their homelands. The late 1840s were particularly rough times in Canada's nascent cities when large numbers of Irish immigrants came to Canada seeking to escape the famines raging in their home country. While many immigrants were absorbed in the rural economy, they were particularly visible in urban areas where they became a normal part of the streetscape. The fact that most were Catholic was especially irksome in the primarily Protestant cities of Ontario.

RISE OF YOUTH CRIMINALITY

Some historians have argued that it was this combination of urban misery and social and moral upheaval that eventually led to juvenile criminality being combined with concerns for the social welfare of children. It was reasonable to link modern explanations of juvenile delinquency (e.g., deprived or broken homes and a lack of skills and resources to compete in the existing opportunity structure) to problems resulting from the growth of industrial society. Many reformers saw the cause of juvenile crime and immorality as lying in social welfare problems that followed from a society quickly losing its agrarian roots.

Post-Confederation

Confederation marks the time point when the colonies and territories united to form the country of Canada, with its own government and laws, pursuant to the *British North America Act* of 1867. Many of the worst social conditions that existed in Europe or the large cities of the United States in the earlier part of the 19th century did not appear until much later in Canada. As an agriculturally based society, Canada's problem with youth crime paled beside that of its neighbour. As one Canadian historian writes,

> lawbreaking by young boys and girls developed in a distinct pattern from the earliest days of pioneer settlement. Much of it was minor in nature, consisting of violations of local ordinances, nuisance offences, vandalism, petty theft, and breaches of the moral laws. Males offended in larger numbers than females, while certain crimes such as prostitution, abortion, and infanticide were primarily committed by females. (Carrigan, 1998: 25)

YOUTH HOMELESSNESS

Interestingly, many social problems that we experience with young people today appeared regularly in the past. Citizens in the growing colonial cities of Halifax, Montreal, and Toronto complained constantly about the problems posed by runaways or "street kids" as we would now call them. One difference in the past was that most of those young people were either orphans or young servants who had run away from their masters. One area of similarity, however, is that many were living on the streets to escape abusive homes only to experience more and different forms of physical and sexual abuse on the streets.

YOUTH PROSTITUTION

Garrison and port towns, such as Halifax, faced particular problems as soldiers and sailors searched for female companionship. Many poor and unskilled adolescent girls were attracted into prostitution. Invariably, the trade was linked to heavy drinking and other forms of vice. Many prostitutes (and young servant girls, for that matter) became pregnant and solved their "problem" through abortion. Frequently, the young women in the sex trade were also involved in minor acts of theft. Either on their own initiative or at the urging of their pimp or brothel owner, they would steal from their often drunk clients. Prostitution was also a major problem in mining and lumber towns, where, again, there were large concentrations of single men, flush with money to spend on payday. Of course, things were not always better in the major cities of central Canada. Kieran (1986: 62) estimates that there were about 140 brothels in Toronto alone at the time of Confederation.

PROPOSED CAUSES OF YOUTH CRIME

By the mid-19th century, many social reformers considered idleness and ignorance—specifically a lack of schooling—to be the primary causes of criminal and delinquent behaviour among young people. Interestingly, idleness was considered a result not just of sloth but also of a lack of education. As Canada was slowly evolving into an industrial economy, the need for workers who had the ability to read, write, and perform rudimentary arithmetic was growing. The demand for unskilled labour was decreasing. Many reformers, such as Egerton Ryerson in Ontario, saw the solution to both the delinquency problem and the labour problem in offering free and universal schooling. Ironically, while the introduction of universal schooling in the 1850s took many young people off the street and provided youth with greater marketable skills, it also created a new class of youthful delinquent—the **truant** (a student who stays away from school without leave or explanation).

PATTERNS OF YOUTH CRIME

The overall pattern of youth crime changed little in Canada from pioneer times until the 20th century. This Canadian experience was quite different from what was typical of many parts of the United States. While it is true that America was primarily rural, there were also large cities where youth crime appeared rampant. Such cities as New York, Boston, and Philadelphia were home to juvenile gangs that often engaged in what might best be described as ethnic warfare. Although quiet by American standards, Canadian cities were a constant concern for the middle class that was very much aware of what was happening south of the border. By the beginning of the 20th century, Canada's population started to become more urbanized, and youth crime was starting to take a higher profile. However, as the historian Carrigan (1998: 104) writes,

> the profile of the typical delinquent of the 1920s changed little from the previous century. Convicted offenders were still predominantly white, male, and Canadian-born. They were urban dwellers, usually from troubled homes, who mixed with bad companions and had repeated run-ins with the law. One not untypical example was a Toronto boy who came from a family of seven. He grew up in poverty and an unkempt home with parents who quarrelled and drank heavily. While still young, his mother deserted the family and the boy started on a path of truancy and petty theft. By the time he was eleven, he had graduated to shop-breaking and stealing automobiles. He was in and out of detention until he eventually reached adulthood. He ended his career in Kingston Penitentiary on a fifteen-year sentence for armed robbery.

While many commentators of the time were quick to focus on youth crime, the situation in Canada seems more of an annoyance than a major social problem from our perspective. It is also worthwhile remembering that, historically, young people made up a much larger segment of the population than they do now. Life expectancies were shorter and birth rates were much higher. Consequently, there were fewer adults in relation to young people than we find today. When we consider that factor, the problem of youth crime appears to have been less of a challenge for Canadian society in the past than it is today.

It is also the case that the economy usually had more room for young people. Educational requirements for employment were different from those we have now. The dexterity and strength of young people were useful, both on the farm and in the factory, where machines were not the complete labour replacement items that they are at present. Furthermore, many young people were accepted into personal service where they worked as servants.

RISE OF YOUTH CRIME IN THE 20TH CENTURY

Juvenile crime increased substantially in Canada through the 1920s and the 1930s. Most of it, however, appears to have consisted of minor property offences. There were, however, increases in the rates of violent crime. Gang behaviour also started to become a more regular part of the urban scene, especially in the bigger cities, such as Montreal and Toronto. As in the United States, many of those gangs revolved around ethnic affiliations. Fortunately, in Canada, juvenile gangs never posed the serious problem that they did in the large American cities.

RESPONSES TO YOUTH CRIME

While youth crime did not take on the same historic proportions in Canada as it did in England or the United States, the formal responses to what crime did exist was drawn from those two countries. The early arrival of English common law in Ontario brought with it the English court system and the jail. Not long before the time of Confederation, however, Ontario's leading citizens started to look to the United States as a source of inspiration for responding to youth crime and for ideas for reforming the existing response.

Institutional Responses

Institutional responses to the problems of delinquent youth have their origins as far back as the 16th century. It is only in the past 150 years or so, however, that most significant developments have taken place. As we noted earlier, the punishment for a young offender was traditionally the same as that for an adult. Often, it consisted of a good whipping or lashing. Prison or jail time generally meant serving one's sentence with adults whatever their crime—whether it was murder, public intoxication, or the inability to pay their debts. Older youth were sometimes transported to the colonies (typically Bermuda in the case of Canada) as were adults. Occasionally, a young person could "avoid" civil punishment by being placed in military service. Of course, for many, life on board a ship or with "the regiment" was not any better than life in prison.

Houses of Refuge

One of the earliest responses to the problem of neglected and wayward youth was the establishment of **houses of refuge** (Barnes, 1972: 201–203). Principally, they kept youth separate from adults and focused on hard work and discipline. They grew out of the juvenile sections of the English workhouses of the 16th and 17th centuries and eventually became common throughout most of Western Europe. Mennel (1973: 3–4) notes that the growth of these houses of refuge marked a shift in the emphasis from family-centred discipline to the institutional control of young people by the state.

The house of refuge idea was apparently brought to America from Europe by John Griscom, a Quaker who travelled widely throughout Europe in the 1820s. The first house of refuge opened in New York State in 1825, but the idea soon spread to neighbouring states. Eventually, however, most juvenile institutions came to take on the characteristics of adult prisons; the facilities were spartan, silence was usually enforced, and strict discipline was maintained. As Sutherland and Cressey (1974: 490) point out, "these institutions were, during the first half-century of their history, primarily prisons, and their principal contribution was the removal of juvenile prisoners from association with adult prisoners."

Institutional reforms were longer in coming to Canada than to many other parts of the world where common law prevailed. Most major cities had jails and other facilities for adults. Few, however, had the type of institutional infrastructure of poor houses and houses of refuge found in Britain or the United States. For example, in 1815, the city of Halifax had a jail along with a regular courthouse. Carrigan (1998: 37) reports that the courts usually imposed 39 lashes rather than allow young offenders to spend time in jail. As he states, "the sanction was preferable to putting them in detention because officials wanted to avoid the expense of providing board and lodging out of the taxpayers' money."

Penitentiaries and Jails

Unlike in England and the United States, the extensive use of penal institutions was relatively late in coming to Canada. The first penitentiary in British North America—the Provincial Penitentiary of the Province of Upper Canada—was opened in Kingston in 1835 based on an American model in Auburn, New York. The penitentiary initially housed both men and women, although separately. In 1934, the Prison for Women (known as "P4W") was opened across the street until its closure in 2000. On September 30th, 2013, the federal government finally closed the men's facility due to "crumbling infrastructure" and "costly upkeep," retiring the "Kingston Pen" maximum security jail into a tourist attraction.

When young offenders were housed in local jails, they faced the same squalid conditions as the adults. The food was poor, sanitation was minimal, and the facilities were crude. When Upper Canada opened its first penitentiary in Kingston in 1835, the courts were ready to supply it with both young and adult prisoners. Conditions in Kingston were never good. Young boys were kept with the general adult male population, and young girls were kept with the adult women. All were subject to lashings for misbehaviour, including several youngsters under the age of 12 years.

What will astonish most readers is that the Kingston Pen also imprisoned offenders as young as eight years of age. One such inmate was Antoine Beauche who was given a three-year sentence in 1845 when he was eight. "This eight year old child received... 47 corporal punishments [the lash] in nine months, and all for offences of the most childish character," according to an 1849 commission headed by a future father of Confederation, George Brown (Schwartz, 2013).

Reform Schools

No matter how poorly these juvenile institutions achieved their goals, it is safe to state that the 19th century was the century of the institution. For most, the ready answer to the "youth crime problem" lay in the institution. Reformers believed that given sufficient hard work, discipline, and moral training, a wayward youth could be moulded into a useful adult citizen. By mid-century, houses of refuge had morphed into training or reform schools where young people were principally taught how to read and write and were provided with skills that would be useful in the job market upon release. Although seemingly archaic by current standards, the evolution of training schools and reformatories marked an innovative chapter in our response to the treatment of youthful criminals. Nineteenth century reformers fought a tough battle to convince legislators and the public (who then preferred a "just desserts" punitive model) that mere punishment was not a sufficient response to the problem of youth crime. Critics saw the investment in training and education as both undeserved and a waste of public resources.

In the late 1850s, new institutions known as "reformatories" started to appear. They were designed to hold young offenders only. The record of the early reformatories is mixed at best. They were often little more than adult jails designed for young people. Historians record much internal turmoil, high rates of escape, chronic mismanagement, and a general lack of progress. Some exceptions have been noted. After a rocky start, the Montreal Reformatory, run by the Brothers of Charity, was viewed as one of the more successful institutions. The Brothers placed great emphasis on trades training so that the young people in their care had a decent chance of getting a job upon release.

The latter part of the 19th century also saw the rise of the industrial school. In 1874, Ontario passed the *Industrial Schools Act*. Ontario opened its first industrial school—the Victoria Industrial School for Boys—in Mimico in 1887. Several years later, in 1892, the Alexandra Industrial School for Girls was opened in Toronto. Industrial schools were designed to fit between the ordinary public schools, which were coming into existence, and the reformatories. Wayward and neglected youth were targeted for the industrial schools as much as young offenders were. As with some reformatories, religious orders and charities as well as the state ran many industrial schools.

Dissatisfaction with Institutions

Not everyone supported children's institutions, least of all the many parents whose children were taken from them. Gradually, reports of cruelty inside the institutions began to circulate in public. Even from the highly acclaimed rural or cottage settings in the United States, there came disturbing reports of juveniles engaging in "unnatural" acts with the farm animals (Mennel, 1973: 107–110). Many observers also began to notice that training schools were often schools for crime rather than institutions where one learned skills for a legitimate career.

The intervention of the state into the family lives of the poor through these "child-saving" institutions became a serious problem. What we must remember is that only occasionally were clear distinctions made between young persons who had actually committed criminal acts and those who were unfortunate enough to have been born to impoverished parents. Despite the intentions of their founders, houses of refuge were often obliged to accept both youth who were committed for criminal acts and those who were committed for vagrancy. Vagrancy was essentially a product of the homelessness of youths, many of whom would "loiter" or beg on the streets. The core of the problem (and one that remains with us even today, to some degree) is that the 19th century viewed poverty almost as a crime, and many of the terms were used synonymously. Thus vagrant, wayward, delinquent, depraved, dependent, vicious, neglected, and many other such adjectives were used to describe basically the same children (Rendleman, 1971: 81).

The non-poor, for the most part, saw little wrong in separating pauper children from their families. Our cultural legacy going as far back as the Elizabethan Poor Laws supported this as a proper and benevolent act, if not a very functional one. Many poor parents, however, could not understand why the state had the right to take their children, especially in instances where the child had essentially committed no crime. The problem became acute in the latter half of the 19th century, in both Canada and the United States, with the mass influx of many Catholic immigrants. First-generation immigrants were especially prone to an impoverished lifestyle. Consequently, their children were prime targets for the Protestant institutions that saw the children as victims of both material and spiritual deprivation. The legal justification presented by reformers for their sometimes high-handed interference in family affairs was the old doctrine of *parens patriae*. *Parens patriae* is a Latin phrase given to the principle that the Crown would intervene to protect persons who were incapable of taking care of themselves. Under this doctrine, the jurisdiction of the Chancery Court could be invoked to intercede on behalf of children when their parents or guardians were neglecting or mistreating them.

Supporters of the 19th century child-saving movement relied heavily on this doctrine for legal support of their activities. Of course, the benevolence of the Chancery Court, which had been initially constituted to protect the property rights of children of the nobility, was highly romanticized to gain widespread popular support for reformers' activities. By drawing on a long and continuous heritage of the state's right to be the ultimate father of the children within its jurisdiction, supporters of juvenile institutions could add a much needed legitimacy to their actions.

Toward the end of the century, however, the use of *parens patriae* to justify removing children from their families came under increased attack as being capricious and unjust. At the same time, there was a growing realization that they were simply not achieving their stated goals. As Mennel (1973: 124) notes,

> by the late nineteenth century, little remained of the enthusiasm and hope which had produced the asylum, the penitentiary, and the reform school. Internal as well as external attacks upon reform schools were indicative of a larger collapse of faith in the healing powers of ... [these places]. By remembering the dimensions of this deterioration of confidence, we can more clearly comprehend the significance of the juvenile court.

THE JUVENILE COURT

The second half of the 19th century was a period of significant social reform. It saw the beginnings of the social welfare movement that gradually improved working conditions and the overall quality of life for most people in much of Western Europe and North America. Many of those reforms and the social institutions that supported them were the result of private charity and philanthropy. Gradually, however, the state started to play an increasingly larger role. This was a period of shifting sentiments where the focus on rehabilitation was taking over the punitive approach. The state supported institutions and passed legislation to limit the punitiveness of criminal law, enhanced child welfare, reduced hours of work, and provided some support for the poor. It should be kept in mind that prior to the early part of the 20th century, what we now recognize as Canada's welfare safety net did not exist. With unemployment came the inability to pay rent or buy food; medical care was largely inaccessible. Private charity was generally the only recourse, and it was severely limited.

With the coming of the 20th century, Canada's largest cities—particularly Toronto—saw the type of rapid growth that had already plagued America's cities. In 1881, Toronto had a population of slightly more than 56,000 people. By 1901, the number of residents in Toronto had increased to a little more than 200,000. While this rapid growth brought economic expansion, it also brought with it a host of social problems, with delinquent and wayward children and youth being regarded as one of the major issues.

Changing Perceptions of Youth

Views of children were also changing, both about how they related to adults and about how they fitted into the social order. Children were seen less as adults in small packages and more as beings who were not only physically but also socially and intellectually less developed than adults. These views of children accelerated around the turn of the 20th century as the young social sciences started to broaden our understanding of human development. Along with the genesis of the academic disciplines of sociology and psychology, this period saw the development of professional social work programs. Canada's first social work program, for example, was opened at the University of Toronto in 1914. All of these disciplines helped to develop a broader understanding of what it meant to be a young person as opposed to an adult and of the contribution of the socio-economic structure to the problems of the day.

Developmental psychologists, for example, provided empirical evidence to show that social and intellectual growth takes place not only in childhood but throughout adolescence. Psychologists suggested that moral development in young people happens in a series of stages. Although there is significant interpersonal variability, the evolution of the individual into a socially, morally, and intellectually mature adult takes time. Other social scientists have made us aware that while many young people may be aware of certain social ideas and terms, such as justice, rights, fairness, and responsibility, their understanding of those terms develops only as they grow older.

Establishment of Youth-Focused Courts

The first formal juvenile court was opened in Chicago in 1899, after the presentation of the innovative *Juvenile Delinquents Act* to the Illinois state legislature the previous year. The juvenile court, it would appear, was an idea whose time had come. Although most jurisdictions were facing increasing difficulties with the manner in which they dealt with troublesome juveniles, Illinois was apparently in a particularly acute predicament. Several court cases in the late 1880s and 1890s began to erode the right of existing legislation to separate wayward youth from their parents in noncriminal situations. At the same time, however, the reformist or "child-saving" movement was still very strong and sought to intercede in the lives of deprived and delinquent juveniles (Platt, 1969). It was, states Mennel (1973: 128), "under these circumstances [that] the legal fraternity in Illinois became concerned about the vacuum of state welfare power and sought a means to reassert the right of the state to assume parental power over delinquent children."

The juvenile court appeared to provide an ideal solution. It recognized the fact that childhood was a special status, qualitatively different from adulthood, and that children were simply not miniature adults. As such, children were protected from the harshness of the criminal sanction under adult courts. Furthermore, the courts could become informal affairs, with the judge acting in the capacity of a wise and judicious parent. The judge's role was not to accuse the child of a crime but to offer assistance and guidance. Because the court was not treating the matter strictly as a criminal issue, the hearing could be held in private, away from the prying eyes of the public and the press.

The new juvenile court also conformed to the rising ideology of the time—that the origins of criminal and anti-social behaviour existed in the mind and social environment of the individual (see Platt, 1969: Chapter 3). By focusing on the causes of criminal and deviant behaviours, the court allowed for a revitalization of the *parens patriae* doctrine and the right of the state to intercede for the juvenile. Attending to young delinquents and youths dwelling in environments that fostered crime or exhibiting delinquent tendencies allowed the court to divert the juvenile from a potential life of adult criminality.

Canadian social reformers did much to implement the new ideas and institutions with which their American counterparts were experimenting. J.J. Kelso, for example, introduced the first Children's Aid Society in Ontario in 1891. Similarly, he organized the Toronto Humane Society as a mechanism for promoting both child and animal welfare. Kelso and his colleague W.L. Scott were among the prime movers in having the Canadian *Juvenile Delinquents Act* introduced in 1908.

The Use of Probation

One of the byproducts of the juvenile court system was the development of community supervision through the use of probation services. Although juvenile court judges were not averse to assigning young people to institutions when deemed necessary, they often resorted to the use of probation officers to provide community supervision. As with the social work movement, the probation movement was viewed as a mechanism for tackling the root causes of crime. Ideally, probation officers supervised the young delinquent in the community and in the family environment. The juvenile court model remained in existence in Canada for over 60 years. During that time, institutions receded as the primary response to delinquency and youth crime and community and family-based intervention ascended. State-sponsored corporal punishment disappeared and the ability of parents to use physical punishment to control their children was severely curtailed.

TEST YOUR KNOWLEDGE

Definitions

Define the following terms:

1. *Actus reus*

_____

_____

_____

2. *Mens rea*

_____

_____

_____

3. Houses of refuge

_____

_____

_____

4. *Parens patriae*

_____

_____

_____

True/False

1. T F Mental incompetence and the lack of intention are no excuse for the commission of a crime.

2. T F Central to what constitutes a crime is the fact that the behaviour must be formally forbidden and punished by the state.

3. T   F   Historically, there has been consistency in the age limit that separates adults from youth.

4. T   F   It is fair to say that the pattern of youth crime in Canada changed little from pioneer times until the early 20th century.

5. T   F   It is only in recent times that many gangs were identified with particular ethnic groups.

6. T   F   Historically, the punishment for a young offender was generally the same as that for adults.

7. T   F   Canada has led the world in developing institutional responses to crime such as training schools and penitentiaries.

8. T   F   Incarceration or imprisonment was not a major way of dealing with youthful crime until the turn of the 20th century.

9. T   F   Most institutions in Canada and especially in Ontario were run by religious orders.

10. T   F   The primary role of the juvenile court judge was not simply to adjudicate guilt or innocence but also to provide guidance and assistance to the young accused.

Multiple Choice

1. A primary factor that separates youthful from adult offenders is the notion that

    a. young people are less intelligent than adults
    b. young people are less able to form criminal intent than adults
    c. young people are incapable of distinguishing between right and wrong
    d. young people are generally smaller than adults and are consequently less capable of creating "harm"

2. The importance of age in making legal distinctions between adults and youth is

    a. age is a good indicator of physical size
    b. age is a good indicator of how much harm a person can commit
    c. age is a main indicator of intellectual development
    d. age is used as an indicator of experience

3. The concept of "age of majority" indicates that

    a. a person has all of the legal rights and responsibilities of an adult
    b. the majority of people in the population are adults
    c. a person has reached the stage of the majority of their intellectual development
    d. a person is too old to be held criminally responsible

4. Corporal punishment

    a. was the only way of dealing with young criminals in 19th-century Canada
    b. was a form of military punishment inflicted on the civilian population
    c. was a term used to indicate how young people entering the military (mostly corporals) were punished in pioneer times
    d. refers to any form of physical punishment

5. Many social reformers, both past and present, link a growth in youth crime to

    a. Canada's inability to lose its agrarian or agricultural roots
    b. the need for farm labour
    c. historical decreases in family size
    d. the increased urbanization of Canadian society

6. Historically, youth crime in Canada was

    a. generally lower than in the United States or England
    b. about the same as in the rest of the industrialized world
    c. much higher than in the United States
    d. lower than in the United States but on par with England

7. Institutional responses to crime (incarceration) has been a major factor

    a. since the 16th century
    b. only in the past 50 years
    c. in about the past 150 years
    d. ever since we started recording observations about youthful criminality

8. One of the most important results of the house of refuge movement was

    a. its shift away from family-centred discipline
    b. it marked a point where a lack of education was seen as the primary cause of youthful crime
    c. that it was the first response to juvenile crime that resulted in a lowering of crime rates
    d. its acknowledgement that the juvenile court system simply did not work

9. A feature that often distinguished industrial schools and other institutions of the latter part of the 19th century from prisons or jails was

    a. their increased effectiveness at preventing crime
    b. their ability to create serious youthful offenders out of minor ones

c. their ability to target the specific needs of a young person

d. their broad scope, which meant that neglected young people were often as likely to be incarcerated as were young offenders

10. The concept of *parens patriae* was used to

a. justify removing young people from their families in order to make them wards of the state

b. arrest and detain parents who abused their children

c. recognize that most parents have little control over their children

d. enforce parental control over children

Short Answer

1. Identify some effects of the Industrial Revolution on women and children.

_____

_____

_____

_____

_____

_____

_____

_____

2. Explain how the relationship between age and criminal responsibility has changed for young people over time.

_____

_____

_____

_____

_____

_____

_____

_____

3. In what ways is the criminal behaviour of young people in pre-20th century Canada different from that after the turn of the 20th century?

_____

_____

_____

_____

_____

_____

_____

_____

4. Describe the various institutional responses to youth crime prior to the 20th century.

_____

_____

_____

_____

_____

_____

_____

_____

_____

5. What was the role of the juvenile court and how did its creation lead to a different response to juvenile crime?

_____

_____

_____

_____

_____

_____

_____

_____

6. Why, over time, was there an increasing dissatisfaction with the use of institutions as a response to the youth crime problem?

    _____

    _____

    _____

    _____

    _____

    _____

    _____

    _____

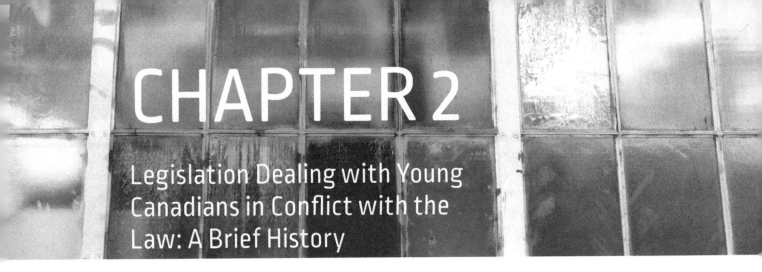

CHAPTER 2

Legislation Dealing with Young Canadians in Conflict with the Law: A Brief History

LEARNING OUTCOMES

Students who have mastered this chapter will have the ability to do the following:

- Distinguish between "common law" and a "penal code."
- Identify what is meant by "legal infant."
- Identify the ways in which young people who committed crimes were treated in the 19th century.
- Describe why, in Canada, dealing with crime requires federal and provincial co-operation.
- Explain why the juvenile court was a type of social welfare agency.
- Articulate the range of behaviours that could lead a person to be found to be "in a state of delinquency."

THE NEED FOR CONTEXT

Students often ask, why is it important to spend time studying "ancient" legal history? Besides the standard academic answer that is good to know about one's heritage, there are some very pragmatic reasons. Legislation is rarely written from scratch. Most laws are either based on previous statutes or are written in reaction to a pre-existing legal environment. In the case of legislation relating to young people, almost all new laws are generated in response to perceived inadequacies or inequities within existing laws. Most new legislation also includes some legacy components from previous legislation. As indicated in Chapter 1, legislation relating to young people in conflict with the law has tended to swing between two basic models: one focused on punishment and due process ("just desserts"), and one based on a rehabilitation or social welfare model of youth justice. Chances are, if someone argues for a change in the law to improve the justice system for young people, we have tried that approach at some point in our history. Few ideas are new and there are few ideas that have not been implemented in the past.

Challenges of Criminal Law

The problem with the criminal law is that it is a fairly blunt instrument that is intended to cover a broad range of circumstances—foreseeable and otherwise. Offences are committed by individuals, with individual circumstances and motivations. As social scientists know, what may be effective, efficient, and equitable at the societal or aggregate level does not always hold at the individual level and vice versa. For example, the punishment for impaired driving is sufficient to make most people abstain from driving while intoxicated, but it doesn't work for everyone. Furthermore, rules do not implement themselves. People choose when and where to invoke them and decide on how they ought to be interpreted. As we will see in this chapter, one of the major criticisms of the *Young Offenders Act* from the Province of Ontario was that it did not allow for the transfer of older youth to adult courts when they had committed serious offences. In fact, that Act did allow for youth to be transferred to adult court. Transfer mechanisms were written into the Act. The "problem" was that for various reasons, Ontario's Crown prosecutors rarely chose to seek such transfers. Despite that fact, fingers were pointed at the "inadequacies" in the legislation when it was the decision-making of the Crown that was at issue.

The Role of Police

Except as lobbyists and private citizens, police officers are expected to enforce the existing laws and not create new ones. Still, it helps to understand why the legal system expects officers to do their job in the manner prescribed. Knowing the context of rules and procedures also helps officers when they are expected to use their judgment. This is particularly the case when they are expected to deal with young people.

THE EARLY YEARS

Legislative History

Until the late 19th century, the laws of Great Britain applied almost directly to Canada. During colonial times, the Canadian legal system treated young people over the age of seven years the same way it treated adults. Canadian practice was similar to British practice, particularly as far as the courts were concerned. If, as Hobbes (1996) contended, life was nasty and brutish, then so was the legal system. Children were exposed to the same laws, the same court procedure, the same judges, and the same punishment, including prisons, as adults.

There were, however, some local differences. In pre-Confederation Canada, one of the earliest signs of special concern for the treatment of young offenders was the passage in 1857 of *An Act for Establishing Prisons for Young Offenders* and *An Act for the More Speedy Trial and Punishment of Juvenile Offenders*. The *Prisons Act* also led to the construction of reformatory prisons in Canada, similar to those that were appearing in Britain and the United States at that time. The second act was concerned primarily with the pretrial conditions of youths who had not yet been convicted of a crime.

At the time of Confederation (1867), Canada inherited the British system of criminal law. A unique characteristic of British criminal law, at that time, was the total absence of a systematic criminal or penal code. Cases in Britain were heard solely under the **common law** system. In 1878, however, a Royal Commission was set up under the initiative of Sir James Fitzjames Stephen to systematize English common law concerning criminal matters and to produce a criminal code.

The Introduction of the *Criminal Code of Canada*

Parliament drafted a Canadian criminal code in 1891, and it was adopted the following year (Mewett and Manning, 1978). Basically, this ***Criminal Code of Canada*** brought together and formalized what had been standard legal practice in criminal matters up to that time. Juveniles were generally subject to the same laws and rules of procedure as adults. One major distinction, however, was the common law rule that an individual's age was a key factor in defining whether or not an accused had the required *mens rea* or intent. This distinction is still with us today and remains one of the most contentious issues surrounding criminal legislation directed at young people. Children under seven years of age were generally excluded from all criminal accountability.

Differences by Age of Accused

1. Under Seven Years
   As was noted in the previous chapter, children under seven were exempt from prosecution.

2. Seven to Fourteen Years
   British common law defined a person between the ages of 7 and 14 years a **legal infant**, a person with limited ability to form criminal intent. This assumption was open to challenge in specific cases, but the burden of proof was placed upon the Crown. To establish criminal liability, the prosecution had to show the court that children had adequate moral discretion and understanding to appreciate the wrongfulness of their actions.

3. Fourteen to Twenty-One
   Common law saw persons between the ages of 14 and 21 years of age inclusive, as being accountable for their actions. This assumption was open to rebuttal. Unlike for persons 7 to 14, the burden of proving a lack of *mens rea* because of age shifted to the defence, rather than the prosecution.

Responses to Youth Imprisonment

In the middle of the 19th century, those children unfortunate enough to be convicted of indictable offences could look forward to the full brunt of Canadian justice. Perhaps the greatest outrages committed on children by the Canadian justice system were those found in the Kingston Penitentiary in the 1840s. From its opening, on June 1, 1835, the penitentiary experienced administrative strife, corruption, and overall mismanagement. Public criticism of the institution was such that, in 1848, a commission was set up by the Governor General, Lord Elgin, to investigate the running of the prison. The commission's report provided a resounding condemnation of the institution's administration.

> The commissioners were especially severe in their condemnation of the treatment of child convicts. They point out the case of 10-year-old Peter Charbonneau, who was convicted on May 4, 1845, and given a seven-year sentence. They said, "… that Charbonneau's offences [in prison] were of the most trifling description, such as were to be expected of a child of ten or eleven (like staring, winking, and laughing); and that for these he was stripped to the shirt, and publicly lashed 57 times in eight months." Then there was the case of convict Antoine Beauche, committed November 7, 1845, for three years: " … this eight-year-old child received the lash within a week of his arrival and that he had no fewer than 47 corporal punishments in nine months, and all for offences of the most childish character …". (Edmison, 1977)

Legislative Responses

As elsewhere, Canadian jails soon achieved a reputation of being harsh and severe institutions. In response to this, the Province of Ontario passed *An Act Respecting Industrial Schools* in 1874, providing an alternative source of residential treatment for "neglected, uncontrolled, and delinquent children" (Hagan and Leon, 1977: 591).

The late 1880s were very eventful years in the field of child welfare legislation in Canada. After the American Humane Society held its annual convention in Toronto, in 1888, the first provincial act dealing with neglected children was passed by the Ontario legislature. Under this Act, "children under 14 years of age could be committed to any society or institution willing to receive them" (MacGill, 1925: 8). The legislation also provided for a special commissioner to try youthful offenders apart from adults. It is interesting to note that concern for the protection of animals came before concerns about children and the law and resources to guard their well-being.

In 1890, Ontario passed two statutes—*An Act Respecting the Custody of Juvenile Offenders* and *An Act Respecting the Commitment of Persons of Tender Years*—both of which further reduced the use of reformatories for children by diverting more juveniles to the industrial schools. Again, it is possible to see the growing disenchantment with institutions in Canada paralleling, though probably not equalling, the intensity of that in the United States and Britain. Other changes in the implementation of the criminal law were also taking place around this time. As previously noted, the first Canadian criminal code was adopted in 1892.

Ontario *Children's Protection Act*

In 1893, Ontario passed the *Children's Protection Act* that "provided for the establishment of Children's Aid Societies and for the commitment of neglected and delinquent children to them by court order" (Scott, 1952: 1). This Act provided an essential element for the success of the juvenile court, which was to be a central component of the juvenile justice system until the mid-1980s. The Ontario legislation, which served as a model for other provinces, provided operational facilities in the form of Children's Aid Societies, through which juvenile courts could dispose of many of their clients. Probation, which became an essential element of the juvenile court, since it provided a clear alternative to institutional supervision, was unknown as such in Canada at this time. The Children's Aid Societies, however, practised a type of probation by supervising the children sent to them through court orders. The first real instance of juvenile probation in Canada seems to have been the appointment of two probation officers (one English-speaking, one French-speaking) by the Children's Aid Society of Ottawa.

THE *JUVENILE DELINQUENTS ACT*

The Canadian *Juvenile Delinquents Act (JDA)* was introduced to Parliament in 1907 and passed into law the next year. It was based on legislation passed in the states of Illinois and Colorado. The architects of the Act, however, found it very difficult to copy and adopt the American statutes in Canada.

Canadian Division of Powers

The *Constitution Act of 1867* (which was originally known as the *British North America Act* or *BNA Act*), is essentially the Canadian Constitution. It called for a clear jurisdictional split between federal and provincial responsibilities—a split aimed at the very heart of the philosophy of the juvenile court. Under the *Constitution Act*, the federal Parliament had sole jurisdiction over criminal law and procedure, but not over the composition of the criminal courts. The provincial legislatures, on the other hand, had jurisdiction over property and civil rights, local and private affairs, and the administration of justice within the province, plus the criminal courts. Thus, it became an extremely complex matter for the authors of the *Juvenile Delinquents Act* to include both the criminal concerns of the federal Parliament and the welfare concerns of the provincial legislatures without infringing upon provincial jurisdiction. This split in jurisdiction remains with us today and accounts for the variability in how young people are handled across the provinces and territories.

Expansion of Criminal Offences

The attempt by Canadian reformers to copy the American experience and reduce the child's involvement with strictly criminal proceedings had unexpected consequences in Canada. They succeeded in broadening the scope of criminal law to include behaviour normally considered "criminal" plus "non-criminal" behaviour, by defining both as "acts of delinquency." Thus, subsection 1(1) of the *Juvenile Delinquents Act* stated that

> "juvenile delinquency" means any child who violates any provision of the Criminal Code or of any Dominion [federal] or provincial statute, or of any by-law or ordinance of any municipality, or who is guilty of sexual immorality or any similar form of vice, or who is liable for reason of any other act to be committed to an industrial school or reformatory under the provisions of any Dominion or provincial statute.

Having made virtually any form of juvenile misbehaviour a criminal act (thus allowing the federal government to intervene in welfare matters through the back door), something had to be done to express the non-punitive philosophy of the juvenile court to soften the "criminal" orientation of the legislation. Thus, section 38 of the *Juvenile Delinquents Act* stated that

> this Act shall be liberally construed to the end that its purpose may be carried out, namely, that the care and custody and discipline of a juvenile delinquent shall approximate as nearly as may be that which should be given by its parents, and that as far as practicable, every juvenile delinquent shall be treated, not as a criminal, but as a *misdirected and misguided child*, and one *needing aid, encouragement, help, and assistance* [emphasis added].

Reliance on Provincial Co-operation

This "liberal" construction of the *Juvenile Delinquents Act* required the co-operation and goodwill of the provincial governments. As we have noted, while Parliament was responsible for enacting the legislation, it depended on provincial resources for its effective application. Thus, despite the theoretical universality of the Act throughout the country, the practical application relied on whatever resources the provinces were willing to devote, or were capable of devoting, to juvenile justice. Throughout most of the history of the *Juvenile Delinquents Act*, there was a great variation in the facilities available across the country (Government of Canada, Department of Justice, 1965: 31).

Scott summarized the major philosophical and ideological underpinnings of the 1908 legislation when he wrote that

> the rights of parents are sacred and ought not to be lightly interfered with, but they may be forfeited by abuse. Paramount to the rights of parents is the right of every

child to a fair chance of growing up to be an honest, respectable citizen. What chance has the daughter of a prostitute, if left with her mother, to be other than a prostitute, or the son of a thief to be other than a thief? ... [W]hy should this girl be condemned, through no fault of her own, to a life of prostitution, or that boy, unwittingly, to a career of crime? The State, too, has rights and ought not to stand idly by while children are trained, either by evil example or by neglect, to disobey her laws. (quoted in Stewart, 1974: 12)

Creation of Juvenile Probation

From a humanitarian point of view, perhaps the greatest benefit gained from the establishment of the juvenile court was the simultaneous creation of a system of juvenile probation as an alternate disposition to incarceration. Yet, the creation of extensive probation services, combined with the fact that very often chance determined whether intervention into a juvenile's life was through welfare agents or the probation service, succeeded in bringing many children into contact with criminal law—children who perhaps ought not to have been there.

Criticism of *Juvenile Delinquents* Act

Youth contact with the criminal law system would not have been a problem if the needs of delinquent as well as neglected children were similar—as the early reformers believed. There was a growing belief, however, that juveniles who committed crimes (especially older juveniles) were different from cases of neglect and ought to be treated differently by social institutions designed specifically for that purpose. Although the juvenile court was under continuous question since its inception (e.g., Hurley, 1905; Waite, 1921), it was only in the 1960s that the underlying philosophy and structure came under broad critical attack. The major offensive against the philosophy and procedure of the court started in the United States but it quickly spread to Canada.

Theory behind a Juvenile Court
"Legal moralists" argue that offenders ought to be punished. Punishment is functional to society because it expresses society's moral indignation regarding socially unacceptable behaviour. The constitutionalists argue for equal treatment under the law and due process.

It is the counterarguments to both positions that form the theoretical foundation of the juvenile court. In other words, the juvenile court is primarily focused on the rehabilitation of youth offenders. First, the juvenile is qualitatively different from an adult and, as such, ought not to be held legally accountable to the same degree as an adult. Second, the aim of the juvenile court is not to adjudicate crime but to prevent crime by interceding in the life of a delinquent. Third, since the juvenile court is not a body whose aim it is to decide guilt or innocence, the issue of individual rights is not relevant. That is, the child does not *need* his or her rights "protected" because the court, in determining its disposition, is considering the best interests of the child. Thus, the court is guarding the child's civil rights, that is, the child's right not to be neglected, not to be exposed to a criminal environment, and to be provided the proper help, care, and guidance so as not to fall into a life of adult criminality.

Juvenile Court as Welfare Agency

The juvenile court was a "court" in name only—functionally it was supposed to be a social welfare agency. Unfortunately, the benevolence of the juvenile court was also dependent upon one's perspective. As Francis Allen (1964: 18) indicates,

> whatever one's motivation, however elevated one's objectives, if the measures taken result in the compulsory loss of the child's liberty, the involuntary separation of a child from his family or even the supervision of a child's activities by a probation worker, the impact on the affected individual is essentially a punitive one. Good intentions and a flexible vocabulary do not alter this reality. This is particularly so when, as is often the case, the institution to which the child is committed is, in fact, a peno-custodial establishment ... the business of the juvenile court ... consists ... [of] dispensing punishment. If this is true, we can no more avoid the problem of unjust punishment in the juvenile court than in the criminal court.

Criminal Versus Non-criminal Delinquents

The response to this criticism, at least by some jurisdictions, was to more clearly distinguish between youths who have been engaged in criminal activities and those who are "non-criminal" delinquents. The New York *Family Court Act* of 1963, for example, created a separate category of youths appearing in front of the family court known as **persons in need of supervision (P.I.N.S.)**. The P.I.N.S. classification was an attempt to deal with "obnoxious" or "undesirable" youthful behaviour that was not strictly of a criminal nature. Thus, the Act stated that

> "juvenile delinquent" means any person over seven and less than 16 years of age who does any act which, if done by an adult, would constitute a crime.
>
> "Person in need of supervision" means a male less than 16 years of age and a female less than 18 years of age who is an habitual truant, or who is incorrigible, ungovernable, or habitually disobedient and beyond the lawful control of parent or other lawful authority. (Presidential Commission on Law Enforcement, 1967)

The Act also defined **neglected minors** as "any minor under 18 years of age ... whose environment is injurious to his welfare or whose behaviour is injurious to his welfare or that of others."

Similar trends were occurring in Canada. As previously noted, the constitutional relationship of the powers of the federal Parliament to the provincial legislatures led to the paradoxical situation of actually "criminalizing" previous social welfare problems when the *Juvenile Delinquents Act* was proclaimed, rather than "socializing" the treatment of criminal behaviour. To impose the Act uniformly throughout the country, the early supporters of the *Juvenile Delinquents Act* had the federal government define all "delinquencies" as criminal offences. As a result, the amorphous "state of delinquency" made no distinctions between serious anti-social behaviours, such as assault or robbery, and minor by-law infractions, such as spitting in the street, or even occasionally, strictly welfare problems, such as being homeless.

It is this historical background of confusion and critical disagreement regarding juvenile delinquency that led the federal government to attempt to change existing juvenile delinquency legislation. A concerted effort was made from the early 1960s onward to develop a juvenile policy around which a consensus could be achieved. That effort manifested itself primarily through the reports of several government committees created to study the issue. Foremost among those was the *Young Persons in Conflict with the Law* and the *Juvenile Delinquency in Canada* documents. Eventually, that reform effort resulted in the passage of the *Young Offenders Act* in 1985 and, more recently, the *Youth Criminal Justice Act* in 2002.

THE *YOUNG OFFENDERS ACT*

The federal government introduced the **Young Offenders Act (YOA)** in Parliament in 1982, and it became law on April 2, 1985. It remained in force until it was repealed with the passage of the current legislation, the **Youth Criminal Justice Act (YCJA)** in 2002. The former *Juvenile Delinquents Act* was designed more as social welfare legislation than criminal legislation. On the other hand, the *YOA* had at once far more limiting and yet far more complex objectives. Fundamentally, it attempted to do four things:

1. Hold young people more accountable for their behaviour.
2. Provide greater protection to society from youthful offenders.
3. Recognize the need to temper the impact of the criminal justice system on young people.
4. Protect the legal rights of young people.

End of Status Offences

Formerly, **delinquency** was a **status offence**. A status offence is an act that is considered to be an offence or crime that would not be an offence if committed by a person who was an adult. Because of their status as young people, juveniles could be considered criminal even if they did something that was not criminal if done by an adult. Young people could be in a "state of delinquency" or be "truant," and the *Juvenile Delinquents Act* defined this state as criminal. Under the *YOA*, there were no status offences, and the provinces had to use child welfare and child protection legislation to address other misbehaviour. By keeping behaviours defined as crimes separate from all other misbehaviour, the seriousness of those behaviours was highlighted.

Parliament meant the *YOA* to protect society from youthful criminals through several measures. Under that Act, the justice system was expected to divert as many young offenders as possible from the formal process. The assumptions here are twofold.

1. The Act would provide more varied programs to be introduced than had existed under the old system. This would give the courts more options for intervention, and hopefully, those options would be more effective than what had been previously available. By providing flexibility in the legislation, the courts could encourage more use of community service orders and victim compensation. The belief was that offenders who are kept closer to the community will become more aware of the social harm they cause.
2. The Act would reserve the formal process for the most serious offenders. Throughout the 1960s and 1970s, a basic criticism of the *Juvenile Delinquents Act* was that it was too lenient on offenders. Many people hoped that the court's dispositions would be more punitive if the formal process were reserved for the most serious offenders.

The *YOA* recognized that young people are different from adults. While the prevailing philosophy of the *YOA* was to enhance accountability, it recognized that young people (even young offenders) needed special protections. This belief went beyond the traditional notion that young persons lacked the social and psychological maturity of adults. Those social scientists who considered themselves *labelling theorists* did an excellent job of influencing the drafters of the legislation. They successfully made the argument that defining young people as *delinquents* or *criminals* is detrimental to both their rehabilitation and their future development. Consequently, Parliament included a provision in the *YOA* prohibiting the publication of the young offenders' identities, restricting access to their records by adult courts, increasing the **age of culpability** from 7 years of age to 12 years, and limiting the length of sentences.

Parliament also put procedures in place to respect further the young person's fundamental legal rights. For example, they included the right to legal representation in the *YOA*. The police were also expected to inform young suspects of their legal rights. Furthermore, police officers would not take confessions without a written waiver or the presence of the young person's lawyer or guardian. Other sections were written to introduce more "procedural fairness" to the process. Thus, the notion of "due process" had a broader application to the young offender than it did to adults.

Key Provisions of the *Young Offenders Act*

In addition to the provisions alluded to above, there are four provisions of the *YOA* that were central: age, alternative measures, rights, and dispositions.

Age

The *YOA* defined young persons as individuals between the ages of 12 and 17 years, inclusive. Under 12 years of age, a person was considered a child and to be dealt with under provincial child welfare statutes. When people reach their 18th birthday, they were considered to be adults. This element of the *YOA* made it substantially different from both historical common law practice and the *YOA*'s immediate predecessor, the *Juvenile Delinquents Act*.

Alternative Measures

The *YOA* outlines a set of alternative measures. **Alternative measures** are ways of dealing with young persons who are in conflict with the law in a manner that reduces continued formal processing in the criminal justice system. They can be initiated by the police before a court appearance, by a judge before a finding of guilt, or by a judge after a finding of guilt. These measures may be used to deal with a young person alleged to have committed relatively minor offences (such as petty theft or minor acts of vandalism) under certain conditions, typically, a first offence. Several restrictions apply, but primarily, young persons must agree that they committed the act in question. The young person must "freely consent" to participate in the program; the young person must be advised of and be given the right to counsel; and, the disposition must take into consideration the best interests of society. The primary function of alternative measures is to divert young offenders from the formal court system.

Rights

Young persons have all the rights that adults have as outlined in the *Canadian Charter of Rights and Freedoms*. Thus, arresting officers have an obligation to notify young offenders of their rights. In addition, young offenders have the right to legal counsel, the right to confer with their parents, and the right to due care while in detention. The handling of young peoples' confessions was much more restricted under the *YOA* than for adults.

Dispositions

The *YOA* contained several sections that relate to the disposition of young offenders. Many dispositions are similar to those available in adult court. For example, the *YOA* allowed for both absolute and conditional discharges, fines, compensation or restitution orders, community service orders, prohibition orders, and probation. Youth court judges could also sentence young offenders to open or secure custody. **Open custody** consisted of removing the young person from his or her home and placing them in a group home for a fixed length of time. **Secure custody** generally implied that the young person is placed in a more restrictive, sometimes jail-type facility with bars and electronic surveillance.

IN THE NEWS

The *Young Offenders Act* Seen as Major Shift from *Juvenile Delinquents Act*

The *Young Offenders Act* took effect 10 years ago this month, and was meant to be a modern answer to the problem of delinquent young people, giving them rights and responsibilities.

The law it replaced, the *Juvenile Delinquents Act,* dated from 1908. The *JDA* had originally been passed at the urging of the "child-savers," who believed young delinquents needed to be rescued from bad families and harmful social conditions. Judges were supposed to consider the delinquent's best interests. (Before that, teenagers and even children could be jailed with adults.)

But several repressive aspects developed under the *JDA.* Truants from school could be sent off to training schools. Sentences from judges were indeterminate, and training-school directors decided when delinquents were ready for society—sometimes not until they turned 21.

Proclaimed on April 2, 1984, the *Young Offenders Act* gives young people the same rights accorded to adults: the right to a fixed sentence, to bail, to due process, and to be informed of those rights.

...

The *YOA* has been shadowed by controversy from its inception. In particular, violent crimes, often involving other young people as victims, have received widespread attention and have prompted scores of petitions calling for tougher sentences.

...

At the same time, academics have produced studies purporting to show that young offenders are more likely to wind up in detention under the current law than under the *JDA,* and for longer periods of time. However, the federal government has dismissed these studies as inconclusive or irrelevant to the task of finding the most appropriate sentences.

The most controversial elements of the *Young Offenders Act* are: It applies only to those 12 to 17.

...

Source: Sean Fine, "Young offenders and the law," *The Globe and Mail*, April 15, 1994, p. A16.

Criticisms of the *Young Offenders Act*

As we have already seen and as we will continue to see, there are many and varied views about how best to deal with young people who come into conflict with the law. Different versions of the *YOA* were considered over more than two decades. Consultations with the provinces were conducted, expert panels were consulted, and a variety of professional and lay groups offered opinions.

From its inception, the *YOA* was criticized. It was criticized, on the one hand, for being too formal in its processing of young offenders, thereby making it more likely that they would see themselves as criminals. It was criticized, on the other hand, for being too soft on young offenders and thereby not "correcting" them and protecting society.

Too Lenient

Most criticisms of the *YOA* reflect differences in opinion over how we should treat young offenders. For example, many people argue that the *YOA* was "too soft" on young offenders. Some saw the minimum age of legal culpability of 12 years as literally allowing child criminals to get away with murder. Many in Ontario believed that the change in the age of adulthood from 16 to 18 years of age resulted in young adult criminals being "mollycoddled." These critics further suggested that the sentences available under the *YOA* were too light—that the maximum available limit for fines should have been higher and that institutional sentences should be longer. It was often heard that light sentences for youthful offenders who commit crimes only serve to encourage crime, not deter it.

Several areas of the *YOA* served as lightning rods for critics. Among the most often cited are the sections that encourage a wide range of non-custodial dispositions and the section dealing with transfer to adult court.

Non-custodial Sentences

To be fair, the *YOA*'s critics generally acknowledged that custodial sentences were not needed for first-time offenders who committed minor offences. Their attention was directed primarily toward "experienced" young offenders who continued to commit ever more serious offences. Even when they are incarcerated, the maximum sentence for a 16- or 17-year-old offender who committed the most serious offence was two years. Worse still, for these critics, once incarcerated, the young offender had the option of not participating in any treatment program.

Transfer to Adult Court

The issue of transfer to adult court, on the other hand, was somewhat misdirected. The *YOA* did allow Crown prosecutors to petition the court to transfer young offenders aged 14 years and over who commit particularly serious offences (such as murder and aggravated sexual assault) to the jurisdiction of the adult courts. It was the youth court prosecutors, however, who were reluctant to use that option. Consequently, some critics argued for *mandatory* transfer to adult court for *all* serious crimes.

Privacy Provisions

Other criticisms were directed at the privacy provisions of the *YOA*. The publication ban on names, for example, was the subject of some objections. Some argued that it placed the public at greater risk, since they were unaware of potentially dangerous young offenders who might be living in their neighbourhood. They also argued that the ban on publicizing names made it more difficult for the police to identify and find serious offenders, especially across police jurisdictions.

Excessive Focus on Youth Rights

Hardline critics of the *YOA* also believed that there was excessive concern for the rights of offenders at the expense of the rights of victims. Such procedures as having to advise young suspects of their rights before questioning, as well as requiring a written waiver or the presence of a lawyer or guardian before the police can seek a confession were common examples of what they saw as "pandering" to civil libertarians. The primary concern of critics was that young people too easily learned how to manipulate the system. We were, they argued, sending the wrong message; that is, it was not important whether you had committed a wrong or not; what was important was that you were only guilty if the case could be proven in court. Criminal responsibility, therefore, became a cat-and-mouse game focused on legal nuances instead of issues relating to right and wrong, culpability, and social harm.

Other Criticisms

Other criticisms of the *YOA* were not directed at the legislation so much as the way in which it was (or was not) applied. Many critics from the rehabilitation or social welfare perspective argued that the Act failed because there were insufficient resources for its implementation. These critics also argued that traditional sentences with an emphasis on punishment and incarceration did not work very well. They often mustered convincing support for the success of alternative dispositions. The problem, they argued, was in the lack of programs, personnel, and facilities to support the *YOA*'s novel provisions.

Ironically, some social welfare critics also saw the growth of legalism—with its emphasis on punishment, procedure, and due process—as a problem. Those who view delinquency as a mental health problem argued that mental health professionals should determine how young offenders are treated—not legal professionals. Lawyers do not treat physical illness, so why should they treat what is arguably a mental illness?

The perceived shortcomings of the *YOA* led to lengthy debate over issues that were not completely resolved with the passing of the *Youth Criminal Justice Act* in 2002.

IN THE NEWS

Unlike *Young Offenders Act*, The *Youth Criminal Justice Act* Appears More Evolutionary than Revolutionary

How should youths be treated by the Canadian justice system?

That question continues to be asked despite a new law, the *Youth Criminal Justice Act*, which takes effect this April 1. Almost everyone agrees the *Young Offenders Act (YOA)* is inadequate.

Canadians are sick and tired of teenagers committing serious, violent crimes and receiving little more than a slap on the wrist.

The assumption was that any law would be better. Which is why it's disappointing that the new legislation is being roundly criticized before it even becomes law.

And it's more the philosophy that's under fire, as opposed to the law itself.

Non-violent crimes and minor assaults, for example, will no longer go through the courts. Judges in youth court will have less sentencing power, and jail time will be a last resort. Youth convicted of violent crimes will be eligible for early release, similar to parole.

Youths will no longer be tried as adults—even for serious crimes—but adult sentences can be imposed following a conviction.

But perhaps the biggest change will be that police officers will have much more responsibility. They must look at a number of alternative measures before a youth is charged.
...

Perhaps critics of the *Youth Criminal Justice Act* believe it doesn't go far enough, that it's not tough enough.

But an-eye-for-an-eye has never been part of Canadian justice.
...

Source: "Time will tell with youth crime legislation," *Orillia Packet & Times*, March 5, 2003, p. A6.

TEST YOUR KNOWLEDGE

Definitions

Define the following terms:

1. *Criminal Code of Canada*

_____

_____

_____

2. Legal infant

_____

_____

_____

3. *Juvenile Delinquents Act (JDA)*

_____

_____

_____

4. Persons in need of supervision (P.I.N.S.)

_____

_____

_____

5. Neglected minors

_____

_____

_____

6. *Young Offenders Act (YOA)*

_____

_____

_____

7. *Youth Criminal Justice Act (YCJA)*

_____

_____

_____

8. Delinquency

_____

_____

_____

9. Status offence

_____

_____

_____

10. Age of culpability

_____

_____

_____

11. Alternative measures

_____

_____

_____

12. Open custody

_____

_____

_____

13. Secure custody

_____

_____

_____

True/False

1.   T   F   Until the late 19th century, the laws of the United States applied almost directly to Canada.

2.   T   F   In colonial times, young people over the age of seven years and adults were treated similarly.

3.   T   F   In colonial times, there were separate prisons for adults and young people.

4.   T   F   Industrial schools in Ontario were in response to treatment in reformatories that was considered to be too lenient.

5.   T   F   Children's Aid Societies were established in Ontario before 1900.

6.   T   F   Welfare concerns are in the provincial jurisdiction.

7.   T   F   The _Juvenile Delinquents Act_ includes sexual immorality and vice in the definition of delinquency.

8.   T   F   The implementation of the _Juvenile Delinquents Act_ depended on the co-operation of the provinces.

9.   T   F   In the _Juvenile Delinquents Act_, there was a clear distinction between criminal acts and other anti-social acts.

10.   T   F   The _Young Offenders Act_ was around for almost 100 years.

11. T   F   The *Young Offenders Act* was designed to keep young persons inside the criminal justice system for as long as possible.

12. T   F   The *Young Offenders Act* generally prohibited the publication of the identity of young persons.

13. T   F   Crimes are defined by the *Young Offenders Act*.

14. T   F   The *Young Offenders Act* was well accepted and did not generate criticism.

15. T   F   Everyone agrees that the names of young offenders should not be published.

Multiple Choice

1. When Canada inherited the English system of criminal law it had the unique feature of

   a. a total absence of provisions for dealing with women who might violate the law
   b. a total absence of systematic penal code
   c. a highly structured and clearly defined criminal code
   d. allowing the penalty of capital punishment of young people for a very broad range of offences

2. English common law defined a person between the ages of 7 and 14 years as

   a. adults
   b. near adults
   c. legal infants
   d. having no ability to form criminal intent

3. In the 19th century, young persons under the age of 12 years in Canada

   a. were not imprisoned
   b. were sometimes lashed (or whipped)
   c. were never placed in the same institutions as adults
   d. were sometimes sent to a prison colony on Vancouver Island

4. Industrial schools were created in Ontario because treatment in reformatories was considered to be

   a. too harsh
   b. too lax
   c. inadequate to deal with girls
   d. too focused on the spiritual needs of young people

5. In Canada, Children's Aid Societies were first established in

    a. British Columbia
    b. Saskatchewan
    c. Ontario
    d. Nova Scotia

6. Canada's constitutional arrangements provide that provincial legislatures have jurisdiction over all of the following except

    a. property and civil rights
    b. local and private affairs
    c. criminal courts
    d. criminal law

7. The crafting of the *Juvenile Delinquents Act* in the early 1900s

    a. was based on a straight application of statutes in Illinois and Colorado
    b. was based on the experience in Australia and New Zealand
    c. was complicated by the differences in political structures between Canada and the United States
    d. was based on a model where each province is responsible for writing its own criminal code

8. The *Juvenile Delinquents Act* defined acts of delinquency, including

    a. both criminal and non-criminal behaviour
    b. any criminal behaviour
    c. only non-criminal behaviour
    d. only those misbehaviours that are recognized as sins

9. The orientation of the *Juvenile Delinquents Act* was to care for young people in conflict with the law in a manner that

    a. was similar to what a parent would do
    b. was the same as an adult
    c. reflected the child's need for corporal punishment
    d. was 30 percent the severity of what an adult would receive

10. Which of the following is not an objective of the *Young Offenders Act?*

    a. hold young people accountable for their behaviour
    b. protection of society
    c. reward the good and punish the wicked
    d. protect the legal rights of young persons

11. Which of the following is required for the use of alternative measures?

    a. that the young person has not really committed a crime
    b. that an appropriate program is not available
    c. that the young person admits guilt
    d. that a fine has already been paid

12. Alternative measures are for all of the following purposes, except

    a. dealing with minor offences
    b. punishing the guilty
    c. dealing with first-time offenders
    d. diverting some young offenders from the criminal justice system

13. The rights of young persons under the *Canadian Charter of Rights and Freedoms*

    a. are less than for adults
    b. are less than those of the police
    c. are the same as everyone else
    d. mostly disappear if they are suspected of having committed a crime

14. Which of the following is not a criticism of the *Young Offenders Act?*

    a. the failure to provide custodial sentences for minor offences by first-time offenders
    b. the maximum sentence of 10 years
    c. the option of not participating in treatment
    d. the publication ban on names of offenders

15. Which of the following best expresses why there are criticisms of the *Young Offenders Act?*

    a. the legislation is totally flawed
    b. the legislation has no roots in our system of criminal justice
    c. there are other well-proven ways of addressing the misbehaviour of young persons that we should be using
    d. reasonable people can reasonably disagree about how to address complex problems

Short Answer

1. Distinguish between a system based on "common law" and one that uses a criminal code.

_____

_____

_____

_____

_____

_____

_____

2. What does it mean to refer to someone as a "legal infant"?

_____

_____

_____

_____

_____

_____

_____

3. Identify two disadvantages of not publishing the names of young offenders.

_____

_____

_____

_____

_____

_____

_____

_____

4. In your opinion, what was the most serious problem with the *Young Offenders Act*, and why do you think that this was so?

_____

_____

_____

_____

_____

_____

_____

_____

5. Describe the role of the court relative to youthful offenders under the *Juvenile Delinquents Act*.

_____

_____

_____

_____

_____

_____

_____

_____

6. Under the *Juvenile Delinquents Act*, what did it mean to be in a "state of delinquency"?

_____

_____

_____

_____

_____

_____

_____

_____

_____

7. Distinguish between "open custody" and "secure custody." What do you suppose would make the difference as to whether a young person would get one of these dispositions rather than the other?

_____

_____

_____

_____

_____

_____

_____

_____

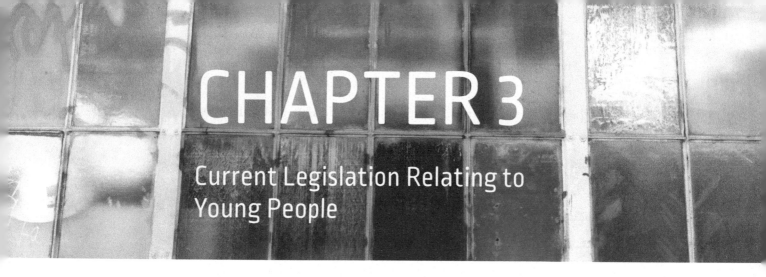

CHAPTER 3

Current Legislation Relating to Young People

LEARNING OUTCOMES

Students who have mastered this chapter will have the ability to do the following:

- Identify federal and provincial responsibilities relative to the creation of criminal law and the prosecution of criminal cases.
- Distinguish between the criteria of defining a young person in conflict with the law under the *Juvenile Delinquents Act* and the *Young Offenders Act*.
- Explain the differences involved in being a "legal infant," a "young person," or an adult.
- Specify the ways in which the *Canadian Charter of Rights and Freedoms* and the United Nations Convention on the Rights of the Child apply to young persons.
- Understand the basic objectives of the *Youth Criminal Justice Act*.
- Articulate the basis for the legal difference between young persons and adults.
- Specify the ways in which young persons are treated differently from adults.
- Describe what the *Child, Youth and Family Services Act* has to do with the behaviour of children.
- Identify some important features of the *Youth Criminal Justice Act*.

THE YOUNG PERSON AND THE LAW

Constitutional Framework

Because of the division of powers outlined in Canada's Constitution, no single level of government is responsible for handling young people who pose a social problem. The *Constitution Act, 1867*,[1] outlines the main divisions of responsibility among federal and provincial governments at sections 91 and 92.

---

1. Prior to the patriation of the Canadian Constitution by the (Pierre) Trudeau government in 1982, the *Constitution Act*, 1867, was known as the BNA or *British North America Act*. Patriation involved transferring the highest authority from the British Parliament to Canada's federal and provincial legislatures.

Federal Powers

Subsection 91(27) of the *Constitution Act* gives the federal government exclusive responsibility for defining criminal behaviour and for deciding what procedures should be followed in criminal cases. The federal government also has the responsibility for prosecuting criminal cases, but it has delegated much of that responsibility to the provinces. The *Criminal Code of Canada* (the *"Criminal Code"*) is the federal legislation which outlines what makes up a crime, what criminal procedures to follow, and how to handle criminals. The *Criminal Code* applies to all persons in Canada including adults and youths and sets out the offences and the corresponding penalties. The *Youth Criminal Justice Act* (*YCJA*)—also federal—indicates how the *Criminal Code* is to be applied to young persons. The *YCJA* creates a separate youth court and establishes a separate set of available punishments. While only federal law can be criminal law, there is other legislation in Canada that regulates behaviour.

Provincial Powers

Various parts of section 92 of the *Constitution Act, 1867*, state that the provinces are responsible for civil matters, licensing, and for the enforcement of provincial laws. Thus, the provinces regulate matters of property and other civil concerns. All provinces and territories in Canada regulate gambling, the consumption and sale of alcohol, the use and sale of tobacco, the conditions for driving motor vehicles, and other behaviours within the provincial realm. All of the separate pieces of legislation set out their own offences and penalties, which typically are fines but may include incarceration. The provinces also set the appropriate procedures for dealing with provincial offences. Section 92(14) of the *Constitution Act, 1867*, mandates that the provinces are responsible for administration of justice, which includes policing and the establishment of civil and criminal courts. The division of power also makes the provinces responsible for most "social" or common welfare issues. The result of the welfare and justice powers is that the provinces are generally responsible for people who misbehave whether or not that behaviour is formally considered "criminal." This includes, for example, people who misbehave because of mental problems (they are handled under the *Mental Health Act*), children who are truant (they are handled under the *Education Act*), or children we see as too young to be handled by criminal law (they are handled under the *Child, Youth and Family Services Act*).

Delegation of Powers

Just as the federal government may delegate some of its responsibilities to the provinces, so too the provinces may delegate some of their responsibilities to municipal governments. Under this arrangement, the provinces give municipalities the power to make and to enforce by-laws. Similarly, they allow many municipalities to have their own police services whose duty it is to enforce criminal law, provincial statues, and municipal by-laws. The result of the constitutional division of powers combined with delegated power means that young persons may be sanctioned for violating federal, provincial, or municipal laws.

Doctrine of Paramountcy

With three levels of government able to make rules governing behaviour, there can occasionally be conflicts. The constitutional doctrine of paramountcy states that where there is conflict, the legislation of the higher level of government will prevail. The general rule is that, to the extent of the conflict, federal law supersedes provincial law, and provincial law supersedes municipal law. Whether or not a law, or part of a law, is paramount to a subordinate law is determined by the courts, but it is still worth understanding that the principle exists.

Incarceration

The *Constitution Act* at section 91(28) empowers the federal government to establish and run penitentiaries. Yet, section 92(6) provides that provinces can establish and maintain prisons for provincial purposes. Adult offenders can be sentenced either to a provincial or federal institution. The federal and provincial governments share responsibilities for adults convicted of offences. Persons receiving a sentence of two years' incarceration or more are the responsibility of the federal corrections system. Persons receiving sentences of less than two years are the responsibility of the provincial correctional systems. Young persons in conflict with the law, however, are the sole responsibility of the provinces.

At times, this peculiar division of responsibility leads to political conflict. The provinces sometimes contend that it is unfair for the federal government to make the rules about young persons who violate the law when the provinces see themselves paying most of the bills. Different provinces have different views on how young offenders should be handled, and they sometimes argue that the federal government's rules do not fit local circumstances. Ontario has been one of the most vocal objectors on this score. In fact, Ontario sought and obtained an exemption that allowed it to delay the implementation of many sections of the *Young Offenders Act* (*YOA*) when it was first introduced. The federal government's response to the provinces is about equity. Ottawa argues that all Canadians should be treated the same whether they live in British Columbia, Ontario, or even (sometimes) Quebec.

The process of consultation over the *YCJA* was long and involved and revealed that there continue to be deep divisions among the provinces on how young violators of the law should be treated. After the *YCJA* was passed by Parliament, it was sent to the Senate for the "sober second thought" exercised in the "upper chamber." Ontario proposed more than 100 amendments for the Senate's consideration—most designed to toughen the language of the legislation. The Senate agreed to none of them.

In a constitutional sense, one of the most interesting features of the *YCJA* is that it allows the individual provinces to enact, or not, wide arrays of provisions that may—and most likely will—lead to quite different ways of dealing with young persons in different provinces. The *YCJA* speaks of uniformity of application across "regions" (*YCJA* 38(2)(b)), which are undefined but seem to allow differences, even within provinces. The principle that the law should apply uniformly appears to be violated. Whether this will lead to constitutional challenges remains to be seen.

As we saw in Chapter 2, in 1908, the federal government tried to deal with some inconsistencies this division of responsibility created by defining most childhood misbehaviour as delinquency. Thus, the *Juvenile Delinquents Act* "criminalized" much behaviour that we might see as wrong, sinful, or immoral, but not necessarily criminal, if performed by an adult.

The introduction of the *YOA* resulted in a reduction of the federal government's control over young people, and this continues in the *YCJA*. A basic principle of the *YCJA* is that of fairness. The writers of both acts believed that consistent definitions of criminality should apply to both young people and adults. Young persons generally should not be held criminally responsible for behaviours that would not be considered criminal if committed by an adult. Thus, the provinces again faced the problem of what to do with non-criminal, but socially unacceptable, youthful misbehaviour. With the *YCJA*, as with the *YOA* before it, Parliament set the minimum age of legal responsibility at the age of 12 years. At the upper end, it imposed a national maximum of 18 years of age for distinguishing young persons from adults.

THE *CRIMINAL CODE* OF CANADA

The *Criminal Code* indicates which behaviours are criminal. It also specifies the procedures law enforcement officials must follow and the maximum penalties for committing a crime. The application of the *Criminal Code*, however, is much more restricted when we are dealing with young persons instead of adults. The definition of what is criminal applies equally to young persons and adults with only legal infants (persons under the age of 12 years) being totally exempt. Many procedures, particularly those that relate to the notification of rights, the acceptance of confessions, and detention, apply only partially to young people. The *YCJA* alters and extends the basic principles that apply to adult cases. Furthermore, the sentences or dispositions outlined in the *Criminal Code* have only partial bearing on the sentences that the youth justice courts might hand out. Again, the *YCJA* specifies the conditions that the youth justice courts can impose on young offenders. Police officers need to be familiar with the offences outlined in the *Criminal Code*, since they form the basis of the substantive law as it applies to young persons.

THE *CANADIAN CHARTER OF RIGHTS AND FREEDOMS*

The ***Canadian Charter of Rights and Freedoms***,[2] which was introduced in 1982, has become an increasingly important document for criminal justice personnel—particularly police officers. The main purpose of the *Charter* is to protect all Canadians, including young people (and police officers), from arbitrary and excessive state intervention in their lives. The *Charter* guarantees, among other things, equality before the law, whatever one's social characteristics (such as age, gender, religious affiliation, or ethnicity), and the right to due process. Sections 8 through 10 of the *Charter* indicate that everyone has the right

- to be secure against unreasonable search or seizure;
- not to be arbitrarily detained or imprisoned;
- to be promptly informed of the reason for being arrested or detained;
- to have and to instruct legal counsel without delay and to be informed of that right; and
- to be released if detention is unlawful or unwarranted.

Many citizens and criminal justice personnel think that minor violations of these Charter rights automatically lead to a case being "thrown out" of court. This is not always the case. For example, subsection 24(2) of the *Charter* allows judges to admit physical evidence even in cases where a confession was improperly obtained. The key issue is whether "having regard to all the circumstances, the admission of it in the proceedings would bring the administration of justice into disrepute." To make this assessment, judges must examine the broader circumstances surrounding the violation of the *Charter*. Part of the misperception here is probably due to differences between Canadian and American jurisprudence. In the United States, constitutional provisions have been more narrowly interpreted. There, taking account of "all the circumstances" is not a consideration.

As we will see in Chapter 5, the courts have also recognized that young persons are usually less aware of their rights than are adults. The courts believe young people are less able than adults to make prudent decisions. Consequently, they have interpreted many fundamental rights outlined in the *Charter* more broadly when applied to young people.

---

2. Available at Government of Canada Justice Laws website: http://laws-lois.justice.gc.ca/eng/Const/page-15.html

THE UNITED NATIONS CONVENTION ON THE RIGHTS OF THE CHILD

The United Nations Convention on the Rights of the Child[3] (UNCRC) is an international legally binding treaty that recognizes that all children under the age of 18 have fundamental human rights. It was adopted by the United Nations in 1989 and since that time 194 countries have signed and ratified the agreement. Canada signed the convention on May 28, 1990, and ratified it on December 13, 1991. Only two countries have not ratified the agreement: the United States and Somalia. It is the expectation that under the convention governments will meet children's basic needs and help them reach their full potential.

The UNCRC contains 54 articles that set out children's rights. Notably, article 12 states that "the child shall in particular be provided the opportunity to be heard in any judicial and administrative proceedings affecting the child, either directly, or through a representative or an appropriate body, in a manner consistent with the procedural rules of national law." This provision is reflected in the *Youth Criminal Justice Act* in section 3(1)(d)(i) regarding the participatory rights of the child when being dealt with under this Act. Respecting and making sure that children are dealt with in an age-appropriate manner that respects their human rights applies throughout from their arrest and questioning, to the type of detention, and the approach of the youth justice court (as further discussed in later chapters).

THE *CHILD, YOUTH AND FAMILY SERVICES ACT*

The *Child, Youth and Family Services Act* (*CYFSA*, 2017) is focused on the protection of children (see Chapter 5 for an extensive discussion). Ontario deals with children under 12 years of age who commit criminal offences under this legislation. Basically, the *CYFSA* is child welfare legislation, and its provisions reflect that underlying philosophy. Consequently, child protection officers (including police/peace officers) are directed to bring a child younger than 12 home or to a place of safety:

> 84 (1) A peace officer who believes on reasonable and probable grounds that a child actually or apparently younger than 12 has committed an act in respect of which a person 12 or older could be found guilty of an offence may bring the child to a place of safety without a warrant and on doing so,
>
> (a)   shall return the child to the child's parent or other person having charge of the child as soon as practicable; or

---

3.   You can read the full convention at the website of the Office of the United Nations High Commissioner for Human Rights at http://www.ohchr.org/EN/ProfessionalInterest/Pages/CRC.aspx

(b)   where it is not possible to return the child to the parent or other person within a reasonable time, shall bring the child to a place of safety until the child can be returned to the parent or other person.

As Bala and Mahoney (1995) point out, "the only legal basis for intervention is if there is serious or repetitive offending behaviour combined with parental unwillingness or inability to provide an appropriate response." Theoretically, an 11-year-old who commits a serious assault would simply be placed in the custody of his or her parents. Usually, however, children who kill or seriously injure someone or who commit more than one serious assault or act of property damage can be subjected to greater intervention. This is also the case where the child's parents either have clearly not provided adequate supervision or have actually encouraged the behaviour. Under these circumstances, the police or a child welfare officer can ask the court to find the child to be "in need of protection" per *CYFSA*, s. 74(2)(l) and (m):

(l) the child is younger than 12 and has killed or seriously injured another person or caused serious damage to another person's property, services or treatment are necessary to prevent a recurrence and the child's parent or the person having charge of the child does not provide services or treatment or access to services or treatment, or, where the child is incapable of consenting to treatment under the *Health Care Consent Act*, 1996, refuses or is unavailable or unable to consent to treatment;

(m) the child is younger than 12 and has on more than one occasion injured another person or caused loss or damage to another person's property, with the encouragement of the person having charge of the child or because of that person's failure or inability to supervise the child adequately.

THE *YOUTH CRIMINAL JUSTICE ACT* AND THE 2012 AMENDMENTS

The *Youth Criminal Justice Act* (*YCJA*) became law on February 2, 2002, replacing the *Young Offenders Act*. It came into force in Ontario on April 1, 2003. The *YCJA* underwent some amendments as contained in the *Safe Street and Communities Act* in March 2012. The principles on which *YCJA* is based echo many of the principles of the *YOA*—for example, protection of society and protection of the rights of young people. However, it goes beyond the *YOA* with an emphasis on prevention and rehabilitation and on sensitivity to the needs of victims. Accordingly, the declaration of principles in subsection 3(1)(a) reads as follows:

the youth criminal justice system is intended to protect the public by

(i) holding young persons accountable through measures that are proportionate to the seriousness of the offence and the degree of responsibility of the young person,

(ii) promoting the rehabilitation and reintegration of young persons who have committed offences, and

(iii) supporting the prevention of crime by referring young persons to programs or agencies in the community to address the circumstances underlying their offending behaviour.

The criminal justice system for young persons must be separate from that of adults, must be based on the principle of **diminished moral blameworthiness**, and emphasize the following:

- Rehabilitation and reintegration
- Fair and proportionate accountability
- Enhanced procedural protection to protect youth rights, including the right to privacy
- Timely intervention that reinforces the link between the offending behaviour and its consequences
- Promptness of enforcement

Within the limits of fair and proportionate accountability, the measures taken against young persons should do the following:

- Reinforce respect for societal values
- Encourage the repair of harm done to victims and the community
- Be meaningful to the young persons, given their needs and level of development, and, where appropriate, involve parents, extended family, the community, and social or other agencies in the young person's rehabilitation and reintegration
- Respect gender, ethnic, cultural and linguistic differences and respond to the needs of Aboriginal young persons and young persons with special requirements

Special considerations that should apply to proceedings against young persons are the following:

- Protection of the rights and freedoms of young persons
- Courteous, compassionate, and respectful treatment of victims
- Victims should be provided with information about the proceedings and given the opportunity to participate
- Parents should be informed of measures and proceedings involving their children and encouraged to support them

Parliament meant the *YCJA* to protect society from youthful criminals through several measures. First of all, the justice system is expected to divert as many young offenders as possible from the formal process. The writers of the Act expected more varied programs to be introduced than existed under the *YOA*. This gives the police, Crown prosecutors, and the courts more options for intervention and, hopefully, those options would be more effective than what had been previously available.

POLICE DISCRETION

Adults

Where adults are concerned, police discretion may be necessary to serve the interests of justice as not all situations fit the letter of the law. Typically what we mean by police discretion is a situation where an officer decides to avoid the judicial process by deciding to investigate no further or to not forward information to the Crown. Where adults are concerned, if police use their discretion, it "must [be] exercised honestly and transparently, and on the basis of valid and reasonable grounds." In determining whether or not grounds are reasonable both subjective and objective factors should be considered (*R v. Beaudry* [2007] 1 S.C.R. 190). In other words, police discretion may be used, but there is the high bar of being able to demonstrate justification for doing so.

Young Persons

The use of discretion where youth are involved is different. Section 6(1) in *YCJA* creates a positive requirement on police to use their discretion as a starting point. That section states that a police officer "shall" determine whether it is appropriate to take no further action, provide a warning, administer a caution, or with the young person's consent, refer him or her to a program. Only after considering these options can more formal steps be taken. The clear objective is to try to keep young people out of the judicial process.

By providing flexibility in the legislation, the courts can encourage more use of community service orders and victim compensation. The belief is that offenders who are kept closer to the community will become more aware of the social harm they cause and be more quickly reintegrated.

The *YCJA* reserves the formal process for the most serious offenders. It does this in two major ways. First, there is an emphasis on diverting many offenders out of the formal system through the use of extrajudicial measures that include warnings, cautions, and referrals to programs, as well as Crown cautions. Second, for many types of offences and for many offenders, there is a presumption against the use of custody as an intervention.

The 2012 Amendments: *Safe Streets and Communities Act*

In 2012, the federal government introduced a number of amendments to various pieces of criminal law legislation (dubbed the "Omnibus Crime Bill"), of which Part 4 applied to the *Youth Criminal Justice Act*. The amendments gave the impression that the federal government was taking a "get tough on crime" approach that included "cracking down" on young offenders. As law professor Nicholas Bala (2015) writes, the focus was actually more of a targeted approach to get tougher on adult offenders, with no real philosophical or practical changes with respect to young offenders:

> Despite the success of the *YCJA* in reducing youth incarceration rates without increasing crime, conservative politicians have continued to invoke "law-and-order" rhetoric to criticize the law, and, as a result, some amendments to the *YCJA* were enacted in 2012. These amendments, however, were a fine-tuning of the Act and not intended to change basic approaches to youth justice in Canada. Some of the more publicized 2012 *YCJA* amendments promote "denunciation" of youth crime and increased emphasis on "protection of the public." However, these were largely symbolic, and some of the less publicized changes actually narrow the grounds for pre-trial detention of adolescents. In contrast to the conservative "get tough on crime law" agenda for adults, which is driving up adult incarceration rates, it seems clear that the federal government does not want Canada to return to its high rates of use of courts and custody for youth criminal justice, if only for financial reasons. While Canada has significantly reduced rates of use of courts and custody, there remain significant challenges about the responses to youth crime in Canada, including the continuing lack of rehabilitative resources and mental health services in community based programs and in custody facilities, high rates of involvement in the youth justice system of Aboriginal and racialized youth, and concerns about conditions in custody facilities. (pp. 127–28)

Thus, the core principles of youth rehabilitation and second chances have prevailed.

Serious Offences

Generally, the 2012 amendments had minimal impact, but concerns that young offenders were not being held sufficiently responsible for serious offences were at the heart of the changes. Therefore, the 2012 amendments to the *YCJA* created three categories of serious offences for youth:

1. Serious Offences
   A *serious offence* is a defined term meaning any indictable offence under an Act of Parliament for which the maximum punishment [if committed by an adult] is imprisonment for five years or more.

2. Violent Offence
   A *violent offence* is also a defined term that requires an element of causing bodily harm, an attempt or threat to cause bodily harm, or an offence in which a young person endangers another person or creates a substantial likelihood of causing bodily harm.

3. Serious Violent Offence

A *serious violent offence* is one of the following: first-degree or second-degree murder, attempt to commit murder, manslaughter, and aggravated sexual assault.

Most notably, the violent offence category was to ensure that a young offender would serve time in custody where it was found that the youth had endangered public safety even if there was no physical harm and/or intent to cause harm. This was in reaction to the Supreme Court of Canada case *R. v. D(C)*, 2005 S.C.C. in which the court had limited the definition of "violent offence" to situations where the young person *actually* caused or attempted to cause or threatened to cause bodily harm. As a result, courts can now impose a custodial sentence on a young person who may have previously been able to escape the "violent" classification (Bala, 2015: 164).

In 2012, Parliament removed the presumptive offence scheme from the *YCJA* while retaining Crown applications for adult sentences for youth. Parliament also amended the adult sentencing provisions to include the following:

- If a young person is 14 years of age or older and is charged with a serious violent offence, the prosecutor must consider applying to the court for an adult sentence. If the prosecutor decides not to apply for an adult sentence, the prosecutor must advise the court. A province may decide to change the age at which this obligation is triggered from 14 to 15 or 16.
- A court can impose an adult sentence only if (a) the prosecution rebuts the presumption that the young person has diminished moral blameworthiness or culpability, and (b) a youth sentence would not be of sufficient length to hold the young person accountable.
- A young person under the age of 18 who receives an adult sentence is to be placed in a youth facility and may not be placed in an adult correctional facility. Once the young person turns 18, he or she may be placed in an adult facility.

Thus, serious offences committed by young persons, who are at least 14 years of age, can result in adult sentences. Each of these is discussed in more detail later in this book (see Chapters 9 and 10).

Overview of the YCJA and Its Key Provisions

This section provides an overview of key aspects of the *YCJA*. Many of these will be discussed in greater detail in the forthcoming chapters, but this discussion will give you an overview of how the legislation works and important highlights for the treatment of young persons who have come into contact with police and the youth criminal justice system.

The *YCJA* is a lengthy document that all police officers need to study. Throughout this book, a serious attempt is made to faithfully represent the elements of the legislation under discussion. Any variation that may exist between this rendition and the

Act must be resolved in favour of the Act. For most purposes, however, it will not be necessary for students to refer to the Act, but it is instructive to check sections of it if questions of interpretation do arise. In addition, it is useful to examine it in order to appreciate how legislation is structured and to be able to follow its requirements.

The *YCJA* recognizes that young people are different from adults. While the prevailing philosophy of the *YCJA* is to enhance accountability, it recognizes that young people (even offenders) need special protections and an emphasis on the opportunity for rehabilitation (see also Chapter 11, "The Criminal Justice System"). This belief goes beyond the traditional notion that young persons lack the social and psychological maturity of adults. Provision of the *YCJA* prohibits the publication of the young offenders' identities, restricts access to their records, and limits the length of sentences. There is respect for the young person's fundamental legal rights, such as the right to legal representation. The police are expected to inform young suspects of their legal rights. Furthermore, police officers cannot take confessions without a written waiver or the presence of the young person's lawyer or guardian. Due process, procedural fairness, and an emphasis on explaining the rights to young persons characterize the *YCJA*.

Young Persons

The *YCJA* defines "young persons" as individuals who are or who appear to be between the ages of 12 and 17 years, inclusive. It is interesting to note that this standard is both subjective and objective. Under 12 years of age, a person is considered a child and must be dealt with under provincial child welfare statutes. When people reach their 18th birthday, they are considered adults. It is important to note, however, that it is the age of the person when the offence is committed that is important—not the person's age at the time of arrest and charge. Thus, someone who commits a sexual assault when 17 years old but is not caught until age 19 years is still considered a young person and falls under the direction of the *YCJA* (see Chapter 6, "Arresting and Questioning Young Persons").

Crimes

The *YCJA* does not describe what makes up a criminal act, but does make distinctions for serious violent offences, violent offences, and serious offences. The *Criminal Code of Canada* defines what is a criminal act. Basically, the law holds young persons accountable for the same behaviours considered criminal if committed by an adult. Furthermore, the same rules of procedure and evidence outlined in the *Criminal Code* and the *Canada Evidence Act* generally apply to young people as they apply to adults. Police officers must, therefore, be familiar with both documents.

Extrajudicial Measures

Immediately after the declaration of principles, the *YCJA* outlines a set of extrajudicial measures. **Extrajudicial measures** are ways of dealing with young persons who are in conflict with the law, in a manner that reduces continued formal processing in the criminal justice system. These measures can be initiated by the police, the Crown prosecutor, or a judge before or after a finding of guilt. Extrajudicial measures may be used to deal with a young person alleged to have committed relatively minor offences (such as petty theft or minor acts of vandalism) under certain conditions, typically, but not necessarily, when they are first offences. These measures range from no further action to referrals by the court. The primary function of non-judicial measures is to divert young offenders from the formal court system through the use of less formal interventions that may be applied in a timely fashion to the ends of prevention, rehabilitation, and reintegration. The secondary function is to reserve courts and other more formal aspects of the justice system for severe offenders and those who cannot benefit from extrajudicial measures (see Chapter 7, "Extrajudicial Measures").

Youth Justice Courts

Under the *YCJA*, any court that deals with a young person is a **youth justice court**. Youth justice courts are means of keeping young offenders separate from adults. In practice, while the courts hear cases involving young persons at different times from those of adult cases, youth justice court judges are Ontario Court (provincial division) judges. Thus, the same judges, court clerks, and Crown attorneys who handle adult cases often handle cases of young persons in the same courtrooms. Young persons are also to be kept in separate holding and detention facilities, although young persons and adults are sometimes kept in adjacent cells (see Chapter 9, "The Youth Justice Court").

Notice to Parents

If the police arrest and detain a young person, the officer in charge has the responsibility to notify the young person's parents or relatives of the arrest as soon as possible. Parents are also to be notified of any summons or appearance notice that requires the young person to appear in court. In practice, courts often postpone proceedings until a responsible adult relative can be identified and notified (see Chapter 6, "Arresting and Questioning Young Persons").

Rights

Young persons have the same rights as adults as outlined in the *Canadian Charter of Rights and Freedoms*. Thus, arresting officers have an obligation to notify young offenders of their rights. Young offenders also have the right to legal counsel, the right to confer with their parents or guardians, and the right to due care while in detention. The handling of young people's confessions is much more restricted under the *YCJA* than it is for adults (see Chapter 6, "Arresting and Questioning Young Persons," and Chapter 9, "The Youth Justice Court").

Procedures

Young persons who are detained have the same right to a bail hearing as adults. Unlike adults, however, young people are not released on their own recognizance. Once a young offender is found guilty, the court may ask for a pre-sentence report. This report generally contains more detailed information on the young person's character and life circumstances that the judge can use when determining an appropriate sentence.

When sentencing a young offender, we expect judges to fit the penalty to the crime. They are to do this while considering mitigating circumstances, the needs of the young person, and the protection of the community (see Chapter 8, "Pre-trial Detention and Processing," and Chapter 9, "The Youth Justice Court").

Sentences

The *YCJA* contains several sections that relate to the sentencing of young offenders. (The *YOA* referred to these as "dispositions.") Many sentences are similar to those available in adult court. For example, the *YCJA* allows for both absolute and conditional discharges, fines, compensation or restitution orders, community service orders, and prohibition orders. There are also provisions for "supervision orders," which are similar to parole for adults, but not the same. Youth justice court judges may also sentence young offenders to custody, of which there are two types. Custody with the least degree of restraint consists of removing the young persons from their homes and placing them in a group home for a fixed length of time; in Ontario, it is referred to as open custody. Custody with a higher degree of restraint, secure custody, generally implies that a sentenced young person is placed in a more restrictive, jail-type facility with bars and electronic surveillance (see Chapter 9, "The Youth Justice Court," and Chapter 10, "Custody and Supervision").

Privacy

We extend young offenders greater rights to privacy than in the case of adults. For example, the police, the press, and the courts are all forbidden to publicize a young offender's identity. Depending upon the sentence imposed, young offenders' records are sealed (but not necessarily destroyed) within one to five years after the young person reaches the age of 18 years. Once they become adults, the young offenders' fingerprints are transferred to a special repository and then destroyed after five years. The *YCJA* is more specific than was the *YOA* about the categories of persons with whom information about young persons in conflict with the law can be shared. It also makes provisions that allow the identification of young offenders to victims (on request, as well as in cases of investigation when the protection of the public is an issue) (see Chapter 8, "Pre-trial Detention and Processing").

Provincial Legislation

So far in this chapter, with the exception of the *Child, Youth and Family Services Act* (Ontario), the laws we have reviewed are all federal. As with federal laws, many provincial laws contain offenses that apply to all people unless an exception is made. The lists of legislation differ by province, but all provinces regulate matters assigned to them by section 92 of the *Constitution Act*. The culpability of young people in provinces also varies across the country but all provinces treat youth differently from adults. For example, in Ontario, the treatment of young persons who have broken provincial or municipal laws is outlined in the *Provincial Offences Act* (*POA*). While that Act is only applicable to Ontario it is illustrative of how provinces view young persons.

Provincial Offences Act, R.S.O. 1990

The *POA* is the procedural legislation under which all provincial (and municipal) offences are prosecuted in Ontario. Part VI of that Act defines youth as persons 12 years or older, but under 16. Youth under 12 cannot be convicted of a provincial or municipal offence. This lines up with the *YCJA* exclusion of youth under 12 from being convicted under the *Criminal Code*. The *POA* is also similar to the *YCJA* in that it limits sentences for young offenders and bans publication of their names.

IN THE NEWS

Brothers, Aged 6 and 8, Crash Parents' Truck at Tim Hortons in Jarvis, ON

An eight-year-old boy and his six-year-old brother escaped unharmed after they allegedly crashed their parents' truck at a Tim Hortons coffee shop in southwestern Ontario.

Provincial police say the boys took the pickup truck around 7 a.m. Thursday. They were hungry for breakfast. They say the eight-year-old, who was driving, lost control of the vehicle in the Tim Hortons' drive-thru in Jarvis, ON, southwest of Hamilton.

The truck hopped the curb and veered into a field where it became stuck.

Police say a Tim Hortons' employee checked on the truck and discovered the children.

No charges were laid and the boys were turned over to their parents.

Source: "Brothers, aged 6 and 8, crash parents' truck at Tim Hortons in Jarvis, ON," The Canadian Press, May 5, 2017. Retrieved from: http://www.cbc.ca/news/canada/hamilton/brothers-aged-6-and-8-crash-parents-truck-at-tim-hortons-in-jarvis-ont-1.4101697

Given the potential for serious consequences of such a young child driving a vehicle, why were no charges laid and the child simply returned to his parents?

Where the *POA* is noticeably different from the *YCJA* is the age at which people are considered adults for the purposes of enforcing provincial offences. In Ontario, that is age 16. It is probably not coincidental that 16 is the minimum age for driving in Ontario. Vehicles and drivers in Ontario are regulated by the *Highway Traffic Act*. According to Ontario statistics, *Highway Traffic Act* offences made up almost half of all provincial offences between April 2015 and March 2017 (http://www.ontario-courts.ca/ocj/files/stats/poa/2017/2017-POA-Statute.pdf). By making the age for adult treatment 16, Ontario is able to treat all drivers as adults in terms of punishment for offences. Given that some highway traffic offences may result in a jail sentence, it is possible for persons under 18 to be given a jail term. This is clearly contradictory to the *YCJA*'s intent. One wonders whether or not a 17-year-old Ontario driver could successfully argue that the doctrine of paramountcy should invalidate the upper age limit under the *POA*.

TEST YOUR KNOWLEDGE

Definitions

Define the following terms:

1. Diminished moral blameworthiness

_____

_____

_____

2. Extrajudicial measures

_____

_____

_____

3. Youth justice court

_____

_____

_____

True/False

1. T F   Persons receiving sentences of two years or more are the responsibility of the provincial corrections system.

2. T F   Provinces, not the federal government, are responsible for local policing.

3. T F   All provinces have the same view of how young persons in conflict with the law should be handled.

4. T F   Persons under the age of 12 years old are to be dealt with under the *Criminal Code of Canada*, rather than under the *Youth Criminal Justice Act*.

5. T F   Procedures regarding the acceptance of confessions are different for young persons from what they are for adults.

6. T F   The *Youth Criminal Justice Act* has been around for so long that it is now almost 100 years old.

7. T F   The *Youth Criminal Justice Act* is designed to keep young persons inside the criminal justice system for as long as possible.

8. T F   The *Youth Criminal Justice Act* generally prohibits the publication of the identity of young persons.

9. T F   Crimes are defined by the *Youth Criminal Justice Act*.

10. T F   The *Youth Criminal Justice Act* is difficult to understand because it contains no statement of principles that would assist interpretation and application.

Multiple Choice

1. In Canada, the responsibility for defining criminal behaviour belongs to
   a. the police
   b. judges
   c. Parliament
   d. the provinces

2. What piece of legislation identifies the procedures to be followed in handling young persons who have committed crimes?
   a. *Youth Criminal Justice Act*
   b. *Young Criminals Act*
   c. *Criminal Code of Canada*
   d. Canadian Constitution

3. Young persons in conflict with the law are the sole responsibility of
   a. the federal government
   b. the provinces

      c. their parents

      d. the Children's Aid Society

4. The *Youth Criminal Justice Act* applies to young people who are

      a. 10–16 years old

      b. 11–17 years old

      c. 12–19 years old

      d. at least 12 years, but not yet 18 years old

5. Whether a person is to be dealt with under the *Youth Criminal Justice Act* is determined by the person's age at the time

      a. the crime was committed

      b. of arrest

      c. of the court case

      d. most of the evidence was collected

6. Children under the age of 12 years who commit serious misbehaviour are dealt with under the

      a. *Criminal Code of Canada*

      b. *Youth Criminal Justice Act*

      c. *Child, Youth and Family Services Act*

      d. *Teenagers Reform Act*

7. Which of the following is *not* an objective of the *Youth Criminal Justice Act*?

      a. hold young people accountable for their behaviour

      b. protection of society

      c. reward the good and punish the wicked

      d. protect the legal rights of young persons

8. Parents of young persons have

      a. a right to be notified if a young person is arrested or detained

      b. no rights

      c. the same rights as the parents of adult criminals and no more

      d. to hire a lawyer before the parents can speak to the young person

9. The rights of young persons under the *Canadian Charter of Rights and Freedoms*

      a. are fewer than for adults

      b. are fewer than those of the police

      c. are the same as everyone else

      d. mostly disappear if they are suspected of having committed a crime

Short Answer

1. Explain why there is sometimes conflict between the federal government and the provinces on how young persons in conflict with the law are to be dealt with.

   _____

   _____

   _____

   _____

   _____

   _____

   _____

   _____

   _____

2. Why does Canada have the *Criminal Code of Canada* as well as the *Youth Criminal Justice Act?*

   _____

   _____

   _____

   _____

   _____

   _____

   _____

   _____

   _____

   _____

3. When it comes to crime, what are the reasons for treating young persons differently from adults?

   _____

   _____

   _____

   _____

   _____

   _____

_____

_____

_____

_____

4. What is the responsibility of a police officer who apprehends a 10-year-old who has committed a serious violation?

_____

_____

_____

_____

_____

_____

_____

_____

_____

5. A young person commits a serious crime three weeks before his 18th birthday. He is arrested nine months later and brought to court after his 19th birthday. Does the _Youth Criminal Justice Act_ apply? If yes, why, and how? If no, why not?

_____

_____

_____

_____

_____

_____

_____

_____

_____

6. What three conditions must apply before a police officer can accept a confession from a young person?

_____

_____

_____

_____

_____

_____

_____

_____

_____

7. Adults can be released "on their own recognizance." Why do you suppose that this does not apply to young persons?

_____

_____

_____

_____

_____

_____

_____

_____

_____

8. What do you suppose would make the difference as to whether a young person would get a particular sentence rather than another?

_____

_____

_____

_____

_____

_____

_____

_____

_____

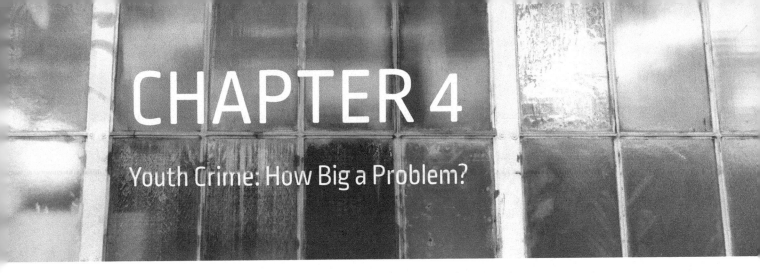

CHAPTER 4

Youth Crime: How Big a Problem?

LEARNING OUTCOMES

Students who have mastered this chapter will have the ability to do the following:

- Explain the value of official statistics on crime.
- Identify and describe key official crime rate measures of youth crime.
- Describe the crime rate patterns associated with youth crime.
- Distinguish between "crimes known to the police" and "crimes cleared."
- Indicate what police discretion is and the extent to which it has an effect on the official rates of less serious and more serious crimes.
- Explain what "self-reports" of crime are and what they tell us about crime that is similar to and different from official statistics.
- Explain what "victimization surveys" of crime are and what they tell us about crime that is similar to and different from official statistics.
- Distinguish among ratios, proportions, and rates.

MEASURING CRIME

Along with the weather, one of the most common topics of conversation is crime. Crime stories are the "bread and butter" of the news media and are the topic of much of our entertainment on television and in the movies. The media has a significant influence on most people's knowledge of how much crime exists and where and when it takes place. The constant diet of crime stories in the newspapers and on television tends to create the conventional wisdom that crime is ever on the increase. It is also part of the conventional wisdom that young people commit more crimes than they did in the past and that they are committing more serious crimes than ever before.

For people working in the criminal justice system, however, the question of how much crime there is in a community has far more practical consequences. Social scientists, such as criminologists and sociologists, use information on the distribution of crime to test explanations of crime. Politicians and planners use crime rates to decide whether there is a need for more police officers or if more courts or prisons should be built. Criminal justice administrators, on the other hand, use crime data to plan the allocation of resources. More police patrols, for example, are generally allocated to areas that have either more crime or more serious crime.

The amount of crime that takes place can be determined in different ways. Each way of counting crime tells us something about the phenomenon. Depending upon our needs, some measures of crime are more useful than others.

Criminologists generally identify four main sources of information on crime.

1. **Official statistics.** The oldest and perhaps most commonly used source of information on crime is what is known as official statistics. Official statistics consist of information on crime collected by official agencies such as Statistics Canada and other groups such as the police, the courts, and the corrections system.
2. **Self-report surveys.** These ask people how much crime they commit.
3. **Victimization surveys.** These ask people if they have been the victims of crime.
4. **Other procedures.** The least frequently used source of information on crime is a residual category of other techniques such items as reports from private security firms, social scientists' field studies on gangs, direct surveillance techniques, and the results of social and psychological experiments.

We will examine each source of information separately with the aim of determining the strengths and weaknesses of those sources of information. We should note at the outset that no single source of data on crime is ideal. Each way of measuring crime has some strengths and some limitations. Each technique tends to give us a different estimate of the "true" amount of crime and each provides a different focus on the issue. Fortunately, criminologists have found that for most purposes, those different ways of measuring crime show similar patterns or distributions of crime even though the total counts do differ (for a detailed discussion, see Maxim and Whitehead, 1997).

Official Statistics

In Canada, the Dominion Bureau of Statistics (now Statistics Canada) started systematically collecting national crime data in the early 1920s. Three basic sources of official statistics are reported: police statistics, court statistics, and prison statistics.

The most commonly reported **official statistics on crime** are police statistics, particularly those referred to as crimes known to police. **Crimes known to the police** consist of just that—a count of all crimes of which the police are aware. For instance, the crime rate is a measure based on the number of *Criminal Code* offences in an area reported to the police per 100,000 population in that area. The Crime Severity Index (CSI) is a measure of police-reported crime that measures both the volume and seriousness of police-reported crime in Canada. The CSI further breaks down the data into violent and non-violent offences. Statistics Canada assigns all crimes a value based on their seriousness with more serious crimes receiving a higher value, and less serious offences a lower value. As a result, more serious offences have a greater impact on changes in the CSI.

Uniform Crime Reporting (UCR) Survey

The police statistics as discussed above are then collected through the Uniform Crime Reporting (UCR) Survey. This survey has been conducted by Statistics Canada since 1962, and is based on nationally defined police-reported crime. Nowadays, criminal incidents are tracked through computer systems that track all police dispatches in response to calls. Keep in mind, not every response is about a crime; police also respond to calls for their assistance when there have been accidents, fires, or other emergency situations that call for police involvement. Every police service across Canada is mandated to submit their UCR data to Statistics Canada. Due to the length of investigations, follow-up, evidence processing, unique internal processes, and the complexity of crime, police services are given until March 31 each year to submit their year-end UCR statistics. Statistics Canada then runs a variety of verification processes, and its tables and reports for the previous year's crime statistics begin to be published near the end of July.

Research shows that about 80 percent of the crimes known to the police result from calls for service from citizens. The remaining amount consists of crimes "discovered" by the police while on patrol or crimes uncovered through police-initiated investigations. Official reports of crimes known to police consist of all offences known to the police minus those determined to be unfounded. **Unfounded crimes** are reported offences that did not take place or were determined to be not real crimes. For example, a report of stolen property may turn out to be simply misplaced property. A stolen car may have been borrowed by one's teenage offspring, and a reported assault may be the result of a prank phone call.

In addition to reporting the crime rate and the CSI, police also provide data on **clearance rates** of crimes cleared. As defined by Statistics Canada (*Juristat*) (2012), the clearance rate

> represents the proportion of criminal incidents solved by the police. Police can clear an incident by charge or by means other than the laying of a charge. For an incident to be cleared by charge, at least one accused must have been identified and either a charge has been laid, or recommended to be laid, against this individual in connection with the incident. For an incident to be cleared otherwise, an accused must be identified and there must be sufficient evidence to lay a charge in connection with the incident, but the accused is processed by other means for one of many reasons.

A crime is most often cleared when an arrest takes place or the crime is otherwise "solved." For example, no arrest may take place in an episode of murder-suicide, but the determination of murder-suicide is enough to result in the case being closed.

National Justice Statistics Initiative (NJSI)

Data collection ultimately requires co-operation between the provincial/territorial governments and the federal government and respective agencies. One such collaborative effort is the survey that is administered as part of the National Justice Statistics Initiative (NJSI). Since 1981, the federal, provincial, and territorial deputy ministers responsible for the administration of justice in Canada, along with the chief statistician, have been working together in an enterprise known as the National Justice Statistics Initiative. The mandate of the NJSI is to provide information to the justice community as well as the public on criminal and civil justice in Canada. Although this responsibility is shared among federal, provincial, and territorial departments, the lead responsibility for the development of Canada's statistical system remains with Statistics Canada.

Youth Specific Data Collection Surveys

Statistics Canada also collects data that is specific to understanding youth crime and sentencing and custody, namely the Integrated Criminal Court Survey and the Youth Custody and Community Services survey.

Integrated Criminal Court Survey (ICCS)

The ICCS is administered by the Canadian Centre for Justice Statistics (Statistics Canada) in collaboration with provincial and territorial government departments responsible for criminal courts in Canada. The survey collects statistical information on both adult and youth court cases involving Criminal Code and other federal statute offences. The data can be reported separately for the youth court portion of the survey where the individuals involved are persons aged 12 to 17 years at the time of the offence. Data are based on a fiscal year (April 1 through March 31).

Youth Custody and Community Services (YCCS) Survey

This survey collects annual data on the delivery of youth correctional services from the provincial/territorial correctional systems. Key themes include: new admissions (commencements) to correctional programs of pre-trial detention, sentenced custody, probation, and other community-based programs. The YCCS survey collects person-based data in three areas: 1) offender (e.g., socio-demographic characteristics such as age, sex, Indigenous identity, etc.); 2) legal status such as sentenced custody, remand, probation, and the characteristics of the status (e.g., aggregate sentence, conditions of supervision, etc.); and 3) events that occur while under supervision (e.g., escapes, temporary absence, releases, breaches of probation, etc.).

Limitations

Police statistics are not perfect indicators of the total amount of crime that is committed in a community. Since most crimes known to police rely on detection by citizens, the onus is placed on citizens to be aware that a crime has taken place and to take the initiative to make a complaint. Victims of crime are among the most likely persons to report crime, but witnesses do so as well. Sometimes, citizens are not aware that a crime has been committed against them. Two patrons in a bar who decide to "step outside" often do not define the situation as an assault. Stolen property may be forgotten or believed to have been mislaid. Occasionally, victims recognize that a crime has taken place but choose not to report it because they are afraid of retaliation, too embarrassed to report it, too indifferent, or are themselves engaged in an illegal activity. For example, few prostitutes report assaults on them committed by their clients, and almost no drug dealers report instances of theft, fraud, or assault.

Despite these limitations, police statistics are often our best indication of criminal activity. At the very least, they are reported on an annual basis and are assumed to have some level of consistency. Police statistics are also used as workload data. That is, they give us a general idea of how much crime the community thinks is important enough to report and the workload faced by the local police.

Counting Crime with Multiple Variables

Even when a crime is reported by a citizen or detected by the police, there remains the difficulty of coming up with a good counting rule. Take the case of three young people who are armed and walk into a convenience store with the intention of committing a robbery. While in the store, they may assault a patron, rob the storekeeper, and do a significant amount of damage to the property. When generating an official report, what do we count? Should we count the number of offenders, the number of victims, or the number of offences? In this brief example, there are three offenders, two victims, and at least three possible offences that took place.

WHAT ARE THE PEAK TIMES FOR YOUTH CRIME?

After-school hours (3 to 6 p.m.) → Violent crime (22%), non-violent crime (20%)

Early afternoon (noon to 3 p.m.) → Drug offences (24%)

Night time (9 p.m. to midnight) → Youth traffic violations (28%)

Source: Z. Miladinovic. (2016). Youth court statistics in Canada 2014/2015. *Juristat* (Catalogue no. 85-002-X). Ottawa, ON: Statistics Canada.

Some cities place curfews on young people, not allowing them out after midnight. What is the pattern you notice around when offences are committed? Would a curfew reduce youth crime? Why? Why not?

While Statistics Canada has produced a detailed handbook for generating counts, the general rule in Canada is to report *incidents* for statistics on crimes known to police. Our example consisted of one incident, and the type of incident (crime) will be defined by the most serious offence determined to have taken place. The other bits of information will eventually appear as official statistics somewhere in the system (for example, the number of offenders), but for all intents and purposes, the official report will remain as that of one crime—in this case, robbery.

Canadian Statistics about Crime

If you are looking for criminal justice data as discussed above, then *Juristat* from Statistics Canada is your most valuable source. *Juristat* publications provide in-depth analysis and detailed statistics on a variety of topics and issues related to justice and public safety. Topics include crime; victimization; homicide; civil, family, and criminal courts; and correctional services. Issues related to community safety and perceptions of safety are also covered. The publication is intended for those with an interest in Canada's justice and public safety systems as well as those who plan, establish, administer, and evaluate programs and projects related to justice and public safety.

IN THE NEWS

Youth Crime Declines with Introduction of the Youth Criminal Justice Act

The rate of criminal charges against young people is at a 10-year low, and the *Youth Criminal Justice Act's* emphasis on reducing the number of accused who end up in court is the reason, Statistics Canada said yesterday.

...

Caseloads in Canada's youth courts declined 17 percent in 2003–2004 from the previous year, the report said. This is consistent with the goal of the *YCJA*—which replaced Canada's *Young Offenders Act* in April 2003—to keep less serious cases out of court, said Nicholas Bala, a law professor at Queen's University.

"This doesn't mean we're seeing a reduction in the level of youth crime in Canada but it means police are, in an increasingly large number of cases, dealing with cases informally, recognizing that that is often a more effective way of holding a young person accountable."

...

Source: Katie Rook, "Fewer youths heading to court, Statscan says; Rate of criminal charges hits 10-year low," *The Globe and Mail*, June 25, 2005, p. A8.

Self-report Surveys

Another source of information on crime is **self-report surveys**. The first surveys that systematically asked a sample of people whether or not they had committed certain types of crimes took place in the 1940s. Since then, social scientists have conducted many studies based on self-reports. Most of those studies have been directed toward young people and inmates. It is likely that if you have participated in a self-report study, it is the one conducted by the Centre for Addiction and Mental Health, which, since 1977, has conducted the Ontario Student Drug Use and Health Survey (OSDUHS). This is a population survey of Ontario students in grades 7 through 12 done anonymously and conducted across the province every two years to identify trends in student drug use, mental health, physical health, gambling, bullying, and other risk behaviours.

As you might suspect, self-report studies indicate that much more crime takes place than is reported in official statistics. When they were first conducted, self-report studies shocked many people when they indicated that almost everyone commits some form of offence at some point in time. In particular, conventional notions that crime was the sole domain of certain social classes and ethnic and racial groups came under challenge. After half a century of self-report research, we can draw two firm conclusions. First, the reality is that everyone does commit some type of criminal act at some point in time. Second, it is also true that what distinguishes those people who get caught from those who do not are the severity and the frequency of the offences they commit. That is, while *everyone* may commit an occasional offence, those persons most likely to show up in the official counts are those who self-report more frequent and more serious criminality.

Thus, for example, self-report studies suggest that as a group, young people from working class backgrounds and from broken homes pose more of a crime problem than do young people from a middle-class background and intact homes. Clearly, there are individual exceptions, since not all working-class kids or kids from broken homes are young criminals, but there are significant differences at the group level. From the researcher's point of view, self-report and victimization studies have the advantage of being able to provide "richer" information about criminality. Official statistics are often only broken down by age, gender, and type of offence. Self-report and victimization studies have the advantage of allowing us to look at other characteristics of young people, such as their social class, ethnicity, intelligence quotient (IQ), and school progress.

Limitations

As with official statistics, however, self-report statistics have their limitations. Self-report studies require young people to perceive that their behaviour fits one of the definitions of crime as outlined in the survey. Often, people forget their misbehaviours (particularly minor ones). Sometimes, respondents lie about or under-report their infractions; at other times, they may exaggerate or report offences they have not committed. This is even the case when researchers promise anonymity on the survey. A common complaint by critics of self-report surveys is that they tend to be loaded with minor offences and with behaviours that may constitute sins, disobediences, and other wrongs, but not crimes. In the past, many researchers have not separated simple "bad acts" from crimes when they have reported the results. This led to the misperception that crime is universal.

Victimization Surveys

Victimization surveys are similar to self-report surveys, except that they ask people whether they have been the victims of offences, not if they have committed them. Victimization surveys are relatively recent developments. The first one of note was conducted in Washington, D.C., in 1967. In Canada, the primary collection of data about victimization is collected through the General Social Survey (GSS), which is the only national voluntary survey of self-reported victimization and is collected in all provinces and territories for people 15 years and over. Statistics Canada conducts this survey by telephone every five years, collecting data about a wide number of aspects that affect citizens' lives in order to monitor changes in living conditions and well-being of its citizens. In 2014, a survey directing participants to an Internet site was piloted. The main objective of the GSS on Canadians' Safety (Victimization) is to better understand how Canadians perceive crime and the justice system and to capture information on their experiences of victimization. The survey allows for estimates of the numbers and characteristics of victims and the types of criminal incidents they experience. Because not all crimes are reported to the police, the survey complements other officially collected crime rates as it measures both those reported to police and those that are unreported. It also helps to understand the reasons as to whether or not people report a crime to the police.

What Do Victimization Surveys Contribute?

As with self-report studies, victimization surveys generally produce higher estimates of the total amount of crime that is committed than we find in official statistics. As a consequence, many criminologists argue that victimization surveys get us closer to the "true" amount of crime that exists—the so-called "dark figure" of crime. Although there is a substantial difference between the estimates of the total amount of crime between official statistics and victimization surveys, there are similarities in both measures. Overall, both official statistics and victimization surveys rank crimes similarly in their order of prevalence.

By their nature, victimization surveys tell us little about the people who commit crimes, since most victims are either unfamiliar with their offenders or the crimes take place when the victims are absent from the crime scene. Most property offences, for example, take place when the victims are away. On the other hand, victimization surveys have provided some insight into the victim–offender relationship, in a situation where both are present at the time of the offence. Usually, these are incidents of crimes against individual persons. Thus, criminologists have learned a great deal more about the dynamics that take place in such crimes as domestic assaults and date rapes (Sacco and Kennedy, 1998).

Victims Are Similar to Offenders

Among the primary findings to come from victimization surveys is the one that young people are more at risk of criminal victimization than are older people. In general, we now know that victims share the same general profiles as offenders. Consequently, victims disproportionately tend to be young males from the working class—the same characteristics that commonly identify offenders. These profiles of victims are interesting, since surveys that tap into peoples' fear of crime suggest that those most likely to be victimized express the least fear of victimization. Usually, the elderly, women, and middle-class individuals express the greatest concern regarding the likelihood of victimization, even though they are, proportionally, less likely to be victimized.

We hold the view that it is the relative lack of fear of crime among those most likely to be victims that puts them at risk. Young males, for example, tend to engage in more reckless behaviour and to frequent locations (such as bars) that put them at greater risk of criminal victimization than in the case of other groups in society. It is the routine activities of one's lifestyle, some criminologists argue, that have the greatest impact on one's risk of victimization.

Reasons for Non-reporting

Victimization surveys also provide the police with other useful information beyond the amount of crime that exists. Most surveys ask people why they do not report crimes that take place—even the relatively serious ones. The most common reasons expressed for non-reporting are that the offences are too trivial to bother the police with and that for some offences, there is nothing the police can do. Less frequently, the reason is that the incident was "personal" or that "nothing was taken." The ability of young persons to report victimization is even more restricted, since they normally do not have the same access to the police as do adults. Young persons who are victimized usually report their concerns to parents, relatives, teachers, and other adults in supervisory roles who then decide whether or not to report the offences to the police.

Young persons face an additional reporting burden when their offender is a relative or an important adult in their lives. This is part of the reason that many incidents of sexual and physical abuse by parents and other adults in supervisory roles, such as coaches and priests, go unreported for so long.

Limitations

While victimization surveys provide more systematic information about crime than do official statistics, they are not perfect. As with self-report surveys, the onus to recognize a criminal event is placed on the citizen. Many victims do not realize that they have been victimized. As we noted earlier, people often assume that stolen property has simply been mislaid or lost. Even when the victim is aware of the event, he or she must also be able to recognize it as a crime. While most people are able to distinguish crimes from other forms of unacceptable behaviour, there are many situations that are difficult to classify. As a consequence, victimization surveys will contain both false positives (instances reported as crimes when they are not crimes) and false negatives (instances that are not acknowledged as such but were in fact crimes). Whether those errors cancel out or bias our results is not known with any degree of certainty.

Other Procedures

Criminologists have many other ways of measuring crime. For example, reports from private security firms are used to gain estimates of how much shoplifting takes place. Banks have estimates of how many credit-card and other frauds take place, even though much of that crime is not reported to the police. Other criminologists conduct field studies with gangs; they "hang out" with groups of young people or interview selected informants. Other sources of information include the use of surveillance cameras on the streets and the use of laboratory experiments. Most of these procedures do not give us better overall estimates of the total amount of crime that is committed. Instead, they enhance our understanding of the who, why, and where of criminal behaviour.

One of the dangers of using some of these procedures is that they can colour our view of the overall problem of crime. For example, field workers who study juvenile gangs can easily be misled into believing that gang membership is more common than it really is. Police officers who work with young offenders often have to remind themselves that most young people are decent kids and not "punks."

PROCESSING COUNTS OF CRIME

The total number of offences that takes place in a community is useful to know for many reasons. It provides an estimate of the size of the crime problem plus an indication of the workload faced by criminal justice personnel. For most purposes, however, raw crime totals are not very useful. Common sense tells us that all else being equal, larger communities would record more offences in total than would smaller communities. Communities with greater proportions of their population in high-crime-prone categories, such as men and young people, will also have higher crime counts. Social scientists usually convert crime counts into different statistics to make them more useful. The most commonly used conversions are ratios, proportions, and rates.

Ratios consist of a comparison of one portion of a population count with another. For example, in a particular city of 350,000 people, 11,371 are arrested for theft involving under $5,000 in a given year. Of that total, 1,391 are women. The ratio of men to women arrested for theft involving under $5,000 is, therefore, 9,980:1,391 or about 7.2:1. In other words, approximately 7.2 men are arrested for one woman.

Proportions consist of the fraction of the population made up by a part of that population. Thus, the proportion of women arrested for theft is 1,391 of 11,371, or approximately 0.12. Multiplying a proportion by 100 gives us a percentage; therefore, 0.12 × 100 or 12 percent of the people arrested in our example community are women.

Rates consist of the number of events in comparison with a standard-sized population or base. Usually, crime rates are based on the standard of 100,000 people, or sometimes, we use a base of 1,000 or 10,000 for more common events. Rates are calculated by the formula:

Events ÷ Population × 100,000 = Rate per 100,000

In this example, we calculate the rate for theft as:

11,371 ÷ 350,000 × 100,000 = 3,249

We read this rate as 3,249 thefts per 100,000 population.

The primary advantage of ratios, proportions, and rates is that we can make comparisons across social and geographical units. Crime rates, for example, allow us to compare cities, nations, or other social groups of different sizes by assuming that the groups have similar population counts.

While they are useful, these statistics do have limitations. One major assumption we make when calculating a rate is that the population in the denominator is similar or homogeneous. When we make this assumption, we calculate what is known as a "crude rate." Different communities, however, may have different population compositions that make the comparison of crude rates a problem. For example, one community might have a higher proportion of young people (who are more prone to crime) than another community. Since the community with proportionately more young people will likely have a higher rate of crime, we find an estimate of the crude rate to be less useful. In those situations, we are inclined to break the population down into smaller groups based on the important crime-related factor. Thus, we might calculate age-specific rates where we estimate the number of crimes per 100,000 people in each age grouping (e.g., people under 15 years; 15–24 years of age; 24–35 years of age, and so on). It is common for social scientists to calculate separate age- or gender-specific crime rates for communities in order to allow for more precise comparisons.

The reluctance of social scientists simply to use crime totals when looking at a community stems from the fact that most things only have meaning when they are compared with something else. For example, the total amount of crime in a community makes much more sense when we look at it in comparison with the total population. The crime rate for Canada takes on more meaning when we compare it with that of another country that has characteristics similar to those of Canada.

STATISTICS ON YOUTH OFFENDERS

Demographics

In Canada, census data is collected every five years. As of the most recent census in 2016, the population of Canada is now 35,151,728. That is up 5 percent from the previous census in 2011. Ontario is the most populous province in the country with 13,448,494 people, or 38.2 percent of the total Canadian population.

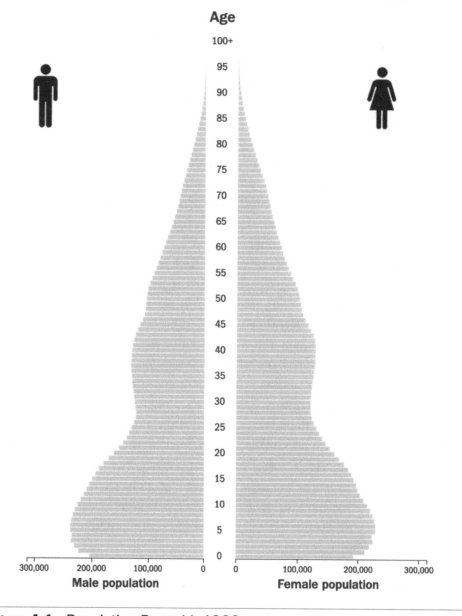

Figure 4.1a Population Pyramid, 1966.

Sources: Statistics Canada, "Census of Population, 1851 to 2016"; Statistics Canada, *Population Projections for Canada (2013 to 2063), Provinces and Territories (2013 to 2038)*. Accessed March 15, 2018, at http://www12.statcan.gc.ca/census-recensement/2016/dp-pd/pyramid/pyramid.cfm?type=1&geo1=01.

Children and youth under the age of 20 represent almost one in four (23 percent) people in Canada. As of July 1, 2010, there were approximately:

- 3.7 million children under the age of 10;
- 1.9 million youths aged 10 to 14; and
- 2.2 million youths between 15 and 19 years of age.
- In 2006, 48 percent of Indigenous people were less than 25 years old, compared to 31 percent for non-Indigenous people. Indigenous youth is one the fastest growing demographics (Public Safety Canada, 2012).

Figure 4.1b Population Pyramid, 2016.

Sources: Statistics Canada, "Census of Population, 1851 to 2016"; Statistics Canada, Population Projections for Canada (2013 to 2063), Provinces and Territories (2013 to 2038). Accessed March 15, 2018, at http://www12.statcan.gc.ca/census-recensement/2016/dp-pd/pyramid/pyramid.cfm?type=1&geo1=01.

It is worthy to note how our population has been changing and shifting over time. These population pyramids (see Figures 4.1a and b) provide an interesting contrast, but also highlight an important demographic that is related to the amount crime in a society. The first data pyramid (Figure 4.1a) is from 1966—50 years prior to 2016 census. Note how the shape of the data features a pyramid shape with the population bulging at the bottom. This was the last year of births associated with the Canadian baby boom, which spanned from 1947 to 1966. Contrast this with the second data pyramid (Figure 4.1b)— this "inverse" pyramid provides a population overview for 2016. Notice how the pyramid is basically turning upside down. The rapidly aging "baby boomers" are quickly nearing, have reached, or just passing the traditional retirement age of 65. Over time, younger people are forming a smaller proportion of the population.

Why Is This Relevant to Crime Statistics?

As we noted earlier, relative to younger persons, older people commit far fewer crimes. While there are many factors that impact crime rates (as you will read), this is one important fact to understand: as people age they commit fewer crimes, and as the population ages, there are fewer crimes overall. As Figure 4.2 shows, police-reported crime in 2013 is at the same level as for 1969. Therefore, while there is a general societal perception that crime has increased, there is considerable evidence to suggest otherwise. Evidence also shows that it has been consistently decreasing for the last 20 years. In addition to the aging population, there are other factors that experts believe are explanations for this decrease, such as inflation (when it goes up, so too do crimes associated with money such as robbery, break and enter, and motor vehicle theft).

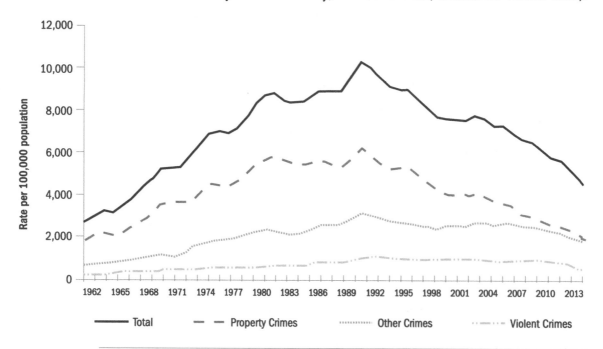

Figure 4.2 Police-reported Crime Rate, Canada, 1962 to 2013

Source: Statistics Canada, Canadian Centre for Justice Statistics, Uniform Crime Reporting Survey.

Changes in alcohol consumption and unemployment rates also have been associated with homicide rates, with increased alcohol and unemployment positively correlated with more murders.

Demographics of Youth at Risk of Offending

Social scientists are aware that there are various factors that put youths *at greater risk* for becoming young offenders. There is a **positive correlation** among these factors and youth who commit offences. In other words, social scientists understand that these risk factors increase the probability of committing crime, but this is not the same thing as "cause and effect." For example, living in poverty does not "cause" crime; rather, living in poverty increases the probability that a youth will commit crime. There are many young people who experience one or a multitude of the following risk factors who will never commit a crime. It is always important to remember this.

Public Safety Canada has collected this data and the factors include the following:

- Living with a single parent
- Living in a step-family
- Being raised by a younger parent
- Living in poverty/low-income household
- Dealing with mental health illness or disorder (affects 10–20 percent of Canadian youth)
- Affected by fetal alcohol spectrum disorder (FASD). It is estimated that 123 to 740 babies are born with FAS as a result of alcohol consumption by the mother during pregnancy. This consumption has permanent impact on brain development.
- Victimization. The highest rates are for youth ages 15 to 17.
- Family contact with a child welfare agency. In one study, 48 percent of youth in open custody and open detention facilities in Ontario reported a history of involvement with child welfare.
- Substance use. Higher cannabis use is amongst youth rather than amongst adults, with the average age of starting to use 15.7 years old. Youth were six times more likely to report harm due to illicit drug use than adults. Furthermore, youth are more likely to report delinquent behaviour when they have consumed alcohol and drugs, had delinquent friends, and reported little parental supervision.
- School dropout rates. Ten percent of young men and 7 percent of young women (defined as 20–24 years old) do not have a high school diploma and are not in school. Indigenous youth are more likely to drop out than non-Indigenous youth (23 percent compared to 7 percent). Only 44 percent of children in foster care graduate from high school, compared to 81 percent of their peers (Public Safety Canada, 2012)

Research has consistently demonstrated that youth are more likely to be accused of crime than adults. Most critically, research has shown that the majority of adult offenders committed their first criminal acts as youth; only a minority of offenders commit a crime for the first time as an adult. That being said, youth crime is lower than the rate for young adults aged 18 to 24, but twice the rate for older adults over the age of 25 years. This isn't to say that committing an offence as a young person leaves them destined to a "life of crime." Most crimes are for minor offences that are highly reflective of inexperience and lack of good decision-making skills that are missing in adolescence. And research on adolescent brain development has identified some interesting insights. Adolescents possess decision-making skills that are as good as adults—when they are not stressed, tired, or in the presence of their peers. For adolescents, whom they "hang out" with is very influential on what types of activities they will engage in, especially criminal ones. Ultimately, most adolescents simply grow out of criminal behaviour as they become adults. It is for these reasons that our society and *Youth Criminal Justice Act* start with the position that young persons lack maturity and are therefore considered less blameworthy or culpable than adults and should be treated differently than adults.

OVER-REPRESENTATION OF INDIGENOUS YOUTH

Increasing concern is being voiced in the over-representation of Indigenous youth in the Canadian youth justice system. In 2014–15, nine jurisdictions in Ontario reported 5,700 youths admitted to correctional services. This was 33 percent of all youth admittances and yet the youth Indigenous population (12 to 17 years) is only 7 percent of the youth population. The *YCJA* principles require alternatives to custody, particularly accounting for the special needs of Indigenous youth. However, these proportions have remained virtually unchanged despite the fact that the number of youths in custody has been decreasing. As Kwok et al. (2017: 19) have concluded: "Indigenous youth over-incarceration appears to be worsening."

The legacy of colonization, the reserve system, and the generational impact of residential schools has had a profound impact on Indigenous culture and its peoples who have had to live and manage the challenges. Efforts to make a formal apology have been made. And legislation is also starting to acknowledge that Indigenous peoples and culture and experiences must be taken into consideration.

The 2017 *Child, Youth and Family Services Act* of Ontario explicitly and cogently states:

> With respect to First Nations, Inuit and Métis children, the Government of Ontario acknowledges the following:
>> The Province of Ontario has unique and evolving relationships with First Nations, Inuit and Métis peoples.
>> First Nations, Inuit and Métis peoples are constitutionally recognized peoples in Canada, with their own laws, and distinct cultural, political and historical ties to the Province of Ontario.
>> Where a First Nations, Inuk or Métis child is otherwise eligible to receive a service under this Act, an inter-jurisdictional or intra-jurisdictional dispute

should not prevent the timely provision of that service, in accordance with Jordan's Principle.

The United Nations Declaration on the Rights of Indigenous Peoples recognizes the importance of belonging to a community or nation, in accordance with the traditions and customs of the community or nation concerned.

Further, the Government of Ontario believes the following:

First Nations, Inuit and Métis children should be happy, healthy, resilient, grounded in their cultures and languages and thriving as individuals and as members of their families, communities and nations.

Honouring the connection between First Nations, Inuit and Métis children and their distinct political and cultural communities is essential to helping them thrive and fostering their well-being.

For these reasons, the Government of Ontario is committed, in the spirit of reconciliation, to working with First Nations, Inuit and Métis peoples to help ensure that wherever possible, they care for their children in accordance with their distinct cultures, heritages and traditions.

The Supreme Court of Canada (*R. v. Gladue*, [1999] 1 S.C.R. 688) has been clear that the courts in their sentencing decisions must consider the systemic or background factors that may have influenced the accused to engage in criminal conduct, and the types of sentencing procedures and sanctions that may be appropriate in the circumstances for the offender because of his or her particular Indigenous heritage or connection. These principles have been further affirmed in *R. v. Ipeelee* (2012 S.C.C. 13, [2012] 1 S.C.R. 433) where the court specifically acknowledged:

When sentencing an Aboriginal offender, courts must take judicial notice of such matters as the history of colonialism, displacement, and residential schools and how that history continues to translate into lower educational attainment, lower incomes, higher unemployment, higher rates of substance abuse and suicide, and of course higher levels of incarceration for Aboriginal peoples.

These same principles must also be applied to Indigenous youth.

Despite these acknowledgements and good intentions, they are not translating well in reducing the disproportionate over-representation of both Indigenous youth and adults in the criminal justice system. As the long list of issues outlines above, good policies to effectively deal with other issues must be addressed in order to have a meaningful impact on rates of offences.

What Kinds of Crimes Do Young Offenders Commit?

In 2014, there were 101,000 youth aged 12 to 17 who were accused of *Criminal Code* offences (excluding traffic) that were reported to police. The youth crime rate was 4,322 per 100,000 youth population. For this time frame, youth made up 7 percent of the population, but they comprised 13 percent of the persons accused of a crime. This includes youth who were charged or recommended for charging, and those youths who were diverted from the formal justice system through extrajudicial measures such as warnings, cautions, and referrals to community programs. This is a typical pattern—young persons account for a disproportionate number of those people processed by the police. As many criminologists have noted, the over-representation of young people among those committing offences appears to be a universal phenomenon. Although the exact ratios may vary somewhat across time and cultures, the overall pattern remains fairly stable.

MEASURING POLICE-REPORTED YOUTH CRIME

The police-reported **crime rate** is comprised of violent crime, property crime, and other *Criminal Code* violations by youth aged 12 to 17 accused in a criminal incident per 100,000 population (both charged and cleared without charge). This rate *does not include* traffic offences or offences under other federal statues, such as drug offences or violations that are specific to the *Youth Criminal Justice Act*. These types of offences are tracked separately.

The Youth Crime Severity Index (YCSI) counts the volume of crime as well as the seriousness of the offences and *does include* traffic violations, drug offences, violations under the *YCJA*, and other federal offences.

Why are children under the age of 12 not included in these crime measures?

Overall, police-reported crime has been steadily falling since 2006, following a general trend of decline since reaching a high in 1991. A large decrease in youth accused of property crimes, particularly for theft under $5,000 and break and enter, is noteworthy.

Youth Offences Are Minor Offences
By and large, police reported youth crime is for minor offences such as the following:

- Theft under $5,000
- Mischief
- Common assault (one of the less serious violent crimes)
- Cannabis possession
- Offences associated with the administration of justice and violations under the *YCJA* (e.g., breach of probation, being unlawfully at large, not complying with conditions of release)

Youth are more likely than adults to be accused in incidents of robbery, theft, break and enter, sexual assault, and sexual violations against children. According to 2014 police-reported data, crime levels peak when individuals who are accused of crime are 17 years old and show a clear and substantial drop after the age of 40-plus age category is reached. This fact is important to note: crimes rates for age cohorts decrease as people get older and mature out of crime.

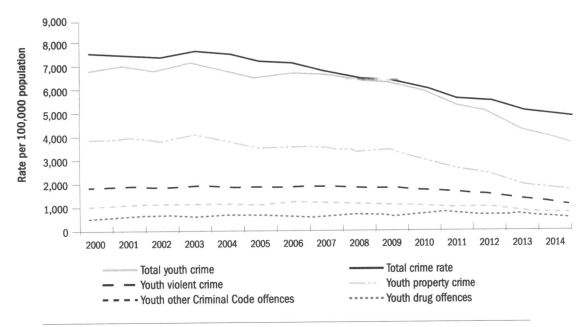

Figure 4.3 Police-Reported Crime and Youth Crimes by Offence Type, 2000 to 2014

Source: Statistics Canada, Canadian Centre for Justice Statistics, Uniform Crime Reporting Survey.

Most of the decrease in the overall charge rate for youth is attributable to a decrease in young persons charged for property crimes. The charge rate for crimes of violence among young people has increased steadily over the past 30 years. Whereas before the mid-1980s more adults were charged proportionately for crimes of violence, the pattern is now reversed. In fact, throughout most of the late 1990s and in the early part of the 2000s, the charge rate for crimes of violence among young persons was almost twice that of adults.

Although the longer term pattern for rates of violent crime has been upward, the overall news is relatively positive. At least as indicated by charge rates, the relative total crime rate and the amount of property crime committed by both adults and young persons is decreasing. The violent crime rate, despite being somewhat higher in historical terms, has levelled off among both young persons and adults over the past decade. While it is not the purpose of this text to explore the underlying causes of criminal behaviour, the consensus among criminologists is that the patterns are due to a combination of real behavioural changes by young people and changes in police activity. This latter element is reflected in an increased willingness by police officers to deal with minor property offences in a non-judicial manner. Regardless, the patterns do not suggest that the need for peace officers will disappear in the near future—something that, we suspect, is good news to those reading this text.

Gender and Crime

Just as the young are over-represented among offenders, so are males. Only about one in four young offenders charged are female. Among adults, the proportion of women both charged and convicted of an offence is less than 20 percent of the total.

Whether young or old, crime is primarily a male activity. Female youth are less likely to be charged by police for both violent and non-violent offences. As might be expected, custodial and other post-sentencing alternatives are heavily oriented toward male offenders. Girls are more likely to be cleared with charge, often with a warning or caution. When the offence is assault or offences related to the administration of justice and violations under the *YCJA*, females and males have similar charging rates.

What Impact Did the *YCJA* Have on Crime Rates?

Legislation can have an impact on official rates of crime, and the *YCJA* is a good example of how legislative policy can impact practice. As you examine the charts above, you will see that 2003 acts as a watershed year for youth crime rates. The rates drop precipitously particularly for those offences targeted in the *YCJA*—minor offences, and especially minor property offences. About the only offences that do not show any difference in charge rates are robberies and possession of stolen property. Offensive weapons charges take a dip in 2003 as do drug charges but then quickly resume to the rate at which they occurred at the turn of the century. While one might argue that the stars were in alignment in 2003 for this decrease in crime, the patterns for these latter offences suggest that the police were adjusting to the new legislation by implementing the new extrajudicial measures and authority to divert young people out of the criminal justice system.

If youth crime has been steadily falling since 2006 and current crime rates mirror those from 1991, why does the perception persist that youth crime is always on the rise and/or getting worse?

What role do the media play in these perceptions?

IN THE NEWS

The Media's Role in Presenting the "Crime Problem"

Defining "news" is a tricky business, given readers' tastes. Editors and writers, after all, must cater to these tastes or they will be out of business. With severe pressures on the newspaper business, those possibilities are not idle matters.

...

Last week, Statistics Canada reported yet again that most crime in Canada remains in decline. There have been a few blips against the trend in recent years, but the general direction of violent crime is down. You would never know it from reading newspapers or watching television. In the newsrooms of the nation, it is an unshakable assumption that crime sells.

In *The Globe and Mail*, to take just one example, a full story about the Statscan report appeared inside the paper at the bottom of a page. That was what we might call a "good news" story. Three other stories that day, all given more prominence, were about various crimes or trials, the "bad news" stories.

The public perception of crime is that rates are rising. We should be vigilant and fearful. Without minimizing the importance of violent crime, it is declining. To what extent, then, are we in the media misleading the public by devoting so much space and airtime to crime, when the underlying story is the reverse of the individually reported ones?

Crime is abnormal behaviour for almost everyone in society. As such, crime is "new," since "news," as it has been defined, is something out of the ordinary, something that is, well, new. Turn that argument on its head. There's nothing at all "new" about crime. It's been with us forever, and always will be. What's really "new"—that is, different—these days is that the rates are falling. So the real news story is to figure out why.

...

Source: Jeffery Simpson, "If we adjusted our definition of 'news,' we'd be better informed," *The Globe and Mail,* July 27, 2007, p. A15.

TEST YOUR KNOWLEDGE

Definitions

Define the following terms:

1. Official statistics on crime

   _____

   _____

   _____

2. Crimes known to the police

   _____

   _____

   _____

3. Unfounded crime

_____

_____

_____

4. Clearance rate

_____

_____

_____

5. Self-report survey

_____

_____

_____

6. Victimization survey

_____

_____

_____

7. Ratio

_____

_____

_____

8. Proportion

_____

_____

_____

9. Rate

_____

_____

_____

10. Positive correlation

_____

_____

_____

11. Crime rate

_____

_____

_____

True/False

1.   T   F   Self-report surveys are an important source of official statistics on crime.

2.   T   F   The oldest and most commonly used source of information on crime is in the form of surveys of victims.

3.   T   F   Each technique (way) of measuring crime produces a *different* estimate of the amount of crime that actually exists.

4.   T   F   Crimes known to police are only those violations of law that the police have witnessed with their own eyes.

5.   T   F   The social categories of persons who least fear crime are those that have the greatest risk of being victims of crime.

Multiple Choice

1. Which of the following sources of official statistics on crime would produce the highest estimates of the amount of crime?

   a.   crimes cleared by arrest
   b.   number of persons incarcerated
   c.   crimes known to police
   d.   persons who are homeless

2. Surveys of victims are particularly helpful because they provide

    a. a good deal of information on those who commit crimes
    b. a good deal of information about those who commit property crimes, even if they provide much less information about crimes against persons
    c. a good deal of information about those who commit property crimes *and* information about the relationships between the offenders and the victims
    d. none of the above

3. Which of the following is a ratio?

    a. 10 percent
    b. 10:1
    c. 100 per 100,000
    d. 10

4. Which of the following is a proportion?

    a. 0.1
    b. 10:1
    c. 100 per 100,000
    d. 10

5. Which of the following is a rate?

    a. 10 percent
    b. 10:1
    c. 100 per 100,000
    d. 10

6. The calculation of crime rates is useful because

    a. all communities are basically the same size
    b. no community changes in size over time
    c. rates allow for the direct comparison of communities of different sizes
    d. the math is easy and it is fun to do

Short Answer

1. For what three purposes can information on rates of crime can be used?

    _____

    _____

    _____

    _____

    _____

    _____

_____

_____

2. By what three agencies are official statistics on crime collected?

_____

_____

_____

_____

_____

_____

_____

_____

_____

3. Identify two advantages of "crimes known to the police" as an indicator of the amount of crime in a city.

_____

_____

_____

_____

_____

_____

_____

_____

_____

_____

4. Discuss the truth or falsity of the following statement and give reasons for your position: "Police discretion is greatest in situations where the offence committed is a minor one."

_____

_____

_____

_____

_____

_____

_____

_____

_____

5.   Why are counts of crime expressed in different ways?

_____

_____

_____

_____

_____

_____

_____

_____

_____

Expressing Counts of Crime

1.   Express the ratio that 80 percent of young persons charged with crime are males. The ratio is: _____.

2.   Express as a rate per 10,000 young persons that 400 younger persons appeared in youth court in a community that had 10,000 people between the ages of 12 and 17 years, inclusive.

3.   Express as a proportion that females commit 20 of every 100 crimes.

4.   Express as a ratio that young males commit 80 percent of property crimes and that young females commit the other 20 percent when such crimes are committed by young persons.

5.   Express as a rate per 10,000 young persons that 800 young persons appeared in youth court in a community that had 20,000 people between the ages of 12 and 17 years, inclusive.

Table-Reading Skills

Based on Table 4.1:

1. The decrease in the number of young persons held in custody (total custody) between 2000/01 and 2004/05 is _____.

2. The *percentage* decrease in number of young persons held in custody (total custody) between 2000/01 and 2004/05 is _____.

3. Assuming there are 1,006,700 young people between the ages of 12 and 17 in 2004/05, the total custody rate would be _____.

4. How would you describe the pattern in pre-trial detention between the years 2000/01 and 2004/05?

Table 4.1 Young Persons Commencing Correctional Services, by Initial Entry Status

	2000/01	2001/02	2002/03	2003/04	2004/05
Total custody	18,139	14,508	11,380	11,563	12,138
Pre-trial detention	3,852	3,218	3,933	3,836	3,149
Total secure custody	1,218	1,079	482	128	12
Secure custody, custody and supervision	—	—	—	128	11
Secure custody, *Young Offenders Act (YOA)*	—	—	—	0	1
Total open custody	1,759	1,284	352	63	20
Open custody, custody and supervision	—	—	—	60	16
Open custody, *Young Offenders Act (YOA)*	—	—	—	3	4
Total community sentences	11,310	8,927	6,613	7,536	8,957
Community sentences, intensive support and supervision	—	—	—	0	0
Community sentences, deferred custody and supervision	—	—	—	159	128
Community sentences, supervised probation	11,215	8,865	6,613	5,683	3,170
Community sentences, other community sentences	95	62	0	1,694	5,659

Source: Adapted from the Statistics Canada CANSIM Table 251-0009.

Table 4.2 Youth Correctional Services, Admissions to Provincial and Territorial Programs, Ontario

	2000	2001	2002	2003	2004
Remand	5,693	6,554	6,368	5,640	8,723
Males	4,915	5,567	5,374	4,805	6,920
Females	778	978	994	835	1,803
Sex unknown		9			
Aboriginal	516	646	260	609	705
Non-Aboriginal	5,177	5,899	6,108	5,031	8,018
Aboriginal identity unknown	9				
Admissions to secure custody	3,359	4,020	1,601	1,222	959
Males	2,786	3,335	1,414	1,054	833
Females	573	685	187	164	126
Sex unknown	0	0	0	4	0
Aboriginal	375	432	79	135	114
Non-Aboriginal	2,680	3,129	1,522	1,083	845
Aboriginal identity unknown	304	459	0	4	0
Admissions to open custody	4,259	4,342	1,507	1,235	1,333
Males	3,455	3,388	1,278	982	1,084
Females	804	959	229	252	249
Sex unknown	0	0	0	1	0
Aboriginal	411	324	64	102	153
Non-Aboriginal	3,384	3,401	1,443	1,132	1,180
Aboriginal identity unknown	464	617	0	1	0
Admissions to probation	16,634	17,909	7,963	11,091	7,824
Males	12,783	13,784	6,471	8,717	6,164
Females	3,851	4,125	1,492	2,374	1,660
Sex unknown	0	0	0	0	0
Aboriginal	1059	1060	576	683	523
Non-Aboriginal	13,685	14,794	7,378	10,408	7,301
Aboriginal identity unknown	1,890	2,100	0	0	0

Note: Fiscal year (April 1 through March 31). Not all variables are applicable to or available for all jurisdictions. Interjurisdictional comparisons of the data should be made with caution.

Data prior to 2002/2003 were submitted by two separate ministries: the Ministry of Children and Youth Services (MCYS) and the Ministry of Community Safety and Correctional Services (MCSCS). The Ontario Ministry of Children and Youth Services (MCYS) is responsible for all young offenders that were between the ages of 12 and 15 at the time of the offence. The Ontario Ministry of Community Safety and Correctional Services (MCSCS) has jurisdiction over all young offenders that were 16 or 17 years of age at the time of the offence.

Source: Adapted from the Statistics Canada CANSIM Tables 251-0010, 251-0012, 251-0015, 251-0016, and 251-0017.

Based on Table 4.2:

5. The *ratio* of males to females who were placed in remand in 2004 was _____.

6. The *proportion* of admissions to probation who were of Aboriginal origin in 2000 was _____, while the equivalent proportion in 2004 was _____.

7. How would you describe the pattern of admissions to both open and secure custody among Aboriginal youth as opposed to non-Aboriginal youth?

8. Describe any changes you see in the proportion of females who are held in remand between 2000 and 2004.

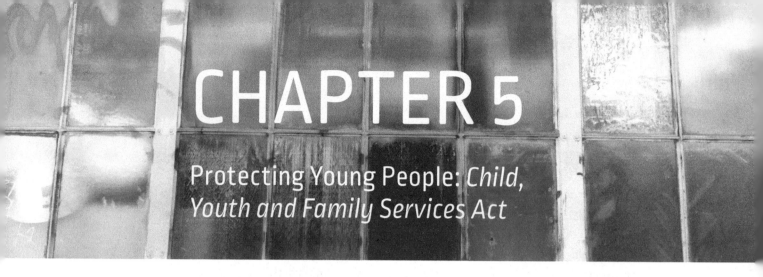

CHAPTER 5

Protecting Young People: *Child, Youth and Family Services Act*

LEARNING OUTCOMES

Students who have mastered this chapter will have the ability to do the following:

- Identify the basic objectives of Ontario's *Child, Youth and Family Services Act*.
- Explain the meaning of the *Child, Youth and Family Services Act* and how it relates to dealing with young persons in conflict with the law and its importance for the police.
- Identify four functions of Children's Aid Societies (CAS).
- Describe situations where a child could be in need of protection.
- Explain the roles and responsibility of the CAS when a child has been apprehended.
- Understand what is meant by the duty to report.
- Know the rights of children in care.

INTRODUCTION

This chapter begins with noting the recent enactment of Ontario's *Child, Youth and Family Services Act* (*CYFSA*), which received Royal Assent June 1, 2017 and is expected to come into force in 2018. It replaces the previous (but very similarly named) *Child and Family Services Act*. Child protection, also known as the child welfare system, is a matter of *provincial or territorial jurisdiction*, and every province and territory has similarly enacted legislation (and often similarly named—e.g., Nova Scotia's *Children and Family Services Act* and British Columbia's *Child, Family and Community Service Act*). As the title of the Ontario legislation highlights, the inclusion of "youth" signifies this Act's deliberate effort to be more inclusive and expansive in addressing the needs and concerns of young people in adolescence. One of the key changes was to raise the age of protection to include youth ages 16 and 17 years in an effort to increase protection services for vulnerable youth in unsafe living conditions, to support their education, and to reduce homelessness and human trafficking. This is also in keeping with the United Nations

Convention on the Rights of the Child, which prescribes protections for children under 18 years of age.

Other changes, as outlined by the Ministry of Children and Youth Services, focused on the following:

- Strengthening the focus on early intervention, helping prevent children and families from reaching crisis situations at home;
- Making services more culturally appropriate for all children and youth in the child welfare system, including Indigenous and Black children and youth, to help ensure they receive the best possible support; and
- Improving oversight of service providers, including children's aid societies, so that children and youth receive consistent, high-quality services across Ontario (Ontario Ministry of Children and Youth Services, 2017).

This chapter focuses on those parts of the Act that are most pertinent to dealing with young persons in conflict with the law and that have the greatest importance for the police, referred to as "peace officers" throughout the Act. To aid in that understanding, we have retained as much of the language of the Act as possible so that you can understand how the legislation is written. Even as we retained much of the original language, we have redressed the number of cross-references to other parts of the Act, and we have clarified the meaning without a long list of definitions. For example, where the *Act* refers to "a society," we have specified that it is the Children's Aid Society (CAS), and where it refers to "peace officer," we have specified peace/police officer.

Due to the focus of this chapter, several parts of the *CYFSA* are not covered here. For example, adoption—as important as it is in other ways—does not fit the present focus.

WHAT IS THE PURPOSE OF THE *CHILD, YOUTH AND FAMILY SERVICES ACT*?

Young people generally—and especially young people who are in conflict with the law—come into the orbit of the *Child, Youth and Family Services Act (CYFSA)* in Ontario or under its counterpart legislation in other provinces. The *CYFSA* has as its "paramount purpose … to promote the best interests, protection and well being of children" who are persons under the age of 18 years [*CYFSA* 1(1)]. This includes the provision of "a service or program for or on behalf of a young person for the purposes of the *Youth Criminal Justice Act* (Canada) or the *Provincial Offences Act*" [*CYFSA* 2(1)—see Definitions—Services at (h)].

The Act also has additional purposes outlined in subsection 1(2), which apply "… so long as they are consistent with the best interests, protection and well-being of children":

1. To recognize that while parents may need help in caring for their children, that help should give support to the autonomy and integrity of the family unit and, wherever possible, be provided on the basis of mutual consent.

2. The least disruptive course of action that is available and is appropriate in a particular case to help a child, including the provision of prevention services, early intervention services and community support services, should be considered.

3. Services to children and young persons should be provided in a manner that
    i.   respects a child's or young person's need for continuity of care and for stable relationships within a family and cultural environment;
    ii.   takes into account physical, emotional, spiritual, mental, and developmental needs and differences among children and young persons;
    iii. takes into account a child's or young person's race, ancestry, place of origin, colour, ethnic origin, citizenship, family diversity, disability, creed, sex, sexual orientation, gender identity and gender expression;
    iv.   takes into account a child's or young person's cultural and linguistic needs;
    v.   provides early assessment, planning and decision-making to achieve permanent plans for children and young persons in accordance with their best interests; and
    vi.   includes the participation of a child or young person, the child's or young person's parents and relatives and the members of the child's or young person's extended family and community, where appropriate.

4. Services to children and young persons and their families should be provided in a manner that respects regional differences, wherever possible.

5. Services to children and young persons and their families should be provided in a manner that builds on the strengths of the families, wherever possible.

6. First Nations, Inuit and Métis peoples should be entitled to provide, wherever possible, their own child and family services, and all services to First Nations, Inuit and Métis children and young persons and their families should be provided in a manner that recognizes their cultures, heritages, traditions, connection to their communities, and the concept of the extended family.

7. Appropriate sharing of information, including personal information, in order to plan for and provide services is essential for creating successful outcomes for children and families.

In brief, the *CYFSA* is focused on the **best interests of the child** and sees the family unit as something to be supported to facilitate the well-being and development of children.

The protection of children is also enunciated in the *Criminal Code* wherein section 215 requires parents to provide for children under the age of 16 with the necessities of life, including food, shelter, and medical treatment. In addition, provincial and territorial statutes, such as the *CYFSA*, require that parents provide appropriate care, supervision, and protection.

HOW OLD DOES A CHILD NEED TO BE TO STAY AT HOME ALONE IN ONTARIO?

We are almost certain that if you were asked this question (and if you asked five people you know) that you would likely get this answer more than any other: 12 years of age. It has somehow become "common knowledge" that 12 is the minimum age requirement, and yet, if you look closely at legislation, such as the *CYFSA*, and you will find no such threshold age. It is very much in the parents' discretion to make the judgment call, keeping in mind that they have the legal obligation to ensure that their child is capable of being alone depending upon the child's level of maturity, comfort, and experience at knowing how to deal with an emergency. Ultimately, the *CYFSA* provides at section 74(2): A child is in need of protection where, (a) the child has suffered physical harm, inflicted by the person having charge of the child or caused by or resulting from that person's, (i) failure to adequately care for, provide for, supervise or protect the child, or (ii) pattern of neglect in caring for, providing for, supervising or protecting the child.

IN THE NEWS

Ontario Passes Legislation to Strengthen Child Welfare and Improve Outcomes for Youth

Province Putting Children at the Centre of Decision-Making

Ministry of Children and Youth Services

Today, Ontario passed legislation to help children and youth across the province thrive and reach their full potential by strengthening and modernizing child, youth and family services.

The *Child, Youth and Family Services Act* makes significant changes to how Ontario provides services to children and youth in need of protection. It puts young people at the centre of decisions about their care, supports more accountable, responsive and accessible child and youth services and strengthens oversight for children's aid societies and licensed residential services. Key areas of change in the act include:

- Raising the age of protection from 16 to 18 to increase protection services for more vulnerable youth in unsafe living conditions, to support their education and to reduce homelessness and human trafficking
- Making services more inclusive and culturally appropriate for all children and youth, including Indigenous and Black children and youth, to ensure every child receives the best possible support

Continued

- Putting a greater focus on early intervention, to help prevent children and families from reaching crisis situations at home
- Improving accountability and oversight of service providers, including children's aid societies and licensed residential service providers, so that children and youth receive safe, consistent and high-quality services across the province.

Supporting children and youth and helping them reach their full potential is part of our plan to create jobs, grow our economy and help people in their everyday lives.

Source: Ministry of Youth and Children Services, «Ontario Passes Legislation to Strengthen Child Welfare and Improve Outcomes for Youth: Province Putting Children at the Centre of Decision-Making,» June 1, 2017. Accessed March 15, 2018, at https://news.ontario.ca/mcys/en/2017/06/ontario-passes-legislation-to-strengthen-child-welfare-and-improve-outcomes-for-youth.html.

Definitions: To Whom Does This Act Apply?

The definitions section of legislation is important. Section 2(1) of the *CYFSA* defines a "child" as "a person younger than 18; ("enfant")."

A "child in care" means a child or young person who is receiving residential care from a service provider and includes

(a)   a child who is in the care of a foster parent, and
(b)   a young person who is
    (i)   detained in a place of temporary detention under the *Youth Criminal Justice Act* (Canada),
    (ii)   committed to a place of secure or open custody designated under subsection 24.1 (1) of the *Young Offenders Act* (Canada), whether in accordance with section 88 of the *Youth Criminal Justice Act* (Canada) or otherwise, or
    (iii)   held in a place of open custody under section 150 of this Act

"Young person" means

(a)   a person who is or, in the absence of evidence to the contrary, appears to be 12 or older but younger than 18 and who is charged with or found guilty of an offence under the *Youth Criminal Justice Act* (Canada) or the *Provincial Offences Act*, or
(b)   if the context requires, any person who is charged under the *Youth Criminal Justice Act* (Canada) with having committed an offence while they were a young person or who is found guilty of an offence under the *Youth Criminal Justice Act* (Canada). ("adolescent")

First Nations, Inuit, and Métis Children

The *CYFSA* preamble also explicitly articulates and identifies respect and obligations for care of First Nations, Inuit, and Métis children to honour their distinct identity and cultures and traditions.

As the Act articulates:

The Province of Ontario has unique and evolving relationships with First Nations, Inuit and Métis peoples.

First Nations, Inuit and Métis peoples are constitutionally recognized peoples in Canada, with their own laws, and distinct cultural, political and historical ties to the Province of Ontario.

Where a First Nations, Inuk or Métis child is otherwise eligible to receive a service under this Act, an inter-jurisdictional or intra-jurisdictional dispute should not prevent the timely provision of that service, in accordance with Jordan's Principle.

The United Nations Declaration on the Rights of Indigenous Peoples recognizes the importance of belonging to a community or nation, in accordance with the traditions and customs of the community or nation concerned.

Further, the Government of Ontario believes the following:

First Nations, Inuit and Métis children should be happy, healthy, resilient, grounded in their cultures and languages and thriving as individuals and as members of their families, communities and nations.

Honouring the connection between First Nations, Inuit and Métis children and their distinct political and cultural communities is essential to helping them thrive and fostering their well-being.

For these reasons, the Government of Ontario is committed, in the spirit of reconciliation, to working with First Nations, Inuit and Métis peoples to help ensure that wherever possible, they care for their children in accordance with their distinct cultures, heritages and traditions.

This is reflected in provisions such as section 80 regarding customary care, which requires the following:

A society shall make all reasonable efforts to pursue a plan for customary care for a First Nations, Inuk or Métis child if the child,

(a) is in need of protection;

(b) cannot remain in or be returned to the care and custody of the person who had charge of the child immediately before intervention under this Part or, where there is an order for the child's custody that is enforceable in Ontario, of the person entitled to custody under the order; and

(c) is a member of or identifies with a band, or is a member of or identifies with a First Nations, Inuit or Métis community.

Functions of Children's Aid Societies

In Ontario, the Ministry of Children and Youth Services designates a Children's Aid Society (CAS) as the agency that is approved to perform a variety of functions with respect to receiving and responding to reports of a **child in need of protection**. In Ontario, there are 47 Children's Aid Societies; nine Children's Aid Societies are Indigenous agencies and three are religious ones (two Catholic and one Jewish).[1] These agencies have investigative responsibilities where there are allegations that a child may be being abused or neglected. They also have connections to services and agencies to help supervise, guide, and support families so that parents can raise their children in a beneficial manner. If deemed necessary, they have authority to bring a child into care and supervise the child's placement in foster care or group home. If a more permanent plan is needed and the child cannot be returned to a parent, the CAS will be part of the process to have a child become a Crown ward and/or be placed for adoption (Crown wardship is further discussed below).

These responsibilities are identified in subsection 35(1). Specifically, the agency is expected to do the following:

(a)   investigate allegations or evidence that children may be in need of protection;

(b)   protect children where necessary;

(c)   provide guidance, counselling and other services to families for protecting children or for the prevention of circumstances requiring the protection of children;

(d)   provide care for children assigned or committed to its care under this Act;

(e)   supervise children assigned to its supervision under this Act;

(f)   place children for adoption under Part VIII (Adoption and Adoption Licensing); and

(g)   perform any other duties given to it by this Act or the regulations or any other Act.

Under a variety of circumstances, there may arise a need for the provision of legal services in child protection matters. In Ontario, legal representation may be provided by the Office of the Children's Lawyer (OCL) [*CYFSA* 17(3)]. The Children's Lawyer is made available "if a society ... or a person, including a child who is receiving child welfare services proposes that a prescribed method of alternative dispute resolution be undertaken to assist in resolving an issue relating to a child or a plan for the child's care." Representation is about due process and respecting and honouring the child's right to his or her own counsel to ensure that matters that involve the child yield an outcome that is in the child's best interests.

What Constitutes a "Child in Need of Protection"?

Part V of the *CYFSA* deals with child protection. The list is quite extensive and

---

1.   See the website for the Ontario Association of Children's Aid Societies (OACAS) at http://www. oacas.org; you can also see an up-to-date list of approved child protection organizations at http://www.oacas.org/childrens-aid-child-protection/locate-a-childrens-aid-society/

wide-ranging, covering the more understood aspects of (a) physical harm, (b) neglect, or (c) sexual abuse, but it also covers (e) children in need of treatment but the parent refuses, and (l) a child has killed or harmed someone. In this part of the *Act*, a child is deemed to be "in need of protection" [*CYFSA* 74(2)] where

(a)   the child has suffered physical harm, inflicted by the person having charge of the child or caused by or resulting from that person's,
  (i) failure to adequately care for, provide for, supervise or protect the child, or
  (ii) pattern of neglect in caring for, providing for, supervising or protecting the child;

(b)   there is a risk that the child is likely to suffer physical harm inflicted by the person having charge of the child or caused by or resulting from that person's,
  (i) failure to adequately care for, provide for, supervise or protect the child, or
  (ii) pattern of neglect in caring for, providing for, supervising or protecting the child;

(c)   the child has been sexually abused or sexually exploited, by the person having charge of the child or by another person where the person having charge of the child knows or should know of the possibility of sexual abuse or sexual exploitation and fails to protect the child;

(d)   there is a risk that the child is likely to be sexually abused or sexually exploited as described in clause (c);

(e)   the child requires treatment to cure, prevent or alleviate physical harm or suffering and the child's parent or the person having charge of the child does not provide the treatment or access to the treatment, or, where the child is incapable of consenting to the treatment under the *Health Care Consent Act, 1996* and the parent is a substitute decision-maker for the child, the parent refuses or is unavailable or unable to consent to the treatment on the child's behalf;

(f)   the child has suffered emotional harm, demonstrated by serious
  (i) anxiety,
  (ii) depression,
  (iii) withdrawal,
  (iv) self-destructive or aggressive behaviour, or
  (v) delayed development,
  and there are reasonable grounds to believe that the emotional harm suffered by the child results from the actions, failure to act or pattern of neglect on the part of the child's parent or the person having charge of the child;

(g)   the child has suffered emotional harm of the kind described in subclause (f) (i), (ii), (iii), (iv) or (v) and the child's parent or the person having charge of the child does not provide services or treatment or access to services or treatment, or, where the child is incapable of consenting to treatment under the *Health Care Consent Act, 1996*, refuses or is unavailable or unable to consent to the treatment to remedy or alleviate the harm;

(h)   there is a risk that the child is likely to suffer emotional harm of the kind described in subclause (f) (i), (ii), (iii), (iv) or (v) resulting from the actions, failure to act or pattern of neglect on the part of the child's parent or the person having charge of the child;

(i)   there is a risk that the child is likely to suffer emotional harm of the kind described in subclause (f) (i), (ii), (iii), (iv) or (v) and that the child's parent or the person having charge of the child does not provide services or treatment or access to services or treatment, or, where the child is incapable of consenting to treatment under the *Health Care Consent Act, 1996*, refuses or is unavailable or unable to consent to treatment to prevent the harm;

(j)   the child suffers from a mental, emotional or developmental condition that, if not remedied, could seriously impair the child's development and the child's parent or the person having charge of the child does not provide treatment or access to treatment, or where the child is incapable of consenting to treatment under the *Health Care Consent Act, 1996*, refuses or is unavailable or unable to consent to the treatment to remedy or alleviate the condition;

(k)   the child's parent has died or is unavailable to exercise custodial rights over the child and has not made adequate provision for the child's care and custody, or the child is in a residential placement and the parent refuses or is unable or unwilling to resume the child's care and custody;

(l)   the child is younger than 12 and has killed or seriously injured another person or caused serious damage to another person's property, services or treatment are necessary to prevent a recurrence and the child's parent or the person having charge of the child does not provide services or treatment or access to services or treatment, or, where the child is incapable of consenting to treatment under the *Health Care Consent Act, 1996*, refuses or is unavailable or unable to consent to treatment;

(m)   the child is younger than 12 and has on more than one occasion injured another person or caused loss or damage to another person's property, with the encouragement of the person having charge of the child or because of that person's failure or inability to supervise the child adequately;

(n)   the child's parent is unable to care for the child and the child is brought before the court with the parent's consent and, where the child is 12 or older, with the child's consent, for the matter to be dealt with under this Part; or

(o)   the child is 16 or 17 and a prescribed circumstance or condition exists.

The Duty to Report

Peace/police officers, like many other professionals such as doctors, teachers, lawyers, and psychologists [see the list at *CYFSA* section 125(6)] have a legally mandated obligation to *immediately* report suspicions of child abuse and/or neglect to the appropriate CAS where there are "reasonable grounds." The *CYFSA* [125(1)] specifically notes:

... if a person, including a person who performs professional or official duties with respect to children, has reasonable grounds to suspect one of the following, the person shall immediately report the suspicion and the information on which it is based to a society:

1.   The child has suffered physical harm inflicted by the person having charge of the child or caused by or resulting from that person's,

(i) failure to adequately care for, provide for, supervise or protect the child, or

(ii) pattern of neglect in caring for, providing for, supervising or protecting the child.

The threshold of **reasonable grounds** applies to suspicion. It does not require that the person with the suspicion conduct any type of investigation. Suspicion is enough to require reporting. The duty is to report **forthwith**, or immediately, and it is clear that waiting two or three weeks to see whether more evidence appears is not the threshold. Furthermore, the **duty to report** is ongoing [*CYFSA* 125(2)]. That is, a person who has additional reasonable grounds to suspect that a child is in need of protection is required to make a further report even if a previous report had been made about the same child. According to the Ontario Association of Children's Aid Societies (OACAS) (n.d.), reports from law enforcement are the primary way in which children come to the attention of the CAS (followed by schools, other Children's Aid Societies, self [mother/father/child], and community caregiver/professionals). OACAS reports that societies are more likely to respond to requests for assistance, child exposure to partner violence, caregiver with a problem, physical force and/or maltreatment, and inadequate supervision.

Critically, the person who has the suspicion is *not* to rely on another person to make the report. For example, if a teacher suspects that a child is abused or neglected, that teacher has the duty to contact the CAS directly. The teacher cannot "report" to the school principal and then leave it to the principal to report to the CAS. Individuals with a duty to report but fail to do so are guilty of an offence if they fail to report a suspicion that is based on information obtained in the course of their professional or official duties [*CYFSA* 125(5)] and can be liable for a fine up to $5,000 [*CYFSA* 125(9)]. It is acknowledged that individuals and other professionals who have a duty to report may have to disclose confidential or privileged information. The *Act* stipulates that there will be no repercussions for having disclosed this type of information provided the person acted in accordance with the *Act* and did so in a way that was neither malicious nor without reasonable grounds for the suspicion [*CYFSA* 125(10)].

RESEARCH IN ACTION: WHY ARE MORE CHILDREN COMING INTO THE CARE OF THE CHILDREN'S AID SOCIETY?

Much has been made of the large number of children taken into care since the mid-1990s. A variety of hypotheses have been offered to account for the increases. Two of these are discussed here: 1) CASs are so concerned with being criticized when they do not remove a child from risks in their home that they take more children into care for less serious reasons than previously; and 2) there are more categories of persons who have a duty to report, and these individuals take their duty more seriously—thus, increased reporting has driven up the overall number of children taken into care.

Whitehead et al. (2004) empirically studied these hypotheses using data from a large CAS in Southeastern Ontario. They compared information on children taken into care in 1995 with those of children taken into care in 2001.

If the first hypothesis is correct, we would expect that in 2001 children are being taken into care at a lower level of risk than were children in 1995. Yet, the data indicate quite the opposite. That is, the children taken into care in 2001 had higher average risk scores than those taken into care six years earlier.

On the second hypothesis, teachers say that they have contributed to the increased numbers of children taken into care because they have become more likely to report. The police say the same. So do other social service and health professionals. Still, others have pointed out that even those who do not have a professional duty to report have increased their reporting behaviour and may be disproportionally responsible for the increases. Whitehead et al. (2004) compared the proportion of cases taken into care in 1995 for each category of reporters, to those in 2001. They find that the relative proportion of reporting is exactly the same in 2001 as it was in 1995. All categories of professionals and non-professionals increased their reporting behaviour, and they did so proportionally. The greater number of cases being reported does not mean that, on average, it is a greater number of less serious cases now being reported. Quite the contrary—the average level of risk in the more recent cases is higher than in the earlier cases.

In brief, what this means is that as a society we have improved our reporting of child abuse and child neglect, and that this improvement is with respect to more severe cases. We have not lowered the threshold at which we are prepared to report. It is also noteworthy that these increases are across the board and do not reflect a change in reporting behaviour in only certain sectors of society.

Circumstances to Be Considered

In subsection 74(3) of the Act, when a person is directed to make a determination or order "in the best interests of a child," the following circumstances, if they are considered to be relevant, must be taken into consideration:

2. Where a person is directed in this Part to make an order or determination in the best interests of a child, the person shall
   (a) consider the child's views and wishes, given due weight in accordance with the child's age and maturity, unless they cannot be ascertained;

(b) in the case of a First Nations, Inuk or Métis child, consider the importance, in recognition of the uniqueness of First Nations, Inuit and Métis cultures, heritages and traditions, of preserving the child's cultural identity and connection to community, in addition to the considerations under clauses (a) and (c); and

(c) consider any other circumstance of the case that the person considers relevant, including

(i) the child's physical, mental and emotional needs, and the appropriate care or treatment to meet those needs,

(ii) the child's physical, mental and emotional level of development,

(iii) the child's race, ancestry, place of origin, colour, ethnic origin, citizenship, family diversity, disability, creed, sex, sexual orientation, gender identity and gender expression,

(iv) the child's cultural and linguistic heritage,

(v) the importance for the child's development of a positive relationship with a parent and a secure place as a member of a family,

(vi) the child's relationships and emotional ties to a parent, sibling, relative, other member of the child's extended family or member of the child's community,

(vii) the importance of continuity in the child's care and the possible effect on the child of disruption of that continuity,

(viii) the merits of a plan for the child's care proposed by a society, including a proposal that the child be placed for adoption or adopted, compared with the merits of the child remaining with or returning to a parent,

(ix) the effects on the child of delay in the disposition of the case,

(x) the risk that the child may suffer harm through being removed from, kept away from, returned to or allowed to remain in the care of a parent, and

(xi) the degree of risk, if any, that justified the finding that the child is in need of protection.

Ultimately, the determination of what it is that is in the best interest of the child is complicated. A young person living in a home environment that is substantially less than optimal is not necessarily helped by removal from that home. When the CAS makes a determination that is in the "best interests of the child" it considers that the removal of a child from a home in some ways also damages that child. The benefits of removal must be an overall improvement for the child. Said differently, "child protection" involves its own set of risks that need to be factored into the decision about the appropriateness of possible interventions. In some cases, the determination is relatively easy to make, such as when the child has experienced life-threatening physical harm or well-documented sexual abuse. In most cases, decisions are far more difficult to make because they involve the balancing of "risks," which are about the probabilities that certain consequences may occur.

It may surprise the reader to learn that Ontario CAS's fielded more than 171,600 calls and referrals, of which 80,815 required investigations in 2014/15. Of the investigations that were completed, 77 percent did not require further protection (OACAS, 2017). The rather high number of cases that did not require further protection should not be construed as a reason to not report one's suspicions, but rather that a potential child in need did receive the outreach needed.

UNDERSTANDING THE TERM "NEGLECT" IN CHILD PROTECTION

The term *neglect* is one of the categories that might warrant a child being identified as in need of protection. According to Nico Trocmé, Director of the School of Social Work, McGill University, neglect is the most frequently reported form of child maltreatment. And extensive research has been extremely clear, neglect has severe negative consequences for children across all domains: "cognitive development, social development, emotional development, number of words spoken, reading capacity" (Trocmé, n.d.).

Trocmé outlines that neglect is a term that has been used for a long time in child welfare but that it tends to be a term that isn't very helpful only on its own. Therefore, Trocmé argues that neglect be viewed as having three separate, but interrelated components, that need to identified and scrutinized in making a determination of neglect:

1. The situation of the parent: Is the parent unable to fully meet the needs of the child due various things such as young age/teen parenthood, mental health issues, addictions, cognitive limitations, or family violence, etc.

2. What are the environmental factors that surround the parent and child? Impoverished families are far less likely to have an extensive network of people and supports that buffer the child from the condition of the parent. Middle-class parents are more likely to have school resources, extended family, paid caregiving and recreation opportunities that act as protective factors for the child and keep the situation from reaching a crisis level of neglect.

3. Resilience of the child: Trocmé identifies that this is considered controversial, but advocates that it is important to look at the temperament and resiliency (i.e., the ability to recover from difficulties) of the child. Some children are more easy going and demonstrate greater resiliency than others and learn to manage. Other children are more vulnerable, and the same family situation can be highly detrimental to this child versus the resilient child.

Ultimately, Trocmé advocates for a multi-layered analysis rather than attributing neglect to only one source: the parent. He views neglect as a collective failure of society rather than solely the fault of the family. He gives the example of a school that sends home a 7-year-old knowing that the single mom works a shift and the child returns home alone. The collective responsibility would be to ensure there is affordable afterschool care for the child. Therefore, neglect has to be viewed as to whether the child's needs are being met through all resources including health care, social services, child care, and schools and not just whether the parent alone has failed to meet the child's needs.

Source: Adapted from Ontario Association of Children's Aid Societies. Nico Trocmé of McGill University discusses why identifying and treating child neglect can be so challenging (n.d.). Available at http://www.oacas.org/2017/10/nico-trocme-discusses-why-identifying-and-treating-child-neglect-can-be-so-challenging/

APPREHENSIONS: ROLE AND RESPONSIBILITIES OF THE CAS

Warrants and Apprehension

A justice of the peace may issue a **warrant** that authorizes a child protection worker to bring a child to a place of safety under subsection 81(2) if the justice of the peace is satisfied that there are reasonable and probable grounds to believe that

(a) the child is younger than 16;

(b) the child is in need of protection; and

(c) a less restrictive course of action is not available or will not protect the child adequately.

Under subsection 81(7), a child protection worker may, *without* a warrant, bring a child to a place of safety (**apprehend** the child), if the worker believes on reasonable and probable grounds that

(a) a child is in need of protection;

(b) the child is younger than 16; and

(c) there would be a substantial risk to the child's health or safety during the time necessary to bring the matter on for a hearing under subsection 90 (1) or obtain a warrant under subsection (2).

For several years, child protection agencies in Canada were unsure as to whom they owed their primary responsibility: the child or the child's parents. This was clarified in 2007 in the Supreme Court of Canada (SCC) case involving a 14-year-old girl referred to as R.D. In this case, the girl claimed that she had been abused by her parents and had been taken into care. The abuse claims appeared unfounded and the parent's assertions that the girl was delusional seemed reasonable. Despite the parents' request that the girl be returned to her parents, the agency involved considered it best that she remain under the care of the state. The girl also consented to being made a permanent ward of the state. The parents and a grandmother sued the child protection agency for $40 million claiming that they were harmed by the custodial treatment of the girl. In this instance, the Court dismissed the case against the agency and made it clear that a child protection agencies' first and primary responsibility is to the child [*Syl Apps Secure Treatment v BD* (2007) 3 S.C.R. 83].[2]

2.   You can read this decision of the SCC on their website at https://scc-csc.lexum.com/scc-csc/scc-csc/en/item/2378/index.do

Peace/Police Officer Powers

To be clear, this section outlines the powers of peace/police officers in the context of child protection. Additional powers with respect to youth justice will be further outlined later in this chapter.

A child protection worker acting to bring a child to safety may call for the assistance of a police officer [s. 81(8)]. Furthermore, the Act explicitly notes that under subsection 81(12) a police officer has the powers of a child protection worker as outlined in subsections (2), (6), (7), (10), and (11), essentially permitting to have the child be medically examined, enter premises with force and search for the child, or enter the premises without a warrant:

81 (13) No action shall be instituted against a peace officer or child protection worker for any act done in good faith in the execution or intended execution of that person's duty under this section or for an alleged neglect or default in the execution in good faith of that duty.

83 (1) A justice of the peace may issue a warrant authorizing a child protection worker to bring a child to a place of safety if the justice of the peace is satisfied on the basis of a child protection worker's sworn information that

(a)   the child is actually or apparently younger than 16, and
   (i)   has left or been removed from a society's lawful care and custody without its consent; or
   (ii)   is the subject of an extra-provincial child protection order and has left or been removed from the lawful care and custody of the child welfare authority or other person named in the order; and
(b)   there are reasonable and probable grounds to believe that there is no course of action available other than bringing the child to a place of safety that would adequately protect the child.

84 (1) A peace officer who believes on reasonable and probable grounds that a child actually or apparently younger than 12 has committed an act in respect of which a person 12 or older could be found guilty of an offence may bring the child to a place of safety without a warrant and on doing so,

(a)   shall return the child to the child's parent or other person having charge of the child as soon as practicable; or
(b)   where it is not possible to return the child to the parent or other person within a reasonable time, shall bring the child to a place of safety until the child can be returned to the parent or other person.

The peace officer must make reasonable efforts to notify the child's parents or appropriate guardian as per subsection 84(2) so the child can be returned. Where it is not possible do that within 12 hours [s. 84(3)], the child is deemed to have been brought to a place of safety under subsection 81(7) [without a warrant] and not under subsection (1) [with a court-ordered warrant].

Crown Wardship

When it is in the best interest of the child, the child can become a **ward of the Crown.** Foster children in Canada are known as *permanent wards*, (*crown wards* in Ontario). When a child's care and protection are placed under protection, the child becomes the legal responsibility of the government. Once a child has been made a Crown ward, he or she is eligible for adoption, kinship care (live with relatives), customary care, legal custody by a family member, independent living situation, or a foster parent/family. Foster parents have an important role to play providing stability and a caring home to support a child or young person's development and well-being. While the legal responsibility for the child or youth remains with Children's Aid, foster parents play an important role in the young person's daily life. Census data from 2011 counted children in foster care for the first time; 29,590 (61.8%) Canadian children under 14 years of age were in care (Statistics Canada, 2012). Children remain under the care of the government until they "age out of care." Each province has different criteria, with provinces like Ontario now offering financial and other supports (e.g., health and dental care) for young adults beyond age 18 provided they are going to school, in training, or working (Ontario Ministry of Children and Youth Services, n.d.). This change in 2014 reflects the challenges that children in care have faced, as most young adults in our modern society need support as they transition from child to fully independent adulthood.

Several detailed procedures are necessary for Crown wardship to be accomplished. It is not an action that is taken lightly by any of the parties. At the end of the day, the CAS needs to satisfy a court of law that the best interests of the child are being served and that there are no other less onerous alternatives that are reasonably available. What follows is a summary of the steps that are involved.

Under subsection 81(1), a CAS may apply to the court to determine whether a child is in need of protection. Then, under subsection 81(2), a justice of the peace may issue a warrant to bring the child to a place of safety. Subsection 81(4) indicates the court may order the child to be produced by those who have custody or that the child should be apprehended by a protection worker or the police. Finally, the determination of whether a child is in need of protection is made at a child protection hearing.

Hearings: Public Excluded, but Limited Role for Media

Subsection 87(4) asserts that hearings will typically be held in the absence of the public. However, subsection 87(5) allows for media representatives (defined at s. 87(1) to include the press, radio, and television media) to be present in lieu of the public per subsection (6) unless they are specifically excluded per subsection (7).

Under these subsections the court may make the following orders:

Selection of media representatives:

(6) The media representatives who may be present at a hearing that is held in the absence of the public shall be chosen as follows:

4. The media representatives in attendance shall choose not more than two persons from among themselves.

5. Where the media representatives in attendance are unable to agree on a choice of persons, the court may choose not more than two media representatives who may be present at the hearing.

6. The court may permit additional media representatives to be present at the hearing.

Order excluding media representatives or prohibiting publication:

(7) Where the court is of the opinion that the presence of the media representative or representatives or the publication of the report, as the case may be, would cause emotional harm to a child who is a witness at or a participant in the hearing or is the subject of the proceeding, the court may make an order,

(a) excluding a particular media representative from all or part of a hearing;

(b) excluding all media representatives from all or a part of a hearing; or

(c) prohibiting the publication of a report of the hearing or a specified part of the hearing.

Prohibition: Identifying a Child

Much like the *YCJA*, which protects the identity of children from the public, the *CYFSA* has similar provisions. Under subsection 87(8), no person shall publish or make public information that has the effect of identifying a child who is a witness or who is a participant in a hearing or the subject of a proceeding. Furthermore, the identity of the child's parent or foster parent, or any member of the child's family shall not be disclosed as that may yield information that identifies the child.

Temporary Care Agreements

Not all children are made permanent wards of the Crown. In most instances, a child's protection begins with a temporary care agreement for their custody and care. One of the underlying principles of child protection is **family reunification,** where it is reasonable and in the child's best interests. The hoped-for scenario where a child cannot be adequately cared for is a temporary arrangement that will allow the parent or caregiver to seek supports and assistance to remedy the circumstances that have prevented the parent from being able to care for the child (e.g., health condition, drug/alcohol addiction, housing, parenting capacity). Children can be brought into care with the parent(s) consent pursuant to a **temporary care agreement** [*CYFSA* 75(1)].

Custody of a child often needs to be addressed before the court is prepared to render its decision on the applications made before it. In such cases, "temporary" orders are made. Before making a temporary order for care and custody, the court must consider whether it is in the child's best interests to make an order to place the child in the care and custody of a person who is a relative of the child, or a member of the child's extended family or community [s.75].

Per section 75(4), a society shall not make a temporary care agreement unless the society

(a)   has determined that an appropriate residential placement that is likely to benefit the child is available; and

(b)   is satisfied that no course of action less disruptive to the child, such as care in the child's own home, is able to adequately protect the child.

Two important notes: (1) children 12 years of age or older must be a party to an agreement involving a temporary order about them [s. 75(2)]; and (2) any agreement terminates upon the child reaching 18 years of age [s. 75(13)].

Ultimately, the goal is to place children in a "forever home." To that end, as much as possible, the legislation puts time limits on temporary orders in order to ensure that children do not linger under a series of temporary orders. Generally, temporary agreements are not to exceed six months [s. 75(5)] and are not to be extended so as to result in a child being in a society's care and custody, for a period exceeding

(a)   12 months, if the child is younger than 6 on the day the agreement is entered into or extended; or

(b)   24 months, if the child is 6 or older on the day the agreement is entered into or extended. [s. 75(6)]

Generally, once that time limit is reached, it is expected that the child will be returned to their parent(s) or that a permanent plan for the child's custody will be made.

Order for Assessment

In the course of a proceeding, the court may order that one or more of the following persons undergo an assessment within a specified time by a person appointed in accordance with subsection 98(1):

1.   The child.
2.   A parent of the child.
3.   Any other person, other than a foster parent, who is putting forward or would participate in a plan for the care and custody of or access to the child.

An assessment may be ordered if the court is satisfied that

(a) an assessment of one or more of the persons specified in subsection (1) is necessary for the court to make a determination; or

(b) the evidence sought from an assessment is not otherwise available to the court.
    [s. 98(2)]

The court order will specify the time to select an assessor and submit the name of the assessor to the court [s. 98(3)]. The court must be satisfied that the person meets the following criteria:

4.   The person is qualified to perform medical, emotional, developmental, psychological, educational, or social assessments.
5.   The person has consented to perform the assessment [s. 98(4)].

If the person does not meet the criteria the court may select and appoint an assessor [s. 98(5)]. The assessor is required to make a written report (typically within less than 30 days) [s. 98(7)] and provide copies to prescribed parties per subsection 98(8). Noteworthy is that a child older than 12 years must also be given a copy of the report "except that where the court is satisfied that disclosure of all or part of the report to the child would cause the child emotional harm, the court may withhold all or part of the report from the child" [s. 98(10)]. Children younger than 12 generally do not receive a copy unless the court considers it desirable [s. 98(9)].

CAS's Plan for a Child

Under section 100, before making an order that would remove the child from the person caring for the child and make the child a ward of the Crown or CAS, the court will obtain and consider a plan for the child's care, prepared by the CAS, that includes the following:

(a)   a description of the services to be provided to remedy the condition or situation on the basis of which the child was found to be in need of protection;

(b)   a statement of the criteria by which the society will determine when its care or supervision is no longer required;

(c)   an estimate of the time required to achieve the purpose of the society's [CAS's] intervention;

(d)   where the society [CAS] proposes to remove or has removed the child from a person's care,

(i)   an explanation of why the child cannot be adequately protected while in the person's care, and a description of any past efforts to do so, and

(ii)   a statement of what efforts, if any, are planned to maintain the child's contact with the person;

(e)   where the [CAS] proposes to remove or has removed the child from a person's care permanently, a description of the arrangements made or being made for the child's long-term stable placement; and

(f)   a description of the arrangements made or being made to recognize the importance of the child's culture and to preserve the child's heritage, traditions and cultural identity.

Under subsection 109(2), where a child is made a ward of the Children's Aid Society, the society shall choose a residential placement that

(a)   represents the least restrictive alternative for the child;

(b)   where possible, respects the child's race, ancestry, place of origin, colour, ethnic origin, citizenship, family diversity, creed, sex, sexual orientation, gender identity and gender expression;

(c)   where possible, respects the child's cultural and linguistic heritage;

(d)   in the case of a First Nations, Inuk or Métis child, is with, if possible, a member of the child's extended family or, if that is not possible,

(i) in the case of a First Nations child, another First Nations family,

(ii) in the case of an Inuk child, another Inuit family, or

(iii) in the case of a Métis child, another Métis family; and

(e)   takes into account the child's views and wishes, given due weight in accordance with the child's age and maturity, and the views and wishes of any parent who is entitled to access to the child.

When a child is under the care of the CAS, the CAS has the rights and responsibilities of a parent for the purpose of the child's care, custody, and control [*CYFSA* 110].

Under section 112, where a child is in extended society care under an order, the society [CAS] shall make all reasonable efforts to assist the child to develop a positive, secure, and enduring relationship within a family through one of the following:

1.   An adoption.

2.   A custody order.

3.   In the case of a First Nations, Inuk, or Métis child,

(i) a plan for customary care,

(ii) an adoption, or

(iii) a custody order under subsection 116 (1).

IN THE NEWS

Child-Care Agencies Often Collaborate with Police

An Oxford County family has been torn apart amidst allegations of sexual misconduct by multiple male siblings.

Three brothers, one on an outstanding warrant, have been charged with sexually assaulting their younger sisters.

On Wednesday in Woodstock's youth court, one of the boys pleaded guilty to sexually touching three of his younger sisters, aged nine, 10 and 11.

The youth, now 18, cannot be named under the *Youth Criminal Justice Act*.

"Police were made aware that five of the young persons in the home were involved in sexual contact with one or more of the male siblings," assistant Crown attorney Michael Carnegie said.

An investigation had also been launched into the father, who was accused of abusing the eldest daughter.

Justice Marietta Roberts sentenced the teen to 18 months' probation. He was also ordered to take counselling and is not to reside with his parents or associate with any female siblings, except for the oldest.

The attacks took place over three years with some incidents occurring in the family's home when the mother was downstairs.

…

In February of last year the oldest daughter reported her father to police for alleged assaults. The Children's Aid Society interviewed all of the girls and the string of sex crimes by the boys in the family came unwound.

…

Source: Carla Garrett, "Brothers charged with sexually assaulting sisters," *Woodstock Sentinel-Review*, September 6, 2007, News Section, p. 3. Reprinted by permission from Sun Media Corp.

CROSSOVER YOUTH

As you transition from reading about children in need of protection to youth justice, it is important to be aware of the concept of **crossover youth**—young people who are engaged with the child welfare system as well as the youth justice system.

*This is an edited excerpt from a 2017 course paper written by Jacob Murray, a St. Jerome's & University of Waterloo undergraduate student, under the faculty supervision of Dr. Denise Whitehead.**

Canadian youth involved in the criminal justice system disproportionately enter the criminal justice system as children in need of protection from the child welfare system. Many of these young people are from socially and economically disadvantaged circumstances, including Indigenous backgrounds (Taylor, 2017). In many instances, the foster care system is ill-prepared to serve the diverse needs of these children and address the neglect and abuse that they have suffered. The compounding of negative circumstances results in many of these young people "crossing over" from the child welfare system into the youth justice system.

The stressors associated with parenting—including being a single parent, meeting economic needs, housing insecurity, and the lack of accessible and affordable daycare can result in poverty, lack of parental supervision, and lack of effective parenting strategies—disproportionately lead children with socially disadvantaged backgrounds to become involved with the child welfare system (Herz et al., 2012). Many of these children are also identified as having experienced physical abuse and corporal punishment (Leschied, Chiodo, Whitehead & Hurley, 2006).

Children in "permanent" foster care encounter new risk factors: residential instability, lack of meaningful relationships, and early contact with alcohol and drugs. Such instability and overexposure to these risk factors can prematurely put children into conflict with the law, as these negative influences fill the void for human connection (Chuang & Wells, 2010; Haight, Bidwell, Choi & Cho, 2016: 2; Ryan, Marshall, Herz & Hernandez, 2008). Relative to their non-foster care peers, youth in care score disproportionately lower on self-esteem and self-efficacy evaluations, as a result of feeling insufficient, unwanted, and unloved (Bala, De Filippis & Hunter, 2013: 9; Finlay, 2003: 4). Subsequently, they become easy prey, as they are sought out by criminal organizations who promise to give these young people a sense of place and purpose (Bala et al., 2013; Finlay, 2003).

The lack of specialized and intensive resources to serve children's complex needs in foster care is highly problematic. Many of these children are not given sufficient resources to be successful and overcome their severe childhood traumas, mental health crises, learning and conduct disorders, and low academic performance (Finlay, 2012: 254; Herz et al., 2012: 17). Limited academic success is of particular concern and is attributed to frequent instruction interruptions, due to frequent placement transfers from foster homes to group homes, and temporary returns to home, before being re-engaged with the foster care system (Leschied et al., 2006: 30).

It has been identified that the lack of a voice in their child protection care and life often leaves children feeling powerless. The children struggle to believe that their wishes are heard, understood and respected despite the provision that allows them to self-advocate (Bala et al., 2013; McCuish, Cale & Corrado, 2017). It has been suggested that inappropriate behaviours serve as a

Continued

means for these young people to assert their opinions and bring attention from their caseworker to alleviate their feelings of isolation from being a child "in the system" (Finlay, 2003).

Children in institutional care lack a sense of home. It has been described that children living in an institutional or group home facility is a "gateway to jail," in part due to the lack emotional support from caring adults (Finlay, 2003). Finlay reports that group homes are often the last resort for children who are not desired by foster families. Typically, these placements are reserved for children over 12 years of age, with histories of violence, and where they are considered too risky to live in a less-intrusive setting (Finlay, 2003: 21). Furthermore, some group home workers lack the educational training to address the complex mental health challenges foster children face, and as such, group homes over-rely on police services to act as disciplinarians. This overreliance on the police prematurely places already vulnerable youth in contact with law enforcement for minor issues (e.g., breaking curfew, verbal altercations with roommates or staff) (Bala et al., 2013: 8; Finlay, 2003: 23).

Group homes also lack the types of supports that many middle-class children receive from their parents. There is a greater expectation that these children provide for their own care and upkeep, such as cooking, self-motivation with school work, and laundry, even though their young age and lack of important life skills adds to their burden to commit to their schoolwork, which can be instrumental in creating a better life for themselves (Bala et al., 2013: 13). Furthermore, these young people, who find themselves in contact with the law, usually lack emotional and financial support (e.g., hiring a lawyer) and find that they must navigate the legal system on their own (Bala et al., 2013: 33). This increases their vulnerability; because children in care lack a support network of parental figures and caring adults, they have a stronger likelihood to be involved with negative peer influences, while being exposed to greater rates of abuse (Bala et al., 2013; Haight et al., 2016). When caring adults are in a child's life, the child is less likely to be held in jail, because their legal guardian can offer the court greater knowledge about the character of the child, their life circumstances, and their life story. Children with biological family support are more likely to receive milder judicial sanctions or probation, whereas children without familial support are at greater risk for long-term incarceration or institutionalization (Haight et al., 2016; McCuish et al., 2017: 142).

Finlay identified that children who have experienced interruptions in primary or secondary care were not sufficiently informed of the reasons for their transfer, leaving children with the sense that were not being heard and, in turn, convinced that "their happiest times were when they lived with their families of origin" (Finlay, 2003: 11). Children in foster care often experience feelings of hopelessness and the lack of adult role models to provide guidance and develop positive life skills (Bala et al., 2013: 40; Lutz & Stewart, 2015). Ambivalent relationships between children in care and adults must be restored and forged so that children can experience success and feel comfortable sharing their lives and concerns with adults. While frequent transfers seem inevitable for children in care, these frequent and abrupt interventions in care can lead children to criminal involvement.

---

* See also Corrado, R.R., Freedman, L.F., & Blatier, C. (2015). The over-representation of children in care in the youth criminal justice system in British Columbia: Theory and policy issues. In R. Carrado, A. Leschied, P. Lussier, and J. Whatley, eds., *Serious and Violent Young Offenders and Youth Criminal Justice: A Canadian Perspective* (pp. 183–197). Burnaby, BC: Simon Fraser Publications.

YOUTH JUSTICE

Part VI of the *CYFSA* deals with youth justice. The new *CYFSA* legislation implements an important change that brings about congruence between the definition of a **young person** with the definition outlined in the *Youth Criminal Justice Act*. Previously, there were two different thresholds—while the *YCJA* was for individuals under 18 years, the previous Ontario legislation in the *Child and Family Services Act* (*CFSA*) applied as follows: a young person means a child who is 12 years of age or more but under 16 years of age, and includes persons 16 years of age or more charged with having committed an offence while 12 years of age or more, but under 16 years of age.

The new *CYFSA*, with its expansive definition of a "youth," now provides as follows: "young person" means

(a) a person who is or, in the absence of evidence to the contrary, appears to be 12 or older but younger than 18 and who is charged with or found guilty of an offence under the *Youth Criminal Justice Act* (Canada) or the *Provincial Offences Act*, or

(b) if the context requires, any person who is charged under the *Youth Criminal Justice Act* (Canada) with having committed an offence while they were a young person or who is found guilty of an offence under the *Youth Criminal Justice Act* (Canada). ("adolescent"). [*CYFSA* 2(1)]

Note that the definition outlined in the *YCJA* is very similar to (a) above:

young person means a person who is or, in the absence of evidence to the contrary, appears to be twelve years old or older, but less than eighteen years old and, if the context requires, includes any person who is charged under this Act with having committed an offence while he or she was a young person or who is found guilty of an offence under this Act. (*adolescent*). [*YCJA* 2(1)]

This alignment in the definitions of young person also brings greater congruence with the United Nations Convention on the Rights of the Child and its goal to protect children under 18—a specified goal as outlined in the preamble to the *CYFSA*: "In furtherance of these principles, the Government of Ontario acknowledges that the aim of the *Child, Youth and Family Services Act, 2017*, is to be consistent with and build upon the principles expressed in the United Nations Convention on the Rights of the Child."

Detention Programs or Facilities

The *CYFSA* provides for the creation and admission of youth to various types of detention facilities. Subsection 145(1) allows the minister to establish and maintain services and programs for youth detention. There are two types specified in the legislation:

1. **Secure temporary detention programs**, in which restrictions are continuously imposed on the liberty of young persons by physical barriers, close staff supervision or limited access to the community.

2. **Open temporary detention programs**, in which restrictions that are less stringent than in a secure temporary detention program are imposed on the liberty of young persons.

Note that the creation of these detention programs must be read in conjunction with the *YCJA* legislation. For instance, in the *YCJA* definitions, a *youth custody facility* "means a facility designated under subsection 85(2) for the placement of young persons and, if so designated, includes a facility for the secure restraint of young persons, a community residential centre, a group home, a child care institution and a forest or wilderness camp."

This is discussed in detail in Chapter 10.

Youth Placement: Which Kind of Detention?

OPEN TEMPORARY DETENTION.
Under subsection 148(1), a young person who is detained under the *YCJA* in a place of temporary detention shall be detained in a place of open temporary detention unless it is determined that the young person is to be detained in a place of secure temporary detention.

SECURE TEMPORARY DETENTION.
Subsection 148(2) states that a young person may be detained in a place of secure temporary detention if the circumstances outlined below apply and if it is necessary to ensure the young person's attendance in court or to protect the public interest of safety:

1. The young person is charged with an offence for which an adult would be liable to imprisonment for five years or more and,

    i.   the offence includes causing or attempting to cause serious bodily harm to another person,
    ii. the young person has, at any time, failed to appear in court when required to do so under the [*YCJA*] or escaped or attempted to escape from lawful detention, or
    iii. the young person has, within the twelve months immediately preceding the offence on which the current charge is based, been convicted of an offence for which an adult would be liable to imprisonment for five years or more.

2. The young person is detained in a place of temporary detention and leaves or attempts to leave without the consent of the person in charge or is charged

with having escaped or attempting to escape from lawful custody or being unlawfully at large.

3. The Provincial Director is satisfied, having regard to all the circumstances, including any substantial likelihood the young person will commit a criminal offence or interfere with the administration of justice if placed in a place of open temporary detention, that it is necessary to detain the young person in a place of secure temporary detention,

    i.   to ensure the young person's attendance at court,
    ii. for the protection and safety of the public, or
    iii. for the safety or security within a place of temporary detention.

Rights of Children and Young Persons in Care

Part II of the *CYFSA* deals with the rights of children and young persons who are **in care.** Every child and young person receiving services under this Act has the following rights:

1. To express their own views freely and safely about matters that affect them.
2. To be engaged through an honest and respectful dialogue about how and why decisions affecting them are made and to have their views given due weight, in accordance with their age and maturity.
3. To be consulted on the nature of the services provided or to be provided to them, to participate in decisions about the services provided or to be provided to them and to be advised of the decisions made in respect of those services.
4. To raise concerns or recommend changes with respect to the services provided or to be provided to them without interference or fear of coercion, discrimination or reprisal and to receive a response to their concerns or recommended changes.
5. To be informed, in language suitable to their understanding, of their rights under this Part.
6. To be informed, in language suitable to their understanding, of the existence and role of the Provincial Advocate for Children and Youth and of how the Provincial Advocate for Children and Youth may be contacted. [*CYFSA* 3]

This rights-based approach to children and young persons places a greater onus on individuals who come in contact with these children and their families, whether through law enforcement or the provision of services to ensure that there is **due process**.

While the general rights of the child and youth are outlined above, it is important to review that children have legislatively protected rights while they are "in care," both as a result of being a child in need of protection or through their detention under the *YCJA*. Some of these rights are the following:

LOCKING UP RESTRICTED.
Under section 5: No service provider or foster parent shall detain a child or young person or permit a child or young person to be detained in locked premises in the course of the provision of a service to the child or young person, except as Part VI (Youth Justice) and Part VII (Extraordinary Measures) authorize.

NO CORPORAL PUNISHMENT.
Under section 4: No service provider or foster parent shall inflict corporal punishment on a child or young person or permit corporal punishment to be inflicted on a child or young person in the course of the provision of a service to the child or young person.

NO USE OF PHYSICAL OR MECHANICAL RESTRAINTS.
Under section 6: No service provider or foster parent shall use or permit the use of *physical restraint* on a child or young person for whom the service provider or foster parent is providing services, except as the regulations authorize.

Under section 7: No service provider or foster parent shall use or permit the use of *mechanical restraints* on a child or young person for whom the service provider or foster parent is providing services, except as Part VI (Youth Justice), Part VII (Extraordinary Measures), and the regulations authorize.

RIGHT OF COMMUNICATION AND TO ADVOCACY.
Under subsection 10(1), a child in care has a right

- (a) to speak in private with, visit and receive visits from members of their family or extended family regularly, subject to subsection (2);
- (b) without unreasonable delay, to speak in private with and receive visits from
    - (i) their lawyer,
    - (ii) another person representing the child or young person, including the Provincial Advocate for Children and Youth and members of the Provincial Advocate for Children and Youth's staff,
    - (iii) the Ombudsman appointed under the *Ombudsman Act* and members of the Ombudsman's staff, and
    - (iv) a member of the Legislative Assembly of Ontario or of the Parliament of Canada; and
- (c) to send and receive written communications that are not read, examined or censored by another person, subject to subsections (3) and (4).

WHEN THE CHILD IS A CROWN WARD.
Under subsection 103(2): The child in care is *not* entitled as a right to speak with, visit or receive visits from a member of his or her family, except under an order for access ..., or an openness order or openness agreement.

WRITTEN COMMUNICATIONS.
Under subsection 10(5): Written communications includes mail and electronic communications in any form (e.g., email, texts).

(3) Subject to subsection (4), written communications to a child in care

(a) may be opened by the service provider or a member of the service provider's staff in the child's or young person's presence and may be inspected for articles prohibited by the service provider;

(b) subject to clause (c), may be examined or read by the service provider or a member of the service provider's staff in the child's or young person's presence, where the service provider believes on reasonable grounds that the contents of the written communication may cause the child or young person physical or emotional harm;

(c) shall not be examined or read by the service provider or a member of the service provider's staff if it is to or from a person described in subclause (1) (b) (i), (ii), (iii) or (iv); and

(d) shall not be censored or withheld from the child or young person, except that articles prohibited by the service provider may be removed from the written communication and withheld from the child or young person.

(4) Written communications to and from a young person who is detained in a place of temporary detention or held in a place of secure custody or of open custody,

(a) may be opened by the service provider or a member of the service provider's staff in the young person's presence and may be inspected for articles prohibited by the service provider;

(b) may be examined or read by the service provider or a member of the service provider's staff and may be withheld from the recipient in whole or in part where the service provider or the member of their staff believes on reasonable grounds that the contents of the written communications,

(i) may be prejudicial to the best interests of the young person, the public safety or the safety or security of the place of detention or custody, or

(ii) may contain communications that are prohibited under the *Youth Criminal Justice Act* (Canada) or by court order;

(c) shall not be examined or read under clause (b) if it is to or from the young person's lawyer; and

(d) shall not be opened and inspected under clause (a) or examined or read under clause (b) if it is to or from a person described in subclause (1) (b) (ii), (iii) or (iv).

PERSONAL LIBERTIES.
Under section 12: A child in care has a right

(a) to have reasonable privacy and possession of their own personal property, subject to section 155; and

(b) to receive instruction and participate in activities of their choice related to their creed, community identity and cultural identity, subject to section 14 regarding parental consent.

PLAN OF CARE.

In accordance with subsection 13(1), a child in care has a right to a plan of care designed to meet their particular needs, which shall be prepared within 30 days of the child's or young person's admission to the residential placement.

RIGHTS TO CARE.

A child in care also has a right [*CYFSA* 13(2)]

(a) to participate in the development of their individual plan of care and in any changes made to it;

(b) to have access to food that is of good quality and appropriate for the child or young person, including meals that are well balanced;

(c) to be provided with clothing that is of good quality and appropriate for the child or young person, given their size and activities and prevailing weather conditions;

(d) to receive medical and dental care, subject to section 14, at regular intervals and whenever required, in a community setting whenever possible;

(e) to receive an education that corresponds to their aptitudes and abilities, in a community setting whenever possible; and

(f) to participate in recreational, athletic and creative activities that are appropriate for their aptitudes and interests, in a community setting whenever possible.

RIGHT TO RESPECTFUL SERVICES: TO BE HEARD AND TO BE REPRESENTED.

Under subsection 15(2): Children and young persons and their parents are to have an opportunity to be heard and represented when decisions affecting their interests are made and to be heard when they have concerns about the services they are receiving.

A child and young person's right to be heard, consulted, and to express his or her views also requires that they be given due weight in the decision-making process [8(2)], and should be considered to the extent that is practical given the child's level of understanding, whenever significant decisions concerning the child are made, including decisions with respect to medical treatment, education and religion and decisions with respect to the child's discharge from the placement or transfer to another residential placement.

FRENCH LANGUAGE SERVICES.

Under section 16, and respecting the bilingual rights of Canadian citizens, all communications and services must be provided in French, where appropriate.

RIGHT TO BE INFORMED.

Under section 9: A child in care who has been admitted to a residential placement has a right to be informed, in a language suitable for the child's level of understanding, of

(a)   their rights under this Part;

(b)   the complaints procedures established under subsection 18(1) and the further review available under section 19;

(c)   the review procedures available for children under sections 64, 65 and 66;

(d)   the review procedures available under section 152, in the case of a young person described in clause (b) of the definition of "child in care" in subsection 2(1);

(e)   their responsibilities while in the placement; and

(f)   the rules governing day-to-day operation of the residential care, including disciplinary procedures.

COMPLAINTS PROCEDURE.

Pursuant to subsection 18(1): A service provider who provides residential care to children or young persons or who places children or young persons in residential placements shall establish a written procedure, in accordance with the regulations, for hearing and dealing with

(a)   complaints regarding alleged violations of the rights under this Part of children in care; and

(b)   complaints by children in care or other persons affected by conditions or limitations imposed on visitors under subsection 11(1) or suspensions of visits under subsection 11(2).

CHILD MAY REQUEST ASSISTANCE FROM THE PROVINCIAL ADVOCATE FOR CHILDREN AND YOUTH.

Pursuant to subsection 18(2), a service provider shall tell the children in care that they may ask for the assistance of the Provincial Advocate for Children and Youth in

(a)   making a complaint

(b)   requesting a further review

REVIEW OF COMPLAINT.

Pursuant to subsection 18(3), a service provider shall conduct a review or ensure that a review is conducted, in accordance with the procedure established under clause (1) (a) or (b), or on the complaint of

(a)   a child in care or a group of children in care;

(b)   the parent of a child in care who makes a complaint;

(c)   another person representing the child in care who makes a complaint; or

(d) a person affected by a condition or limitation imposed on visitors under subsection 11(1) or a suspension of visits under subsection 11(2), and shall seek to resolve the complaint.

RESPONSE TO COMPLAINANTS.

Pursuant to subsection 18(4), upon completion of its review under subsection (3), the service provider shall inform each person who made the complaint, whether as an individual or as part of a group, of the results of the review.

FURTHER REVIEW.

Pursuant to subsection 19(1), where a person referred to in subsection 18(3) makes a complaint, whether as an individual or as part of a group, and is not satisfied with the results of the review conducted under that subsection and requests in writing that the Minister appoint a person to conduct a further review of the complaint, the Minister shall appoint a person who is not employed by the service provider to do so. Under subsection (2), a person appointed under subsection (1) shall review the complaint in accordance with the regulations and may do so by holding a hearing.

TEST YOUR KNOWLEDGE

Definitions

Define the following terms:

1. Best interests of the child

   _____

   _____

   _____

2. Child in need of protection

   _____

   _____

   _____

3. Reasonable grounds (duty to report)

   _____

_____

_____

4. Forthwith

_____

_____

_____

5. Duty to report

_____

_____

_____

6. Warrant

_____

_____

_____

7. Apprehension

_____

_____

_____

8. Ward of the Crown

_____

_____

_____

9. Family reunification

_____

_____

_____

10. Temporary care agreement

_____

_____

_____

11. Crossover youth

_____

_____

_____

12. Young person

_____

_____

_____

13. Secure temporary detention program

_____

_____

_____

14. Open temporary detention program

_____

_____

_____

15. In care

_____

_____

_____

16. Due process

_____

_____

_____

True/False

1. T   F   The *CYFSA* recognizes that parents may need help in caring for their children.

2. T   F   Under the *CYFSA*, Indigenous people are not entitled to provide their own child and family services.

3. T   F   Children in the care of the CAS are eligible to be represented by the Office of the Children's Lawyer.

4. T   F   A child is not "in need of the protection" if there is only a risk of physical harm, but no evidence of actual harm.

5. T   F   Parents are expected to adequately supervise the children under their care.

6. T   F   A child protection worker is not allowed to call on the assistance of the police.

7. T   F   Under some parts of the *CYFSA*, a police officer has the powers of a child protection worker.

8. T   F   Before taking action with respect to a child who appears to be under the age of 12, the police officer must first collect evidence that clearly indicates that the child has not yet reached the age of 12.

9. T   F   Children who are under the age of 12 and have been apprehended by the police because they have committed a serious offence need to be returned to their parents as soon as is practicable.

10. When a child is made a ward of the Children's Aid Society, the society shall choose a placement that

    T   F   represents the least restrictive alternative

    T   F   is in the same neighbourhood as the child's parents

    T   F   respects the religious faith in which the child was raised

    T   F   is close to the home of the child's friends

    T   F   respects the child's cultural heritage

    T   F   takes into account the child's wishes

    T   F   takes into account the wishes of all parents

    T   F   takes into account the financial situation of the foster parents

11. T   F   Under the *CYFSA*, the presumption is that if a young person is to be detained that it will be in a place of secure temporary detention.

12. With respect to each of the following, a young person can be detained in a place of secure temporary detention if

    T   F   it is necessary to ensure attendance at court

    T   F   it is necessary to protect the public

    T   F   the young person needs to be taught a lesson

    T   F   the young person deserves to be punished

13. T   F   Foster parents are allowed to use corporal punishment in the discipline of a child who needs it.

14. T   F   Children in care have the right to be informed that they can speak to the police.

15. T   F   Children in care have the right to be informed that they can talk to their parents.

Multiple Choice

1. The *Child, Youth and Family Services Act* (*CYFSA*) applies
   a. only to persons under the age of 12
   b. only to persons under the age of 14
   c. only to persons under the age of 16
   d. only to persons under the age of 18

2. Which of the following is *not* a "paramount purpose" of the *CYFSA*?
   a. to promote the best interests of children
   b. to see to it that children receive the discipline that they need
   c. to promote the well-being of children
   d. to promote the protection of children

3. The *CYFSA* has as one of its purposes to recognize a course of action that is available and appropriate and should be considered if it is also
   a. proven in the literature to be effective
   b. least costly to the province
   c. the least disruptive
   d. two of the above

4. Which of the following are responsibilities of those who provide services to children?
   a. an opportunity for parents, but not children, to be heard
   b. an opportunity for children, but not parents, to be represented
   c. decision made according to clear and consistent criteria
   d. all of the above

5. When, under the *CYFSA*, a person is directed to make a determination "in the best interests of the child," which of the following circumstances need to be taken into consideration?
   a. the child's emotional needs
   b. the child's religion
   c. the child's views and wishes
   d. all of the above

6. A justice of the peace may authorize that a child be brought to a place of safety if there are reasonable and probable grounds to believe that
   a. the child is in need of protection and asks to be protected
   b. a more restrictive course of action is not available
   c. the child is in need of protection
   d. two of the above

7. When a child under the age of 12 is apprehended by the police because the child has committed an act that a person over the age of 12 could be found guilty of an offence, the peace/police officer

   a. shall return the child to the child's parent
   b. shall take the child into police custody
   c. shall take the child to the Children's Aid Society
   d. shall return the child to the child's parent within 48 hours

8. No one is allowed to publish identifying information about which participants in a child protection hearing?

   a. the subject of the hearing
   b. the child's parents but not foster parents
   c. a witness but not other participants who are children
   d. two of the above

9. Rules concerning the presence of the media take into account the possibility of emotional harm to

   a. only the child who is the subject of the proceedings
   b. only a child who is a witness
   c. the parents of the child
   d. none of the above

10. Those who have a duty to report a child in need of protection must

    a. ensure that they have evidence before they report
    b. report what they suspect on reasonable grounds
    c. report what they have been told by other persons who are their friends
    d. report the incident to their immediate supervisor

11. Which of the following has a duty to report and would be guilty of an offence if he or she failed to report a suspicion that is based on information obtained in the course of his or her professional duties?

    a. dentist
    b. firefighter
    c. university professor
    d. all of the above

12. Which of the following is *not* a type of facility or program that may be established under the *CYFSA*?

    a. secure temporary detention program
    b. secure custody facility
    c. permanent custody facility
    d. open custody facility

13. Secure temporary detention may be appropriate if the young person is charged with an offence for which an adult would be liable to imprisonment for five years or more and

   a.   the offence includes causing serious bodily harm to another person
   b.   the young person has escaped from detention
   c.   the young person is from a prominent family
   d.   two of the above

14. Which of the following is *not* a right of a child in care?

   a.   receive well-balanced meals
   b.   see their parents
   c.   receive good quality clothing
   d.   participate in athletic activities

15. When children are informed of their rights the way the information is provided should take into account which of the following?

   a.   suitability of language
   b.   the child's level of understanding
   c.   both of the above
   d.   none of the above

16. Who of the following has the right to file a complaint that a service provider has violated the rights of a child in care?

   a.   the child in care
   b.   the child's parent
   c.   another person representing the child
   d.   all of the above

Short Answer

1.   Identify three purposes of the *CYFSA*.

   _____

   _____

   _____

   _____

   _____

   _____

   _____

2. Identify four functions of Children's Aid Societies.

    _____

    _____

    _____

    _____

    _____

    _____

    _____

    _____

3. Identify three situations where a child could be deemed to be "in need of protection."

    _____

    _____

    _____

    _____

    _____

    _____

    _____

    _____

4. When a person is directed to make a determination "in the best interests of a child," certain circumstances may be taken into consideration. Identify five of them.

    _____

    _____

    _____

    _____

    _____

    _____

    _____

    _____

5. A police officer apprehends a young person who is throwing stones at and damaging passing cars. The young person looks as though he might be under the age of 12. Identify two things that the police officer should do.

_____

_____

_____

_____

_____

_____

_____

_____

6. The *CYFSA* makes it possible for the media to be present or excluded from a child protection hearing. In your opinion, the decision to include or exclude should be based on what considerations?

_____

_____

_____

_____

_____

_____

_____

_____

7. When a child is made a ward of the Children's Aid Society, what are the terms of choosing a residential placement for that child? Identify five considerations.

_____

_____

_____

_____

_____

_____

_____

_____

8. The duty to report involves suspicion based on reasonable grounds. Identify two situations that meet this test without there being clear and convincing evidence of abuse or neglect.

_____

_____

_____

_____

_____

_____

_____

9. Name five occupational categories that under the *CYFSA* would be guilty of an offence if they failed to report a suspicion that is based on information obtained in the course of their professional or official duties.

_____

_____

_____

_____

_____

_____

_____

10. In your own words, indicate what it means for a child to be "in care" of the Children's Aid Society.

_____

_____

_____

_____

_____

_____

_____

11. Why do you suppose that there are rules about who, and under what circumstances, the mail of a child in care can be opened?

_____

_____

_____

_____

_____

_____

_____

_____

12. How are foster parents supposed to discipline children who are in care if they are not allowed to use corporal punishment?

_____

_____

_____

_____

_____

_____

_____

_____

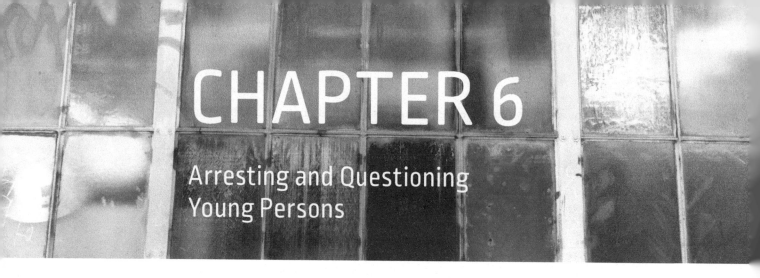

CHAPTER 6

Arresting and Questioning Young Persons

LEARNING OUTCOMES

Students who have mastered this chapter will have the ability to do the following:

- Explain what is meant by a "young person" under the *Youth Criminal Justice Act*.
- Identify the rights of the accused under the *Canadian Charter of Rights and Freedoms*.
- Distinguish between "indictable offences" and "summary offences."
- Distinguish between an "appearance notice" and a "summons."
- Explain the rules for taking statements from young persons.
- Explain the techniques that can be used to determine whether young persons understand the rights that have been stated to them.
- Understand the reasons why there are special protections for young persons.
- Describe the circumstances under which parents need to be notified.
- Explain the procedure to be used with persons under 12 years of age.
- Explain the responsibilities of a peace officer who apprehends a person under 12 years of age.

ARRESTING YOUNG PERSONS

The basic rules that govern the arrest and questioning of adults also apply to young offenders. Thus, for example, it remains good practice to touch the person you are arresting in order to indicate that you are "holding" them under arrest. The *Youth Criminal Justice Act* (*YCJA*) places additional requirements on the police to make sure that they protect the rights of the young person. Those requirements extend to include the admissibility of statements made by young persons if they decide to enter a "not guilty" plea in court.

Points to Consider

Relevant Law

The relevant law that guides arrest and questioning is found in the *Criminal Code of Canada*, the *Canadian Charter of Rights and Freedoms*, and the *YCJA*. In many ways, the *YCJA* gives the police much more flexibility with respect to arrest than they have when dealing with adults.

Article 12 of the United Nations Convention on the Rights of the Child (UNCRC) is reflected in the *YCJA*. For example, subsection 3(1)(d)(i) provides that young persons have a "right to be heard in the course of and to participate in the processes … that lead to decisions that affect them."

Encouragement of Extrajudicial Measures

Both the statement of principles and many sections within the *YCJA* encourage the use of informal and extrajudicial measures. The *YCJA* requires peace officers to consider not laying charges for the less serious cases, where a first-time offender is involved. In these instances, the law is satisfied if less formal and effective measures have been used. The *YCJA* recognizes that for many young people, simply being spoken to by the peace officer may be a deterrent. This is particularly the case when the young person's parents are willing to take an active role in dealing with the young person's misbehaviour.

Child, Youth and Family Services Act

The latter part of this chapter will deal with some aspects of Ontario's *Child, Youth and Family Services Act* (*CYFSA*). Strictly speaking, children who are under 12 years of age cannot be arrested. They can, however, be apprehended. We will examine some sections of the *CYFSA* since arrest and apprehension both result in the young person being placed in police custody, even if for only a short period.

Who Is a "Young Person"?

The *YCJA* defines a *young person* as someone "who is or, in the absence of evidence to the contrary, appears to be 12 years of age or more, but under 18 years of age" [*YCJA* 2(1)]. The jurisdiction of the youth justice court extends to persons who are more than 18 years of age but who were under 18 years of age when they committed the offence.

Uncertainty as to a Young Person's Age

Where there is some question about the offender's age, a parent's word is normally accepted. The *YCJA* also allows proof by standard documentary procedures, such as the submission of a birth certificate. Occasionally, young offenders lie about their age. Typically, this might be an attempt by someone over 17 years of age to avoid adult court. In these instances, the peace officer must start treating the offender as a young person and not an adult. Practically, this involves segregating the young offender from other adults in custody and extending the rights provisions under the *YCJA*, including notifying the young person's parents. The opposite also occurs when some young offenders claim to be older than they are to avoid having the peace officer notify their parents.

Mistakes as to Age

Because substantial differences exist in how we handle the cases of adult and young persons, the *YCJA* has provisions that avoid the loss of testimonial evidence when mistakes are made about the person's age. Under subsection 146(8), the youth justice court may accept statements or waivers given by young persons when it is believed that they are 18 years or older due to misrepresentation of their age. The courts have also decided that when the peace officers apprehend or charge adults for offences they committed as young persons, the peace officers are not bound by all the restrictions imposed by the *YCJA*. Typically, this means that all the protections surrounding the questioning of young persons need not apply.

Basic Rights of the Accused

The sections on legal rights (sections 7 through 14) of the *Canadian Charter of Rights and Freedoms* (*CCRF*) outline the general guidelines within which justice must be carried out. The basic principle is outlined in section 7, which states that we should not deprive anyone of their life, liberty, and security, "except in accordance with the principles of fundamental justice." Among those principles of fundamental justice are the following rights:

- To be "secure against unreasonable search or seizure" [*CCRF* 8]
- To be "informed promptly" why they are being arrested or detained [*CCRF* 10(a)]
- To have access to legal counsel without delay [*CCRF* 10(b)]
- To be informed that they have the right to legal counsel, [*CCRF* 10(b)] to *habeas corpus*—the right to be brought before a justice within a reasonable time
- To determine whether their detention is lawful or necessary [*CCRF* 10(c)]
- To be informed of the specific charges against them [*CCRF* 11(a)]
- To be tried within a reasonable time [*CCRF* 11(b)]
- Not to be denied reasonable bail without just cause [*CCRF* 11(e)]
- Not to be subjected to any "cruel and unusual treatment or punishment" [*CCRF* 12]

These rights apply equally to young persons and adults.

Arrest

It is important to understand that the *Criminal Code of Canada* (*CCC*) distinguishes among three types of offences as there are different implications depending on the seriousness of the offence (starting with the arrest stage). The three types of offences are: (1) indictable offences, (2) summary offences, and (3) dual or "hybrid" offences.

Indictable offences are usually the most serious offences. Specifically, **indictable offences** are those for which the potential penalty is either greater than six months in jail or a fine of more than $2,000. More often, indictable offences carry sentences of two or more years' imprisonment (including life). Occasionally, the *CCC* does not indicate a maximum sentence for an indictable offence. For such offences, the maximum sentence is set at five years under section 730 of the *CCC*.

Summary offences are those for which the potential penalty is "to a fine of not more than two thousand dollars or to imprisonment for six months or to both" [*CCC* 787(1)]. **Hybrid offences**, such as some types of assault, can be treated as either summary or indictable offences. The distinguishing feature is usually how much harm or damage has been done. It is up to the Crown prosecutor to decide how to handle these cases.

Sections 494 to 502 of the *CCC* outline the law that allows peace officers to make arrests for criminal offences. From the law's point of view, "arrest" is a means of compelling a person to appear before a justice of the law. The law does not consider arresting an adult a form of punishment, although it may occasionally serve that function socially. The *YCJA*, however, recognizes that being arrested may have a significant impact upon many young persons. Consequently, the *YCJA* allows peace officers the option of not compelling young persons to appear before the youth justice courts when they believe it is in the best interests of the young person and the community. These situations occur mostly when the young person has committed a minor offence, has little history of offending, and appears to be genuinely sorry about the deed.

There are times, however, when compelling a young person to appear in court is the appropriate course of action. Arresting a young person is based on the rules for arresting an adult. Because different individuals and different circumstances require different levels of "compulsion," the law provides for different procedures for compelling an appearance. According to the *CCC*, a person may be compelled to appear before a justice by

- issuing an appearance notice [*CCC* 496],
- issuing a summons [*CCC* 509],
- arresting a person *without* a warrant by any person [*CCC* 494(1)] and by a peace officer [*CCC* 495(1)], or
- arresting a person with a warrant [*CCC* 513].

Appearance Notices
A peace officer may issue an appearance notice to a person for an offence listed under section 553 of the *CCC*, for a hybrid offence, or for a summary conviction offence. In fact, subsection 495(2) of the *CCC* lists situations where officers are not to arrest a person who has committed one of those types of offences without a warrant. Officers should not make an arrest when no need exists to do any of the following:

- establish the identity of the person;
- secure or preserve evidence;

- prevent the continuation of or prevent an offence; or
- make sure a person does not "fail to attend in court."

Essentially, appearance notices are "issued by a peace officer to a person not yet charged with an offence." Section 501 of the *CCC* indicates what should be included in the appearance notice. Form 9, which appears at the back of the *CCC*, provides a sample of what an appearance notice should contain.

Summonses

Section 509 of the *CCC* sets out the requirements for summonses. Summonses are used for summary and hybrid offences. They cannot be used when an indictable offence has taken place. Unlike an appearance notice, a summons shows that the peace officer has charged a person with committing an offence. Form 6, at the back of the *CCC*, provides an outline of a typical summons.

Arrest without a Warrant

Sections 494 and 495 of the *CCC* present the conditions for arresting someone without a warrant. A peace officer may arrest a person without a warrant if the person is found committing an indictable offence. Peace officers may also arrest without a warrant when, on "reasonable grounds," they believe a person "has committed or is about to commit an indictable offence." Furthermore, an officer may arrest a person without a warrant if the officer believes a warrant of arrest or committal is outstanding for that person.

Arrest with a Warrant

Arrest with a warrant is justified under section 513 of the *CCC*. Section 511 shows what needs to be included in the warrant. Form 7 in the *CCC* presents both the structure of a warrant and a listing of the reasons for which the court issues a warrant. Primarily, warrants are issued when a person fails to appear in court when asked to do so, when a person tries to avoid the serving of a summons, or when a person escapes or attempts to evade custody.

Jurisdiction to Execute a Warrant

For adults, officers normally only execute warrants in the territorial jurisdiction of the court or justice that issues them. The primary exception is when they are involved in a fresh pursuit. Section 145 of the *YCJA*, however, allows youth court warrants to be executed anywhere in Canada.

QUESTIONING THE YOUNG PERSON

Asking questions is one of the primary investigative tools available to a peace officer. Officers ask questions for many purposes, but ultimately, most officers question an accused in order to obtain a confession. For an adult suspect, a signed confession is one of the most helpful things an officer can provide to the Crown for its presentation of a case. When dealing with young offenders, however, statements tend not to be very useful in supporting the case. While this is a practical reality in many situations, it does not mean that one should not proceed to take statements when one can. While few statements might be used as evidence in the youth court, a statement might give the officer more insight into the incident—even to the point of deciding that the young person's involvement was not what it first seemed. Providing a statement might also be the first step in a process that allows young persons to come to grips with their culpability.

Requirement for Proper Procedures

Since questions and confessions play such an important role in the criminal justice process, there are strict rules surrounding both. Questions, particularly those directed at young people, can only provide useful information if asked in the right manner, at the right time, and under the right circumstances. Similarly, confessions must be given "freely and voluntarily" in order to be acceptable as evidence. This is not a book on dealing with either investigation or interrogation techniques. Consequently, we will not pursue the details of those issues. What we need to do, however, is to examine how those normal techniques of peace officer procedure need to be modified to deal with young people.

Right to Remain Silent
One of the main differences between Anglo-American law, which forms the basis of Canada's legal system, and other legal systems is the right of the accused to remain silent. Traditional common law has long acknowledged that accused persons cannot be forced to testify in court and that both accused persons and witnesses cannot be forced to give self-incriminating evidence. So important is that concept to our view of justice that we have incorporated it into our *Charter of Rights and Freedoms* [sections 11(c) and 13].

The broader concept of the right of the accused to remain silent under other circumstances was recognized in the Hebert case, which was heard in the Supreme Court in 1990 (*R v. Hebert* [1990] 2 S.C.R. 151). In that case, Madame Justice McLachlin placed the right to silence within the context of one of the fundamental rights outlined in section 7 of the *Charter of Rights and Freedoms*. Essentially, the Supreme Court's stance is that accused persons should have the freedom to choose whether or not they wish to speak to the authorities or to refuse to make a statement. The right of the accused not to make a statement does not prohibit the peace officer from speaking to the accused. The peace officer can encourage the accused to make a statement, particularly in light of available physical evidence. The key feature, however, is that the statement must be an informed one that is given freely and voluntarily. Statements taken under a threat (even an implied one) or statements made under a promise or inducement from the peace officer or other officers of the court will likely not be admissible in court.

The onus is not on the accused to prove that the statement was not given voluntarily. If asked, the onus is on the Crown to show how the statement was given freely.

WHAT CONSTITUTES A THREAT, INDUCEMENT, OR COERCION?

What constitutes a threat, inducement, or coercion (particularly an implied one) differs from one situation to another. Salhany (1997: 197), however, provides some examples of statements that have been judged by the courts on various occasions to constitute a threat. These, for example, include the following statements:

- "It would be better for you if you told us what happened."
- "You will be arrested if you do not tell us where the stolen goods are."
- "You had better tell the truth."
- "It is necessary to give an explanation."

However, phrases such as the following have been seen as acceptable (Salhany, 1997: 198):

- "Be sure to tell the truth."
- "Be a good girl/boy and tell the truth."

Salhany (1997: 199–200) also indicates that it is easy for officers to unintentionally make promises or inducements that can invalidate the acceptance of a confession. Offering to speak to the judge about a lighter sentence if the accused person confesses and offering to arrange for therapy if a confession is forthcoming have been seen as inducements. This is even the case if the officer is making the offer in good faith and in what might be seen as in the best interests of the accused.

HOW DOES THIS APPLY TO YOUNG PERSONS?

While peace officers must exercise procedural care when questioning adults and taking their confessions, they must exercise extra care when dealing with young persons. The basic procedures in these areas apply to both adults and young people. The *YCJA* and the courts have imposed further rules on interactions between the peace officer and young persons.

Taking a Statement

Although interpersonal dealings with young offenders may sometimes be more difficult than dealing with adult offenders, most cases involving young persons can be disposed of more easily. Young persons have less experience and less well developed judgment than adults. Because of this, it is very important that peace officers take young persons' statements correctly. Inadequate attention to the details of taking statements can easily result in a straightforward case becoming a series of problems.

STATEMENTS MADE TO PEACE OFFICERS AND "PERSONS IN AUTHORITY"

The same basic rules that apply to adults for collecting evidence apply to young persons. There are, however, two subsections of the *YCJA*—146(2) and 146(4)—that impose additional considerations on the taking of statements. The rules for taking the statements of young persons apply to both peace officers and what the law defines as another "person in authority." Generally, a **person in authority** is someone who is considered to have a "direct role in the administration of justice or prosecution of offences" (Bala, 1997: 123). This would normally include probation officers and anyone who is a peace officer. So far, the courts have not regarded parents, teachers, school principals, physicians, or psychiatrists as persons in authority (Bala, 1997: 119–123). This distinction is important because the specific rules of caution outlined under subsection 146(2) of the *YCJA* apply only to peace officers and persons in authority.

Statements made to other persons are subject to the normal rules of evidence. The court will usually accept them even if those "other persons" do not provide the normal cautions beforehand.

Subsection 146(2) of the *YCJA* states that no written or oral statement given by a young person to either a peace officer or a person in authority is admissible against the young person unless certain conditions apply. Specifically, those conditions are the following:

- The statement is voluntary.
- The young person is told before giving a statement, in language appropriate to the young person's age and understanding, that
  - the young person is under no obligation to give a statement,
  - any statement given may be used as evidence in court,
  - the young person has the right to consult legal counsel,
  - the young person has the right to consult a parent, relative, or another adult who might provide assistance, and
  - any statement they make must be made in front of their legal counsel or another appropriate adult, unless they desire otherwise.
- Before giving the statement, the young person must be given a reasonable opportunity to
  - consult with legal counsel,
  - consult with a parent, adult relative, or another appropriate adult chosen by the young person, and
  - make the statement in the presence of that parent, adult relative, or another adult.

How to Inform Young Persons of Their Rights

Some police services give peace officers a card outlining the main points that the officer needs to tell the young person. This is generally a good procedure. There are, however, some limitations to that approach. The main problem is that a standard explanation is not appropriate for all young persons. The *YCJA* requires the peace officer to explain the young person's rights to them in a language that is appropriate to their age and ability to understand. Some police services use a detailed form to track the explanations provided to young persons as well as the responses received. This is an important issue that we will cover in more detail in the next section of this chapter.

It is good practice to advise the young person of their rights at several points in the arrest process. For example, the arresting officer should inform the young person of the charge and of his or her basic rights. The arresting officer should provide the same information again when turning the young person over to the officer in charge and, if the young person is temporarily detained, the rights should be repeated upon release.

Exceptions

There are two exceptions to the need for an officer to give young persons a formal explanation of their rights. The first involves spontaneous oral statements made by the young person [*YCJA* 146(3)]. If the young person "blurts out" a confession or details of the case before the officer has a reasonable opportunity to comply with the subsection 146(2) requirements, that statement may still be admissible. In those circumstances, however, the officer must inform the young person of his or her rights as soon as is practical. Failure to do so will likely invalidate any further statements. The courts have often interpreted this section narrowly, usually favouring the young person. At the very least, the circumstances under which the statement was made must be consistent with being voluntary and spontaneous. Any element of duress will generally invalidate the statement (Bala, 1997: 124–25).

Generally accepted examples would include situations where the officer is unaware that the young person was involved in an offence, but the young person makes an impulsive confession. Another example might be a candid admission when an officer first encounters the young person. An officer might ask the question, "What are you people doing here?" and the answer to it might be an admission of guilt.

The second exception occurs when the *young person chooses to waive his or her rights*. In such instances, the peace officer has informed the young person of his or her rights, but the young person decides that he or she does not want to consult with counsel or parents before giving a statement. In this situation, subsection 146(4) requires that the waiver to be either videotaped or presented by the young person in writing. If the waiver is written down, the young person must state that the peace officer has informed them of his or her rights, and the young person must sign the document.

The special requirements outlined by subsection 146(2) of the *YCJA* only apply to young persons. Consequently, if the offender is over 18 year of age when a statement is made, the provisions of subsection 146(2) do not apply, even if the offender was under 18 years of age when the offence took place.

Explanations Appropriate to the Young Person's Age and Understanding

Social scientists have made us aware that while many young people may be aware of certain social ideas and terms, such as justice, rights, fairness, and responsibility, their understanding of those terms evolves only as they become older.

Abramovitch et al. (1993; 1995) conducted research into how well young offenders understand their right to legal counsel when the peace officer advised them about it. Their conclusions are that most young persons claim to understand the advice given to them concerning their rights to silence and legal counsel, but the reality is that they have far less appreciation of the meaning attached to those warnings than do adults. Overall, young people have less understanding of the meanings of legal notions than do adults. They are also less likely to appreciate the consequences of giving up or waiving their rights.

Factors that Impact Understanding

Social scientists have also studied factors that go beyond the more limited ability of young people to understand legal concepts than in the case of adults. Disproportionately, being in conflict with the law is related to poor school performance and lower intelligence quotient (IQ) scores. There is still debate in the criminological literature over whether lower IQ or poor school performance causes delinquency; however, few dispute the fact that there is a relationship between these factors. Thus, despite the apparent worldliness, brashness, and knowledge of legal jargon exhibited by many young offenders (probably because they watch crime dramas), often they have little real appreciation of what is actually happening to them.

It is easy for peace officers, regularly exposed to legal jargon, to assume that everyone else has the same level of understanding of those ideas as they have. This is particularly the case when confronted with a "smart aleck" young person who is spouting knowledge about his or her rights. The fact is that we have chosen to create a society based on law. Legal experts have created and defined many of the concepts included in our laws. Unfortunately, the emphasis is on precision, rather than on whether the language is understandable to the average adult citizen, let alone to immature young people.

Peace Officers Must Comply with the "Spirit" to Inform

Subsection 146(2)(b) of the *YCJA* is designed to address this problem of differing levels of understanding among young persons. It is also one area where the courts have paid a great deal of attention. The key phrase in that subsection is that the young person's rights must be *"clearly explained … in language appropriate to his or her age and understanding."* The courts have made it clear that peace officers are to comply fully with the spirit of this section. Consequently, "rattling off" a statement of the young person's rights to silence and to counsel from a preprinted card is generally considered unacceptable.

In the 2008 decision of *R. v. L.T.H.*, Supreme Court Justice Fish clearly outlined the necessity of ensuring that the questioning of youth suspects by peace officers is handled appropriately when he noted:

> Young persons, even more than adults, are inclined to feel vulnerable when questioned by peace officers who suspect them of crime and can influence their fate. Parliament has for that reason provided them by statute with a complementary set of enhanced procedural safeguards in s. 146 of the *Youth Criminal Justice Act* ... procedural and evidentiary safeguards available to adults do not adequately protect young persons, who are presumed on account of their age and relative unsophistication to be more vulnerable than adults to suggestion, pressure and influence in the hands of peace interrogators.

Immature Persons or Persons with Mental Disabilities

Young persons who seem particularly immature or who appear to have mental disabilities require special attention. While the judgment of what language is appropriate is obviously subjective, the courts are demanding increasingly that officers provide objective evidence that they have made the attempt. The statement outlined below might be used as a good starting point. It covers the main points that need to be included in a caution. As indicated in the previous section, it is a good practice to restate the caution several times.

Does the Young Person Understand the Explanation?

There are several ways in which the peace officer can show that the youth was given an **age-appropriate explanation**. For example, the officer might ask the young person a series of questions to "test" the young person's grasp of the explanation. We list a series of such questions below the two cautions. The restatement of the young person's rights in different words is also helpful. Law professor Nicholas Bala (1997: 115) suggests that an officer might ask the young person to state in his or her own words his or her rights as the young person understands them. A further suggestion is to ask the young person to write out the cautions in his or her own words. Some police services provide facilities for audiotaping and videotaping the cautioning segments of interviews with young persons.

Caution Examples

The following are two examples of cautions that might be given to young persons, which outline their legal rights. They cover the main points that we need to include in a caution. The first version includes some wording used in the *YCJA*. According to the Flesch-Kincaid grade level index, it is written at a grade 10 level of understanding. We have rewritten the second version to simplify the vocabulary and the syntax. The rewritten version conforms to a grade 8 level of understanding as measured by the index.

INFORMING YOUNG OFFENDERS OF THEIR RIGHT TO COUNSEL

(Grade 10 Version)

It is my duty to tell you that you have the right to talk to a lawyer and to your parents or another adult relative. If they are not available, you may speak with some other adult you feel can assist you. If you speak to any of these people before giving a statement, they must be present while the statement is being taken, unless you do not want them to be present. You have the right to telephone any lawyer you wish. You also have the right to free advice from a Legal Aid lawyer. If you are charged with an offence, you may apply to the Ontario Legal Aid Plan for assistance. 1-800-555-5555 is a toll-free number that will put you in touch with a Legal Aid lawyer for free legal advice right now.

INFORMING YOUNG OFFENDERS OF THEIR RIGHT TO COUNSEL

(Grade 8 Version)

It is my duty to tell you that you have the right to talk to a lawyer. You can also talk to your parents or to another adult relative. If they are not available, you may speak with another adult you feel can help you. If you speak to any of these people before giving a statement, they must be with us when we are taking the statement. However, they do not need to be present if you do not want them to be here. You have the right to telephone any lawyer you wish. You also have the right to free advice from a Legal Aid lawyer. If we charge you with an offence, you may apply to the Ontario Legal Aid Plan for help. The toll-free number for a Legal Aid lawyer is 1-800-555-5555. That number will put you in touch with a Legal Aid lawyer for free legal advice right now.

> Do you understand what I have just said?
>
> Do you want to call a lawyer now?
>
> Do you want to have a lawyer here with you?
>
> Do you want to speak with one or both of your parents?
>
> Do you want to have one or both of your parents here with you?
>
> If a parent is not available, do you want to speak to an adult relative?
>
> Do you want to have an adult relative here with you?
>
> If an adult relative is not available, do you want to speak to another adult?
>
> Do you want to have an adult here with you?

NOTIFICATION TO PARENTS

When a peace officer arrests and keeps a young person in custody, section 26 of the *YCJA* obliges the officer to provide a **notification to a parent** of the young person as soon as possible. The parent must be contacted and told, either orally or in writing, *where* the young person is detained and the *reason* for the arrest. If the parents cannot be contacted, the officer in charge at the time of the detention should try to contact another adult relative who knows the young person and is likely to help him or her. If no other relative can be contacted, notice of the arrest may be given to another adult who knows the young person and is likely to assist him or her. Examples of other adults in this case include members of the clergy, scoutmasters, and older siblings.

Notification of Appearance Notice or Summons

It is also necessary to notify a parent of the young person if an appearance notice or a summons is issued. Notice must also be given when the young person makes a promise to appear or enters into a recognizance.

That notice must include the following:

- the young person's name,
- the charge,
- the time and location of the appearance, and
- the fact that the young person has the right to be represented by counsel.

It is the responsibility of the officer in charge to send that notice, in writing, as soon as possible. Again, when a parent cannot be located, the notice may be sent to another adult relative or to another adult who knows the young person and is likely to help him or her.

Confusion as to Who Should Be Notified

There will be situations where confusion exists as to whom a notice should be given. In these cases, subsection 26(5) allows a youth justice court judge (or a justice of the peace when a youth justice court judge is not available) to decide who the appropriate recipient of the notice is.

Consequences of Failure to Ensure Proper Notice

The failure to send proper notice under subsection 26(2) may invalidate any further proceedings against the young person. The *YCJA*, however, provides youth justice court judges a great deal of latitude in this matter. Several options available to youth justice court judges are outlined under subsection 26(11) such as adjourning the proceedings or proceeding without notice.

Parents Can Be Compelled to Attend

Under section 27 of the *YCJA*, judges can compel a young person's parents to appear at the hearing if it is deemed necessary. Parents who fail to appear may be sanctioned.

PERSONS UNDER 12 YEARS OF AGE

In Ontario, young persons who are under 12 years of age are dealt with under the *Child, Youth and Family Services Act* (see the extensive discussion in Chapter 5). As was discussed in the previous chapter, the *CYFSA* is child protection legislation and not criminal legislation. From a policing point of view, the key element of the *CYFSA* is that it covers children who are under 12 years of age.

Duties of the Peace Officer

The duties of peace officers are outlined in some detail under the *CYFSA*. Most importantly, peace officers must recognize the fact that no matter what young persons under 12 years may have done, they are not offenders. From the law's perspective, they are not, and must not be treated as, young criminals.

Peace Officers Have Discretion

Perhaps the most important section of the *CYFSA* for policing is section 84. Under subsection 84(1), peace officers may apprehend young people under the age of 12 years without a warrant if they "could be found guilty of an offence." Clearly, this section gives peace officers a considerable amount of discretion. When discretion is allowed, there will be occasions when decisions that are not agreeable to everyone are made. In these cases, peace officers are protected from personal liability under subsection 86(6) of the *CYFSA* "for any act done in good faith in the execution or intended execution" of their duty.

Bring Child to Parents or "Place of Safety"

Officers who apprehend a child must return the child to a parent or guardian as soon as it is practical [84(1)(a)]. Where the child cannot be returned in a reasonable amount of time, a peace officer may detain the child in a "place of safety" until returning the child becomes possible [84(1)(b)]. Subsection 84(2) makes it clear that the parents must be notified as soon as possible whenever a child is in custody.

Other Types of Apprehensions

There are other circumstances where the *CYFSA* allows peace officers to take the initiative when dealing with children. Peace officers may apprehend young people they think have left or escaped the "lawful care and custody" of the Children's Aid Society. There are also times when it will become obvious that a child is being abused, neglected, or otherwise mistreated. These situations are most likely to arise when the police are called to investigate a domestic dispute. In these circumstances, peace officers may apply to the courts under subsection 40(4) of the *CYFSA* for a hearing to decide if the child is "in need of protection."

Police Assistance

Other situations arise where peace officers are asked to assist child protection workers. For example, the police may be called to help a child protection worker when a warrant authorizes the apprehension of a child. Peace officers may also be called upon to execute warrants to "bring a child to a place of safety."

TEST YOUR KNOWLEDGE

Definitions

Define the following terms:

1. Indictable offences

_____

_____

_____

2. Summary offences

_____

_____

_____

3. Hybrid offences

_____

_____

_____

4. Person in authority

_____

_____

_____

5. Age-appropriate explanation

_____

_____

_____

6. Notification to a parent

_____

_____

_____

True/False

1. T F   All of the laws that are relevant to the questioning of young persons are found in the *Youth Criminal Justice Act*.

2. T F   An 11-year-old person cannot be arrested.

3. T F   Youth justice court warrants may be executed anywhere in Canada.

4. Indicate whether the items below are rights under the *Canadian Charter of Rights and Freedoms.*

 T F   To be secure against unreasonable search or seizure.

 T F   To be informed of the right to marry.

5. Before giving a statement, a young person must be told that

 T F   there is no obligation to give a statement

 T F   the statement may be used in court

 T F   the young person has the right to legal counsel

 T F   the statement can be withdrawn after it is signed

 T F   the young person has the right to consult with other young persons who may have been accused of the same crime

6. T F   Youth justice court judges can compel a young person's parents to appear at a hearing.

7. T F   Legally, persons under the age of 12 years are never offenders.

Multiple Choice

1. Laws that guide arrest and questioning of young persons are found in

   a. the *Criminal Code of Canada*
   b. the *Youth Criminal Justice Act*
   c. the *Canadian Charter of Rights and Freedoms*
   d. all of the above

2. Which of the following should peace officers consider when deciding to lay a charge?

   a. the gender of the young person
   b. the age of the young person
   c. the seriousness of the offence
   d. all of the above

3. When there is uncertainty about a person's age, it is best to

   a. treat the person as an adult
   b. afford the protections that would apply under the *Youth Criminal Justice Act*
   c. incarcerate the person until the matter of age is cleared up
   d. send the person to a mental hospital

4. Indictable offences carry potential sentences of

   a. two or more years of imprisonment
   b. fines only
   c. no more than six months of imprisonment
   d. no more than six months of imprisonment and a $2,000 fine

5. Which of the following, according to the *Criminal Code of Canada*, is not a way to compel a person to appear before a justice?

   a. issuing a charge for a crime
   b. issuing a summons
   c. arresting a person without a warrant
   d. arresting a person with a warrant

6. Which of the following is a "person in authority"?

   a. peace officer
   b. school principal
   c. physician
   d. all of the above

7. Statements should be taken from young persons

   a. as quickly as possible
   b. before they speak to their parents

    c. only when certain conditions are met

    d. in private and without the distraction of other adults present

8. Young persons must have their rights explained to them in language that is

    a. French in Quebec and English in the rest of Canada

    b. the same as that used for adults

    c. appropriate to their age and ability to understand

    d. the same for every young person

9. In a situation where a young person waives rights to consult with counsel, a parent, or another adult, what must the peace officer do?

    a. videotape the waiver or have the young person present it in writing

    b. wait 12 hours

    c. wait 24 hours

    d. get a second peace officer to be in the room

10. A peace officer who keeps a young person in custody must contact the parents of the young person

    a. within 12 hours

    b. within 24 hours

    c. as soon as possible

    d. by registered mail

11. When a parent is given notification that a young person is being kept in custody, which of the following is information to which parents have a right?

    a. the reason for the arrest

    b. the names of the other young persons also under arrest

    c. the location where the young person is detained

    d. two of the above

12. If an appearance notice or summons is issued, the peace officer in charge must notify the parents of the young person of

    a. the charges

    b. time and location of the appearance

    c. the right of the young person to be represented by counsel

    d. all of the above

13. If there is confusion over who is to receive notice, who is charged with deciding?

    a. a youth justice court judge

    b. the staff sergeant

    c. the Crown prosecutor

    d. all of the above

14. The *Child, Youth and Family Services Act*

   a. defines no role for the peace officers with respect to children under 12 years
   b. allows a peace officer to arrest some children under the age of 12 years if they escape from the Children's Aid Society
   c. allows a peace officer to apprehend children under age 12 years in certain circumstances
   d. forbids a peace officer from executing warrants in cases of children under age 12 years

Short Answer

1. Under what circumstances, when a crime has been committed, should the peace officer not make an arrest?

   _____

   _____

   _____

   _____

   _____

   _____

   _____

   _____

2. List three conditions under which a peace officer may arrest someone without a warrant.

   _____

   _____

   _____

   _____

   _____

   _____

   _____

   _____

3. List three reasons warrants are issued.

   _____

   _____

   _____

_____

_____

_____

_____

_____

4. A peace officer approaches a young person who makes an immediate statement of admission to a crime. What is the next thing that the peace officer should do? Explain why.

_____

_____

_____

_____

_____

_____

_____

_____

_____

5. Why is there a concern that young people must have their rights explained to them clearly?

_____

_____

_____

_____

_____

_____

_____

_____

6. Discuss the following statement: "If we make people aware of their rights, they will never tell us anything important."

_____

_____

_____

_____

_____

_____

_____

7. What kinds of things can a peace officer do to ensure that young persons understand the rights that have been explained to them?

_____

_____

_____

_____

_____

_____

_____

_____

Exercise: You Be the Judge

The arrest of a young person places far more onus on a peace officer than does the arrest of an adult. Young persons must be clearly informed of their rights and must be told that any statement must be taken in the presence of a lawyer or adult unless the young person clearly indicates otherwise. What follows is a case recently addressed by the Supreme Court of Ontario relating to the matter.

Facts of the Case
A 17-year-old was charged with robbery and use of a disguise in the commission of an indictable offence. The peace officer informed the respondent that he had the right to have a lawyer, or other specified adult with whom he consulted, present when he gave his statement. The exchange between the peace officer and the young person was the following:

Q: Do you want to speak with or consult a lawyer?

A: Don't think I need to.

Q: Do you want to have a lawyer here with you?

A: Nope. [Shakes head.]

Q: If your parent or parents are not available, do you want to speak with an adult relative?

A: No.

Q: If an adult relative is not available do you want to speak with or consult another adult?

A: No.

Q: Do you want to have a parent ... an adult relative or another appropriate adult here with you?

A: No.

Q: Okay ... Scott this is called the Waiver of Rights. I'll read this to ya and then I'll explain it to ya, okay?

It says I've been given the opportunity to obtain immediate free advice from a Legal Aid Lawyer and the opportunity to speak with or consult a lawyer and or my parents or in the absence of a parent an adult relative or in the absence of a parent or adult relative any other appropriate adult. I have been informed that I have the right to have any of these people with whom I have consulted present when making a statement. These rights have been explained to me and I understand them.

A: [Nods head.]

Q: So you understand that?

A: Yep. [Nods head.]

Q: Okay.

How Would You Rule?

Did the peace officer adequately execute (discharge) the requirement, under subsection 146(2)(b)(iv) of the *YJCA*, to explain to the young person that any statement given to the peace officer was required to be made in the presence of a consulted third party, unless the young person desired otherwise?

In other words,

(a) Did the peace officer act properly?

(b) Did the peace officer discharge that responsibility as required?

What are the reasons for your answers?

The Decision of the Ontario Court of Appeal

Here is what the what was found at the trial, and subsequently reflected in the 2007 decision at the Ontario Court of Appeal in the case of *R. v. S.S.*, 2007 O.N.C.A. 481 (CanLII).

The trial judge found that the information provided to the young person did not conform with subsection 146(2)(b)(iv) of the *Youth Criminal Justice Act*, which required the peace officer to tell the young person that any statement had to be taken in the presence of a lawyer or adult with whom the young person had consulted, unless the young person desired otherwise. The young person was acquitted.

The Crown appealed. The question on appeal was whether telling the young person about his or her right to have a third party present was equivalent to explaining to the young person that any statement given to the peace officer was required to be made in the presence of a consulted third party, unless the young person desired otherwise. The appeal of the Crown was denied on the grounds that the failure to tell the young person about the requirement was a breach of subsection 146(2)(b)(iv). That breach denied the respondent (young person) important information that would have enabled him to decide whether to consult a third party. On a plain reading of the legislation, there was an important distinction drawn between a "right" of a young person on the one hand and a "requirement" put on the peace officer on the other. The distinction was consistent with the purpose of protecting young people in light of their lack of maturity and their susceptibility to yield to authority

CHAPTER 7

Extrajudicial Measures

LEARNING OUTCOMES

Students who have mastered this chapter will have the ability to do the following:

- Distinguish between judicial and extrajudicial measures.
- Identify the extrajudicial measures that the police must consider.
- Explain the conditions under which extrajudicial measures are presumed to be adequate.
- Explain the meaning of extrajudicial sanctions.
- Identify the conditions under which extrajudicial sanctions may be used.

EXTRAJUDICIAL MEASURES

The cornerstone of the *Youth Criminal Justice Act* (*YCJA*) is its emphasis on **extrajudicial measures** (EJM)—meaning "outside the court." The fundamental principle is to hold the young person *accountable* without proceeding through the formal court process. Many such measures were allowed under the *Young Offenders Act* (*YOA*), in the sense that it was silent about them, and the YOA provided for what it called "alternative measures." The *YCJA*, in contrast, *requires that the use of extrajudicial measures (or non-court measures) be considered in some circumstances and that non-judicial measures be ruled out as inappropriate before judicial measures are used.* This reflects the intent of the Parliament of Canada in the preamble to the *YCJA* that states that Canada should: "have a youth criminal justice system that … reserves its most serious intervention for the most serious crimes and reduces the over-reliance on incarceration for non-violent young persons." Typically, EJMs are favoured for first-time non-violent offenders, but are also used extensively with repeat offenders, as appropriate.

It is the clear intention in the *YCJA* that less formal means are to be preferred over more formal ones and that the presumptive burden falls to the police, the Crown, and the judges to determine why the non-judicial measures are inappropriate in the given instance.

There are two broad types of extrajudicial measures:

1. Those that are used prior to a charge being laid, which are applied by the police; and
2. Those that are post-charge, called Crown cautions and extrajudicial sanctions, which are applied by the Crown prosecutors and youth justice courts, respectively.[1]

Pursuant to section 5 of the *YCJA*, extrajudicial measures should be consistent with the following objectives:

*   Provide an effective and timely response to the offending behaviour.
*   Encourage the repair of harm caused to the victim and the community.
*   Encourage the involvement of families, victims, and the community.
*   Respect the rights of young persons.
*   Be proportionate to the seriousness of the offence.

In the sections that follow, we examine the requirements of the *YCJA* with respect to extrajudicial measures and their impact on the behaviour of the police, Crown prosecutors, and the court.

Appropriateness of Extrajudicial Measures

The *YCJA* leaves it to the police to decide whether the use of an extrajudicial measure is appropriate, but the appropriateness must be determined in the context of the principles of section 4 of the *YCJA*:

(a) extrajudicial measures are often the most appropriate and effective way to address youth crime;

(b) extrajudicial measures allow for effective and timely interventions focused on correcting offending behaviour;

(c) extrajudicial measures are presumed to be adequate to hold a young person accountable for his or her offending behaviour if the young person has committed a non-violent offence and has not previously been found guilty of an offence; and

(d) extrajudicial measures should be used if they are adequate to hold a young person accountable for his or her offending behaviour and, if the use of extrajudicial measures is consistent with the principles set out in this section, nothing in this Act precludes their use in respect of a young person who

---

1.   It is up to each province to decide whether and how programs of extrajudicial sanctions will be established. The *YCJA* does not exclude that such sanctions may be initiated at the level of the police, but it appears more likely that it would occur mainly at the level of the Crown prosecutor and at youth justice court.

(i)   has previously been dealt with by the use of extrajudicial measures, or

(ii)   has previously been found guilty of an offence.

Extrajudicial Presumption

In this context, the police must recognize that the *YCJA* has a presumption or bias in favour of extrajudicial measures for a broad range of offences. The emphasis is on holding young persons accountable for their behaviour and not on punishing them. Further, there is a clear preference for interventions that are timely. A discussion with the young person's parents today is preferable to having it dealt with by the court in a month's time. Again, the police must consider the responses that they will have to produce under cross-examination by defence counsel if they consider the "timely" response to not be adequate and go ahead and charge the young person.

POLICE

Police Discretion

The police have always had discretion to deal with those who come into conflict with the law in ways that stop short of laying a charge. The most obvious cases involve relatively minor incidents where the offender has not previously been in trouble. The police may take no further action, give the offender a warning that further infractions will lead to a charge, or take a young person home and speak to the parents about what happened in this instance and the implications for the future. Generally speaking, the more serious the offence, the less police discretion is exercised. Similarly, the more prior involvements with the law and the more serious the offences, the less likely it is that a simple warning will be used.

The use of police discretion is limited by the *YCJA*; it is not eliminated. The limits favour the use of non-court measures and open the police to serious cross-examination on the reasons for not using an extrajudicial measure. Warnings, cautions, and referrals issued by the police require that a young person is alleged to have committed an offence, but they do not require that the young person admit that the allegation is true. Referral to a program or agency requires the consent of the young person, but does not require an admission of guilt.

Basic Principle: Least Intrusive Measures First

The *YCJA*, in keeping with its general approach of first trying the least intrusive measures, makes specific provisions for doing nothing, warnings, cautions, and referrals to programs or agencies.

Doing Nothing

When no offence is alleged to have occurred, the police may decide to do nothing further. There are circumstances when an offence is alleged to have occurred, but in the judgment of the police, doing nothing further is the best way to deal with the situation. The *YCJA* requires that the police officer at least consider the appropriateness of doing nothing further. When an offence is alleged to have been committed by a young person, the *YCJA* requires that warnings, cautions, and referrals be considered as sufficient prior to starting judicial proceedings.

Warnings and Cautions

Warnings and cautions are not specifically defined in the *YCJA*, but their meaning can be inferred as follows.

Police warnings are informal notices (admonitions) issued to a young person by a police officer. They may be made at the point of contact, or they might take place as part of a discussion with the parents of the young person. Warnings are, therefore, a more serious intervention than "doing nothing further," but a less serious intervention than issuing a caution.

Police cautions, as in the case of warnings, stop short of laying a charge, which could lead to judicial proceedings. Cautions are notices to young persons and their parents about the offence that has been alleged. The *YCJA* makes provisions that each province may establish a "program" to "administer cautions." Even without such a program, the police are still required, under the *YCJA*, to consider whether a caution would be an appropriate way of dealing with a given instance. Presumably, a program to administer cautions would require formal "paperwork," perhaps including a letter to the parents as well as a mechanism for tracking persons who have received a caution. Ideally, the information would not be restricted to a single police service, but be available across jurisdictions. (Note: Police cautions are distinct from Crown cautions, which are discussed further down.)

Referral to a Community Program

Another option that a police officer must consider when a young person is alleged to have committed an offence is referral to a community program. **Referral to a program** or agency means referral to a service in the community that may help the young person to avoid committing offences. Such referrals are considered to be a more serious intervention than a caution, but still stop short of starting judicial proceedings. Referrals may only take place with the consent of the young person. Community programs include police-based diversions programs such as Youth Intervention Program, community accountability programs such as Restorative Justice (discussed in Chapter 11), recreational programs such as Boys & Girls Clubs and sporting clubs, and substance use treatment programs.

Police Conferences

Pursuant to section 19 of the *YCJA* police may conduct a conference to obtain advice on appropriate measures. The conference is designed to understand the youth and his or her situation better by generating more ideas on the case, suggesting creative solutions, organizing coordinated services, and seeking more involvement from the victim or other community members.

IN THE NEWS

Case for Extrajudicial Measures

A homeowner chased and caught a 13-year-old after watching him try to steal Christmas lights from a backyard tree Saturday night about 7:15. The homeowner saw two people in the backyard stealing the lights and called out. The youths fled, but the homeowner ran after them and nabbed one. Police were called and identified the second youth. Both will write letters of apology and do several hours of community service for the homeowner... . Police have powers under the new *Youth Criminal Justice Act* to take "extra-judicial measures" to deal with these sorts of matters... .

Source: "Walkerton: Light thieves now indebted to owner," *Owen Sound Sun Times*, January 6, 2004, p. A7.

Notes about Extrajudicial Measures

Failure by Police to Use Extrajudicial Measures

The *YCJA* provides that a police officer shall consider the use of such measures as warnings, cautions, and referrals to a program before proceedings with a charge. The *YCJA*, however, provides no consequences for failure to consider these things. That is, failure to consider does not interfere with proceeding with a charge. It does not end there, however, for the police officer. If called to testify, a police officer who did not consider extrajudicial measures can expect to face stiff cross-examination by the defence lawyer. Failure to consider, when addressed on the witness stand, does have consequences, which may include embarrassment as well as a weakening of the Crown's case. It is important, therefore, that such alternatives be considered, even in situations where they may be quickly discarded as inappropriate.

Repeat Offenders

The *YCJA* is specific that extrajudicial measures are not to be restricted to first-time offenders. Young persons who previously received an extrajudicial measure must be considered for further ones. Even a previous finding of guilt does not preclude the use of extrajudicial measures. The *YCJA* identifies circumstances where extrajudicial measures are "presumed to be adequate to hold a young person accountable for ... offending behaviour." Extrajudicial measures are required if the offence is non-violent and the young person has not been previously found guilty of an offence. Evidence about warnings, cautions, and referrals, or that the police took no further action in respect of an offence, is *not admissible* for the purpose of proving prior offending behaviour.

Lack of Tracking Data

The 2012 amendments to the *YCJA* now require that police forces keep track of their use of the extrajudicial measures they use with young persons. Yet, the lack of inter-jurisdictional tracking of extrajudicial measures at the provincial level continues to be a large gap in understanding its impact on whether it has been effective in reducing youth recidivism (re-offending). As Kwok et al. (2017: 29) discuss:

> Data currently collected by the *Ontario Youth Justice Program* only reflects youth who have been sentenced through the criminal justice system. Data is not collected on youth who have been diverted from the system through extrajudicial measures. It is impossible to assess recidivism rates for youth who have received extrajudicial measures because there is not an integrated tracking mechanism that interfaces with the *Ontario Youth Justice Program*. Essentially, it is impossible to prove positive outcomes if community organizations don't have access to follow-up data on the youth they work with.

CASE BRIEF

Indigenous Extrajudicial Measures (EJM) Program

Shane, 16, is an Indigenous young man who lives with his mother in social housing. The family is on social assistance.

When Shane was eight years old and his sister was two years old, his family moved from their First Nations community to a nearby city in Southwestern Ontario. His father left the family when he was 10, and his mother has suffered from depression since then. His younger sister was taken into care at the age of four under a voluntary agreement with Child Welfare Services. Unfortunately, his sister died in care six months later due to an unfortunate car accident. Shane has had a history of self-harming behaviour after his father left the family and the loss of his sister. He was struggling in school and claimed to be affiliated with an Indigenous urban gang as a fringe member.

One day Shane was hanging out with a friend who was his "big brother" in the gang. The two of them went into a large electronic retail store. A staff of the store witnessed Shane's friend have a conversation with him in front of the cell phone accessories aisle. The friend then left the store by himself. Shortly after Shane's friend left, Shane started putting some cell phone accessories in his backpack and headed out of the store. Shane was stopped at the exit by a security guard who searched Shane's backpack and found unpaid cell phone accessories in the amount of $500. Both Shane's mother and the police were called.

Shane was taken to the police station, where he had a meeting with his mother and an Indigenous police officer. During the intake interview, Shane shared that he still struggles with issues of loss over his younger sibling, the absence of his father, and displacement from this home community and culture. After talking to Shane and his mother and understanding more about his family background and situation, the police officer decided to not press charges. Instead, the officer offered Shane an opportunity to participate in an extrajudicial measures (EJM) diversion program that is designed for Indigenous youth.

The program Shane was referred to has been running for 15 years and has supported hundreds of youth to regain community and cultural connections. Youth involved in the program build relationships with Elders and peer mentors. It offers healing supports through a sweat lodge and counselling to work through unprocessed grief and loss. The program also offers referral services for Shane's mother to support her on her healing journey. The program takes a restorative approach to youth justice and hosts healing and sharing circles that can include family and community members. Shane will have support to finish school as well as opportunities to learn skills and enroll in a program that provides on-the-job training. Shane agreed to voluntarily participate in the EJM program and contacted the community agency that runs the program to get started.

Source: S.M. Kwok, R. Houwer, H. HeavyShield, R. Weatherstone, and D. Tam. 2017. *Supporting Positive Outcomes for Youth Involved with the Law.* Pg. 11. Youth Research and Evaluation eXchange (YouthREX). Toronto, ON.

CROWN PROSECUTORS

Crown prosecutors exercise discretion with respect to the cases that they prosecute. In the exercise of such discretion, a variety of factors are taken into consideration, such as the quality of the evidence, the availability of witnesses, the likelihood of a successful prosecution, and whether the goals of the criminal justice system are being served (these will be addressed in greater detail in Chapter 11). None of this depends on the *YCJA*. The *YCJA* does provide means for Crown prosecutors to deal with young persons in conflict with the law: Crown cautions and extrajudicial sanctions.

Types of Extrajudicial Measures

Crown Caution

The *YCJA* makes provision for provinces to establish a program that authorizes prosecutors to administer **Crown cautions** to young persons, rather than starting or continuing judicial proceedings. The *YCJA* does not explicitly give a name to such cautions, but it is implicit that they are Crown prosecutor cautions. They are given after the police have referred the case to the Crown. Most typically, the caution is in the form of a letter to the youth and the youth's parent(s).

Crown Conference

Like the use of the police conferences described above, Crown prosecutors can similarly hold conferences to understand the youth better and explore appropriate options [*YCJA* 19].

Extrajudicial Sanctions

The *YCJA* provides that provinces may choose to implement a set of extrajudicial measures that take the form of a program of extrajudicial sanctions. **Extrajudicial sanctions** are formal interventions administered to a young person who has been accused of an offence but where the process is a non-court (extrajudicial) one.

TYPES OF EXTRAJUDICIAL SANCTIONS

The terms and conditions of an extrajudicial sanction agreement should be confined to those that are reasonably achieved within a three-month period time limit. The terms and conditions should be fair, proportionate, and a relevant response to the alleged offence. Examples include:

- A verbal or written apology to the victim
- An essay or research assignment
- Attend school or maintain employment
- Participation in a police/Crown conference
- Participation in a victim-offender mediation program
- Community service work or direct service to the victim (maximum of 50 hours and the youth must conduct the work; money in lieu is not permitted)
- Full or partial restitution or compensation to the victim
- Counselling
- Supervision by Probation for the purpose of completing the agreement

CONDITIONS

Several conditions must be met before extrajudicial sanctions may be used [*YCJA* 10]:

1. The young person must be alleged to have committed an offence.
2. The young person cannot satisfactorily be dealt with by warning, caution, or referral because of the seriousness of the offence, the nature and number of previous offences, or any other aggravating circumstances.
3. The sanction must be part of a "program of sanctions" authorized by the province/territory.
4. The person who is considering whether to use the sanction is satisfied that it would be appropriate, having regards for the needs of the young person and the interest of society.

5. The young person accepts responsibility for the alleged offence (this is not the same as pleading guilty).
6. The young person fully and freely consents to the sanction.
7. The young person has been advised of the right to be represented by a lawyer and given reasonable opportunity to a lawyer.
8. There is sufficient evidence, in the view of the Crown, to proceed with prosecution.
9. Prosecution is not barred by law.
10. The young person does not deny participation or involvement in the commission of the offence.
11. The young person does not express the wish to have the charge dealt with by a youth justice court.
12. The parents of the young person receiving the sanction are informed of the sanction.

Notes about Extrajudicial Measures

Admissions as Evidence
Admissions, confessions, or statements accepting responsibility for acts or omissions that are made by young persons as a condition of being dealt with by extrajudicial measures are not admissible in evidence against any young person in civil or criminal proceedings [*YCJA* 10(4)].

Right of Victim to Be Informed
When a young person receives an extrajudicial sanction, the victim has a right to request and to be provided with information as to the identity of the young person and how the offence was dealt with [*YCJA* 10(4)]. This subsection does not provide a right for the victim to be consulted before the sanction is determined. The province will need to decide who the appropriate authority will be to provide the information; it could be the police.

It should be noted that while the *YCJA* allows victims to be informed of the identity of the young person when an extrajudicial sanction is used, there is no such provision when other extrajudicial measures, such as warnings, cautions, or referrals, are used.

YOUTH JUSTICE COURT

A judge of the youth justice court can decide that a young person is best dealt with through extrajudicial measures and may order this be done. All the conditions for the use of extrajudicial sanctions must still be met if such sanctions are to be used.

What Happens to the Charge after Completion of the Extrajudicial Sanction?

If a charge has been laid, the Crown adjourns the case until the youth has substantially complied with the extrajudicial sanction, which is normally completed within three to six months. Once compliance has been demonstrated, the charge will be "stayed," meaning that the Crown will not pursue the charge in court.

If the youth does not comply with the sanction or does not complete it, the Crown may choose to proceed with the charge and prosecution in court.

LOOKING AHEAD

Extrajudicial measures take many forms. Typically they involve the young person in a set of activities that are organized in such a way as to engage the young person in one or more processes that may lead to insight or awareness about the seriousness of what he or she has done and the risks and consequences of future law-violating behaviour. The same is true of extra-legal sanctions. In both cases, there tends to be an emphasis on making reparations for misbehaviour and, very frequently, include the idea that other persons should be part of the process. It is for these reasons that many communities have put in place restorative justice initiatives that in some cases are used as extrajudicial measures, in other cases as extrajudicial sanctions, and in still other cases for both. In Chapter 11, restorative justice is discussed within the context of the objectives of the criminal justice system and its particular application to youth justice with its emphasis on rehabilitation and reintegration into the community.

IN THE NEWS

Adults and Young Persons May Be Dealt with Differently for Same Offence

Ottawa police were last night in the process of laying a *Criminal Code* charge of mischief against a 23-year-old man after a man was photographed urinating—while smiling and gesturing at the camera—on the National War Memorial on Canada Day.

Police also plan to pursue "extrajudicial measures" under the *Youth Criminal Justice Act* against two youths also accused of urinating at the memorial, meaning they would be assigned to community service or some other form of restitution.

Source: "Urinator faces mischief charge," *Kingston Whig-Standard*, July 7, 2006, p. 9.

SUMMARY

Extrajudicial measures include the following:

1. Taking **no further action** (i.e., a decision is made by the police officer that no further response to an incident is required);

2. A **warning** from police (such warnings are intended to be informal warnings and are an example of a traditional exercise of police discretion);

3. A **caution** from police (cautions are more formal warnings that may typically involve a letter from police to the young person and the parents and in some cases may require the young person and parents to appear at the police station for a meeting to discuss the incident);

4. A **referral** from police to a community program or agency designed to help youth avoid committing offences (such referrals may only be made with the consent of the young person);

5. A **Crown caution** (such cautions are similar to police cautions but are issued by Crown prosecutors after police have referred the case to them); and

6. An **extrajudicial sanction** (sanctions are applied through more formal programs set up by the provinces and territories). (Government of Canada, 2015)

TEST YOUR KNOWLEDGE

Definitions

Define the following terms:

1. Extrajudicial measures

_____

_____

_____

2. Police warning

_____

_____

_____

3. Police caution

_____

_____

_____

4. Referral to a program

_____

_____

_____

5. Crown cautions

_____

_____

_____

6. Extrajudicial sanctions

_____

_____

_____

True/False

1. T F   Extrajudicial measures are penalties imposed by persons who are not judges.

2. T F   The more serious the offence, the less discretion police have in dealing with it.

3. T F   Warnings are to be used for situations where the young person is not alleged to have committed an offence, but where there is concern about what may happen in the future.

4. T F It makes little difference to Crown prosecutors or defence counsel whether the police have considered extrajudicial measures.

5. T F Referral to a program by the police requires that the young person admit responsibility for the alleged offence.

6. T F Extrajudicial sanctions are applied in situations where the young person has been extra bad and failed at previous programs.

7. For each of the following indicate whether it is true or false that this is a condition that must be met before an extrajudicial sanction may be used:

   T F The young person must have a previous finding of guilt.

   T F Warning, caution, and referral were not considered by the police.

   T F The young person pleads guilty to the offence.

8. T F Admissions of responsibility that are made by young persons as conditions of being dealt with by extrajudicial measures are admissible in criminal proceedings.

Multiple Choice

1. Which of the following is not an extrajudicial measure under the *YCJA*?

   a. police warning
   b. Crown caution
   c. police referral to a program
   d. extrajudicial sanction

2. Warnings and cautions can only be used by the police if the young person

   a. admits to having been involved in an offence
   b. is alleged to have committed an offence
   c. is represented by counsel, a parent, or a responsible person
   d. all of the above

3. The *YCJA* provides that provinces may establish programs

   a. that would allow the police to use cautions
   b. to administer cautions
   c. that would eliminate warnings in favour of more formal cautions
   d. all of the above

4. Referral to a program or agency is for the purpose of

   a. a mild, rather than a severe, punishment
   b. assisting the young person to avoid committing offences
   c. easing the burden on parents
   d. all of the above

5. Under the *YCJA*, which of the following is a police officer *not* required to do when a young person is alleged to have committed an offence?

   a. consider using a caution
   b. lay a charge
   c. consider referral to a program
   d. consider taking no further action

6. Crown cautions, if they are to be used,

   a. must be part of a program established by the province
   b. require that the young person denies involvement with the alleged offence
   c. requires that the young person has already received two or more police warnings or police cautions
   d. all of the above

7. Extrajudicial sanctions are

   a. informal interventions
   b. to be considered when prosecution is otherwise impossible
   c. only used if the young person denies involvement in the alleged offence
   d. none of the above

8. Which of the following is *not* a condition for the use of an extrajudicial sanction?

   a. that the needs of the young person are addressed
   b. that the interests of society are addressed
   c. that the needs of the victim are addressed
   d. that the sanction is appropriate

9. In order for an extrajudicial sanction to be used, which of the following is true about the involvement of legal counsel? The young person

   a. must be advised of the right to be represented by counsel
   b. must consult with counsel
   c. must have counsel that is independent of the counsel of parents
   d. all of the above

10. When a young person receives an extrajudicial sanction, which of the following does the victim have a right to request?

    a. the address of the young offender
    b. consultation about the type of sanction to be used

c. information on how the offence was dealt with

d. all of the above

Short Answer

1. If you were a police officer, describe two situations where giving a warning or caution to a young person would seem appropriate.

2. If you were a police officer, identify two situations where you consider that referral to a program would be appropriate and identify the type of program to which you would refer in each case.

3. Identify five conditions that must be met before an extrajudicial sanction may be used.

_____

_____

_____

_____

_____

_____

4. Why do you suppose admissions or confessions that are made by a young person as a condition of receiving an extrajudicial measure are not admissible against the young person in civil or criminal proceedings?

_____

_____

_____

_____

_____

_____

_____

_____

_____

5. What rights does a victim have when a young person is dealt with by way of an extrajudicial sanction?

_____

_____

_____

_____

_____

_____

_____

_____

_____

CHAPTER 8

Pre-trial Detention and Processing

LEARNING OUTCOMES

Students who have mastered this chapter will have the ability to do the following:

- Explain the underlying philosophy of the *Criminal Code of Canada* with respect to the speed with which a detained person needs to be brought before a justice.
- Explain the presumption with respect to the detention of young persons.
- Identify the reasons for which a young person can continue to be detained.
- Describe what is involved in a Promise to Appear.
- Explain the requirement for release to a responsible person and the responsibilities of that person.
- Explain the circumstances under which young persons may be detained with adults.
- Identify the purpose of bail hearings.
- Explain the conditions under which it is permissible to fingerprint and photograph young persons.
- Describe whom is covered by the ban on publication.
- Identify the time limits within which records of young persons must be destroyed.
- Explain the accessibility of records of young persons.
- Explain the appropriateness of conditions of release.
- Describe "reverse onus."

PRE-TRIAL DETENTION

Following an arrest, one of the fundamental principles of the criminal justice system is that a person accused of crime is presumed innocent until found guilty. Generally, this presumption favours the release of an accused (often with various conditions, as outlined below). In some cases, however, legislation, including the *Youth Criminal Justice Act*, permits the court to keep an accused young person in custody prior to his or her trial. This is known as **pre-trial detention**.

As you read in the previous chapter, the *YCJA* favours release of most youth who come into conflict with the law and are therefore not held in pre-trial detention. Considerable effort is expended to handle youth cases outside of the formal court process through extrajudicial measures, such as police warnings or referrals to community programs. Police may also choose to release the young person back into the community while waiting for the case to be dealt with in court. If a bail hearing is held, a court will decide whether to release the young person into the community, often under strict conditions that must be obeyed through the use of an undertaking or recognizance.

The *Criminal Code of Canada* and the *YCJA* outline the basic rules of procedure for arresting and detaining a young person. The specifics of how those rules are implemented will vary from one location to another and, of course, will change over time. Nationally, some provisions of the *YCJA* differ from province to province. Differences also occur among provinces in terms of programs that may be established for cautions, conferences, and pre-charge screening.

If police want to keep a youth in custody pending trial, the *YCJA* sets out the permitted grounds for pre-trial detention.

Grounds for Pre-trial Detention

Under s. 29(2) of the *YCJA*, a youth may be detained prior to trial only if *all* of the following criteria are met:

1. The youth has been charged with a "serious offence" (i.e., an offence for which an adult could be imprisoned for five years or more if convicted) *or* has a history of outstanding criminal charges or findings of guilt under the *YCJA*;
2. The court is satisfied that detention is necessary to ensure the young person's attendance in court, to protect the public, or in exceptional circumstances, to maintain public confidence in the justice system; and
3. Releasing the youth into the community with conditions would not be sufficient to address the court's concerns.

The *YCJA* at s. 29(1) specifically states that pre-trial detention cannot be used as a substitute for child protection, mental health, or other social measures. This means, for example, that a homeless youth cannot be kept in custody simply because he or she has no place to live.

Local Policies and Procedures

New police officers need to find out from their supervisors how local conditions have been adapted to meet the requirements of the *YCJA*. Some of those conditions will involve the physical layout of buildings; other conditions will relate to the availability of support personnel and the practices of local Crown prosecutors and judges. In some municipalities, for example, uniformed officers do not fill out much paperwork beyond a summons. Officers in an adjoining jurisdiction, however, may be responsible for filling out most of the necessary forms. Even experienced officers who transfer from one jurisdiction to another will take some time to get "the lay of the land."

How the CCC Applies to the Arrest and Detention of Young Persons

When it comes to detention, the *YCJA* introduces specific considerations, different from those that apply to adults that need to be taken into account. The general rules for arrest and detention are presented in sections 494 to 503 of the *CCC* and have an influence on how detention is handled for youth pursuant to the *YCJA*.

Without Delay
The underlying philosophy of the *CCC* is that we should not detain accused persons any longer than necessary after being arrested. This is consistent with the long history of *Writs of Habeas Corpus*[1] that have been an integral part of English common law for several centuries. *Writs of Habeas Corpus* are used to ensure that an accused person is brought before the courts within a reasonable amount of time to examine the legality of the detention. Section 503 of the *CCC* requires that an arrested person be brought before a justice "without unreasonable delay." Where a justice is readily available, this means within 24 hours at most. Where a justice is not available, the person is to be brought before a justice "as soon as possible."

Subsection 503(4) also states that

> A peace officer or an officer in charge having the custody of a person who has been arrested without warrant as a person about to commit an indictable offence shall release that person unconditionally as soon as practicable after he is satisfied that the continued detention of that person in custody is no longer necessary in order to prevent the commission by him of an indictable offence.

Temporary Detention without a Warrant
Sections 497 and 498 of the *CCC* detail the circumstances surrounding temporary detention. Section 497 deals with situations where a peace officer arrests a person without a warrant for an indictable offence, a hybrid offence, or for one punishable on summary conviction (see Chapter 6 to review). This section makes it clear that normally and as soon as is practical, the officer shall "release the person from custody with the intention of compelling his appearance by way of summons" or by issuing an appearance notice.

---

1.   A *writ of habeas corpus* is Latin for to "produce the body." At common law, it is a court order to a person or agency holding someone in custody (such as a warden) to deliver the imprisoned individual to the court issuing the order and to show a valid reason for that person's detention.

Section 498 outlines the situation for persons arrested and taken into custody without a warrant. Again, for offences that may be handled by summary conviction and for hybrid offences and less serious indictable offences, the officer in charge must normally release the accused. The accused person's appearance in court is assured through the issuance of a summons, a promise to appear, or by posting surety (that is, money [not to exceed $500] or other action or promises to the court), depending upon the individual circumstances of the offence and the accused.

Exceptions to release provisions exist and they are specified in sections 497 and 498 of the *CCC*. These exceptions occur when it is necessary to establish the person's identity, preserve evidence, or prevent the continuation or repetition of this or another offence.

Presumption for Release of Youth

One of the objectives of the *YCJA* is to reduce the amount of time that young persons are incarcerated during the pre-trial stage. As with the *CCC*, the *YCJA* provisions are based on the presumption that the young person will be released. Arrest and detention are measures to deal with exceptional circumstances.

Three principles are at the heart of this approach.

1. The least restrictive means should be used to ensure that the young person will appear in court.
2. The young person is presumed to be innocent until there is a finding of guilt.
3. That pretrial detention is not to be used as a form of punishment as the *YCJA* clearly specifics—and courts have previously decided.

Factors to Be Considered in Releasing the Accused

To decide which procedure is most appropriate for releasing the accused, the officer needs to assess several factors. Clearly, the severity and circumstances surrounding the immediate offence need to be considered. It would be unwise, for example, to release a young man into his parent's custody if he was just charged with assaulting his mother or sister. There may, however, be another responsible person into whose custody the young person might be released without posing a threat to either the mother or the sister. The police are required to consider whether such options exist. On the other hand, releasing the same individual to a parent after his having committed a minor assault against an acquaintance or a stranger might pose little danger to the victim or others. In order for a young person to be placed in the care of a **"responsible person"** [*YCJA* 31(1)], two conditions must be met:

1. The "responsible person" agrees in writing to care for and be responsible for the attendance of the young person in court, as well as comply with any other conditions that the judge may specify. [*YCJA* 31(3)(a)]
2. The young person agrees, in writing, to comply with the arrangement as well as any other conditions that might be specified. [*YCJA* 31(3)(b)]

Another significant factor to consider is the *young person's record*. To assess the record, the officer should check with the Canadian Police Information Centre (CPIC) and with the local database for prior police contacts and convictions. An officer who is undecided about whether to release a young person may find the decision less difficult if the young person has a history of not appearing in court.

Police Decision Making for a Show-Cause Hearing

One of the important decisions a police officer will make is whether to start a formal criminal process against the young person. Note, this is done when the officer has decided *not* to use extrajudicial measures or other sanctions. In most instances, the youth will not be held in detention, but there will be measures designed to ensure that the youth returns for the hearing. Typically, the youth will be released on an **appearance notice**. This document is given to the accused by police after being charged, telling the youth to appear in court on specific day and time to answer to a criminal charge. The accused will sign a **promise to appear**—a notice promising to appear before the court for trial on a the specific date. It might also include an **undertaking**, which is a set of conditions on the promise to appear, or a **recognizance,** wherein the youth agrees to such things as parental supervision, school attendance, or a curfew. Finally, the young person may be required to sign a recognizance as a formal agreement by the accused that acknowledges a debt to the Crown up to $500. The accused may be required to pay a deposit in order to be released on bail. Ultimately, the youth is released to a parent or other responsible person.

If the youth is not released to a parent or responsible person, the police may detain the accused pursuant to sections 497–498 of the *CCC*. Reasons for detention include to mitigate the risk that the accused might not attend court, preserve evidence, establish identity of the accused, or prevent the continuation of offending or a further offence.

CASE BRIEF

Interim Release of a Youth to a "Responsible Person"

R. v. J.D.G.V., 2010 SKPC 077 (CanLII)
(A decision of the Provincial Court of Saskatchewan Youth Justice Court)

This case considers the interim release of a youth to a "responsible person."

ISSUE: The Crown, who bears the onus that a young person should be detained, argued that rather than release the youth to the care of a responsible person, he should be held in detention due to the violent circumstances of the alleged offence.

Continued

THE FACTS: The youth had been the front door "lookout" during a premeditated violent home invasion involving five other individuals, all of whom were under the direction of an adult known as the "big boss." The plan was to rob a known drug dealer of money and drugs. Approximately two months later the youth was involved with two other young people in another preplanned robbery and assault causing bodily harm—the youth assaulted the victim with a beer bottle. The proceeds of the robbery were split among the youth with the majority of the money going to the "big boss."

The Court ordered the preparation of a Judicial Interim Release Report (JIR) and an updated one four days later. These reports are routinely used in youth justice court in Saskatoon and carry a great deal of weight in decision making. The JIR recommended the release of young person with conditions. The JIR noted the following:

- J.D.G.V. is 17 years of age.
- The alleged offences occurred during a time when J.D.G.V. was not in his parental home. He had moved out because he found his mother's home too strict. He is now prepared to live in her home and abide by her rules.
- His mother is prepared to have him return to her home and she will provide strict supervision. She is prepared to call the police if he does not comply with court-ordered conditions.
- Prior to arrest he was not working or going to school.
- He has expressed a willingness to participate in any programming or counselling as his youth worker may recommend.
- J.D.G.V. acknowledged a problem with marihuana and is willing to attend programming. The role of marihuana and/or alcohol ingestion in relation to these offences is not clear.
- At the time of the initial JIR the young person had a job lined up. The updated JIR ... indicated that the job is no longer available. However, it indicates that a youth pastor/worker (who appeared with the mother in Court) is prepared to spend 15 hours per week with the young person. He can provide counselling and will help J.D.G.V. find a job.

The Judicial Interim Release Reports proposed release under supervision of that program. The youth worker will be available to the mother and the youth pastor and it is expected that they will work co-operatively in providing the necessary supervision.

DECISION: The personal, family, and community circumstances warranted that the young person be released pursuant to s. 31(1) and there was "substantial reassurance with respect to concerns for the protection of the public and confidence in the administration of justice."

What factors do you think were persuasive in the judge's decision to release the youth?

Additional Considerations for Release

In addition to its emphasis on the use of a "responsible person" as an alternative to pre-trial detention and the presumption of release, the *YCJA* includes two other considerations:

1. It prohibits the use of detention as a substitute for mental health, child welfare, child protection, or other social measures.
2. It has a presumption against detention, if the young person could not be sentenced to custody when found guilty of an offence.

Release Except When Not in the Public Interest

Except for the most serious crimes, the police officer must remember that the presumption is that release will take place, unless the police officer has reasonable grounds to believe that detention is in the public interest. The public interest has regard to all the circumstances of the situation, including the need to accomplish the following:

1. Establish the identity of the young person
2. Secure evidence about the offence
3. Prevent the commission of an offence
4. Ensure the safety of a victim or witness
5. Have reasonable grounds to believe that the young person will attend court

APPEARANCE BEFORE A JUDGE: THE SHOW-CAUSE HEARING

If a young person continues to be detained by the police in spite of the various provisions that require or allow release, the young person must be brought before a youth justice court judge or justice of the peace *without unreasonable delay* and within 24 hours of arrest [*CCC* s. 503] for a **show-cause hearing**. Here, too, there is the presumption that the young person brought before a judge should be released and that the release should be without conditions. It is the *burden of the Crown* to show-cause why detention is justified (see the Case Brief above). This onus is reversed to the defence/accused—a **reverse onus**—such that the defence now has the burden to meet the standard of proof as to why the young person should be released. The onus of who has to meet the burden is set out in s. 515(6) of the *Criminal Code* and includes situations such as when the youth failed to attend court, breached an undertaking or recognizance, or has been charged with a serious indictable offence.

Police will be involved in preparing the Crown package—a presentation of any police evidence that would be of assistance to the Crown prosecutor who will argue to "show-cause" why the accused should be detained. If detention is not justified, the judge must release the young person *without conditions*, unless the Crown can show-cause as to why conditions are justified.

Under the *YCJA*, the judge is required to presume that detention is not necessary for the protection of the public if the young person could not, on being found guilty, be sentenced to custody.

The three criteria for the use of custody as a sentence require that the young person has done one or more of the following:

1. Committed a violent offence
2. Failed to comply with two or more custodial sentences
3. Committed an indictable offence for which an adult would be liable to imprisonment of more than two years and has a history that indicates a pattern of findings of guilt.

The *YCJA* requires that the judge inquire about the possible availability of a "responsible person" as an alternative to detention.

The release of the young person may be subject to the following:

1. An undertaking with conditions
2. A recognizance, which is a promise to do something, typically appear in court, that may be with or without sureties
3. A recognizance without sureties and with conditions

Conditions of Release

Conditions of release fall into three categories:

1. Those that shall not be used
2. Those that should not be used
3. Those that are allowable

Shall not: Conditions of release are not to be selected on the basis of their being punitive or therapeutic.

Should not: Conditions of release should not be vague, for example, "obey house rules," or so broad as to make successful compliance unlikely.

Allowable: Allowable conditions of release are specified in the *CCC*, subsection515(4), and include the following:

1. Report at specified times to, for example, the police
2. Remain within a specified jurisdiction
3. Not communicate with persons or go to places specified in the order
4. Comply with "other reasonable conditions" specified in the order

With respect to "conditions," the *YCJA* is concerned that the nature of the conditions does not unnecessarily place the young person in the situation of "reverse onus."

Reverse onus refers to the onus or burden shifting to the young person to show cause why release is justified. Reverse onus is created when there is a failure to meet a condition or recognizance. Conditions that are unnecessary or vague may elevate the risk of the young person becoming in a reverse onus situation. This is inconsistent with the *YCJA* where the dominant presumption is in favour of release.

As in many other areas, the *YCJA* augments the basic procedures that apply to adults. Those additional elements in the *YCJA* highlight the special status of young persons. The temporary detention of young persons is one area where adult and youth practices differ substantially, and it is to that issue that we turn next.

TEMPORARY RESTRAINT, TEMPORARY DETENTION, SECONDARY CAUTIONS, AND BAIL

Temporary Restraint

The issue of detaining young offenders comes up both before and after their appearance in youth justice court.

The *YCJA* has two major emphases on detention:

1. There is a broad presumption against detention (covered in the previous section); and
2. If there is to be detention, young persons are to be kept separate from adults. The *YCJA* is clear that we are not to house young offenders with adults, whenever possible. Of course, circumstances do arise where complying with this restriction is impossible. Typically, one such set of circumstances arises when the young person is in temporary restraint. **Temporary restraint** is when the young person is in the custody of a police officer before a youth court justice can remand the young person to a regional detention centre [*YCJA* 30(1), (2)].

What are the issues surrounding the temporary restraint of young persons before their appearance in youth justice court? The *YCJA* outlines the basic rules underlying the detention of young persons. Young persons who are detained must be held in specially designated youth facilities, *separate from adult offenders*. Yet, this is not always done in Canada, frequently justified on the basis that vast geography makes such "specialized" accommodations impractical. Yet, housing youth with adults runs contrary to article 37 of the United Nations Convention on the Rights of the Child, which stipulates that children must be housed separately from adults.

There are, however, some exceptions to this rule. Young persons may be held under the supervision and control of a police officer while they are being transferred from one location to another. Normally, that transfer would be from a designated youth detention area to youth justice court. A youth justice court judge may also waive the location requirements if "the young person cannot, having regard to his own safety or the safety of others, be detained in a place of detention for young persons." Another exception occurs when "no place of detention for young persons is available within a reasonable distance" [*YCJA* 30(3)].

The general provision that young people must be held in special areas separate from adults does not apply at the point of arrest. Specifically, subsection 30(7) states that these provisions

> do not apply in respect of any temporary restraint of a young person under the supervision and control of a peace officer after arrest, but a young person who is so restrained shall be transferred to a place of temporary detention
>
> … as soon as is practicable, and in no case later than the first reasonable opportunity after the appearance of the young person before a youth justice court judge or a justice… .

The need for the exemption from keeping young persons separate from adults becomes obvious when we examine the practicalities of policing. For example, if a police officer arrests a young person for committing an offence with an adult accomplice, it is often difficult for the arresting officer to arrange to have the two accused transported in separate cruisers. Consequently, if a 16-year-old and a 19-year-old are arrested for having just committed a break-and-enter, it is permissible for the arresting officer to place both persons in the back seat of the cruiser to transport them to the police station.

Summary

Situations where the young person is considered in temporary restraint include the following:

1. Transportation to the police station after being arrested.
2. Being held in the police station while waiting to be interviewed.
3. Being in lockup while waiting to be released.
4. Waiting to be taken before a youth court justice.
5. All situations where the young person is transferred between the regional detention centre and the court.

Of course, it is good practice to keep young offenders separate from adults, whenever possible. Some police services in larger centres, for example, have clearly separated areas for interviewing and holding young persons. Unfortunately, this degree of physical separation is not always possible in smaller centres or in situations where many young persons are arrested in a short period.

Temporary Detention

Temporary detention, on the other hand, normally refers to the period when the young person is in a detention centre before sentencing. Typically, a young person will be kept in detention if the young person has committed a very serious offence or has a history of non-appearance and was denied bail as a consequence.

Temporary detention includes the periods that a young person spends waiting to be tried and any time he or she is detained while being tried. Two key provisions relate to temporary detention. First, the young person must be kept separate and apart from adults. This provision includes separate washroom facilities. Second, the young person must have all the benefits and privileges extended to adult offenders.

The only exception to the rule about separation from adults is when a youth justice court judge or a justice decides that the young person may pose a risk to his or her own or another person's safety, or a suitable place for detaining young people is not available within a reasonable distance.

A young person who is detained must have his or her person and clothing searched before the youth can be left alone. This includes temporarily locking a young person in an interview room. Young females must only be searched by a female officer.

Privacy to Talk to a Lawyer

While not strictly an issue of detention, it should be remembered that a suspect and his or her lawyer have the right to conduct their conversations in private. Normally, the officer in charge will provide an interview room for this purpose. Such facilities need not be extended to parents or other persons who may wish to converse with the suspect. The decision to extend such privileges is at the discretion of the officer in charge.

Secondary Caution to Charged Person

As discussed in the previous chapter, getting a young person's statement admitted as evidence during a trial is very difficult. Nevertheless, officers should attempt to obtain a statement, even if they expect that it will do little to convict the offender in court. Some statements do make it into the court record, and sometimes, the process of making a statement helps "convince" the young person that accepting some sanction is the wisest solution. Statements also give the officer an opportunity to assess the offender's immediate physical and emotional conditions. The officer might also gain some insight into the young person's domestic (home) situation. This is useful information when considering whether and under what terms to release the young person.

Interviews with the accused are occasionally useful in redirecting the investigation toward another perpetrator or an accomplice. At the very least, going through the process hones and sharpens the officer's interview and questioning skills. Most formal statements are taken in rooms that are specially set aside for that purpose, and they are often equipped with a video recording device.

Secondary Caution

When the interview takes place, the officer should again advise the young person of his or her legal rights. At this point, it is also essential to give the young person what is known as a "secondary caution." This **secondary caution** is to help ensure that the young person has not been pressured or coerced into giving a statement. That is, the young person is giving the statement freely and voluntarily. Typically, a secondary caution would be worded in the following way:

> *If you have spoken to any police officer or to anyone with authority or if any such person has spoken to you in connection with this case, I want it clearly understood that I do not want it to influence you in making a statement.*

> *Do you understand what I have just said?*

As with the primary caution, the wording needs to be adjusted to fit the young person's ability to understand the points being made (also discussed in Chapter 6). Consequently, it is necessary to ask the question in different ways and to ask the suspect to explain what he or she thinks the caution means. The exact wording of the officer's caution and the young person's response should be copied into the officer's notes.

If a statement is given, the video tape of the statement will undoubtedly be played in court. Defence counsel will scrutinize the tape to ensure that there were no real or apparent inducements offered and that the young person was not being coerced. This scrutiny generally goes far beyond that for adult cases, and the interviewing officers' words, demeanour, and body language will all be called into question.

Bail Hearings and Release on Bail

Young persons who commit particularly serious crimes, are charged with multiple offences, or have a history of non-appearance are generally detained by the police. In addition, young persons are also not released where the *CCC* forbids the release of adults (e.g., charges of murder). In these instances, the decision of whether or not to release the young person is made at a bail hearing.

A **bail hearing** is a judicial process where it is decided whether and under what circumstances a person charged with an offence will be released. **Bail** refers to the *financial conditions* on which a person will be released with a promise to appear in court. Bail money may be forfeited if the defendant fails to appear.

Either a justice of the peace or a youth justice court judge may preside over a bail hearing. Justices of the peace, however, cannot preside when young persons are charged with offences under section 469 of the *CCC*: murder, conspiracy to commit murder, or being an accessory after the fact to murder.

Review of a Bail Order

Where a justice of the peace cannot preside, a youth justice court judge holds the hearing. A youth justice court judge can also review the order of a justice of the peace upon the request of the young person, the young person's counsel, or the Crown. Notice must be given two days ahead of time, and the hearing is made *de novo*. In other words, the second hearing is not an appeal of the decision made by the justice of peace; it is treated as a totally new or original application for bail.

The standard provisions outlined in section 515 of the *CCC* relating to surety apply to young persons as well as to adults. A **surety** is a person who agrees to vouch for the accused's return to court for a trial, and to pay a certain amount of money if the accused does not show up. There is, however, one significant option of interest to police officers that is open to the youth justice court that does not apply to adults. A youth justice court judge or a justice may decide to place the young person in the care of a responsible person as outlined in section 31 of the *YCJA*. This provision is only used when other forms of release (such as a notice to appear) are not applicable and the young person would otherwise be kept in detention.

Recall from earlier in this chapter that the section 31 provision is used when the responsible adult "is willing and able to take care of and exercise control over the young person, and … the young person is willing to be placed in the care of that person." The responsible person must indicate in writing that he or she will supervise the young person and assume the responsibility for making sure the accused appears in court. That person must also agree to whatever other conditions the judge may impose. If the young person breaks any of those provisions, or the responsible person can no longer supervise the young person, the supervising adult must notify the police of the situation. If no responsible adult comes forward, the young person will be remanded in detention until the scheduled court appearance or until another bail hearing is requested.

The court can remove a young person from the care of the responsible person if that person becomes unwilling or unable to exercise care and control over the young person. The supervising adult, the young person, or "any other person" may apply to the youth court to have the responsible person relieved of the responsibility. In this instance, an arrest warrant is issued for the young person, who is then compelled to appear in court.

IN THE NEWS

A Case for Detention in Hindsight

It was a youth crime that shocked an entire community.

On October 14, 2004, a Toyota Camry driven by teaching assistant Theresa McEvoy was broadsided at a Halifax intersection by a Chrysler LeBaron driven by a 16-year-old youth, instantly killing a 52-year-old mother of three.

Continued

What was so galling to the people of Halifax was not just that the young man, Archibald Billard, had stolen the car and was so high on marijuana that he did not know how fast he was going. It was also the fact that two days before the crash, he had been released from jail even though he was facing charges stemming from a high-speed police chase two weeks earlier and other alleged offences.

Mr. Billard eventually was given an adult sentence of 5 1/2 years in custody after pleading guilty to criminal negligence causing death. But his case is the subject of an ongoing public inquiry that is focusing a bright light on the *Youth Criminal Justice Act*, the federal law that makes it difficult to keep young offenders in jail unless they commit serious, violent crimes.

…

Criminologists and prosecutors say the new act is doing what it was designed to do: jailing young people only for serious violent offences, or in a limited number of other exceptional circumstances. But some also say it is too restrictive, making it tough to keep people such as Mr. Billard off the street.

Source: Richard Blackwell, "Adult crime, adult time? N.S. case fuels debate; A teen driver high on pot hits another car, killing its driver," *The Globe and Mail*, April 1, 2006, p. A9.

RECORDS

Fingerprinting and Photographing

Section 113 of the *YCJA* allows police officers to fingerprint and photograph young persons under the same general conditions that apply to adults under the *Identification of Criminals Act*. In other words, an officer may fingerprint and photograph young persons if the officer charges them with committing an indictable or a hybrid offence. Fingerprinting or photographing a young person is only permissible, however, if they have been charged or convicted of an offence. It is *not* permissible to fingerprint or photograph a young person who has been charged with a summary offence only.

This situation is at odds with some practices involving adults. For example, adults are occasionally asked to provide fingerprints to aid in an investigation. A typical situation might be when unidentified prints are found at a crime scene and several possible suspects exist. Those suspects may be encouraged to exclude themselves from the investigation by providing fingerprints that can be compared with those found at the crime scene.

For less serious indictable offences, a young person may be released from custody and given a notice requiring appearance at a later date for the fingerprints and photographs to be taken. For more serious cases, the fingerprinting and photographing are usually done when charges are laid. If a young person accused is required to appear at a later date, notice of that must also be given to the young person's parents or guardian. Normally, failure to appear for fingerprinting is an offence under section 145 of the *CCC*. Bala (1997: 135, fn. 7) notes, however, that in the case *R. v. K.(P.A.)*, Justice Scott ruled that a youth could only be convicted under this section if a copy of the notice to appear had been provided to the youth's parents.

Police Records

A police service that is involved in the investigation of any offence alleged to have been committed by a young person may keep a record of that offence as well as the original copy of fingerprints or photographs of the young person [*YCJA* 115(1)].

When a young person is charged with committing an offence that could cause an adult to be photographed, fingerprinted, or otherwise measured, the investigating police service may provide a record relating to the offence to the Royal Canadian Mounted Police (RCMP). If the young person is found guilty of the offence, the record shall be provided to the RCMP [*YCJA* 115(2)].

The RCMP has a central repository, known as the Canadian Police Information Centre (CPIC), which holds information on offences where there has been a finding of guilt of a young person, keeping the file or records of offenders for the identification of offenders [*YCJA* 115(3)]. In addition to CPIC, the RCMP central repository contains a number of specialized repositories, such as the following: the Criminal Intelligence Service of Canada (CISC); the national DNA data bank, which includes DNA profiles from unsolved crimes; a convicted offender index, which includes DNA profiles from young offenders; and the "special records repository," which includes prohibition orders made under section 51 of the *YCJA* (prohibition from possessing certain weapons).

Most critically, section 118 of the *YCJA* severely restricts access to these records where it would identify a younger person, unless authorized or required by the Act.

CASE BRIEF

Use of Fingerprints for Later Case as an Adult

R. v. A.S. 2013 BCPC 0373

THE FACTS: A man was robbed and assaulted in his car after being "pulled over" by people impersonating police with fake lights and one person presenting himself as a plainclothes police officer at the passenger door. In committing the crime, he had touched the car door. An RCMP officer was able to successfully lift the fingerprints, which were then run through a database, subsequently linking them to the sealed file of a youth offender who had been

Continued

in possession of a small amount of marijuana—a summary offence (*Note: It is not permissible to fingerprint for a summary offence—the judge noted that the new officer had made a mistake in understanding the nature of the offence for possession of a small amount of marijuana, and continued to make the same mistake four years later during his testimony*). The fingerprint evidence was central to the initial identification and locating of the accused as an adult. Without the fingerprints, the Crown had no case.

ISSUES: The accused asserts that his fingerprints as a young offender were improperly taken in 2009, thus violating his right to be secure against unreasonable search and seizure pursuant to s. 8 of the *Charter*. Was it permissible for the police to use his fingerprints to help them in solving the crime in 2012 when A.S. was an adult?

DECISION: The fingerprints were not obtained lawfully in 2009. Being a summary offence, there was no power to take the prints. Furthermore, A.S. was a young person at the time and access to the records expires after a time period, except in very limited circumstances that were not present in A.S.'s case. In addition, the records were to be destroyed pursuant to section 128(3) of the *YCJA*, which had not been done in the case of the A.S.'s records.

> Does this case properly reflect the intentions of the YCJA to enact safeguards to protect access to records so that young offenders do not have their crimes follow them into adulthood?

Government Records

A department or agency of any government in Canada may keep information that it obtains for any of the following purposes:

1. Investigation of an offence alleged to have been committed by a young person
2. Use in proceedings against a young person
3. Administering a youth sentence or other order
4. Considering whether to use extrajudicial measures
5. As a result of the use of extrajudicial measures to deal with a young person [YCJA 116(1)].

Other Records

Persons or organizations may keep records of information that they obtained as a result of the use of extrajudicial measures and/or for the purpose of participating in the administration of a youth sentence [*YCJA* 116(2)].

Period of Access

The length of time that the record of a young person can be accessed depends on the nature and result of the charge. These periods are summarized in Table 8.1.

Table 8.1 Period of Access to the Records of a Young Person [*YCJA* 119(2)]

Disposition	Period of Access
Extrajudicial sanction	Two years after the young person agrees to be subjected to these sanctions
Acquitted	Two months after the expiry of time for an appeal
Charge dismissed	Two months after the dismissal e
Found guilty and receives an absolute discharg	One year after the finding of guilt
Charge stayed	One year if no proceedings taken against the young person for that period of time
Found guilty and receives a conditional discharge	Three years after the finding of guilt
Found guilty of a summary conviction offence	Three years after the youth sentence has been completed
Found guilty of an indictable offence	Five years after the youth sentence has been completed
Subsequent convictions	Time extended
Presumptive offences (per the 2012 amendments, a youth may no longer be charged with these offences, but there may be holdovers from when youth could be charged)	May be retained indefinitely
Serious violent offences	Additional five years
If over 18 years and commits subsequent offence and young person's crime-free period has not expired	Record becomes part of adult record and adult rules apply

Protection of Privacy

A major distinction between how we handle adult offenders and young offenders relates to the issue of privacy. It is permissible to publish the names of adults charged or convicted of an offence. It is also normal practice for local newspapers to assign a court reporter to cover the more interesting cases heard in court. In fact, the right to a public trial is a fundamental aspect of our legal system. Public and open trials, we believe, are one way of making sure that the power of the state is limited and that the courts do not engage in abusive and arbitrary procedures. The *YCJA*, on the other hand, is written from a perspective that sees publicity as detrimental to the personal and social well-being of the young person. Consequently, there are strict limitations on the public release of information (called **publication**) relating to the offence, hearing, adjudication, disposition, or appeal of a young person.

The prohibition, **publication ban,** in subsection 110(1) of the *YCJA* is clear: "no person shall publish the name of a young person, or any other information related to a young person, if it would identify the young person as a young person dealt with under this Act." This includes not only young persons who are found guilty, but also young persons who are under investigation or charged, as well as young victims or witnesses. The issues at hand may be sensitive for them, and they may be intimidated by the public attention to their testimony. The reputation of the witness or victim may also be adversely affected by publication.

CASE BRIEF

Disclosure versus Privacy

Toronto Police Service v. D.(L.) 2016 ONSC 5500

ISSUE: What happens when police officers are alleged to have assaulted a young person and must defend themselves in a disciplinary hearing?

As noted above, the protection of young offenders' privacy is deemed paramount under the *YCJA*.

In *Toronto Police Service v. D.(L.)* 2016 ONSC 5500 the question of whether a police officer had a valid interest in having the records of youth disclosed was debated in the courts.

THE FACTS: A police officer was the subject of disciplinary proceedings based on an allegation by a young person that the police officer had assaulted him while the youth was in custody. The officer brought an application under the *YCJA* for disclosure of the young person's youth records in order to assess the young person's credibility of the allegations he had made against the police officer. The youth court judge dismissed the application, ruling that the principle of *diminished moral responsibility* pervades the *YCJA* and the records were irrelevant to the determination of the young person's credibility.*

The police officer appealed.

DECISION: The appeal judge held that the records should be disclosed. The young person was the not the accused but rather the witness who had made serious allegations against a police officer who was facing disciplinary proceedings. In this case, it was determined that the officer's rights to *procedural fairness* to be able to answer the allegations as completely as possible overrode the principle of diminished moral responsibility when the situation was such that the young person was essentially the accuser rather than the accused.

The judge ruled that the officer had a "valid and substantial interest" pursuant to s. 123(1)(a) of the *YCJA* in having the young person's records disclosed.

---

*To read a copy of the first judgment, see *Toronto (City) Police Service v. D.(L.)*, [2015] O.J. No. 4143, 2015 ONCJ 430.

Two judges couldn't agree on how this should be handled. What is your opinion?

Exceptions to the Non-publication Rule

The *YCJA* provides detailed exceptions to the general rule of non-publication and these have to do with the following: receipt of adult sentences; information made available in the course of the administration of justice; seeking public assistance in apprehending a young person; and where the young person is not over 18 years and not in custody and wants the information made public.

The first four of these exceptions are clarified below:

1. *Adult sentence.* The *YCJA* permits the publication of names of all young persons who have received adult sentences for murder, attempted murder, manslaughter, aggravated sexual assault, or repeat violent offences or any other criminal offences [*YCJA* 110(2)(a)].
2. *Violent offence.* Where a young person has received a youth sentence for a violent offence and a youth justice court has ordered the lifting of a publication ban [*YCJA* 110(2)(b)].
3. *Administration of justice.* Publication made in the course of the administration of justice where the purpose is not to make the information known to the community is allowed [*YCJA* 110(2)(c)].
4. *Seeking public assistance.* Publication of the name of a young person allows authorities to seek public assistance in apprehending a young person who is dangerous. An application needs to be made to a youth justice court judge, and counsel for the young person does not have to be informed (this is called *ex parte*). The order is operative for only five days. The fact that the police must make application to a judge means that a clear process must be followed by the police and that they cannot simply take it upon themselves to publish the information [*YCJA* 110(4)(a) & (b)].

In summary, the ban on publication does not mean that records cannot be kept, and identifying information regarding young persons and witnesses cannot be passed from one person to another. The *YCJA* exempts situations where the information is used for the administration of justice. In other words, it is permissible for police officers and other justice personnel to identify young persons when they are engaged in standard investigative practices. They may also provide information in the young person's file to court workers, corrections personnel, or youth workers, who may, for example, provide extrajudicial measures.

Nothing in the *YCJA* prevents an officer from inadvertently identifying young offenders by arresting them in a public place. For example, arresting a young person at school in the view of other students is not considered a violation of privacy. The decision about when and where to arrest a suspect rests with the individual police officer.

Accessibility of Records

Section 119 of the *YCJA* allows a broad range of people access to young persons' records before the expiry of the time limits placed on the records. Young persons and their counsel, for example, are granted automatic access to the young persons' youth justice court records.

The *YCJA* has a list of persons, groups, or institutions that may seek access to youth records and a list of the purposes of such access. That is, information requirements vary under individual circumstances of individual cases.

Subsection 119(1) recognizes access by the following:

1. Young persons, their counsel, parents, or adults the court permits to assist them.
2. Crown prosecutor.
3. Any judge, court, or review board.
4. Justice officers to assist in an investigation.
5. Persons administering extrajudicial measures or sanctions or prepares reports under the Act.
6. Provincial Director.
7. Those participating in a conference.
8. Victim.
9. Coroner, privacy or information commissioner, ombudsman, or child advocate.
10. Government officials.
11. An accused person or his counsel who needs it to make a defence.
12. Official agents of the federal government for statistical or security and other purposes.

Victim Access

Unlike youth court records, however, police and other government records relating to the young person are made available at the discretion of the agency keeping the records. Thus, police officials may allow victims access to all or parts of the record of a young person who has been charged or convicted of an offence, if, in their judgment, it will help the victim.

Lawyer Access

The lawyer or counsel of the accused young person will often request access to the police file. This file will likely contain the names and addresses of witnesses. As a matter of courtesy, some departments routinely ask witnesses (or more likely their parents) if they mind having their names and addresses revealed when such requests are made. Many police officers will also inform witnesses that they are under no obligation to speak with the offender's counsel if they do not wish to do so. It is also standard procedure to inform the Crown's office when these requests are made.

Access to Other Entities

In addition to the individuals and agencies cited above, the *YCJA* provides for the sharing of information with other entities. Access is given for particular circumstances or specific purposes so it is expected that the custodian of the records, for example, the police, will exercise discretion, as will the court, when an application is made. Insurance companies may be granted access to investigate a claim arising out of an offence. School authorities may receive a portion of a record that is relevant to ensure compliance with a court order or ensure the safety of staff, students, or other persons or to facilitate the young person's rehabilitation. On the other hand, in the 2000 decision *Re: F.N.*, the Supreme Court of Canada upheld an appeal forbidding the Roman Catholic School Board of St. John's from routinely distributing the youth court docket to local school boards. Fundamentally, the Supreme Court agreed that this practice violated the non- disclosure provisions of what was then the *YOA*. The distribution of "tailored" information, however, with respect to specific offenders, is acceptable.

SUMMARY: PUTTING IT TOGETHER

There is no one typical criminal event: crimes differ, offenders differ, and circumstances differ. How police officers deal with a young person who commits a minor act of vandalism or shoplifting will be very different from how they handle a serious assault or drug offence. To illustrate the many steps an officer might follow in arresting a young offender, however, we will consider an example of a call to investigate a theft under $5,000. The steps in this example are charted in Figure 8.1.

The crime: In this example, two male suspects are caught trying to steal some electronic appliances from a discount store. The total value of the goods is approximately $1,900. One suspect is a 17-year-old, and the other is a 19-year-old. The manager of the store observed the suspects, and the store's security camera recorded the act. The manager and two salespeople detained the suspects as they exited the store.

We will focus on those aspects of the arrest that illustrate the difference between the handling of a young person and that of an adult.

Arrest of a young person and an adult for a theft under $5,000

(17–year–old)   (19–year–old)

Both are told reason for arrest

↓

Both are read right to counsel

Right to counsel explained
in a language appropriate to
the age and understanding
of young person

Ask for an explanation of the right to counsel

↓

Record the explanation of the right to counsel for proof of
understanding in court

↓

Search both prisoners

↓

It is permissible to put both prisoners in the rear of the same cruiser,
since the young person is considered to be in temporary restraint

↓

Note the names of all persons in authority who came in contact
with the suspects

↓

Transport the suspects to the police station and turn them over
to the officer in charge

↓

Separately present each suspect to the officer in charge

Give the young person the right
to counsel again and assist
him/her in exercising that right

↓

Phone the parents of the young
person to notify them of the
arrest and ask them to pick up
their son/daughter

Give both suspects the opportunity to speak to counsel

↓

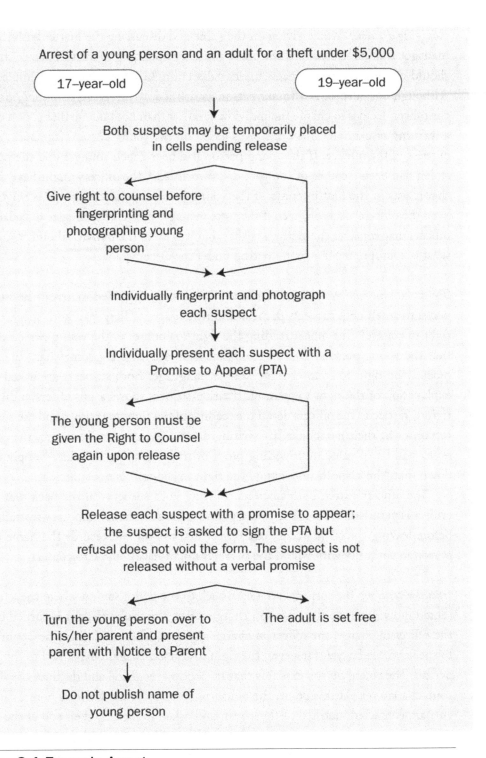

Figure 8.1 Example Arrest

Charging decision: After arriving on the scene and discussing the matter with the store manager and the salespeople, the police officers responding to the call decide that they should charge the two suspects under subsection 322(1) of the *CCC* (simple theft). Although one suspect is a young person as defined by the *Youth Criminal Justice Act*, the officer decides to charge the individual, rather than not take further action or issue a warning or caution. This decision is based on the young person's age and the seriousness of the offence. If the young person had been much younger and the property stolen had been a couple of compact discs worth $30, the officers might have decided that it was in the best interests of the young person not to charge. This might have been the officers' decision, even if the store manager pressed for charges to be laid. The officers may consider the victim's wishes, but it is up to the individual officer to decide what is appropriate for a young person under the circumstances.[2]

The arrest and reading of rights: Once the officers have decided to arrest the two suspects, they tell both suspects the reason for their arrest. They read both suspects their right to counsel. The officer reading the right to counsel to the young person decides that the young person's level of comprehension seems to lag somewhat. The officer repeats the right to counsel using simpler language. Both suspects are asked for an explanation of the right to counsel. If either suspect shows a misunderstanding, the right is restated. The officers detail the reading of the right to counsel and the suspects' responses in their notebooks. By writing down the responses verbatim, the officers' notes will be of value in providing proof of understanding in court. Simply noting down that "the suspects understood the right to counsel" is not sufficient.

The officers search both suspects. Putting both suspects in the back seat of the cruiser is permissible, since the young person is considered in temporary restraint. Just before leaving the crime scene, one officer takes notes and records the name of any person in authority with whom the suspects might have come into contact.

Initial detention: The suspects are taken back to the police station where they are presented individually to the officer in charge. Once the adult offender is turned over to the officer in charge, the officer in charge asks him if he would like the opportunity to speak with a lawyer. However, the right to counsel is again explained to the young person. The young person explains that he "knows the drill" and declines the offer to contact a lawyer. At this point, the officer phones the young person's home. The parents are contacted, notified of the arrest, and asked to pick up their son at the police station. Both suspects are now placed in holding cells while waiting to be released. In this instance, the police station has a separate corridor just for young offenders, and this is where the 17-year-old is held. The 19-year-old is placed in the general holding area used for adults.

Fingerprinting and photographing: Since the theft is a hybrid or dual offence under section 334(b) of the *CCC*, both suspects will be taken for fingerprinting and photographing. While the 19-year-old is processed in the standard manner, the young

---

2. Of course, the manager and the store owner have the option of laying a private information.

person is once again explained his right to counsel and given the opportunity to call counsel. Although the suspects were involved in the offence together, they are kept separate while the fingerprints and photographs are taken.

Decision to release from detention: In this case, the identity of the suspects is known, the issue of protecting evidence is not an issue, and neither suspect appears to pose a threat to others. A check of the records and the immediate demeanour of the suspects do not suggest that they will fail to appear in court. Consequently, the officer in charge decides to release both suspects with a Promise to Appear. Again, both suspects are processed separately. In the instance of the adult suspect, the suspect and the officer in charge simply sign the appearance form. After the paperwork is completed, the adult offender is set free.

Informing the parents of the youth. A few minutes later, the young person's parents arrive at the station. The officer in charge uses this opportunity to explain the situation to the parents and to explain the right to counsel again. While the officer is explaining the availability of legal aid's 1-800 number, the 17 year-old explains that he "knows the drill" and will speak with Ms. Blackstone of the law firm of Winnem and Luzem when he gets home. The young person agrees to sign the *Promise to Appear* form in the presence of his parents. Once done, the officer in charge presents the parents with a *Notice to Parents*. When that is completed, the officer in charge turns the young offender over to his parents, and they leave the station.

Publication in the newspaper: As a last point, a reporter from the local newspaper enters the station and thinks he recognizes the two suspects. When asked if these are "the two characters" that were involved in the theft at the discount electronics store, the officer in charge explains that one suspect is an adult and the other is a young offender. The reporter then asks for and receives the full name of the adult suspect for possible publication but is reminded by the officer in charge that he cannot publish the name of the young offender.

TEST YOUR KNOWLEDGE

Definitions

Define the following terms:

1. Pre-trial detention

_____

_____

_____

2. Responsible person

_____

_____

_____

3. Appearance notice

_____

_____

_____

4. Promise to appear

_____

_____

_____

5. Undertaking

_____

_____

_____

6. Recognizance

_____

_____

_____

7. Show-cause hearing

_____

_____

_____

8. Reverse onus

_____

_____

_____

9. Temporary restraint

_____

_____

_____

10. Temporary detention

_____

_____

_____

11. Secondary caution

_____

_____

_____

12. Bail hearing

_____

_____

_____

13. Bail

_____

_____

_____

14. Surety

_____

_____

_____

15. Publication

_____

_____

_____

16. Publication ban

_____

_____

_____

True/False

1. T F In order to follow the *Criminal Code of Canada*, it is important to detain adults as long as possible.

2. T F The *Youth Criminal Justice Act* requires that young persons be detained for a lesser period of time than adults.

3. T F Accused persons are to be brought before a justice any time it is convenient for the police.

4. T F A young person's record can be consulted when making the decision of whether or not to release the young person.

5. T F Under the *YCJA*, arrest and detention are among the usual ways that a young person involved in an offence is dealt with.

6. T F If a young person is detained by the police, the young person must be brought before a youth justice court judge or justice of the peace within six hours.

7. T F The judge must presume that detention is not necessary for the protection of the public if the young person could not, on being found guilty, be sentenced to custody.

8. T F Custody may be considered a sentence if the young person failed to comply with a non-custodial sentence.

9. T F Custody may be used as a sentence if the young person committed an indictable offence and would be liable to imprisonment of more than two years and has a history of findings of guilt.

10. T   F   Conditions for release should not be punitive.

11. T   F   It is when the secondary caution is being given that it is acceptable for a police officer to offer to "go easy" on the young person in exchange for co-operation.

12. T   F   Bail hearings are only about money.

13. T   F   If a responsible person cannot be found, it may be necessary to keep a young person accused of a crime in detention.

14. T   F   Young persons may be fingerprinted, but not photographed, by the police.

15. T   F   The preferred procedure under the *Youth Criminal Justice Act* is to fingerprint young persons before they are charged.

16. T   F   It is a violation of the *Youth Criminal Justice Act*'s prohibition on publication if a police officer tells her husband that one of the youths in the neighbourhood was charged with assault.

17. T   F   In order to publish the name of a young person the police must apply to youth justice court for permission.

18. T   F   Records of young offenders are generally kept for a shorter period of time than the records of adults.

Multiple Choice

1. Which of the following is not a sufficient reason to not release a young person?

a. to establish the person's identity
b. to get the youth to give up the names of the other persons involved in the crime
c. to preserve evidence
d. to prevent the repetition of this offence

2. When deciding to release a young person, which of the following should the police officer be satisfied with?

a. that the accused will probably appear in court
b. that the accused is of no danger to a victim
c. that the accused is of no danger to others
d. all of the above

3. Which of the following must occur before a young person is released in the care of a "responsible person"?

    a. the police officer must issue a warning to the young person
    b. the Crown prosecutor must give consent
    c. the "responsible person" must agree in writing to care for and be responsible
    d. the parents of the young person must consent

4. Which of the following does not constitute grounds for the detention of a young person?

    a. need to establish the identity of the young person
    b. need to secure evidence about the offence
    c. the parents of the young person are divorced
    d. the safety of a witness is an issue

5. A young person who continues to be detained by the police must be brought before a youth justice court judge or justice of the peace

    a. without unreasonable delay
    b. within 24 hours
    c. both of the above
    d. none of the above

6. Which of the following apply when a young person is brought before a youth justice court judge or justice of the peace?

    a. the presumption that the young person will be released
    b. if released, the release should be without conditions
    c. the burden is on the Crown to show why detention is justified
    d. all of the above

7. A youth justice court judge is required to presume that detention is not necessary for the protection of the public, unless the young person

    a. has already received a police caution
    b. is assumed of having committed a theft under $1,000
    c. is accused of having committed a violent offence
    d. is accused of having committed a theft over $1,000

8. Which of the following is an appropriate condition of release under the *YCJA*?

    a. requirement to attend a treatment program
    b. requirement to obey the rules of the house of the responsible person
    c. regular attendance at church
    d. report at specific times to the police

9. Reverse onus, when it comes to young persons,

    a. should be encouraged
    b. should be avoided
    c. is highly desirable
    d. can only occur if the young person was previously referred to a program

10. The police may house young offenders with adults

    a. never
    b. any time as long as it is during the day
    c. when doing otherwise is impossible
    d. for a maximum of 24 hours

11. Which of the following is not a consideration at a bail hearing?

    a. the seriousness of the offence
    b. the suffering of the victims
    c. the family situation of the young person
    d. the risk of flight

12. Once fingerprints and photographs of young persons are taken, they may be retained

    a. for no longer than 12 months
    b. until the young person reaches the age of 18 years
    c. forever
    d. none of the above

13. To which categories of people who fall within the legal age that defines a young person does the *Youth Criminal Justice Act's* ban on publication apply?

    a. offenders
    b. victims
    c. witnesses
    d. all of the above

Short Answer

1. Identify three pieces of information that should be found on a Promise to Appear form.

    _____

    _____

    _____

    _____

    _____

_____

_____

_____

2. Describe the procedure that applies for fingerprinting a young person charged with a summary offence.

_____

_____

_____

_____

_____

_____

_____

_____

3. Identify four circumstances under which it is permissible for a police officer to detain a young person with adults.

_____

_____

_____

_____

_____

_____

_____

_____

4. Why must young offenders who are detained and are about to be left alone be searched?

_____

_____

_____

_____

_____

_____

_____

_____

5. You are a police officer who is testifying in court. You are being asked by defence counsel about whether and how you provided the young person with a secondary caution. Identify three questions that might be put to you as a way of challenging whether you did it correctly.

_____

_____

_____

_____

_____

_____

_____

6. What makes a bail hearing for a young person different from one that is for an adult?

_____

_____

_____

_____

_____

_____

_____

7. Identify three circumstances in which it may be appropriate to publish the name of a young person.

_____

_____

_____

_____

_____

_____

_____

_____

8. Why do you suppose the *Youth Criminal Justice Act* has provisions for the destruction of records of young persons?

_____

_____

_____

_____

_____

_____

_____

Exercise 1: You Be the Judge

Here are two cases that were heard by the Supreme Court of Canada. Each of the cases that follow was heard when the *Young Offenders Act* (*YOA*) was in place. The legal issues involved in these cases are the same in the *Youth Criminal Justice Act* (*YCJA*) as they were under the *YOA*. Therefore, these decisions will continue to apply fully. Given your knowledge of the *YCJA*, the principles on which it is based, and the *Charter of Rights and Freedoms*, answer the following questions about how you would have decided the case. The Court's decisions are summarized at the end of each exercise, but answer the questions before you read the court's decisions.

The Facts: A young person was charged with second-degree murder of a cab driver. His great-aunt, a First Nations band-elder with little formal education, accompanied him on his arrest to the police station. The young person regarded her as his mother. The police informed her that there would be time to look for a lawyer on their arrival at the police station, but on their arrival, both were taken to an interview room, where the investigating constable began taking a statement over the course of four and a half hours. Prior to taking the statement, a "Statement to Person in Authority" form was completed. The officer tried to explain the right to counsel, the right to have an adult present, and the fact that any statement could be used in proceedings against the accused. A statement was made without the advice of a lawyer. Later, the young person, at his request, met with his lawyer for half an hour. The next day, the young person informed the investigating constable that he had information to add to his statement. After the young person finished speaking with his lawyer, he and the constable went through the process of completing the "Statement to Person in Authority" form. The young person indicated that he did not want a lawyer or other adult present. The second statement included an exchange about the plan the young person and his co-accused had to murder a cab driver.

Questions

1. Should the *first* statement have been admitted as evidence?

   _____ Yes _____ No

   Indicate the reasons for your decision.

   _____

   _____

   _____

2. Should the *second* statement have been admitted as evidence?

   _____ Yes _____ No

   Indicate the reasons for your decision.

   _____

   _____

   _____

3. Does it make a difference to you that the same police officer was involved in taking the first and second statements in terms of the admissibility of the second statement?

   Indicate the reasons for your decision.

   _____

   _____

   _____

4. Does it make a difference if the police officer used information contained in the first statement in the questions posed to the young person at the time the second statement was taken?

   Indicate the reasons for your decision.

   _____

   _____

   _____

The S.C.C. Decision

The trial judge excluded the first statement, but not the second. The Supreme Court [in *R. v. I. (L.R.) and T. (E.)*] ruled that the second statement must be excluded as well. The following are edited excerpts of the reasoning provided by the Supreme Court.

> With respect to the first statement, neither the young person nor his great aunt appreciated the consequences of his act of confession, despite the fact that young person had had previous dealings with the police. If waiver had been in issue, the young person would not have had sufficient information concerning the extent of his jeopardy to make an informed and valid decision as to whether or not to speak with a lawyer. Accordingly, neither section 56 of the *YOA* [see s. 146 of the *YCJA*] nor section 10(b) of the *Charter* were complied with, and the first statement was inadmissible on this ground as well.
>
> The admissibility of the second statement was affected by the grounds for exclusion of the first statement. A parent is not an alternative to counsel, unless the right to counsel is waived. Section 56 of the *YOA*, which appears to provide that a parent or other adult may be an alternative to counsel, must be interpreted in a manner consistent with both the section 10(b) of the Charter right to counsel and the provision in section 11 of the *YOA* [see s. 25 of the *YCJA*] requiring that counsel be available.
>
> The determination of whether or not a young person validly waived his or her section 10(b) of the Charter right to counsel is not to be based simply on what the police told the young person but upon the young person's actual awareness of the consequences of his or her actions. The police need not advise an accused, as a matter of course, of the maximum penalty he or she might face. The phenomenal difference in potential consequences faced by the young person in youth court as opposed to adult court, however, mandates that a young person be aware of the possibility (where it exists) that he or she will receive an adult sentence, and the potential result of this in terms of stigma and penalty. The particular characteristics of young offenders make extra precautions necessary in affording them the full protection of their Charter rights.
>
> Under the rules relating to confessions at common law, the admissibility of a confession which had been preceded by an involuntary confession, involved a factual determination, based on factors designed to ascertain the degree of connection between the two statements. These included the time span between the statements, reference to the previous statement during questioning, the discovery of additional

incriminating evidence subsequent to the first statement, the presence of the same police officers at both interrogations and other similarities between the two circumstances. A subsequent confession would be involuntary if either the tainting features that disqualified the first confession continued to be present or if the making of the first statement was a substantial factor contributing to the making of the second statement. An explanation of one's rights either by a police officer or counsel may not be of use in the face of a strong urge to explain away incriminating matters in a prior statement.

Here, there was not only a close temporal relationship between the statements but also the second statement was a continuation of the first, and the first statement was a substantial factor leading to the making of the second. The statements were taken less than a day apart by the same officer.

There was no evidence that the police, in the interval between the two statements, had gathered further evidence tending to incriminate the appellant to which the appellant might be asked to respond. There was also continuous reference by the police officer throughout the second statement to information given in the first statement. All the evidence leads to the conclusion that the second statement was a continuation of the first. Communication with counsel did not make this conclusion unnecessary.

Exercise 2: You Be the Judge

Here is a set of facts that the Supreme Court of Canada had to work with. Given your knowledge of the *YCJA*, the principles on which it is based, and the *Charter of Rights and Freedoms*, answer the following questions about how you would have decided the case. The court's decision is summarized at the end, but answer the questions before you turn to the answer.

The accused was charged under the *Young Offenders Act* with theft. He was 17 years old at the time of the alleged offence. He voluntarily made an inculpatory written statement (admitting involvement) to a person in authority after having been cautioned and advised of his rights under the *Canadian Charter of Rights and Freedoms*. He was 18 years old when he made the statement. The police treated him as an adult and did not advise him that he had a right to have an adult person in attendance when he made the statement. Section 56(2) of the *YOA* [see s. 146(2) of the *YCJA*] provides that a statement given by a young person to a person in authority is not admissible unless certain conditions are met, including the requirement that the young person be advised of his or her right to have an adult person in attendance when making the statement.

Questions

1. Should the statement have been admitted as evidence?

   _____ Yes _____ No

2. Indicate the reasons for your decision.

_____

_____

_____

The S.C.C. Decision

The Supreme Court [in *R. v. Z. (D.A.)*], as reflected in the edited version of the ruling provided below, decided the following:

> The section 56(2) of the *Young Offenders Act* [see s. 146(2) of the *YCJA*] does not apply to statements made by an accused 18 years of age or older. Both the express words used by Parliament and the overall scheme and purpose of the *Act* support this conclusion. The term "young person" is defined in section 2 as a person at least 12 years old but under 18 years. The definition is further extended to include any person charged under the *Act* with having committed an offence while between the ages of 12 and 18 years.
>
> The concern over ensuring that all accused are similarly held accountable for the mistakes of their youth does not dictate that all the special protections afforded under the *Act*, regardless of the age of an accused. In enacting certain of the *Act*'s special protections, Parliament has sought to address concerns specific to a youth, rather than an adult.

There is clearly nothing underlying the purpose of section 56(2) [*YCJA* 146(2)] requiring its application to an adult accused. The aim of section 56 [*YCJA* 146] is to protect adolescents who, by virtue of their lack of maturity, are not likely to fully appreciate their legal rights and the consequences of making a statement to the police. These concerns do not arise with respect to an accused over the age of 18 years. No further protection beyond that already afforded under the *Charter* and common law is necessary to ensure that any statement made by an adult accused is truly voluntary. As such, the context of section 56(2) [*YCJA* 146(2)] does not require that the term "young person" therein be interpreted to include a person over the age of 18 years.

CHAPTER 9

The Youth Justice Court: The Trial and Sentencing

LEARNING OUTCOMES

Students who have mastered this chapter will have the ability to do the following:

- Describe the purpose and principles that guide sentencing under the *YCJA*.
- Describe the difference in the roles of defence counsel and Crown prosecutors.
- Articulate how the principles of denunciation and deterrence apply to young persons.
- Distinguish between a pre-sentence report, pre-sentence assessment, and conference.
- Describe the role of a youth justice court judge.
- Understand what goes on at a youth justice court trial.
- Understand the purposes and principles of youth sentences.
- Describe the range of youth sentences.
- Explain the circumstances under which a young person may receive an adult sentence.

JURISDICTION: YOUTH JUSTICE COURT

Adult court is for persons 18 years of age and older. When young persons, between the ages of 12 and 17 years, are in court, the court is always a *youth justice court* and the judge is always a youth justice court judge. It makes no difference what the name of the court is or the level of the court in each province [*YCJA* 13(2)]. Under the *Youth Criminal Justice Act* (*YCJA*), there is no such thing as the transfer of a young person to adult court no matter what the charge under the *Criminal Code*. Young persons may be given adult sentences, as we will see later, but this occurs in a youth justice court. Part 2 of the *YCJA* sets out the organization of the youth criminal justice system.

The Main Players

While the *YCJA* recognizes the unique status of young persons, the youth justice court is basically modelled after the ordinary courts. That is to say, they are fundamentally *adversarial*, and the requirement of *due process* that forms the basis of the ordinary courts also forms the basis of the youth justice court. Structurally, this means that professional lawyers—a Crown counsel, and a defence counsel representing the accused—will present the two sides of the case. The youth justice court judge must apply the requirements of the *YCJA*. Many of these requirements are different from the rules that apply to adults with respect to a wide range of issues, including frequency of instructions about right to counsel, publication of information, and type and length of sentence. Fundamentally, however, the youth justice court judge plays the same role as a judge in adult court, with one important exception. The major departure for the youth justice court judge is that the judge has to consider whether the matter at hand is best dealt with through *extrajudicial measures*, including an extrajudicial sentence. That is, the *YCJA* requires that the youth justice court judge consider the merits of dealing with the young person in a non-court manner. Such considerations *do not* apply in adult court. A more thorough discussion of extrajudicial measures can be found in Chapter 7.

Defence Counsel

The centrality of legally trained professionals (particularly defence counsel) in court to deal with young people is relatively new in Canada. Under the *Juvenile Delinquents Act*, young people were entitled to legal representation, but the participation of lawyers was not encouraged. Legal representation was the exception, rather than the rule. Legal representation of young persons was really introduced with the *Young Offenders Act*, and it continues with the *YCJA*.

Lawyers are officers of the court as well as their client's legal representative. The primary role of the defence counsel is to represent the legal interests of the accused, but also to serve the court honourably in the administration of justice. The job of the young person's lawyer is to ensure that the young person's legal rights are preserved and respected. Defence lawyers do not represent society, or even young persons' parents; their sole client is the young person.

RIGHT TO COUNSEL.

As emphasized in previous chapters, the *YCJA* requires the police to inform young persons of their right to consult and to retain counsel at almost every step in the legal process. The *YCJA* is clear that young persons need to be notified of their right to legal counsel and that they need to be given the opportunity to retain such counsel. Section 25 of the *YCJA* states, "a young person has the right to retain and instruct counsel without delay." That right can be exercised "at any stage of proceedings against the young person." This right is also printed on summonses, warrants, notices, and other documents given to the young person. If the police wish to question the young person, counsel must be present or the young person must sign a legal waiver. Even young persons whom the police bring into the station for a breathalyzer test must be given the opportunity to consult counsel before the test can be given. Even if a police officer obtains a written waiver, the waiver is voided once the young person requests counsel. Once the young person has passed through police custody, the *YCJA* requires the youth justice court to remind the young person of the right to counsel at several stages in the proceedings.

As listed in subsection 25(3) of the *YCJA*, they are the following:

- Pre-trial detention hearings
- Adult sentence hearings
- Trials
- Hearings to consider the application for a continuation of the custodial portion of youth sentence
- Hearings to determine whether the young person has breached condition(s) of community supervision
- Hearings to set the conditions of conditional supervision
- Hearings to determine whether the suspension of conditional supervision is appropriate
- Reviews of a youth sentence
- Reviews of the level of custody

Young persons do not have to exercise this right. If, however, the young person is not represented by counsel, the youth justice court may choose not accept a plea, unless the following occurs:

1. The youth justice court judge ensures that the young person understands the charge.
2. If it applies, the youth justice court judge explains the consequences of being liable to an adult sentence and explains the process for applying for a youth sentence.
3. The youth justice court judge explains the options available to the young person.

If the court is not satisfied that the young person understands these things, then the court must direct that the young person be represented by counsel.

WHEN THE YOUNG PERSON CANNOT AFFORD A LAWYER.
If the young person is not able to contact or obtain private counsel, the *YCJA* requires the court either to refer the young person to the provincial legal aid plan or to appoint a counsel [s. 25(4)]. In some larger centres, *duty counsel* will often provide initial advice to young persons if they appear in court without a lawyer. A duty counsel lawyer is either an employee or contractor for the court and provides on-the-spot, no-charge advice to an unrepresented accused.

The ability of young persons to request counsel for even relatively minor offences has raised concerns about cost in many jurisdictions. The *YCJA* indicates that the provinces are not prevented from establishing rules to recover costs of appointed counsel from young persons or their parents [*YCJA* 25(10)]. The *YCJA* considers that a conflict of interest might exist for lawyers whom the young person's parents have hired and paid to represent the young person. In situations where a youth justice court judge sees "the interests of the young person and his parents are in conflict," the judge "shall ensure that the young person is represented by counsel *independent of his parents*" [*YCJA* 25(8)].

ADVICE.

The first advice that most defence counsel will likely give their clients is to *remain silent* and not to co-operate with the police beyond providing their full name and age. As legal advocates, they can present evidence of their client's innocence such as mistaken identity or an alibi. Lawyers can also challenge any evidence or testimony presented, even if they believe their client is guilty. Lawyers can also make challenges under the *Charter* if they believe that the police violated their client's rights and/or due process during the investigation. Such violations can lead to the exclusion of evidence, which leaves the possibility that the charges will be dismissed if the exclusion results in too little evidence for a conviction. These are all legitimate aspects of a defence counsel's job, particularly if their client advises them to do so.

FACILITATE EXTRAJUDICIAL MEASURES.

Under the *YCJA*, there are even more options available to defence counsel than under previous legislation. The emphasis on the use of extrajudicial measures in the *YCJA* means that defence counsel have multiple points in the criminal justice system where they can attempt to have their clients dealt with in a more or less formal manner. These points occur at the level of the police (warning, caution, referral to program or agency), the Crown prosecutor (Crown cautions), and the youth justice court (extrajudicial sanctions).

The Crown Prosecutor

As in ordinary court, the primary role of the Crown prosecutor is to represent the government's (Crown's) case before the court by presenting evidence and arguments. The Crown in youth justice court also carries out most of the same functions as in adult cases. For example, Crown prosecutors often advise police officers about the specific charges to lay. They also screen cases to ensure that there is sufficient evidence to proceed with a charge. Usually, the Crown will review both the *substantive* case against the young person (whether the facts exist to prove guilt and warrant the sanctions) and the *procedure* followed by the police in the arrest (whether fair processes were followed to ensure that the accused's rights were respected).

ONUS ON CROWN TO FIRST PURSUE EXTRAJUDICIAL MEASURES.

This is an additional feature added by the *YCJA*. The Crown now needs to satisfy itself that the police considered the options of taking no further action, warning, caution, and referral to a program, and that the circumstances of the case warrant is being raised to their level. The Crown must also consider whether a *Crown caution* would be the appropriate disposition of this matter (review Chapter 7).

Where an extrajudicial measure is possible, the Crown will often discuss the case in more detail with the arresting officer. The goal here is to obtain as much information as possible about the officer's knowledge of the accused, the victim, and any witnesses. It is common for individual police officers to get annoyed with Crown prosecutors who choose not to proceed with a particular case. We must remember that the Crown is responsible for presenting the case in court, and poor evidence or faulty procedure will only lead to both the Crown and the arresting officer being embarrassed in court (e.g., think back to the Case Brief presented in Chapter 8, in which the police officer improperly fingerprinted a young offender). Experienced Crown attorneys are usually good judges of what the local courts will or will not accept. In some circumstances, the Crown will drop the immediate charges but will ask the police to lay them again after the proper procedures are followed.

PROFESSIONAL CONDUCT.

It is sometimes difficult for new officers to understand that different laws and rules of professional conduct govern Crown and defence counsels. They are lawyers, governed by professional codes of conduct as established by the law societies for the province in which they are licensed and practise. The primary role of defence counsel is to follow their client's instructions. Thus, many counsel believe that questioning every element of evidence and pursuing every technical defence open to them is their ethical obligation—even if they know that their client has done the deed. Their job is not to second-guess what might be in the "best interests" of their client, their client's parents, or society. Crown counsel, on the other hand, are restrained professionally from taking a "win at all costs" approach. Their role is to present the government's case to the court and allow the court to judge its merits. Crown counsel are also expected to use their professional judgment about what is in society's best interests.

It is this obligation—to consider the best interests of society—that will lead the Crown to drop charges if the offence is a minor one and the cost to the participants is high. For example, the Crown may choose not to proceed with the case if witnesses are required to travel long distances or will otherwise be severely inconvenienced.

PLEA BARGAINS.

The Crown will also use its judgment when agreeing to reduce charges if the offender agrees to enter a guilty plea to a lesser offence. The **plea bargain** is a trade-off, where both attorneys weigh the likelihood of conviction against the cost of conviction to the accused and the cost of prosecution to the community.

Hybrid, summary, or indictable offence?

Another duty of the Crown is to decide how to proceed with hybrid offences. Until otherwise elected, hybrid offences are treated as indictable offences in both adult and youth justice court proceedings. Many consequences of proceeding by indictment are the same for young persons as for adults. The potential sentence associated with an indictable offence is more severe than if the case is handled summarily. The main difference between adult court and youth court, however, is that the youth court handles indictable offences procedurally the same way as summary offences. Section 143 of the *YCJA* indicates that indictable offences and offences punishable on summary conviction "may be charged in the same indictment and tried jointly." In many situations, the police charge offenders with more than one offence. Because of the uniformity of procedure in youth court, listing both indictable and summary offences on the same information is possible.

Crown must provide disclosure.

Yet another obligation of the Crown is to provide **disclosure**. The basic rules of disclosure that apply to adult cases also apply to those of young persons. In general, the Crown must disclose its *entire* case—including evidence and the names of potential witnesses—to the young person's counsel before the trial. The defence, on the other hand, is under *no obligation* to disclose anything to the Crown. Because of the confidentiality rules surrounding young persons, the range of persons who may be privy to disclosure is generally more restricted in cases involving young persons than in cases of adults.

The Judge

Judges in youth justice court have the same general rights and responsibilities as judges in ordinary courts. It is the primary role of the judge to "manage" the proceedings in the courtroom. The judge is also responsible for the following:

1. Determining that proper procedure was followed in laying the charges, including that all requirements identified in section 146 on the admissibility of evidence were followed.
2. Determining that the young person is aware of, and has had opportunity to, obtain and consult with counsel.
3. Resolving disputes between lawyers over the admissibility of evidence.
4. Determining guilt or innocence.
5. Determining the advisability of an extrajudicial sentence.
6. Sentencing the offender after a finding of guilt.

Youth court judges also intervene in the trial process more frequently than a judge would in the case of an adult. The *YCJA* mandates part of this intervention. For example, it is the responsibility of the judge to ensure that young defendants are aware of the nature of the charges against them, even if they are represented by counsel. Youth court judges also have more latitude in intervening if they suspect the young person is suffering from a mental deficiency or a mental disorder.

Judges intervene most actively when they believe that the young person's counsel is not doing an adequate job of representing the client. In these situations, the judge may be more proactive in assessing the value of evidence and in questioning witnesses. Judges are loath, however, to become too involved in the "non-judicial" aspects of the trial, since doing so can place them in seriously conflicting roles. Furthermore, instances of too much judicial activism provide ready grounds for appeal. Fortunately, the availability of duty counsel, in most courts, and the provisions of the *YCJA* that allow a judge to direct that the young person be provided with legal counsel remove the need for much judicial intervention.

In larger centres, the youth justice court judge who presides over the bail hearing may *not* preside over the trial. Once a trial starts, however, the same judge who hears the trial must be the one who passes judgment. If this is not possible, then under section 131, the replacement judge may proceed with the sentencing if adjudication (has given a judgment or decision) has been made or "if no adjudication has been made, recommence the trial as if no evidence had been taken."

The Police

The arresting officer is usually present in court to act as a witness and to review the evidence with the Crown prosecutor. Officers are typically not present when the young person has negotiated a plea beforehand. Police officers are also able to provide other information to the Crown about the victim, the witnesses, and occasionally the accused. This extended role of the police is important because a broader range of evidence is admissible in youth justice court than in adult court. If the court continues or postpones the case, the Crown might also confer with officers over available dates.

PRE-TRIAL AND TRIAL MATTERS BEFORE THE COURT

The accused young person may make other appearances before a youth court judge that are not part of a full-fledged trial. In Chapter 8, the topic of bail was discussed as an example of one type of appearance. There are many other matters and stages of decision making to determine whether to proceed to trial that will be adjudicated before a youth court judge.

Statistics Canada collects data for the outcomes of matters heard in youth court. Notice in Table 9.1 that a guilty verdict was assessed in 18,704 cases or roughly 60 percent of the cases heard. Only a very small minority were acquitted: 1.4 percent. The most interesting item to note is that 41 percent of the cases (13,492) were stayed or withdrawn. Having a case stayed or withdrawn is not the same as *acquitted*—acquitted is a "not guilty" finding and the case cannot be reopened by the Crown. While generally a case that is *stayed* is seldom brought back before the court, the Crown does have one year within which it can reopen the matter if, for instance, new evidence has come to light, or a witness is now available. A matter that has been *withdrawn* by the Crown is typically done so where there were no reasonable and probable grounds to lay the

Table 9.1 Court, Youth Cases by Decision, by Province and Territory

| | 2014/2015 | | | | |
	Total all decisions	Guilty	Acquitted	Stayed or withdrawn	Other[1]
	Number of cases				
Total offences	**32,835**	**18,704**	**467**	**13,492**	**171**
Total Criminal Code	26,553	14,624	413	11,371	144
Criminal Code (without traffic)	26,012	14,190	398	11,280	143
Crimes against the person	9,743	5,405	269	4,004	64
Homicide	25	15	1	5	4
Attempted murder	22	10	0	11	1
Robbery	1,459	801	35	614	9
Sexual assault	630	375	43	205	7
Other sexual offences	655	397	36	217	5
Major assaults	2,074	1,279	47	738	9
Common assaults	2,743	1,376	41	1,314	12
Uttering threats	1,746	955	45	735	11
Criminal harassment	174	78	12	83	1
Other crimes against persons	215	119	9	82	5
Property crimes	10,735	5,408	80	5,206	41
Theft	3,586	1,620	24	1,924	18
Break and enter	2,537	1,597	18	915	7
Fraud	364	228	3	133	0
Mischief	2,096	975	13	1,100	8
Possession of stolen goods	1,856	821	18	1,010	7
Other property crimes	296	167	4	124	1
Administration of justice	3,520	2,214	15	1,274	17
Other *Criminal Code* offences	2,014	1,163	34	796	21
Criminal Code traffic	541	434	15	91	1
Impaired driving	242	200	11	30	1
Other *Criminal Code* traffic	299	234	4	61	0
Other federal statutes	6,282	4,080	54	2,121	27
Drug possession	1,761	676	21	1,064	0
Other drug offences	903	511	13	377	2
Youth Criminal Justice Act/ Young Offenders Act	3,450	2,765	19	641	25
Residual federal statutes	168	128	1	39	0

Note: A case that has more than one charge is represented by the charge with the "most serious offence" (MSO). In Newfoundland and Labrador, the terms "acquittal" and "dismissed" are used interchangeably, resulting in an under-count of the number of acquittals in that province.

1. Includes final decisions of found not criminally responsible and waived out of province or territory. This category also includes any order where a conviction was not recorded, the court's acceptance of a special plea, cases which raise Charter arguments and cases where the accused was found unfit to stand trial.

Source: Statistics Canada, CANSIM, table 252-0064, Catalogue no. 85-002-X

charge and/or there is no reasonable likelihood of conviction, thus putting an end to the matter. The "Other" category contains dispositions that included the accused was not criminally responsible, special pleas, and where the accused was found to be unfit to stand trial.

Stages and Phases in Court Proceedings

First Appearance

When an indictment (charge) is laid against a young person, he or she must appear before a youth court judge who reads the information or indictment. The judge will do a number of things: inform the young person of the right to counsel if the youth is appearing without a lawyer, make sure that the young person understands the charge against him or her, advise the young person of his or her rights, and advise the young person if the charge might be one for which an adult sentence can be imposed. If the judge is not satisfied that the young person sufficiently understands the issues and implications at hand, and where there is no defence counsel, the judge must enter a plea of not guilty and proceed to trial.

Entering a Plea

Most criminal matters in both youth and adult court are resolved without proceeding to trial. Where the accused elects to *plead guilty* without a trial the court can advance directly to the sentencing stage. One will also hear of the "plea deal," or "plea bargain," wherein the accused agrees to accept guilt for a lesser offence or lesser number of offences with the understood implication that this will also result in a lighter sentence. Where the individual is making this election, it is required that the judge conduct a *plea inquiry* to ensure that the person has made this election voluntarily, admits the elements of the offence, and that the court is not bound by any plea bargain or agreement that has been negotiated with the Crown (ultimately the judge always retains final authority in that regard, although the court is generally guided by the Crown's suggestions). In youth court, if the judge has any concern about whether the guilty plea does not match the facts, leaving the court concerned that the youth may not in fact be guilty, the court must proceed to trial. This type of "second guessing" is not done in the adult court.

Of course, the accused can also enter a *plea of not guilty* and proceed to trial. But even this option is not the final decision—there are many opportunities for the accused to change his or her mind and plead guilty or accept a plea bargain.

Preliminary Motions

Both defence counsel and the Crown can raise issues prior to trial for which they want the court's ruling. The preliminary motions and applications involve procedural matters and applications under the *Charter*. Many preliminary motions focus on requests for change of venue (to change the location of the courthouse for the trial), whether to join or separate the counts (charges), and similarly for multiple accused. There may also be motions by defence counsel for Crown disclosure.

Diversion Out of Court

Because the *YCJA* requires the police to consider warnings, cautions, and referrals to programs, it is rare that the young person will be in court for a first offence or a non-serious alleged offence. Similarly, the requirement that the Crown consider a Crown caution as an extrajudicial measure should keep less frequent and less serious alleged offenders out of court. This is precisely in keeping with the intent of the *YCJA*, which seeks to reserve court proceedings for the more serious cases.

Judge and Jury Election

Perhaps the main difference between youth justice court and ordinary court is that the youth court follows summary procedures whatever the offence. Being charged with a summary offence means that the youth will be tried in a provincial court, with a judge alone (no jury option), proceeding without an indictment; and, as a "lesser" offence, the accused is not fingerprinted or photographed.

There is an exception to which a young person may elect to have a jury trial: where the youth is accused of first- or second-degree murder, is at least 14 years of age at the time of the offence, and the Crown has elected to pursue an adult sentence. In such a case, the youth court judge must advise as follows:

> You have the option to elect to be tried by a youth justice court judge without a jury and without having had a preliminary inquiry; or you may elect to be tried by a judge without a jury; or you may elect to be tried by a court composed of a judge and jury. [*YCJA* 67(2)]

Preliminary Inquiry

For serious offences, the accused youth will also have to make a decision about whether to have a **preliminary inquiry**—an opportunity for the Crown to present its case so that a determination can be made whether there is sufficient evidence to proceed to trial. The preliminary inquiry is in essence a test of the Crown's evidence. Cases that lack sufficient evidence, and where it is unlikely that the prosecution will meet the high burden of proof beyond a reasonable doubt, do not proceed to trial [*YCJA* 67(7)]. Where the youth does not elect to have a preliminary inquiry, the court will set a date for trial.

Adjournments

As with ordinary court, the actual trial may follow one of several routes. Both defence and Crown counsel have the right to ask for an adjournment. Defence counsel are likely to ask for an adjournment if they are late coming to the case or if they need further disclosure from the Crown. Crown counsel usually asks for an adjournment if the case is serious and there are problems relating to witnesses. When the Crown makes such a request, most defence counsel will move for a dismissal of the charges. The decision of whether to proceed or not rests with the judge.

SIGNIFICANT CHANGE IN THE LAW IN 2012

Prior to the *YCJA* 2012 amendments, there was a category of offence called a **presumptive offence**. The Supreme Court ruled that this presumption was unconstitutional (*R. v. D.B.*, 2008 S.C.C. 25), and this concept was abolished in the 2012 amendments. Prior to this ruling and pursuant to s. 2(1) of the unamended *YCJA* a presumptive offence was:

> committed by a person who has attained at least the age of 14 years and the offence falls into one of the following categories: first-degree murder or second-degree murder; attempt to commit murder; manslaughter; aggravated sexual assault; or a serious violent offence for which an adult is liable to imprisonment for more than two years, after having had at least two judicial determinations at different proceedings that the young person has committed a serious violent offence.

The commission of one these serious crimes came with the presumption that an adult sentence would be imposed unless the Crown gave notice to seek a youth sentence or the youth could persuade the court that a youth sentence would hold the youth accountable.

How Does Youth Court Compare to Adult Court?

By and large, there are many similarities of youth court with the ordinary adult court. That being said, there are also important differences that are worth highlighting. Most of these differences reflect the intention to understand the particular vulnerabilities of being a young person and the intention of the *YCJA* to "protect" youth from being involved in a process they do not understand.

Youths Must Appear

Unlike adults, all young persons *must* appear in person before the courts, whatever the charge. For many offences, particularly the less serious ones, adults who are charged may choose not to appear personally in court if they are represented by a lawyer or paralegal.

Public Access

For the most part, the rules of procedure that govern cases tried in ordinary or adult court apply to the youth court. Formality in the youth justice courts varies more than one would find in the ordinary courts. One area where this is most apparent is in the "openness" of the court. We expect ordinary court proceedings to be public affairs and it is only under exceptional circumstances where judges will exclude spectators. Indeed, the *Canadian Charter of Rights and Freedoms* enshrines the *right to a public hearing*.

In the youth justice court, judges are freer to decide who should be allowed in the court and under what circumstances. They may allow only those immediately concerned with the offence or those who are legally entitled to participate in the trial in court. It is also common for judges to exclude witnesses from the courtroom when others are giving testimony. This is done to minimize witness "contamination," where one witness is influenced by the testimony of another. In other instances, some judges will exclude children (those under 12 years of age) from viewing the proceedings, even if they are siblings of the accused. For many judges, the protection of the young person's privacy is a prime consideration, but the protection of victims and witnesses is also to be considered.

Judges who hear cases of 16- and 17-year-olds, however, are often likely to retain public access to the proceedings. While the *YCJA* does not permit anyone to publish the names of any young person who may appear before the courts, many judges do not consider awareness of the case by individual members of the community to pose a serious problem.

Courtroom Decorum

Youth justice court judges also differ considerably with respect to the decorum they expect in their courtrooms. Some judges will not allow participants to appear before the bench in T-shirts, shorts, or sandals. Others are less concerned with dress and will only draw the line when offensive logos are displayed. Judges can enforce decorum in the courtroom through statutory references to contempt. They can exclude young persons who are disruptive in court under section 650 of the *Criminal Code of Canada*. Section 15 of the *YCJA* gives youth justice court "the same power, jurisdiction, and authority to deal with and impose punishment for contempt against the court as may be exercised by the superior court of criminal jurisdiction."

Understanding the Charges

Another difference between adult court and youth justice court proceedings occurs when the trial starts. After the charges are read, the judge must be satisfied that the young person understands the charges. If, in the judge's opinion, the young person does not understand the charge, then the *YCJA* obliges the judge to enter a *plea of not guilty* for the accused and a full trial must go on. Where the judge is satisfied that the young person does understand the charges, the judge may accept a plea of guilty or not guilty.

Not Guilty by Reason of Insanity

While it is rare, young offenders have the same option as adults in entering a plea of not guilty by reason of insanity. Section 34 of the *YCJA* also allows the youth court, "at any stage in the proceedings," to ask for a medical or psychological assessment of the young person. This assessment can be requested by the defence counsel or the Crown. It is the judge's decision as to whether it will be ordered. The court alone can also require it if

- "the court has reasonable grounds to believe that the young person may be suffering from a physical or mental illness or disorder, a psychological disorder, an emotional disturbance, a learning disability or a mental disability";

- the young person shows a pattern of repeat offending; or
- the charge is one involving serious violent offence.

Medical or Psychological Assessments

Section 34 assessments are more often called for at the *disposition stage* (i.e., the sentencing stage). Fortunately for the administration of justice, most young offenders enter into a plea bargain even when they enter an initial plea of not guilty. Even a small increase in the proportion of young offenders who appear before the courts entering a plea of not guilty would soon clog the court system. The high proportion of guilty pleas is perhaps a testimony to the efficiency and good judgment of most police officers and Crown prosecutors. It remains to be seen as to the number of cases that start in court and end with an extrajudicial measure.

Evidentiary Threshold

Where the accused enters a plea of not guilty, the court proceeds in a manner similar to that observed in adult cases. As in a criminal trial, the evidence must show guilt "beyond a reasonable doubt." The civil law criterion—the less onerous "on a balance of probabilities"—is not sufficient for conviction. A main difference one observes in the youth justice court is the higher percentage of young witnesses. This should come as no surprise, given the age of the defendants. The law has long recognized that the testimonies of youthful and, particularly, child witnesses need to be handled differently from those of adult witnesses. Consequently, special provisions exist in the *YCJA* for handling both young witnesses and their testimonies.

Child and Youth Witnesses

Witnesses serve the same function in the youth court as they do in the adult court. Because witnesses are more likely to be children or young persons, there are some special provisions relating to them. For example, under section 151 of the *YCJA*, the trial judge must instruct children (those under 12 years of age) "as to the duty of the witness to speak the truth and the consequences of failing to do so." They also give this instruction to witnesses who are young persons if the judge believes it is necessary. Failure to give these instructions to a child can form grounds for appeal.

As previously noted, the identity of young persons who are witnesses is subject to the standard ban on publication. One advantage of this ban is that it protects young witnesses from having their own records publicized.

SENTENCING

As with adults, the process of sentencing is separate from the process that determines guilt. Once the young offender is found guilty of the charge, the question becomes one of what the appropriate sentence should be. The range of available sentences is much broader in youth court than in adult court and includes extrajudicial sanctions and judicial sanctions, which extend from absolute discharge to custodial requirements.

Purpose and Principles of Sentencing

Under section 38 of the *YCJA*, the purpose of youth sentences is to hold young persons accountable through just sanctions that ensure meaningful consequences for them and promote their rehabilitation and reintegration into society, thereby contributing to the long-term protection of the public.

Sentencing principles emphasize that a youth sentence must:

- not be more severe than what an adult would receive for the same offence;
- be similar to youth sentences in similar cases;
- be proportionate to the seriousness of the offence and the degree of responsibility of the young person; and
- within the limits of a proportionate response, (a) be the least restrictive alternative, (b) be the sentencing option that is most likely to rehabilitate and reintegrate the young person, and (c) promote in the young person a sense of responsibility and an acknowledgement of the harm done by the offence.

Principle of Proportionality

This is a basic principle wherein less serious offences should result in less severe consequences, and more serious offences should result in more severe consequences.

Under the *YCJA*, the **principle of proportionality** also applies to rehabilitative measures. Rehabilitative measures are often imposed in order to address the underlying problems that appear to have caused the young person to commit an offence. The *YCJA* does not permit longer or more harsh sentences, even if they are for the purpose of rehabilitation. For example, a young person who has committed a relatively minor offence but has serious psychological needs that seem to have contributed to the behaviour should receive a sentence that reflects the seriousness of the offence and not the seriousness of the psychological needs.

Principles of Deterrence and Denunciation

In 2002, the *YCJA* did not articulate that **specific deterrence** (i.e., to deter the specific youth from committing offences) or **general deterrence** (i.e., deter others from committing offences) were objectives of sentencing. Yet, deterrence has been a fundamental objective of adult sentencing in the *Criminal Code*. The *YCJA* also did not provide for the adult sentencing objective of denunciation (i.e., public condemnation).

In 2012, Parliament amended the *YCJA* to permit a youth sentence to include the objectives of denunciation and specific deterrence, with the provisos that a sentence must be a proportionate response or is consistent with the purpose of sentencing and the mandatory sentencing principles mentioned above, such as choosing a sentence that is most likely to rehabilitate the young person.

Other Principles

Additional principles to be considered:

1. Sentences should be similar in a "region" (the *YCJA* does not define region).
2. All available sanctions, other than custody, should be considered for all young persons, with particular attention to the circumstances of Indigenous young persons.
3. The sentence must be the "least restrictive" that is capable of achieving the purpose outlined above.
4. The sentence must be the "one" that is "most likely" to rehabilitate and reintegrate the young person.
5. The sentence must promote a sense of "responsibility" and an "acknowledgement" of harm done to the victims and the community.
6. The sentence must consider the degree of participation in the commission of the offence.
7. The sentence must consider the harm done to the victims and whether it was intentional or reasonably foreseeable.
8. The sentence must consider whether reparations have been made to the victim or the community.
9. The sentence must consider the time spent in detention.
10. The sentence must consider the previous findings of guilt.
11. The sentence must consider any other aggravating or mitigating circumstances.

Information Gathering: Determining What Is Best for the Youth

Before handing down a sentence, the judge may request additional information that could help the court to ensure that the twin objectives of the young offender system are met: (1) the protection of the community, and (2) the needs of the young person in conflict with the law. The community needs protection from future victimization, and the young person's needs are met when an intervention is provided that reduces the likelihood of coming into further conflict with the law. Where judicial sentences are involved, the court may adjourn its decision while waiting for a pre-sentence report or a pre-sentence assessment to be prepared.

The Pre-sentence Report

Under subsection 39(6) of the *YCJA*, the court must ask that a **pre-sentence report** be prepared during the sentencing process if the judge is contemplating a custodial disposition. The youth justice court may request a pre-sentence report in other circumstances when the court believes it is advisable. Practically, this has come to mean that the court will order a pre-sentence report if the young person's counsel insists on one. Defence counsel are generally of the opinion that an outlining of the youth's problems in a pre-sentence report can moderate the sentences that the court might impose. Furthermore, they believe these reports can result in a disposition that is more likely to be helpful to the young person.

Pre-sentence reports are usually prepared and written by probation officers or "youth workers." The report is a narrative of the young person's involvement with the

law, the family history as far as the probation officer knows it, and the person's progress while on probation. It can be presented to the court either in writing or, if defence
counsel provides a waiver, orally. Copies are made available to the judge, the young
person, his or her counsel, the prosecutor, and the young person's parents. Once sentenced, a copy of the pre-sentence report will be forwarded to the custodial facility
along with the young offender.

Subsection 40(2) details what needs to be included in the report:

- Results of interviews with the young person, the young person's parents and,
  where possible, members of the young person's extended family
- Results of interviews with the victim, where possible
- Information on the young person's age, maturity, character, attitude, and will-
  ingness to make amends
- Information on the relationship between the offender and the offender's fami-
  ly, including how much control the parents might have over the young person
- Any plans the young person might have to get his or her life back on track
- Any history of offending
- A history of any extrajudicial sanctions and their outcome
- A history of the young person's school attendance and performance

Pre-sentence Assessments

In some situations, there is concern that the young person may be suffering from disturbances that are severe enough for the court to consider them when making a disposition. Section 34 of the *YCJA* indicates the conditions under which the court can order
a **pre-sentence assessment** of the medical, psychological, or psychiatric condition of
the young person.

The purpose of a section 34 assessment under the *YCJA* is to make available to
the youth justice court, including Crown and defence counsel, recommendations
about sentences. Those recommendations are based on a clinical understanding of the
emotional, cognitive, and social functioning of the young person who has come into
conflict with the law, along with the needs of that person, the individual and social
risks posed, and the need for intervention.

A full court-ordered assessment typically consists of four stages:

1. *Information gathering* consists of a clinical case history and a battery of cognitive, personality, and diagnostic tests that may be administered over a period
   of days or weeks. Interviews are also conducted with parents and others who
   may have information on the youth's functioning.
2. *Interpreting* the various dimensions of assessment (e.g., cognitive functioning,
   personality, emotional functioning, social functioning, and risk of recidivism).
3. *Integration* of the information.
4. *Recommending* options that provide direction and are reasonable.

The court orders section 34 assessments in only a minority of cases, probably less than 5 percent. There seems to be considerable variation from area to area, and from judge to judge, about how extensively they are used. Avison and Whitehead (1997) and Whitehead and Avison (1998) examined their use in London, Ontario, and found that there was a high level of satisfaction with the assessments and the purpose they serve. Judges as well as Crown and defence counsel found them useful in reaching agreement on what kind of sentence would be appropriate. Defence counsel also found them helpful in dealing with the young person's parents on the question of what they should request.

None of the parties saw the assessments as a means of "getting the kid a free ride." Indeed, it was widely acknowledged that a defence counsel who might be looking for a non-custodial sentence would be least likely to initiate such a request because if a custodial sentence were recommended, it would carry much weight.

According to Whitehead and Avison (1998), such assessments have two major advantages: 1) They increase the likelihood of reaching agreement on what an appropriate sentence should be. The parties express confidence that they are meeting the needs of the young person while they protect the community. 2) Section 34 assessments make it possible to avoid custodial sentences in some cases and, in other cases, to have shorter custodial periods than would have been likely without an assessment. The clinical judgments of psychologists and, sometimes, but less often, psychiatrists about the potential for violence or recidivism make a significant difference. In addition, the recommendations made by these professionals for courses of intervention that involve a series of steps (some custodial, some non-custodial, and some therapeutic) allow for a more comprehensive approach to addressing the needs of the young person.

Youth Justice Committees and Conferences
Prior to the *YCJA*, the use of **conferences** was increasing in many parts of Canada in order to assist in the making of decisions regarding young persons who were involved in the youth justice system. They are now officially sanctioned pursuant to s. 19 [*YCJA*]: A youth court judge as well as other officers of the court such as a police officer, Crown counsel, justice of the peace, or youth worker may request that a conference for the purpose of decision making be held. The mandate of these conferences is to give advice on appropriate extrajudicial measures, conditions for judicial interim release, sentences, a review of sentences, and reintegration plans.

Conferences can take the form of family group conferencing, youth justice committees, community accountability panels, sentencing circles, and inter-agency case conferences. Conferences provide an opportunity for a wide range of perspectives on a case, more creative solutions, better coordination of services, and increased involvement of the victim and other community members in the youth justice system.

A conference can be composed of a variety of people, depending on the situation. It can include the parents of the young person, the victim, others who are familiar with the young person and his or her neighbourhood, and community agencies or professionals with a particular expertise that is needed for a decision. A conference can be a restorative mechanism that is focused on developing proposals for repairing the harm done to the victim of the young person's offence. It can also be a professional case conference in which professionals discuss how the young person's needs can best be met and how services in the community can be coordinated to assist the young person.

It is important to note that a conference under the *YCJA* is not an authorized decision-making body—it only provides advice or recommendations to a decision maker, such as a judge or a prosecutor. The recommendations can be accepted by the decision maker but only if they are consistent with the *YCJA*.

YOUTH SENTENCING OPTIONS

After duly hearing the evidence and reaching a decision, or accepting a guilty plea, and after having requested and obtained any pre-sentence reports, assessments, and recommendations from a conference committee, the judge will arrive at the final decision as to the sentence that will be imposed on the young offender. There are three broad types of sanctions available to the youth justice court under s. 42 of the *Youth Criminal Justice Act*:

1. In-court sanctions
2. Community-based sanctions
3. Custody and supervision

- Reprimand
- Absolute discharge
- Conditional discharge   } In-court sanctions
- Fine, not exceeding $1,000
- Restitution order for specific (not general) damages

- Prohibition or seizure order
- Community or personal service order   } Community-based sanctions
- Probation
- Intensive support and supervision

- Non-residential programs
- Custody and supervision   } Custody and supervision
- Intensive rehabilitative custody and supervision

In-court Sanctions

Reprimand
A **reprimand** is a statement by the youth justice court judge that indicates to the

young person that the law has been violated. The statement may indicate the severity with which it could be dealt and the reasons why, on this occasion and in these circumstances, the judge considers that the young person should have learned the appropriate lesson.

Absolute Discharge

An **absolute discharge** is just what it implies. The court releases a young person with no obligations or restrictions on their freedom. As Platt (1991: 142) points out, however, an absolute discharge in the youth justice court does not have the same impact as one given in an ordinary court. Platt points out that "it is incorrect to request that an absolute discharge be granted to a young person so that he or she can avoid a criminal record." In fact, an absolute discharge carries the same implications for the retention of a youth justice court record as any other sentence. Consequently, if a young person reappears in court on another charge, the fact that he or she has been given an absolute discharge is admissible at the sentencing stage. The judge must also be assured that this disposition is "in the best interests of the young person and not contrary to the public interest." Absolute discharges cannot be combined with any other disposition.

Police officers who believe a young offender is worthy of this disposition can improve the young offender's chances of obtaining an absolute discharge. To do so, they must make their views known to the Crown or give evidence in support of the defendant. Experienced defence counsel can often improve their client's chances of obtaining a discharge by involving the young person in giving an apology to the victim, paying for damages, and getting involved in some positive community activity.

Conditional Discharge

A **conditional discharge** allows for the young person "to be discharged on any conditions as the court considers appropriate." A typical condition imposed by the court would be that the offender remain at work or return to school and be supervised. Once the young person fulfills the conditions imposed, the sentence result in an absolute discharge.

Fine

A **fine** is a financial penalty. The young person can be fined an amount no larger than would be required of an adult for a similar offence. The maximum fine under the *YCJA* is $1,000 [*YCJA* 42(2)(d)], and the mandatory minimum fines stated in the *Criminal Code of Canada* do not apply to young offenders. In fining the defendant, the judge must consider the young person's ability to pay the fine. The court will not use this option if the young person has no savings and no source of income (such as a part-time job). Often, small fines are used with another disposition. For more significant fines, youth justice court judges will usually allow the young offender to make periodic payments. Some jurisdictions also allow offenders to work off fines by becoming involved in some form of community service. Youths who do not meet their fine obligations must explain the situation to the court. Failure to appear can result in an arrest warrant being issued, and judges can always substitute a more severe sentence. Young persons who default on a fine, however, cannot be incarcerated.

Restitution and Compensation

The courts can order the young person to make restitution or pay compensation for any property taken or damaged during the commission of the offence. **Restitution** involves returning any property that may have been taken to its rightful owner. **Compensation** usually involves a monetary payment when the offender cannot make restitution or it is inappropriate in the circumstances. It can also involve "compensation in kind" by way of personal service.

Subsections 54(4) and 54(6) indicate, however, that the person to be compensated needs to be consulted and must agree to the compensation. One difference between compensation orders for young persons and adults is that compensation must be for specific damage and not general damages [*YCJA* 42(2)(e)]. Otherwise, the same basic conditions that apply to fines apply to compensation orders. Thus, the judge must consider the offender's ability to pay. As with fines, restitution and compensation orders are often used with other sentences, such as probation.

Prohibition

Prohibition means that the youth justice court can also prohibit or forbid a young person from owning something that they could otherwise legally possess, if it were not that they had been involved in the commission of the offence. For example, the court may disallow a young person from having any of the following in his or her possession: firearm, crossbow, prohibited weapon, restricted weapon, prohibited device, ammunition, or explosive substance. Property may also be forfeited and seized. A young computer hacker may find that he is no longer in possession of his personal computer. The youth court is not bound by mandatory minimums attached to some prohibitions identified in the *Criminal Code of Canada*. The court is obliged, however, to provide a maximum time up to a period of two years after the completion of a custodial portion of a sentence or, if the young person is not subject to custody, after the time the young person is found guilty of the offence. [*YCJA* 51(4)].

Community-based Sanctions

Community Service Orders

Community service orders (CSO) are used increasingly in the youth justice system. A judge may require the young person to perform up to 240 hours of community service. The community service cannot be extended beyond one year. Furthermore, the judge must determine that the young offender "is a suitable candidate for such an order" and "the order does not interfere with the normal hours of work or education of the young person" [*YCJA* 54(7)(b)].

Community service orders are a means for young offenders to "pay off" property damage that resulted from acts of vandalism. Judges generally use CSOs to make young offenders more aware of the consequences of their actions and to make them "give something back" to their communities. Thus, the court may require a young person who has victimized an elderly person to perform work around a retirement home.

Occasionally, the judge may impose a *personal service order* where the offender must work directly for the victim. This is most often used when the victim is a corporate entity, such as a store in which the offender shoplifted, or a car dealer where the young offender was caught slashing tires. The same time limits for a CSO apply in these situations.

Most communities have a *community service coordinator* who works out of a local probation office. Community service is generally sponsored by a non-profit or service organization, such as a youth club, Native centre, or service club. Often, the John Howard Society plays a significant role in coordinating and supervising young people serving CSOs. Young persons who fail to abide by a CSO may be charged with the offence of failure to comply. This is a summary offence, and the young person is liable to a maximum sentence of six months in open custody.

Probation Order

The youth court may impose a **probation order** on the young person *for a period not exceeding two years for most offences.* This is extended to three years where the sentence for an adult would be life sentence. If the young person commits another offence while on probation, the court can extend the period of probation. Young persons may serve probation orders either *continuously or intermittently,* and they generally include subsidiary conditions. In Ontario, a professional probation officer usually supervises probation orders.

Probation conditions.

Subsection 55(1) of the *YCJA* indicates the conditions that must appear on the probation order. These are that the young person must "keep the peace and be of good behaviour" and must "appear before the youth justice court when required to do so." Subsection 55(2) specifies conditions that the judge may impose on the order.

These possibilities include the provisions that the young person

- is bound by the probation order and must report to a designated probation officer, must notify the court or probation officer of any change in address, employment, or education status,
- must remain in a specific locality or jurisdiction,
- must try to obtain and maintain employment,
- must attend school or a suitable training program,
- must reside with a parent or other designated adult who is willing to take responsibility for the young person,
- must reside at a specific location, and
- must comply with any other reasonable conditions set out by the court.

The courts tailor probation orders to suit the particular circumstances of the offender. They may require offenders from homes with little supervision to report to their probation officer regularly. In extreme situations, the courts may ask the young person to reside in a specific home. In more stable circumstances, the order may not require reporting beyond the initial contact. Some probation officers are excellent at finding an effective "program" for a troubled young offender. Others, for workload reasons and otherwise, do little more than see the young person biweekly for a 20-minute chat.

The schooling provisions may pose particular problems for a community. Many young offenders are "problem cases" for school officials and have long histories of suspensions and expulsions. Many judges correctly perceive the young person's need for schooling, but most schools do not have adequate facilities for handling tough cases. Often, calls from school officials to the police involve problems with young people who are already on probation. For many young offenders on probation, there is constant conflict with their probation officer, school officials, and the police. Ultimately, many of the worse cases report back to court, where the only viable alternative becomes custody.

Most young offenders complete their probation orders successfully. Some clearly do not. Where the young person consistently breaks a probation order or has no intention of complying with it, the probation officer may charge the young person with a "failure to comply with a court order." A breach of probation is the only offence relating to noncompliance with a sentence that can lead to a sentence of secure custody.

Intensive Support and Supervision Program (ISSP)

An **Intensive Support and Supervision Program (ISSP)** is a clinically focused, community-based program for young offenders. This sentencing option is used if the Provincial Director has determined that an alternative to custody is needed for young persons who are found guilty of a criminal offence and who are diagnosed with a mental health disorder(s) or developmental delay, or both (dual diagnosis). Such programs are to address the needs of the young person and contribute to rehabilitation and reintegration without placing society at risk.

Non-residential Program

The judge's order may be for the young person to attend a non-residential program, if the Provincial Director has determined that a program to enforce the order is available, for a maximum of 240 hours over a period of not more than six months.

The *YCJA* does not specify the specific conditions that "intensive support" or "non-residential" programs must have. As with all else in the *YCJA*, however, the expectation is that the programs will assist young persons in areas of their life where they have needs. Some such programs may well focus on life skills, others on anger management, and still others on rehabilitation from alcohol or drug abuse. The *YCJA* leaves it to individual communities to put in place the programs that may be of the greatest assistance to young persons and to Provincial Directors and judges to determine their appropriateness in given circumstances.

Table 9.2 Court, Youth Cases by Types of Sentence, by Province and Territory

	2014/2015			
	Intensive support and supervision	Probation[1]	Attendance at non-residential program	Fine
	Number			
Total offences	**251**	**10,660**	**149**	**520**
Total Criminal Code	**209**	8,938	106	313
Criminal Code (without traffic)	**206**	8,738	106	197
Crimes against the person	**107**	3,564	39	19
Homicide	**0**	3	0	0
Attempted murder	**0**	5	0	0
Robbery	**41**	541	5	0
Sexual assault	**3**	269	2	2
Other sexual offences	**6**	292	1	0
Major assaults	**32**	871	15	4
Common assaults	**9**	779	8	9
Uttering threats	**12**	652	7	2
Criminal harassment	**1**	61	0	1
Other crimes against persons	**3**	91	1	1
Property crimes	**53**	3,453	40	82
Theft	**13**	894	22	41
Break and enter	**18**	1,185	8	9
Fraud	**2**	159	3	3
Mischief	**5**	564	3	17
Possession of stolen goods	**11**	536	3	12
Other property crimes	**4**	115	1	0
Administration of justice	**32**	981	20	80
Other Criminal Code offences	**14**	740	7	16
Criminal Code traffic	**3**	200	0	116
Impaired driving	**0**	58	0	99
Other Criminal Code traffic	**3**	142	0	17
Other federal statutes	**42**	1,722	43	207
Drug possession	**1**	323	4	38
Other drug offences	**8**	398	4	5
Youth Criminal Justice Act/ Young Offenders Act	**33**	981	35	158
Residual federal statutes	**0**	20	0	6

Notes: A case that has more than one charge is represented by the charge with the "most serious offence" (MSO). Cases can have more than one sentence. Therefore, sanctions are not mutually exclusive and will not add to 100%.

1. Since 2004/2005 for the Northwest Territories, the number of custody orders have been under-reported and the number of probation orders have been overreported by unknown amounts due to clerical procedures. The majority of custody orders were captured as probation.

Source: Statistics Canada, CANSIM, table 252-0067, Catalogue no. 85-002-X.

Statistics on Sentencing

Statistics Canada collects data on the types of sentences that are meted out in youth court. As Table 9.2 outlines, in 2014/2015 one can look at the type of offence and the sentence that was imposed.

IN THE NEWS

Judge Gets Creative and Issues an Unusual Sentence

A 12-year-old boy from Alberta pleaded guilty to assault with a weapon and possession of a weapon after he was caught brandishing a knife while threatening another youth and trying to steal money.

The youth's sentence ... to practice basketball.

During the court proceedings the judge canvassed the circumstances of the boy's under-privileged life. The boy talked about his desire to play basketball, even though he doesn't play on a team or even own a basketball.

The judge noted that the youth did not have a criminal record and had spent seven days in custody. The youth was placed on probation for 12 months and ordered to practice dribbling and shooting a basketball for at least five hours a week. The judge instructed the court sheriff to provide a ball to the boy before he was released.

Source: Delon Shurtz, "Alberta boy, 12, who chased youth with knife sentenced to practice basketball." *The Star*, September 15, 2016. www.thestar.com/news/canada/2016/09/15/judge-sentences-alberta-boy-12-to-basketball-practice.html

Was this sentence in line with the stated objectives of the *Youth Criminal Justice Act*?

Custody and Supervision

Judges may also sentence young persons to periods of **custody and supervision**. Section 39 stipulates that a young person shall not receive a custodial sentence as a youth sentence, unless one or more of the following apply:

    (a)   committed a violent offence;

    (b)   has failed to comply with non-custodial sentences;

(c)   has committed an indictable offence for which an adult would be liable to imprisonment for a term of more than two years and has a history that indicates a pattern of either extrajudicial sanctions or of findings of guilt or of both under this Act; or

(d)   in exceptional cases where the young person has committed an indictable offence, the aggravating circumstances of the offence are such that the imposition of a non-custodial sentence would be inconsistent with the purpose and principles set out in section 38.

It needs to be emphasized that we are still dealing with youth sentences, *not* adult sentences for which young persons may qualify. Under the *YCJA*, orders are for custody and supervision means that it is for a period of *incarceration* plus a period of *supervision*. The supervision period is to be one-half as long as the custody period. The idea is that the supervision part of the sentence will assist in the young person's rehabilitation and reintegration into society.

The length of these custody and supervision orders varies by the severity of the offence. The total of the *periods is not to exceed two years*, unless the offence is a serious, violent one.

Serious Violent Offence
A **serious violent offence** means an offence under the *Criminal Code*:

(a)   first-degree murder or second-degree murder (section 231 or 235)

(b)   attempt to commit murder (section 239);

(c)   manslaughter (section 232, 234, or 236); or

(d)   aggravated sexual assault (section 273).

A **violent offence** means

(a)   an offence committed by a young person that includes as an element the causing of bodily harm;

(b)   an attempt or a threat to commit an offence referred to in paragraph (a); or

(c)   an offence in the commission of which a young person endangers the life or safety of another person by creating a substantial likelihood of causing bodily harm. (*infraction with violence*)

A **serious offence** means an indictable offence under an Act of Parliament for which the maximum punishment is imprisonment for five years or more.

Mental Illness and Psychological Disorders
If a youth suffers from mental illness or psychological disorder, the youth justice court may make an order for **intensive rehabilitative custody and supervision** [*YCJA* 42(7)].

Such orders may only be made when the following conditions are met:

A youth justice court may make an intensive rehabilitative custody and supervision order under paragraph 42(2)(r) in respect of a young person only if

(a) either
   (i) the young person has been found guilty of a serious violent offence, or
   (ii) the young person has been found guilty of an offence, in the commission of which the young person caused or attempted to cause serious bodily harm and for which an adult is liable to imprisonment for a term of more than two years, and the young person had previously been found guilty at least twice of such an offence;

(b) the young person is suffering from a mental illness or disorder, a psychological disorder or an emotional disturbance;

(c) a plan of treatment and intensive supervision has been developed for the young person, and there are reasonable grounds to believe that the plan might reduce the risk of the young person repeating the offence or committing a serious violent offence; and

(d) the provincial director has determined that an intensive rehabilitative custody and supervision program is available and that the young person's participation in the program is appropriate.

Deferred Custody and Supervision Order (DCSO)

Carrington et al. (2011: 300) have noted that this important and innovative non-custodial sanction is rarely researched or written about, even though the **deferred custody and supervision order (DCSO)** can "reduce the use of custody yet also ... generate public and professional criticism when it is imposed for a serious crime of violence." The *YCJA* at subsection 42(2)(p) permits a DCSO no longer than six months. In addition, subsection 42(5) adds to additional restrictions: That the young person is found guilty of an offence that is *not* a serious violent offence; and the order is consistent with the purpose and principles as set out in section 38 and the custody restrictions of section 39. Criticism of this section (and the adult counterpart known as the Conditional Sentence of Imprisonment) has focused on whether these should not be available for serious crimes of violence (Carrington et al., 2011: 303). The legislature responded to these criticisms by eliminating discretion in adult court for "serious personal injury" and terrorism offences. A similar approach has been adopted in the *YCJA*—the DCSO may *not* be used for a "serious violent offence." According to Carrington et al., this has produced an incongruent outcome: A young offender who commits a violent offence may not be given a DCSO but can still be given a lesser sanction such as an extrajudicial measure or any other non-custodial sanctions that are allowed in youth court. See the following Case Brief to see how the courts have been interpreting this issue.

CASE BRIEF

When Is a Deferred Custody and Supervision Order Appropriate?

The legislative intent was to remove the DCSO as a sentencing option for youths who commit serious violent offences. But the legislation does not stipulate that a judge is barred from imposing a lesser sentence. That is where the courts have come into play.

In *R. v. K. (P.K.),* the Alberta Court of Appeal in a 2006 decision was asked to review the decision of a provincial court that had imposed a probationary sentence on a youth who had committed a brutal and unprovoked assault after concluding that a DCSO was not permissible by law. This struck the Alberta appeal court as absurd—that the message was that since you cannot offer a greater sentence, that you impose a lesser sentence. Justice Cote concluded that the legislative presumption should be that one imposes a heavier sentence, not a lighter one, and clear reasons should be provided if this is not followed. The Court of Appeal set aside the probation order and imposed an 11-month prison term.

The Ontario Court of Appeal faced a similar situation in *R. v. K.L.* [2009 ONCA 602]. A 15-year-old was found guilty of assault causing bodily harm. K.L. had been the ringleader in organizing a group of other youths who deliberately planned an attack that injured an 18-year-old when they knocked him unconscious and he was severely beaten. This offence is deemed to be a serious violent offence. Since a DCSO was prohibited, the provincial court ordered two years of probation. The Crown appealed. The Court of Appeal granted the Crown's appeal and overturned the sentence on the grounds that the probationary sentence did not address the issue of the *proportionality principle*—"that the punishment should fit the crime." The sentence was set aside and the youth was sentenced to six months' custody and supervision, and six months' probation.

From the above discussion, it can be seen that the number of sentencing options available under the *YCJA* to deal with the most serious cases has increased in comparison with the *Young Offenders Act*. Again, this is in keeping with the objective of the *YCJA* to focus court (i.e., judicial) responses on the most serious cases and to use extrajudicial measures for the rest.

The *YCJA* also makes provision for young persons to receive "adult sentences."

Adult Sentences

An important feature of the *YCJA* is that it identifies a category of offences for which the Crown may make an application to the youth justice court of its intention to seek an adult sentence [*YCJA* 64(1)]. A young person may only be subject to an adult sentence if the young person is found guilty of an offence that is one of a pattern of repeated serious violent offences or of an offence for which an adult would receive over two years in jail, the young person is 14 years or older, and the Crown has rebutted the presumption of diminished moral blameworthiness or culpability of the young person. An adult sentence can only be sought and ordered when a young person has been found guilty of one of the serious violent offences, such as:

- first or second degree murder
- attempt to commit murder
- manslaughter
- aggravated sexual assault

If the Crown intends to seek an adult sentence, the Crown must give notice to the young person and to the youth justice court prior to the young person entering a plea [*YCJA* 64(2)].

IN THE NEWS

Youth Receives Adult Sentence for His Mother's Murder

His maternal grandmother begged Justice Alex Sosna for an adult sentence so that she and her family could feel safe.

His paternal grandmother begged the judge for a youth sentence that would give the young man convicted of killing his mother another chance.

In the end, Cody Barnoski, 17, received an adult sentence for his first-degree murder conviction. Sosna also lifted the ban on the publication of Barnoski's name, since "the seriousness of this offense and the public interest in this matter supersede the privacy interests of the young person."

The adult sentence is life with no possibility of parole for seven years, served in a secure youth facility. Once released, he will remain under parole supervision for life. Barnoski is also subject to a DNA order and a life-time weapons prohibition.

One deciding factor in his sentencing is the fact that, until Wednesday, Barnoski had expressed no remorse …"In imposing the life sentence, I have considered the seriousness of the offence and Cody's pivotal role in the planning and deliberate murder of his mother, which he personally carried out."…

The boy grew up in an atmosphere of domestic violence and substance abuse, interspersed with days at a time left in the care of relatives while his parents were out socializing. He [defence counsel] related reports of years of truancy, bullying and disruptive behaviour, perhaps at least partly attributable to the fact that his father left when he was seven and his mother moved around so much that he attended nine different schools. He also reported numerous pleas made by school and social-service authorities to his mother for interventions and counselling—recommendations she never followed up.

At the trial, court heard that Barnoski and his mother grew apart as he grew up—and as she began pursuing her own educational, employment and romantic opportunities. By the time he was 14, he had begun abusing marijuana and tensions were fatally high.

The grave that would eventually hide Michelle Barnoski's body was dug some days in advance of her murder, which was apparently precipitated by her son's fear that they would be moving again, away from a girlfriend to whom he was attached.

Michelle Barnoski suffered a broken hand and forearm before she was shot in the nape of the neck in 2008. She was still alive but immobilized when seven more bullets hit her head and face.

The crime scene was cleaned up, her car hidden, the evidence disposed of, alibis concocted and the mother reported missing. Her body was eventually found buried in the back yard ...

"I strongly urge the authorities to implement all necessary and available counselling, not only for Cody Barnoski's rehabilitation but also to provide the protection that the community requires," the judge urged.... "Mr. Barnoski, I can only wish you good luck," Mr. Justice Sosna said.

Source: C. Nasmith, "Youth gets adult sentence for mom's murder." *London Free Press*, September 30, 2010. Available at http://www.torontosun.com/news/canada/2010/09/30/15537801.html

If the young person does not oppose the application by the Crown, an adult sentence shall be imposed [*YCJA* 64(5)].

If the Crown gives notice that an adult sentence will not be sought, the court shall order that the young person is not liable to an adult sentence and order a ban on publication.

The decision as to the merits of the application for a youth sentence or for an adult sentence is made at a **sentencing hearing**. This hearing takes place after the issue of guilt has been decided. At the sentencing hearing, the Crown, the defence, and the parents of the young person are given an opportunity to be heard [*YCJA* 71].

In making its decision on applications, the youth justice court must consider the following:

1. The seriousness and circumstances of the offence.
2. The age, maturity, character, background, and previous record of the young person.
3. Other factors the court considers relevant.

4. Whether a youth sentence is of sufficient length to hold the young person accountable for the offending behaviour.

5. A pre-sentence report.

The **onus**, or burden of proof, is on the Crown. When the court makes a decision, it "shall state the reasons for the decision." When a young person who is subject to an adult sentence is sentenced to imprisonment, that incarceration must be in a youth custody facility separate from adults or in a provincial correctional facility for adults or a penitentiary [*YCJA* 76(1)]. If the young person is under the age of 18 years, however, the placement should be in a youth custody facility [*YCJA* 76(2)(a)], and if the person is aged 18 years or over, in a provincial correctional facility [*YCJA* 76(2)(b)]. Usually, no young person would remain in a youth facility after attaining the age of 20 years [*YCJA* 76(9)].

Adult sentences, while provided for in the *YCJA*, are meant to be used in exceptional cases, where it is clearly demonstrated that a youth sentence is not long enough to hold the youth accountable. When an adult sentence is considered necessary it should still be lighter than the average sentence imposed on adults in order to reflect the greater dependence and reduced maturity of youth.

TEST YOUR KNOWLEDGE

Definitions

Define the following terms:

1. Plea bargain

_____

_____

_____

2. Disclosure

_____

_____

_____

3. Preliminary inquiry

_____

_____

_____

4. Presumptive offence

_____

_____

_____

5. Principle of proportionality

_____

_____

_____

6. Pre-sentence report

_____

_____

_____

7. Pre-sentence assessment

_____

_____

_____

8. Conference

_____

_____

_____

9. Reprimand

_____

_____

_____

10. Absolute discharge

_____

_____

_____

11. Conditional discharge

_____

_____

_____

12. Fine

_____

_____

_____

13. Restitution

_____

_____

_____

14. Compensation

_____

_____

_____

15. Prohibition

_____

_____

_____

16. Community service order (CSO)

_____

_____

_____

17. Probation order

_____

_____

_____

18. Intensive support and supervision program (ISSP)

_____

_____

_____

19. Custody and supervision

_____

_____

_____

20. Serious violent offence

_____

_____

_____

21. Intensive rehabilitative custody and supervision

_____

_____

_____

22. Deferred custody and supervision order (DCSO)

_____

_____

_____

23. Adult sentence

_____

_____

_____

24. Sentence hearing

_____

_____

_____

25. Onus

_____

_____

_____

True/False

1. T F In adult court, it is professionals who present the two sides of the case, but in youth justice court, there are no professionals.

2. T F When a parent or another responsible adult is present, it is not necessary to remind a young person of right to counsel; having said it once is enough.

3. T F Young persons are eligible to apply for legal aid.

4. T F A young person who is brought into the police station for a breathalyzer test has a right to consult counsel before the test can be given.

5. T F When the case of a young person gets to court, there is no longer a role for the police.

6. T F It is for any of the most serious offences that a young person can elect to have trial by jury in youth court.

7. T F Trial by jury is a right of all Canadians as long as the charge against them involves a violation of the *Criminal Code of Canada*.

8. T F Typically, the youth justice court is held in private without any member of the public allowed to be present.

9. T F Pre-sentence reports are usually prepared by the police officer who made the arrest.

10. T   F   Once a young person receives an absolute discharge, that discharge cannot be admitted again in court.

11. T   F   The purpose of a youth sentence is to appropriately punish the young person for the harm done.

12. T   F   A youth justice court judge may require a young person to perform up to 240 hours of community service.

13. T   F   Community service orders are reserved for those 16 and 17 years old and never used for those 14 and 15 years old.

Multiple Choice

1. Defence counsel must be mindful that their job includes representing

   a.   the young person who is their client
   b.   society
   c.   the criminal justice system
   d.   two of the above

2. Under the rule of "one lawyer per family," young persons are represented by

   a.   the lawyer of their parents' choosing
   b.   the lawyer who represents their parents
   c.   both of the above
   d.   none of the above, because there is no such rule

3. In youth justice court, the role of the Crown prosecutor is

   a.   very different from what it is in adult court
   b.   not much different from what it is in adult court
   c.   focused on the needs of the young person because of the *YCJA*
   d.   two of the above

4. Which of the following is *not* a responsibility of the judge in youth justice court?

   a.   determining that proper procedure was followed in laying the charges
   b.   resolving disputes over the admissibility of evidence
   c.   determining guilt or innocence
   d.   ensuring that defence counsel has made full disclosure to the Crown

5. In the youth justice court, a young person may elect to have a trial by jury

   a.   for any serious offence
   b.   only when both parents consent
   c.   for first- or second-degree murder if the Crown is seeking a youth sentence
   d.   none of the above

6. Young persons must personally appear before the youth justice court

    a. only for violent offences
    b. only for charges of serious offences
    c. only if their lawyer is not present
    d. for all charges

7. In the youth justice court, judges may consider the protection of the privacy of all but which of the following?

    a. the police
    b. the young person who is charged
    c. victims
    d. witnesses

8. The *YCJA* seeks to reserve court proceedings for

    a. more serious cases
    b. young persons who have already received two or more warnings
    c. young persons who are second-time offenders
    d. two of the above

9. In the youth justice court, the standard for a finding of guilt is

    a. the guilt is "beyond a reasonable doubt"
    b. the guilt is "on the balance of probabilities"
    c. the standard changes with the merits of each individual case
    d. there is no formal finding of guilt

10. Which of the following is not a concern of the *YCJA* when it comes to sentencing?

    a. protection of society
    b. holding young persons accountable for their behaviour
    c. ensuring that young people show respect for the judge and officers of the court
    d. the mental and emotional health of the young person

11. Which of the following is *not* likely to be found in a pre-sentence report?

    a. results of interviews with the young person
    b. results of interviews with the accomplices of the young person
    c. information on the young person's age and attitude
    d. plans the young person might have about the future

12. There is no reason to believe that pre-sentence assessments are found to be useful by

    a. judges
    b. defence counsel
    c. Crown prosecutors
    d. young persons

13. Which of the following may *not* be used as a condition of probation?

    a. report to a probation officer
    b. try to obtain employment
    c. attend school
    d. love, honour, and obey parents

14. Which of the following conditions is *not* permitted in a probation order?

    a. must remain in a specific city
    b. must try to obtain employment
    c. must reside in a specific location
    d. all of the above are permitted

Short Answer

1. Identify two advantages to the Crown for entering into a plea bargain.

2. Identify two advantages for the defence in entering into a plea bargain.

3. Describe the responsibility of the Crown and of the defence counsel with respect to disclosure.

_____

_____

_____

_____

_____

_____

4. What do you consider to be the most important difference between the responsibility of a judge in a youth justice court and a judge in an adult court? Why is it so important?

_____

_____

_____

_____

_____

_____

_____

_____

5. Identify three features of a trial of a young person that may be different from a trial for an adult.

_____

_____

_____

_____

_____

_____

_____

6. Identify two ways in which witnesses who are young persons are treated differently from adult witnesses.

_____

_____

_____

_____

_____

_____

_____

_____

7. What are the principal differences between pre-sentence reports, pre-sentence assessments, and a conference?

_____

_____

_____

_____

_____

_____

_____

_____

8. Discuss the following statement: "There is no reason to believe that the _Youth Criminal Justice Act_ is interested in the protection of society."

_____

_____

_____

_____

_____

_____

_____

9. You are a police officer who has questioned and arrested a young person. You are going to be a witness if the case goes to court. On the basis of your discussions with the young person and her family, you form the view that an absolute discharge could be the right disposition in this case. What would you do next?

_____

_____

_____

_____

_____

_____

_____

_____

10. What value do you suppose a restitution or compensation order has as part of a disposition for a young offender?

_____

_____

_____

_____

_____

_____

_____

_____

11. You are a police officer who is asked to speak to a community group. Its members are upset about community service orders because they think that it is simply a way of going soft on young offenders. They ask you, "What use are they anyway?" How do you respond?

_____

_____

_____

_____

_____

_____

_____

12. Several things are to be taken into consideration when a youth justice court imposes a youth sentence. Identify seven of them.

_____

_____

_____

_____

_____

_____

_____

_____

13. Under what conditions may an adult sentence be imposed on a young person?

_____

_____

_____

_____

_____

_____

_____

_____

Exercise: You Be the Judge

A Case for Adult Sentences

Of the tens of thousands of young people across Canada who appear before the courts, only a very few represent individuals whose behaviour warrants an adult sentence. Needless to say, those cases are heavily covered by the press, capture people's imaginations, and come to define the "typical" case for crusading politicians and many members of the public.

The following case is useful in illustrating some of the facts and circumstances that need to be considered in deciding whether a young person should receive an adult sentence. We have also provided a longer summary of the case. This is to give the reader some idea of the range of factors the courts must consider. The case involves a young person who took part in a home invasion type of robbery during which a man was shot and nearly died.

The following outlines the 2007 Ontario case known as *R. v. Lights* [2007 ONCJ 173 (CanLII)].

The Facts

Lights entered pleas of guilty to the following offences arising from this incident: 1) aggravated assault; 2) break and enter of a dwelling house; 3) use of a firearm while committing an indictable offence; 4) breach of recognizance (house arrest); and 5) breach of probation (firearms prohibition).

The offences arose from a break-in committed by Lights and three others, who ransacked a house looking for guns they believed to be in the house. The victim, a 22-year-old, returned home while the break-in was in progress. He saw someone in his room, placing things in a bag. He became enraged and struggled with the intruder, who quickly called for help from the others. Two or three other males came to the rescue. The victim was beaten with a baseball bat and then shot, but was unable to positively identify any of his assailants. The investigation led the police to Lights, whom they arrested in a residence in which a search warrant was executed and where two sawed-off firearms were found. One was forensically determined as the gun used to shoot the victim. Lights' precise role during this break-in could not be determined. The Crown could not prove beyond a reasonable doubt that he was the person who fired the gun. Indeed, the evidence suggests that he was not the actual shooter. Nevertheless, Lights played an integral role in the break-in and attack.

At the time of these events, Lights was subject to a recognizance order entered into just 48 hours earlier, which included a house arrest condition. He was also subject to a probation order, which included a condition that he not possess any weapons. By his involvement in the offences, Lights breached both orders.

A few days after the near-fatal home invasion, Lights was involved in another very serious incident involving a firearm. In this instance, he entered pleas of guilty to: 1) robbery while using a firearm; 2) failure to comply with a recognizance (house arrest); 3) possession of a prohibited weapon with ammunition readily available; and 4) possession of a weapon without authorization. The take from this attack was substantial. The victim was a jeweller who lost $4,000 in cash, personal jewellery worth $30,000, a Cartier watch worth $40,000, and other pieces. He also lost two wallets, one of which was very expensive. The victim's wife had a necklace ripped from her neck. A ring was also stolen from her, her identification, and approximately $450 in cash. When the police executed the warrant, five people ran outside. One of these people was Lights. At the time, he was wearing one of the stolen chains and had one of the victims' wallets. Approximately $2,775 in Canadian currency and $564 in US currency was recovered, most of it from Lights' person. The police also found two guns in a box under a staircase. One was the sawed-off gun used during the previous home invasion.

Again, Mr. Lights' precise role in this group of offences is unknown. The Crown was not able to prove that he was the person who carried the gun or knife, nor whether he was personally responsible for assaulting the victims. Nevertheless, he was one of the individuals who participated in the robbery and attack.

CIRCUMSTANCES OF THE OFFENDER

Mr. Lights was almost 17 years old at the time of the offences. He was 18 years old at the time of his sentencing. The court was provided with a great deal of information concerning Lights, which included a pre-sentence report, expert psychiatric reports, in-person evidence, and the submissions of counsel.

The judge noted that there is some disagreement in the evidence as to how to best address Lights' situation. There are, however, large areas of consensus. It is agreed that

Lights had had a difficult home life. His parents split up when Lights was very young. He spent a good portion of his youth moving back and forth between his parents' homes. At the age of 14, he asked the Children's Aid Society (CAS) to take him into care, as he did not wish to live with either parent. With both parents, he proved difficult to control, acting out in various anti-social, and sometimes, criminal ways. He demonstrated similar behaviour while in the care of the CAS. Lights maintains contact and has good relations with both of his parents, as well as with his father's partner. It was clear to the court these relationships are complicated. Still, his family supports him.

Lights' Criminal History
At the time of pleading guilty, Lights had a youth court record consisting of the following:

- November 20, 2002, sentenced to 12 months of probation for mischief.
- August 16, 2003, sentenced to 12 months of probation for failure to comply with a recognizance.
- October 13, 2003, sentenced to 12 months of probation for possession of marijuana.
- April 29, 2004, found guilty of (1) mischief; (2) fail to comply with a recognizance; (3) carrying concealed weapon; (4) possession of schedule II substance; (5) fail to attend in court; and (6) fail to comply with undertaking. He received a total sentence of 12 months' probation.
- May 3, 2004, sentenced to 12 months of probation for carrying a concealed weapon.
- November 17, 2004, sentenced to 12 months of probation for the offence of robbery. (Lights approached a young person in his neighbourhood and asked him for $5. When the youth refused, Lights threatened to "knock out" the victim.)
- May 18, 2005, sentenced to time served and 12 months of probation after spending 267 days of pre-trial custody for (1) break and enter; (2) robbery; (3) robbery with a firearm; (4) point firearm; (5) possession of prohibited weapon; (6) fail to comply with probation; and (7) possession of a restricted weapon.

Questions
1. On the basis of this evidence, should Lights receive an adult sentence?
   Yes _____ No _____ Not Sure _____

2. What are your reasons for your answer?

   _____
   _____
   _____

If more information would be helpful, what type of information would that be?

_____

_____

_____

3. At this point, does Lights have a right to have more information provided to the court before a decision is made?

Yes _____   No _____   Not Sure _____

4. What are your reasons for your answer?

_____

_____

_____

The Decision

The judge had ordered that a pre-sentence report be prepared, as well as a psychological assessment under section 34 of the *YCJA*. He also had available a previous report prepared for a prior sentencing. It contained detailed history of Lights' difficult family circumstances and his early years. Lights witnessed domestic violence directed toward his mother by one of his mother's boyfriends. From Grade 1, he was in trouble at school, stealing from and bullying other students. There is some suggestion that, as a child, Lights suffered with Attention Deficit and Hyperactive Disorder (ADHD), but his mother was not comfortable with the use of medication to address this concern, so nothing was ever done about it.

The psychiatrist variously described Lights as being of average intelligence and being "fairly bright and engaging." Lights displayed good interpersonal skills and good verbal ability. Lights was said to have the capacity to achieve scholastically, but had not applied himself. Lights had some Grade 9 credits, some of which he obtained while in custody.

In both reports, and in testimony before the court, the psychiatrist reported troubling conclusions regarding Lights' risk of re-offending. The first report, based on scoring of risk prediction inventories, said that Lights' risk to re-offend was "high," especially in light of his callousness, lack of remorse, and his tendency to minimize his role in his offences. The second assessment concluded that Lights' risk had increased to being "very high." This change was due to Lights' further criminal involvement and his poor institutional behaviour while incarcerated pending sentence.

The psychiatrist observed that Lights seemed to have expressed more remorse and empathy toward his victims this time around, but his more recent offences involved more planning (as opposed to being impulsive) and that planned (or instrumental) aggression is harder to treat than reactive aggression.

The second report provided balancing of the factors both for and against sentencing Lights as an adult. There were many factors in favour of keeping him in the youth system. He had exhibited some improved behaviour at times. Developmentally he was still an adolescent and hence his novelty-seeking and poor judgment might improve as his brain matures over time. He did have several strengths that could be capitalized upon in vocational rehabilitation in youth correctional settings. He articulated a wish to change his life, use programming to become more pro-social, and had goals to be an electrician or some vocation. He acknowledged that he had had an anti-social and narcissistic attitude in the past, and had poor decision-making skills. He also expressed some regret for the impact on the victims. It was possible that his experiences within the last year of custody had convinced him that change was in order, despite his turbulent and highly anti-social past.

Nevertheless, he had had the chance last year and resumed his old lifestyle. Hence, he needed help with individual counselling for problem-solving, cognitive skills, addictions work, anti-social attitudes, vocational rehabilitation, and extra educational support to finish high school.

THE SENTENCE

The judge decided in favour of an adult sentence despite the fact that Lights' precise role during this break-in could not be determined. The Crown could not prove beyond a reasonable doubt that he was the person who fired the gun. Indeed, the evidence suggests that he was not the actual shooter. Nevertheless, Lights played an integral role in the break-in and attack on the person shot. At the time of these events, Lights was subject to a recognizance entered into just 48 hours earlier, which included a house arrest condition. He was also subject to a probation order, which included a condition that he not possess any weapons. By his involvement in the offences, Lights breached both orders.

THE APPEAL OF HIS SENTENCE

This story continued to evolve: Mr. Lights appealed his adult sentence to the Ontario Court of Appeal [2011 ONCA 163 (CanLII)], which dismissed his appeal as follows: "We have carefully reviewed the trial judge's reasons. We see no error in the trial judge's decision to sentence the appellant as an adult, nor his decision to impose a sentence of eight years less credit for time served to be served in a youth facility."

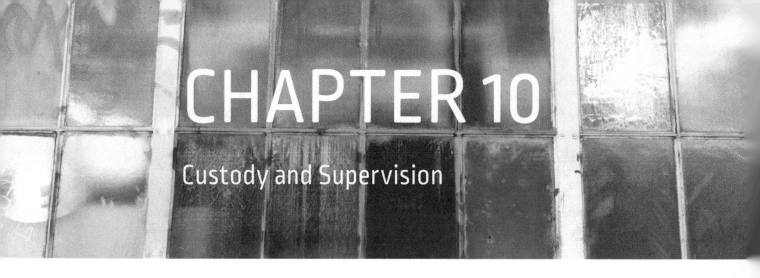

CHAPTER 10

Custody and Supervision

LEARNING OUTCOMES

Students who have mastered this chapter will have the ability to do the following:

- Describe the difference between "least degree of restraint" and "higher degree of restraint."
- Identify the things to be taken with consideration in deciding the appropriate degree of restraint in a custodial decision.
- Distinguish between "re-integrative leave" and "day release."
- Explain the role of conditional supervision in dealing with young persons.
- Describe and explain the difference the use of mandatory conditions involved in orders of conditional supervision.
- Identify and describe the conditions under which extraordinary measures in custody may be used.
- Explain the circumstances under which a police officer may arrest a young person under an order of conditional supervision.
- Explain the role of case management in dealing with youth in custody.
- Explain why a range of service options is useful in dealing with young persons.

CUSTODIAL PROVISIONS

Levels of Custody

Part 5 of the *Youth Criminal Justice Act* (*YCJA*) sets out the provisions with respect to custody and supervision. The purpose of the system of custody is the protection of society through "safe, fair, and humane" restraints that will assist the rehabilitation and reintegration of young persons into the community [*YCJA* 83 (1)]. At the same time, the young person is to be held accountable in a manner that is proportionate to the seriousness of the offence and the degree of responsibility of the young person. The legislative framework is constructed by the federal government (e.g., the *YCJA*), but it is the provinces and territories that have carriage of administering youth correctional services in Canada.

Degree of Restraint

The *YCJA* requires that there be at least two "levels" of custody [s. 85]. Formerly, these were referred to as "open custody" and "secure custody," but the *YCJA* does not use these words. The two levels of custody in the *YCJA* are distinguished by the "degree of restraint" that they impose on the young person. One level of custody is referred to as the one with the "**least degree of restraint**," and the other level is referred to variously as "more than a minimal degree of restraint," "a higher degree of restraint," and "increased degree of restraint." We will use the expression **higher degree of restraint** to refer to the level of custody that is greater than the least degree of restraint.

Ontario's youth facilities are administered under the Ministry of Child and Youth Services and legislated via Ontario's *Child, Youth and Family Services Act* (*CYFSA*). Ontario uses the more well-known terms "open custody" and "secure custody" to distinguish between the two levels of detention. Pursuant to subsection 145(1) of the *CYFSA*, the minister has responsibility to establish these facilities. Open custody facilities, with the least degree of restraint, are smaller residences, generally located in the community, where youth live under supervision. They must remain with staff at all times, unless they have an approved leave from the facility. Secure custody has more than a minimal degree of restraint and is characterized by facilities that are separated from the community by security fencing and other security features. Supportive programs and activities are available within open and secure custody facilities for youth (e.g., decision making and problem solving, victim awareness, education, dealing with drug and alcohol abuse, self-control and anger counselling, learning basic life skills, such as how to express feelings and listen to others, playing sports and other recreation, taking part in social programs). Throughout this chapter, both sets of terms will be used.

Principles in Choosing the Degree of Restraint Required

Among the principles to be applied in using custody to achieve its purposes are the following [s. 83(2) (a)–(e)]:

- the least restrictive measures consistent with the protection of the public, of personnel working with young persons and of young persons be used;
- young persons sentenced to custody retain the rights of other young persons, except the rights that are necessarily removed or restricted as a consequence of a sentence;
- the youth custody and supervision system facilitate the involvement of the families of young persons and members of the public;
- that custody and supervision decisions be made in a forthright, fair and timely manner, and that young persons have access to an effective review procedure; and
- that placements of young persons where they are treated as adults not disadvantage them with respect to their eligibility for and conditions of release.

One of the primary principles is that youth must be detained separately from adults [*YCJA* 84]. If, however, the youth attains the age of 18 while serving his or her sentence, the Provincial Director may seek to have the individual transferred to an adult correctional facility to serve out the remainder of the sentence where it is in the best interests of young person or the public interest [*YCJA* 92(1)].

The *YCJA* leaves it to each province to determine the nature and types of facilities that will provide the two levels of restraint. It is up to the **Provincial Director** (a term found in the *YCJA*) to determine which facility and which levels of restraint best serve the needs of the young person and the community under the *YCJA* [ss. 83(3) and (4)]. The term applies to a fairly broad category of persons. It means a person, a group, or class of persons or a body appointed by a province to perform functions under the *YCJA*. For example, persons in charge of probation services as well as persons in charge of provincial correctional facilities are "Provincial Directors." There is not, therefore, a single Provincial Director of Ontario; there are many individuals and groups who hold that designation.

Least Degree of Restraint Facilities

The types of facilities that are likely to be considered as providing the least degree of restraint that may be suitable for a custodial sentence are a community residential centre, group home, child care institution, or forest or wilderness camp. Although it is considered to have the least degree of restraint, residents are not permitted to leave the facility, unless staff accompanies them or they have an authorized temporary release. Whenever possible, it is expected that such facilities should be near the community in which the young person lives. This should help with the reintegration of the young person into the community by making it easier for the young person to remain in contact with parents and local schools.

Some least degree of restraint facilities resemble adult halfway houses in that they do not have an "institutional look." This allows them to blend into their neighbourhood. In these residences, young persons are expected to perform some typical household duties, such as keeping their sleeping areas tidy, occasionally helping to cook meals, washing dishes, and taking out the trash. Some facilities have classrooms and teachers who are available daily; many use temporary absence provisions to allow residents to attend local schools.

Higher Degree of Restraint Facilities

Higher degree of restraint facilities are places that afford a higher level of containment of young persons. In Ontario, such facilities are locked settings surrounded by a security fence. This gives them the look of an "adult prison." Staff supervision is greater than in least degree of restraint facilities, and movement within the facility is also restricted. Typically, the residents' rooms have locks on the doors so that they can be "locked down" at night.

Higher degree of restraint facilities have regular classrooms, and most have segregation rooms for those who have serious behaviour problems or who commit violations of the rules of the institution. Young persons who are placed in higher degree of restraint facilities are those who pose a significant risk to themselves or to others.

We can expect that what constitutes "least" as compared with "higher" degree of restraint will vary both within and across jurisdictions. There are limits, however, on how these definitions can be applied. Bala (1997: 241) reports a Nova Scotia case, where the government attempted to use a former adult jail as a youth facility. It was classified as an open as well as closed custody facility, with "open custody" meaning that the cells were unlocked. The courts did not share the Nova Scotia government's view of what open custody meant.

Terms of Custody

Many readers would undoubtedly have seen television broadcasts and movies that depict the system of justice in the United States. It is common for American judges to impose indeterminate sentences where they sentence the offender from, say, seven to ten years in prison. Indeterminate sentences do not form part of the legal landscape in Canada.[1]

Nearly all periods of incarceration are determinate—that is, a definite time limit is assigned. Each province has to decide whether judges will determine level of restraint for custodial sentences or whether an administrative approach will be taken, and it is decided by the Provincial Director. If it is to be done by the Provincial Director, then there will be provision for an independent Custody Review Board. Subject to review are those cases where a young person would be placed in a facility that has more than a minimal degree of restraint or where there is to be a transfer of a young person to a higher or increased degree of restraint. The *YCJA* leaves it to the Provincial Director to decide the appropriate level of custody, unless the province decides otherwise.

Regardless of who makes the decision, subsection 85(5) identifies the "appropriate level of custody" as the one that is "least restrictive" to the young person, having regard to the following:

(a) ...(i) the seriousness of the offence and the circumstances in which that offence was committed,

(ii) the needs and circumstances of the young person, including proximity to family, school, employment and support services,

(iii) the safety of other young persons in custody, and

(iv) the interests of society;

(b) that the level of custody should allow for the best possible match of programs to the young person's needs and behaviour, having regard to the findings of any assessment in respect of the young person; and

(c) the likelihood of escape.

YOUTH CORRECTIONAL STATISTICS IN CANADA

A fundamental principle underlying the *YCJA* is to minimize intervention by the state in the lives of young persons. Consequently, police officers must consider, and reconsider, their decision to charge. Once charged, considerations must then be made as to what is the least invasive intervention that will achieve the objectives of

---

1. An exception being sentences for dangerous offenders [*CCC* 753(4)].

rehabilitation and reintegration. The *YCJA* sees incarceration as a tool of last resort. One way to see if the courts are de-emphasizing custodial dispositions is to review current data. Statistics help to track if custody is being used more or less over time, thus allowing insight into how the principles of the *YCJA* are being implemented.

HOW IS YOUTH IN CORRECTIONS MEASURED?

Youth corrections data is composed of two parts: the number of youth in custody and the number of youth under a community supervision order. Typically, youth in facilities is counted daily, while youth under community supervision is counted and reported monthly via the Youth Corrections Key Indicator Report. These counts are then averaged to arrive at the annual average daily custody and community counts that are reported.

The *youth incarceration rate* is the average number of youth in secure or open custody per day for every 10,0000 individuals in the youth population (12–17 years old). This rate includes youth in sentenced custody, youth in Provincial Director Remand being held following the breach of a community supervision condition, youth in pre-trial detention awaiting trial or sentencing, and youth in other temporary detention.

Other data is collected from two sources discussed in Chapter 4: The Youth Custody and Community Services Survey (YCCS) (e.g., age, gender, Indigenous identity) and the Integrated Correctional Services Survey (ICSS) (collects data on socio-demographic characteristics of both adults and youth who are in the federal and provincial/territorial correctional systems).

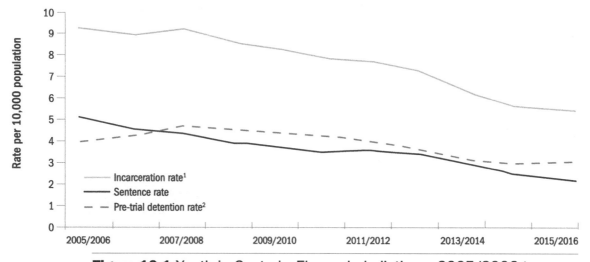

Figure 10.1 Youth in Custody, Eleven Jurisdictions, 2005/2006 to 2015/2016

1. Incarceration rate includes sentenced custody, pre-trial detention, Provincial Director remand, and other temporary detention.
2. Pre-trial detention is to hold a young person temporarily in custody, while awaiting trial or sentencing. It is equivalent to remand for adults.

Source: J. Malakieh (2017). "Youth correctional statistics in Canada, 2015/2016," Chart 1. *Juristat* (Cat. No. 85-002-X). Ottawa, ON: Statistics Canada. Retrieved from http://www.statcan.gc.ca/pub/ 85-002-x/2017001/article/14702-eng.pdf

In 2015–16, there were a total of 8,455 youths aged 12 to 17 who were supervised in either a custody or a community program throughout Canada (Malakieh, 2017) (see Figure 10.1). This was down 11 percent from 2014–15 and down 33 percent from five years earlier. Given the discussion in Chapter 4, which highlighted overall declining crime rates for youths, this data is in keeping with the overall trend of fewer youth offending. Other trends also remain the same. Males account for three-quarters of youth admitted to correctional services and 56 percent of youth admissions to correctional services involve youths aged 16 and 17. Youth aged 12 and 13 years form only 4 percent of admissions.

Indigenous Youth

Indigenous youth continue to be over-represented in the correctional system. There were 5,642 Indigenous youth admitted to correctional services in 2015–16, representing 35 percent of admissions (see Figure 10.2). The principles of the *YCJA* required that youth courts consider alternatives to custody, with particular focus on the social circumstances of Indigenous youth. Despite this there is still a disconnect—in 2015–16, 54 percent of Indigenous youth were admitted to custody versus 44 percent for non-Indigenous youth, up from 52 percent the reporting year prior, and up from 48 percent in 2011–12. In other words, the proportion has grown over time, not diminished. This pattern repeats for female Indigenous youth, where they accounted for 43 percent of all female youths admitted to correctional services in 2015–16 (up from 38 percent in 2011–12). In contrast, male Indigenous youth accounted for 31 percent of all male youth admitted.

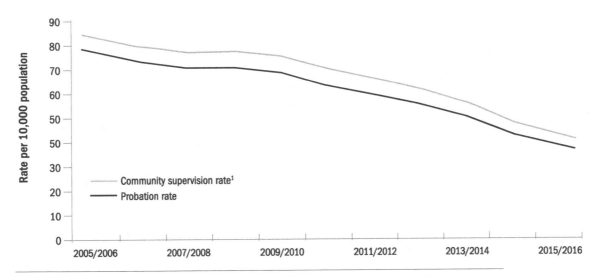

Figure 10.2 Youth in Community Supervision, Seven Jurisdictions, 2005/2006 to 2015/2016

1. Includes probation, deferred custody and supervision, intensive support and supervision and community portions of custody sentences.

Source: J. Malakieh (2017). "Youth correctional statistics in Canada, 2015/2016," Chart 2. *Juristat* (Cat. No. 85-002-X). Ottawa, ON: Statistics Canada. Retrieved from http://www.statcan.gc.ca/pub/85-002-x/2017001/article/14702-eng.pdf

Length of Stay

Figure 10.3 shows that the length of time youth spend in pre-trail detention has decreased slightly from five years earlier. In 2015–16, 79 percent of youth spent one month or less, with 53 percent there for less than one week. For youth released from sentenced custody, 45 percent were there for one month or less, with 91 percent in custody for six months or less. One-half (51 percent) were supervised on probation for one year or less. Females spend less time under correctional supervision: 85 percent were released from pre-trial detention after one month or less, compared to 76 percent of male youth.

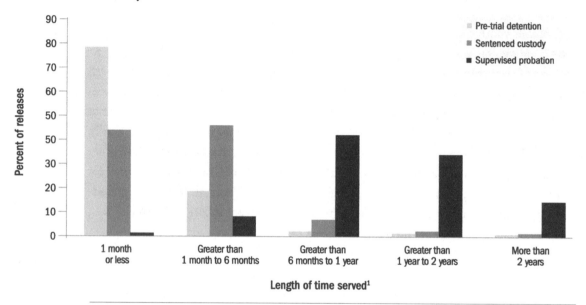

Figure 10.3 Time Served by Legal Hold Status, Nine Jurisdictions, 2015/2016

1. Releases with unknown time were excluded.

Source: J. Malakieh (2017). "Youth correctional statistics in Canada, 2015/2016," Chart 4. *Juristat* (Cat. No. 85-002-X). Ottawa, ON: Statistics Canada. Retrieved from http://www.statcan.gc.ca/pub/85-002-x/2017001/article/14702-eng.pdf

Relationship Custody

The importance that positive relationships play in assisting youth in custody addresses a fundamental need that young people have for connections to people to support positive life changes and important emotional development. Like all children, young people respond best when high demands are coupled with high levels of warmth and responsiveness. In the parenting research, this is called *authoritative* parenting. This is in contrast to *authoritarian* parenting practices that are often high in punishment and other types of disciplinary practices, but low in warmth, conversation, and explanation. Prison is all about authoritarian rules and implementation. For youth in custody, their ability to mature, grow, and develop trust in people is contingent upon them having positive interactions with adults and mentors in whom they can entrust their feelings, hopes, and fears.

The Residential Services Review Board (2016) in their research about the experiences of youth in custody summarized as follows:

> Youth Justice Services reports that they are committed to the use of a relationship custody approach, directed at fostering respectful, caring relationships between staff and young people and enabling staff to provide effective, evidenced based interventions to benefit youth. … Some secure custody centres appear to struggle with mitigating the total control context of custodial cultures and processes and experience challenges in optimizing care. There is some indication that the size of the facility contributes to a youth-centred, therapeutic focus and the ability to establish positive relationships with young people, with smaller facilities often more able to accomplish these objectives.
>
> Young people that we spoke with indicated that their experiences varied. They indicated that they always knew whether a staff member genuinely cared about them. Some staff made a particular effort to express an interest in the youth, to build trust and respect, listen to them and to establish a relationship. As indicated in the report *It Depends Who's Working*[2] released by the Provincial Advocate for Children and Youth, young people reported that their experience in custody varied according to which staff were working. The staff in some facilities were described by young people as being more caring overall and the youth experience at that facility was more positive as a result.

Extraordinary Measures While in Custody

The use of mechanical restraints and secure isolation and other intrusive measures is permitted where a youth is held in secure custody or secure temporary detention. Nevertheless, use of such practices is challenging and not without controversy and concerns for such extreme measures. It is considered a controversial practice for adult offenders in prison, and presents even more concerns when used with children.

Mechanical Restraints

Mechanical restraints are permitted pursuant to subsection 156(1) of the *CYFSA*, where the youth is in secure custody or secure temporary detention. The specific reference to "secure" custody means that they are not permissible at all in open custody facilities. Restraints may *not* be used for the purpose of punishment. The conditions for their use are if there is imminent risk:

      i. the young person or another person would suffer physical injury,

      ii. the young person would escape the place of secure custody or of secure temporary detention, or

      iii. the young person would cause significant property damage.

---

2.   Provincial Advocate for Children & Youth. 2013. *"It Depends Who's Working": The Youth Reality at the Roy McMurtry Youth Centre.* Toronto, ON: Office of the Provincial Advocate for Children and Youth.

Restraints may also be used when transporting a youth from secure custody or secure temporary detention to another place of custody or detention or to and from court or the community [*CYFSA* 156(3)].

Secure Isolation

Under the *CYFSA* [173], placing a young person in secure isolation is permitted by putting the child in a *de-escalation room,* when the behaviour of the youth presents imminent risk of serious harm to another person/property and when no less restrictive method is practicable to manage his or her behaviour. It is not permitted to be used for punishment.

The usual practice is that there is a one-hour time limit with continuous supervision of the youth. Where it is deemed necessary, youth under the age of 16 can be kept in secure isolation for a maximum of 8 hours in any one day or 24 hours in a week. Youth 16 years of age or over cannot be held over 72 hours unless approved by a Provincial Director. Anytime a youth is kept for more than one hour, there are protocols for reviewing the youth in isolation at prescribed intervals. While in secure isolation, youth retain all of the rights they have under the *CYFSA.*

A comprehensive review by the Residential Services Review Panel (2016) discussed the systematic review conducted by the Office of the Provincial Advocate for Children and Youth of Ontario (PACY) and noted:

> The review found that while there is a general trend across the province of declining use of secure isolation ...a pattern of high use continues to be observed in some facilities ...The review also noted that the conditions for confinement for the use of secure isolation were being inconsistently applied across facilities, with some young people being held longer than the maximum periods, and that the conditions of confinement did not reflect the basic rights of young ...the Advocate cited feedback of youth who had experienced isolation that spoke to concerns about basic needs being met while in isolation—such as access to fresh air, hygienic practices and supplies (showers and toileting), adequate food—and the lack of mental stimulation ...The review indicated that the implications of secure isolation can be severe, potentially causing serious mental health issues including anxiety, depression, anger, increased risk of self-harm and suicide, and may be especially harmful to people with mental health disorders.
>
> An increasing body of literature showing that secure isolation can change brain activity and result in symptoms within seven days was cited to underscore this point (PACY, n.d.[3]). Further, a review of international literature by the Advocate revealed consensus that secure isolation not be used at all with adolescents because of the potential implications for mental health and safety ...
>
> The facilities we visited that make minimal use of secure isolation were clear that establishing rapport and effective relationships with youth; a rehabilitative, youth-centred culture; working to de-escalate youth who are acting out; and engaging with youth, make a significant difference in the need to use secure isolation.

---

3. Reports from the Office of the Provincial Advocate can be retrieved from https://www.provincialadvocate.on.ca/main/en/publications/.

Secure Treatment Program

Mental health disorders and substance abuse and addictions provide complex challenges that often must be treated in order to address the underlying causes that may be associated with a young person who is committing crime. The *CYFSA* [ss. 158–168] sets out the provisions for committing a youth to a secure treatment program.

Commitment to a secure treatment program requires that it be done as an emergency admission [*CYFSA* 171] or by court order [*CYFSA* 164]. For a child less than 16 years of age, the application for a court order can be brought by a parent or a Children's Aid Society if the child is under a protection order, or by another person who has legal responsibility for the child. For a young person 16 years of age or older, the application brought by a parent can only be done with the child's consent. The youth can also bring the application on his or her own behalf, or a Children's Aid Society or physician can make an application. The court may order that an assessment be conducted to help make a determination as to the appropriateness and necessity of a secure treatment program.

The following conditions must be considered by the youth court in making a determination to order commitment to a secure treatment program [*CYFSA* 164]:

- the child has a mental disorder;
- has caused, attempted to cause, or by words or conduct made a substantial threat to cause serious bodily harm to themself or another person, or has caused or attempted to cause a person's death;
- the secure treatment program would be effective to prevent the child from causing or attempting to cause serious bodily harm to themself or another person;
- treatment appropriate for the child's mental disorder is available at the place of secure treatment to which the application relates; and
- no less restrictive method of providing treatment appropriate for the child's mental disorder is appropriate in the circumstances.

Where the child is younger than 12, the court shall not make an order unless the minister consents to the child's commitment.

Review of Sentences

When young persons are committed to periods of custody beyond one year, they must be automatically returned to the youth justice court for a review of the sentence at the end of the first year [*YCJA* 94(1)]. Section 94 of the *YCJA* also provides for reviews "on request." Reviews may be initiated by the Provincial Director and will take place if requested during the period of incarceration by the young person, the young person's parent, or the Attorney General. To be eligible for a review, the youth sentence must be for less than one year, and meet the following criteria:

- The young person must have served at least 30 days in custody from the date of the sentence.
- The young person must have served at least one-third of the period of the sentence.
- At any point in time, where a youth justice court is satisfied that there are grounds for review.

If a young person receives a sentence of more than one year, then the youth is eligible for a review if he or she has served six months after the date of the most recent sentence. A young person's sentence can be reviewed on any of the following grounds [94(6)]:

- The young person has made sufficient progress to justify a change in sentence.
- The circumstances that led to the youth's sentence have changed materially.
- New services or programs are available that were not available at the time of the sentence.
- The opportunities for rehabilitation are now greater in the community.
- On such other grounds as the youth criminal justice court considers appropriate.

This mandated review assessment is, what we might call, asymmetrical. That is, the courts can shorten the young person's period of custody, but the court cannot lengthen the sentence unless the young person commits another offence. No review will be heard if the young person's case is being appealed.

A major distinction between how adults and young persons are handled while in custody relates to release provisions. Adult correctional officials have the authority to modify the offender's term in custody significantly by granting parole. Provincial officials in charge of young persons do not have that authority. Any change to the young person's custody can only be made by the youth justice court. Thus, the youth justice court is far more involved in the young person's sentence and treatment than are ordinary courts with adult offenders.

Re-integrative Leave

Principles and Purpose

The Ontario Ministry of Children and Youth Services published a report in 2015: *Supporting Effective Transitions for Ontario Youth*. The ministry highlighted its commitment toward youth justice programs and services "in order to create a service continuum that reduces reoffending, contributes to community safety and prevents youth crime through rehabilitative programming, holding youth accountable, and creating opportunities for youth at risk"(5). This report noted that this was a follow-up to a 2012 goal of *Ontario's Youth Action Plan* (YAP) "to foster safer communities and give young people the support and opportunities they need to succeed" (Hoskins & Meilleur, 2012, p. 6). Part of the YAP initiative was to assist youth with the social, behavioural, familial, and other circumstances that have led to the youth to be in conflict with the law.

A core component of reintegration planning is the use of case management to establish a plan for school, work, home, and the community, with the end goal of reducing the risk of reoffending.

Case Management
It is current practice to assign a case manager (usually a probation officer) to every offender who receives a disposition resulting in custody or probation. Probation officers, as well as facility staff and service providers, are responsible for collaborating with the youth, family, and other key people in putting together a risk/needs assessment and a case management plan within 30 days of the young offender receiving a disposition from the youth court. A plan of care is also provided for young persons who are in a custodial facility for more than 30 days. The plan of care outlines the services to be provided to the young person and the young person's response to treatment. It is to be continually revised as the youth moves through and out of the justice system and/or needs change.

Young offender services, accommodations, and programs are delivered using a case management model that is designed to address the individual needs and circumstances of each young person focusing on aspects such as culture, diversity, gender, and mental health. Ideally, case management should allow for a coordinated effort so that services are efficient, seamless, and comprehensive. Furthermore, there are efforts to support youths as they transition out of the justice system as well.

Treatment services vary across the facilities, but within the system, there is a broad range of programs available, including the following:

- Psychological and psychiatric therapy
- Education, literacy, and life skills
- Employment counselling
- Chaplaincy services
- Counselling for alcoholism, substance abuse, and anger control
- Recreation
- Discharge planning

The ministry has identified the following reintegration best practices:

- Increased engagement and participation by the youth and their family
- Placing the youth and family at the centre of service provision
- Fostering youth leadership
- Strengthen service collaboration through an interdisciplinary plan
- Strengthen communities to support youth success

Leave Provisions
Section 91 of the *YCJA* allows for **re-integrative leaves** and day releases. Re-integrative leaves may be allowed for not more than 30 days. Re-integrative leave is at the discretion

of the Provincial Director; it allows the young person to be absent from custody with or without an escort. It is used for medical, compassionate, or humanitarian purposes or for the purposes of rehabilitation or reintegration into the community. For example, such leaves may be given when a close relative of the young person is ill or if he or she requests to attend a relative's funeral. A young person may receive re-integrative leave when some medical service is required that cannot be provided at the institution.

Another form of re-integrative leave is generally known as **day release**. Day releases usually allow the young person to leave the institution during the day to perform some duty and then return at night. The exact days and time for these releases are at the discretion of the Provincial Director. The *YCJA* identifies several reasons for allowing a day release. These include the following:

- Attend school.
- Continue employment, or perform domestic or other duties for the family.
- Participate in employment or training related programs.
- Attend outpatient treatment programs.

The appropriate authority may revoke these leaves at any time. Young persons who do not return once their re-integrative leave has been revoked or, who fail to follow any conditions applied to the absence, may be arrested without a warrant and returned to custody.

Conditional Supervision

Section 96 of the *YCJA* provides that a young person being held in custody may be released from custody and placed under conditional supervision if the Provincial Director is satisfied that the needs of the young person and the interests of society would be better served. The Provincial Director must make such a recommendation to the youth justice court. Further, all youth sentences imposed under subsection 42(2)(n) contain provision for a portion of their sentence (one-third) to be served under supervision in the community.

A **conditional supervision order** [*YCJA* 105] allows a young person to serve part of the sentence in the community with a set of restrictions or "conditions," by which the youth must abide. Conditional supervision is meant to allow for a gradual release of the young person from custody back to the community. Conditional supervision orders are generally more restrictive than probation orders, so they give the youth justice court a greater degree of control when dealing with sentences.

The mandatory conditions to be imposed on the young person are outlined in subsection 105(2) and require that the young person do the following:

(a) keep the peace and be of good behaviour;

(b) report to the provincial director and then be under the supervision of the provincial director;

  (c)   inform the provincial director immediately on being arrested or questioned by the police;

  (d)   report to the police, or any named individual, as instructed by the provincial director;

  (e)   advise the provincial director of the young person's address of residence and report immediately to the provincial director any change

      (i) in that address,

      (ii) in the young person's normal occupation, including employment, vocational or educational training and volunteer work,

      (iii) in the young person's family or financial situation, and

      (iv) that may reasonably be expected to affect the young person's ability to comply with the conditions of the sentence; and

  (f)   not own, possess, or have the control of any weapon.

When warranted the youth court may add in other conditions as outlined in subsection 105(3):

  (a)   on release, travel directly to the young person's place of residence, or to any other place that is noted in the order;

  (b)   make reasonable efforts to obtain and maintain suitable employment;

  (c)   attend school or any other place of learning, training or recreation, that is appropriate, if the court is satisfied that a suitable program is available;

  (d)   reside with a parent, or any other adult that the court considers appropriate, who is willing to provide for the care and maintenance of the young person;

  (e)   reside in any place that the provincial director may specify;

  (f)   remain within the territorial jurisdiction of one or more courts named in the order;

  (g)   comply with conditions set out in the order that support the needs of the young person and promote the reintegration of the young person into the community; and

  (h)   comply with any other conditions set out in the order that the court considers appropriate, including conditions for securing the young person's good conduct and for preventing the young person from repeating the offence or committing other offences.

A prime difference between probation orders and conditional supervision orders is the ability of the authorities to apprehend the young person who breaks a condition of the order. Young persons are in violation of a probation order if they actually breach a condition and adequate evidence exists to prove the breach. Under a conditional supervision order, however, it is sufficient to revoke the order, if there are "reasonable grounds to believe that a young person has breached or is about to breach a condition of an order."

Once the young person's order is suspended by the Provincial Director, the young person may be remanded to custody if the Provincial Director believes it is appropriate. Once the young person is in remand, the correctional authorities have 48 hours to either cancel the suspension or refer the young person to the youth justice court for a review.

The Provincial Director may also have a warrant issued for the apprehension of the young person [*YCJA* 107(1)]. Any police officer may execute those warrants anywhere in the country per subsection 107(2). Police officers have the authority under subsection 107(3) to arrest a young person without a warrant if they have reasonable grounds to believe that a warrant is outstanding. Once a young person has been arrested, the young person is to be brought before the Provincial Director "without unreasonable delay" and, in any event, within 24 hours [*YCJA* 107(4)(a)].

Custodial Alternatives

Wilderness Programming

While most custodial facilities follow a traditional design, there have been experiments with alternative arrangements. Project DARE (Development through Adventure, Responsibility and Education) is based on the Outward Bound wilderness program and is located in Ontario at Algonquin Park. This therapeutic program stresses the value of meeting physical challenges in order to enhance the young person's self-confidence. Ontario Probation officers can refer for admission male youths aged 13 to 18 sentenced to open custody. The program works to address complex issues that the boys have faced such as substance abuse, family conflict, school truancy, depression, and lack of motivation. Every student participant receives a Case Management and Reintegration Plan.

"Boot Camp"

Ontario experimented with a "boot camp" variant called Project Turnaround (1997–2004). Project Turnaround was based on a paramilitary model with a strong focus on discipline and structure. The project was based on several programs that have been introduced in the United States. The primary objectives of the program were to teach self-discipline, personal responsibility, and respect by learning how to cooperate while living with others. Strict discipline is defined by "highly structured, 16-hour days that stress mandatory education and life skills development, earned privileges, rigorous physical activities, community service work projects, and minimal idle time" (Carr and Ecker, 1996). Staff and residents dressed in uniforms. It was discontinued when the site was deemed uninhabitable due to mould coupled with the introduction of the *YCJA* in 2003, a change in government and its high price tag even though it was considered to be successful and respectful of the young persons who participated.

CONCLUSION

Custody, whether open or secure, is more of an opportunity than an intervention. Given the *YCJA* preference for non-custodial dispositions, custody occurs in circumstances that are serious enough to warrant having young offenders live apart from their families. Being in a custodial facility means that varying degrees of control are imposed on the comings and goings of young persons. In the case of open custody, the conditions of its continuation are clear, and there is the threat that violation of these conditions (e.g., stay in school, stay out of trouble) can lead to re-appearance in court and a more restrictive custodial sentence.

Secure custody is also an opportunity. Some stimuli that may trigger problem behaviour may be removed and there is the opportunity to expose the young persons to programs and services that may help them learn ways of dealing with problems in living without engaging in law-violating behaviour. Some of these programs and services are educational, others are vocational, and still others are therapeutic. For example, some institutions offer anger management, addictions counselling, and a variety of interventions of the mental health variety.

Young offenders have the right to refuse treatment. This is a controversial provision that is not favoured by some professionals. Nevertheless, what it means is that while young people are in custody, there is the opportunity to expose them to the option of such services. They may also meet the people who would deliver them and even begin one or the other of these programs, with the option to drop out at any point of their choosing.

When the system works well, staff members who work in custodial facilities use the information in the predisposition reports and the recommendations from predisposition assessments to formulate a plan of action for dealing with the young person during custody. Mental health issues are frequently prominent, and there is considerable variation in the extent to which custodial facilities have access to support services from trained clinicians (Avison and Whitehead, 1998).

It is paradoxical that, on the one hand, custody is used to deal with the needs of the young offender and the community, while, on the other hand, we allow young persons to decide whether they will participate in treatment. The very mental health issues (e.g., aggression, poor impulse control, immaturity, depression) that contribute to their receiving custodial dispositions can only be addressed programmatically if the young offender agrees. By virtue of their age, let alone their emotional state, they are, arguably, in a poor position to judge their own needs for treatment.

Consequently, except for the physical control provided by a custodial disposition, the success of interventions depends heavily on those who work in these facilities. The extent to which they can earn the trust and respect of the young people in their care influences the likely success of various programs and services in making a difference in the life—and, later, career—of each young person.

TEST YOUR KNOWLEDGE

Definitions

Define the following terms:

1. Least degree of restraint

   _____

   _____

   _____

2. Higher degree of restraint

   _____

   _____

   _____

3. Provincial Director

   _____

   _____

   _____

4. Re-integrative leave

   _____

   _____

   _____

5. Day release

   _____

   _____

   _____

6. Conditional supervision order

   _____

   _____

   _____

True/False

1. T   F   "Least degree of restraint" when applied to a custodial facility means that the residents are allowed to come and go as they please, but only during the day.

2. T   F   A facility with a "higher degree of restraint" means that the extent of restraint or control is greater than in a facility with a "lower degree of restraint."

3. T   F   In contrast to the United States, the practice in Canada is to have indeterminate sentences.

4. When a custodial disposition is made, the following are to be taken into account:

   T   F   The highest level of restraint possible.

   T   F   The safety of the young person.

5. T   F   Facilities that provide custody for young persons in conflict with the law in Ontario are all privately operated.

6. T   F   All facilities are required to have the same treatment services.

Multiple Choice

1. Which of the following is least consistent with a facility in a higher degree of restraint?

   a. community reintegration
   b. "lock down"
   c. classrooms
   d. secure isolation room

2. If a young person turns 18 years while serving a term of custody

   a. the term of custody ends
   b. the offender is automatically transferred to a correctional facility for adults
   c. the term continues with the possibility of transfer to an adult correctional facility
   d. the term of custody is automatically extended so that custody will last for at least 12 additional months

3. Changes to a young person's custody can be made by

    a. correctional officials
    b. the Provincial Director
    c. the youth justice court
    d. the Crown prosecutor

4. Young persons who do not return once their re-integrative leave has been revoked may be

    a. arrested only with a warrant and returned to custody
    b. arrested without a warrant and returned to their parents' home
    c. arrested without a warrant and returned to custody
    d. arrested and subjected to treatment

5. Conditional supervision orders allow young persons to

    a. serve dispositions to secure custody in open custody
    b. hold a job or go to school while living in a secure custody facility
    c. serve the remainder of their sentence in the community
    d. serve the remainder of their custodial disposition with almost no conditions imposed on them, except for staying out of trouble

Short Answer

1. Describe the underlying reasons for having facilities that provide custody with the least degree of restraint.

    _____

    _____

    _____

    _____

    _____

    _____

    _____

    _____

2. Identify five factors that are to be taken into account when a sentence is to be served in a facility with a higher degree of restraint.

    _____

    _____

    _____

    _____

_____

_____

_____

_____

3. Identify four purposes for which re-integrative leaves may be granted.

_____

_____

_____

_____

_____

_____

_____

_____

4. Identify five mandatory conditions to be imposed as part of a conditional supervision order.

_____

_____

_____

_____

_____

_____

_____

_____

5. Identify four purposes for which day release may be granted.

_____

_____

_____

_____

_____

_____

_____

_____

6. Under what conditions may a police officer arrest a young person who is under an order of conditional supervision?

_____

_____

_____

_____

_____

_____

_____

_____

7. Identify two things that a probation officer must do within 30 days of a young person receiving a sentence.

_____

_____

_____

_____

_____

_____

_____

_____

8. Discuss critically the following statement: "Defence counsel and the police cannot help but disagree strongly on the need to provide so many different types of services to young persons in conflict with the law."

_____

_____

_____

_____

_____

_____

_____

9. Describe and discuss the importance of "relationship custody" in the approach to assisting youth in custody.

_____

_____

_____

_____

_____

_____

_____

_____

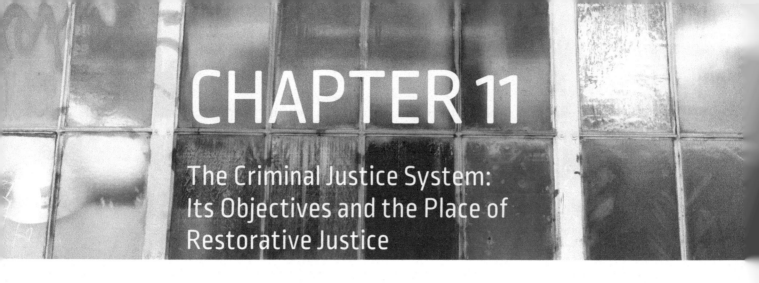

CHAPTER 11

The Criminal Justice System: Its Objectives and the Place of Restorative Justice

LEARNING OUTCOMES

Students who have mastered this chapter will have the ability to do the following:

- Identify and define seven objectives of the criminal justice system.
- Identify the compatibility of the objectives with one another.
- Explain how each objective is addressed in the youth justice system.
- Discuss the special place of restitution in the youth justice system.
- Define restorative justice.
- Identify the three perspectives from which restorative justice sees the effects of crime.
- Identify the roles of the various persons involved in a restorative justice conference.
- Indicate what goes on in a restorative justice conference.
- Indicate the purpose of the Canadian Victims Bill of Rights.

THE OBJECTIVES OF THE CRIMINAL JUSTICE SYSTEM

In Canadian society, as in other countries that trace their legal systems back to English common law, there is not a unitary view of the purpose or objective of the criminal justice system. What we have is a set of ideas as to the purpose of criminal law and the system (e.g., police, Crown, courts, jails, and prisons) that supports it. As we will see later, these "ideas" are different, and they are sometimes inconsistent with each other. That is, acting based on one may mean rejecting, in whole or in part, another.

What are these ideas or views that we hold about the purposes or objectives of the criminal justice system? Commentators have outlined several purposes of the criminal justice system: restraint, retribution, specific (individual) deterrence, general (societal) deterrence, symbolism, rehabilitation, and restitution.

Restraint

The objective of **restraint** is to protect society by incapacitating the individual from committing further crimes. In varying degrees, parole, probation, house arrest, and imprisonment are forms of restraint. Cutting off the hand of a pickpocket, and castrating rapists, are forms of restraint from different times and places. Capital punishment is the ultimate form of restraint.

Retribution

While many people consider retribution to be the same as revenge, they are, in fact, different. Revenge knows no boundaries: you push, I shove; you slap, I punch; you stab, I shoot. **Retribution**, in contrast, is measured. It means to give back to the perpetrator in equal measure what was done to or taken from the victim. The perpetrator should suffer the same pain as was inflicted on the victim. Its formal expression goes back at least as far as the Code of Hammurabi (1700 BC) where the expression of justice takes the form of "an eye for any eye and a tooth for a tooth." For some types of crimes, especially those involving personal injury, the criterion of the Code is difficult to meet in a society that is not willing to inflict pain in the form of flogging or the severing of one or more body parts. We can address some crimes involving money or property on this basis. It needs to be noted, however, that retribution is not about giving back to the victim, but about giving back to the offender the pain or loss that the offender inflicted on others.

Specific Deterrence

Specific deterrence, sometimes called *individual deterrence*, is the idea that there can be interventions in the form of punishment or pain of some sort that, if inflicted on the perpetrator, will make it less likely that the crime will again be committed. That is, because of having directly experienced some punishment (e.g., formal processing, fine, or restriction of freedom), the individual will not recidivate to avoid the punishment that is found aversive. The intervention causes the perpetrator to do a set of calculations and discover that the cost outweighs the advantage of breaking the law.

General Deterrence

In contrast to specific deterrence, **general deterrence** (societal deterrence) is the idea that when other members of society experience vicariously, not personally, the punishment of an offender, they will be less likely to commit that offence themselves.

Symbolism

Some believe that the presence of laws and the fact that violators are processed serves an important **symbolic** value for society. These are expressions of our mores (i.e., societal customs and conventions); what we say as a society that we do not like, or wish not to tolerate and, consequently, place on our unacceptable list of human behaviour. Even in the relative absence of enforcement or in the unlikelihood of conviction (e.g., simple possession of drugs), we see the presence of these laws in the *Criminal Code* as an important symbol of our values and of our ideas of right and wrong.

Rehabilitation

Rehabilitation, as the name suggests, is about making the person "able again" to live a life that does not depend on crime. Whether it is about making someone able "again" or able for the first time, **rehabilitation** involves a set of interventions (things done to, for, or with people) to change that person so he or she will function as a law-abiding member of society. The nature of the interventions that we consider rehabilitative is broad and varied. Some interventions are educational or emotional, increasing the likelihood of earning a legitimate living. Some are therapeutic in character, designed to address alcohol or drug dependency, gambling addiction, mental health issue, or anger management problems. Still others are about changing attitudes, which are emotional predispositions to react in certain ways to particular stimuli. They may involve some or all of attitudes toward women, the legitimacy of law, the dignity of other persons, respect for authority, or seeing oneself as a person whose behaviour has a real impact on others. In brief, the notion of rehabilitation, sometimes thought of as treatment, involves interventions that change the offender to reduce the likelihood of recidivism.

Restitution

For our purposes, the last of these ideas or views about the purpose of criminal law is restitution. **Restitution** is about giving back. It is about restoring the victim to the original state or condition, before the crime that victimized. To restore is to make whole again. Sometimes making the victim whole again appears easy. If an offender steals $100 and $100 is returned, restitution—at least financially—has occurred. If emotional injury or physical injury is involved, the return of the $100 does not restore the victim to wholeness. Some potential forms of restitution could involve further contact between the offender and the victim that the victim might not find congenial. Court-ordered free babysitting for a child molester, for example, is a non-starter. Senior citizens whose property has been vandalized may not much care to have the young perpetrator painting their fence or cutting their lawn. Some attempts at restitution have been with us for some time, as with a restitution order where the conviction carries a lifetime order to repay the victims for their loss. The problem with such orders is that few offenders have the capacity or resources to repay their victims. They may also lack motivation to do so.

Over the past 30 years or so, many jurisdictions have moved in the direction of paying more attention to restitution. These steps have taken various forms, some of which are as follows: victim impact statements, victim compensation schemes, plea bargains, and restorative justice initiatives.

Victim Impact Statements

The *Canadian Victims Bill of Rights* came into force on July 23, 2015. This Act gives every victim the right to present a victim impact statement and to have the Court or Review Board take it into account when sentencing an accused person or when making other decisions about a person found not criminally responsible. Any person who has been physically or emotionally harmed, has had property damaged, or lost money as a result of offence may prepare a **victim impact statement**. The *direct victim* is the person who encountered the loss or injury, personally. *Indirect victims* are relatives (spouse, parents, siblings, children) who also suffered because of what happened to the victim. Both direct and indirect victims offer these statements to the court at the sentencing stage of the trial. The statements give victims the opportunity to tell the court and the offender of the depth and seriousness of their injury and how it has affected their life, relationships, health, finances, and trust in others. Victims must be permitted to read the statements, in person, in the courtroom, if they choose. Victims can also read their statement with a support person nearby, from behind a screen, or outside the courtroom via closed circuit television—whatever makes the victims the most comfortable. The statements can also be read by the Crown prosecutor, police, or victim services personnel. Victim statements can also be prepared and read at Review Board hearings.

Rules usually do not allow the statements to recommend what the appropriate sentence should be, but the Court must take the statement into account when sentencing the offender. It does allow victims to address the consequences of the victimization, which, most often, is not allowed during the trial part of the case. The courts see this as a form of restitution, in that direct and indirect victims feel that they too have had their day in court so that their experiences may be reflected in the sentence. In this sense, victim impact statements have elements of both retribution and restitution.

Victim Compensation Schemes

Some jurisdictions have provisions for victims of crime to be compensated. In Ontario, we have the **Criminal Injuries Compensation Board**. It is a quasi-judicial tribunal, created and funded by the Government of Ontario. It receives formal requests for financial compensation from victims of crime for the pain, suffering, funeral expenses, lost income, and cost of the injuries that they have sustained. Typically, awards are not large, but they are a step in the direction of making victims "whole again." The funds distributed do not come from the perpetrators of crime; the government allocates money to the board as part of its yearly budgeting process. Other financial assistance programs include Financial Assistance for Families of Homicide Victims Program, Victim Quick Response Program, and the Vulnerable Victims and Family Fund.

Victim Supports

Ontario Victim Services works to ensure that victims of crime are treated with respect and receive the information and services they need. These services include the following:

- Domestic Violence Court Program
- Family Court Support Worker Program
- Help for child victims
- Internet Child Exploitation Counselling Program
- Legal services
- Partner assault response programs
- Support services for male survivors of sexual abuse
- Sexual assault/rape crisis centres
- Victim Crisis Assistance Ontario
- Victim/Witness Assistance Program

These services are funded through the Victims' Justice Fund (VJF). Funds for the VJF is collected from victim fine surcharges imposed on fines under the *Provincial Offences Act* as well as the federal victim surcharge, which is imposed on *Criminal Code* and *Controlled Drugs and Substances Act* offences. In 2014–15, over $47 million was collected. Pursuant to the *Victims Bill of Rights*, money paid into the VJF is used to assist victims of *Criminal Code* offences by supporting programs that provide services to victims and by making grants to community agencies that help victims. VJF funding cannot be used to provide direct compensation to victims; this is done through the Criminal Injuries Compensation Board.

Plea Bargains

Our criminal justice system depends on the majority of persons accused of crime pleading guilty. If all accused persons pled not guilty and demanded trials, our criminal justice system would grind to a halt. Not enough Crown Attorneys, judges, court rooms, or court days exist to handle such a caseload. Accused persons will not plead guilty simply to benefit the court or the system as a whole. They need some incentive. The incentives are provided as part of a **plea bargain**, that is, an agreement between the Crown prosecutor and the defence attorney to plead guilty in exchange for certain concessions. This bargain may be struck along several dimensions. The Crown can reduce the number of charges (e.g., 12 originally, but plead guilty to one or two). The severity of the charge may be reduced—rather than run the risk of being found guilty of break and enter theft, an offender may agree to plead to a lesser charge of being in possession of stolen goods. The defence can make an offer of partial or, more likely, full restitution of money fraudulently obtained. This offer could lead to a sentencing recommendation to the court that the Crown and defence attorney make jointly. Restitution, when it is possible, can be a critical element in a defendant securing a favourable plea bargain.

Restorative Justice Initiatives

Restorative justice initiatives may, theoretically, be put in place during any part of the criminal justice process. For adults it occurs post-charge and pre-trial, but it is sometimes done following a guilty plea and before sentencing. We will discuss restorative justice initiatives in greater detail in a later section of this chapter. For now, consider them as creating opportunities for the victim and the offender to come together so that the victim may show the nature, extent, and consequences of the harm received. Offenders have the opportunity to express sorrow, shame, or other emotions for the consequences of their behaviour. Restorative justice is intended to be restorative for both the victim and the offender. As we will see, the community is also expected to be a beneficiary.

Summary

These seven ideas about what the objectives of the criminal justice system are quite different one from the other, because they tend to have different foci (some on the offender, others on the victim, and still others on the broader society) and different means of reaching their objective. Sometimes, we may target a particular intervention at two or more objectives: a lengthy prison term may restrain, individually deter, generally deter, and be seen as retributive. In other cases, the pursuit of one objective may be at cross-purposes or, at least, interfere with one or more other objectives. If the focus is on rehabilitating the offender, little may be accomplished by way of retribution, general deterrence, or restitution.

Take the opportunity to visit court on a day when sentencing is argued. You will find that both the Crown prosecutor and the defence attorney will, one by one, go through this list of objectives of criminal justice and show to the court why each should or should not be given weight in the sentence. Not surprisingly, the two will express quite different views and show why the features of this case (perpetrator, victim, circumstances, record of the perpetrator, etc.) support a reliance on one or more of these objectives and not on some others.

When the judge produces reasons for sentencing, these same objectives of criminal justice will be reviewed and there will be an indication of which ones weighed more prominently concerning the facts of this case.

YOUTH CRIMINAL JUSTICE SYSTEM

The objectives of the criminal justice system identified above apply to adult offenders. They apply differently to young people in conflict with the law. Under the *Youth Criminal Justice Act (YCJA)*, interventions with young persons are, initially, aimed at restoring (or bringing for the first time) the young person to a state or condition that the young person can function effectively in society. The 2012 amendments of the *Safe Streets and Communities Act*, allow the courts to consider "specific deterrence" and "denunciation" in sentencing. General deterrence was not included in the reforms as a factor to be considered.

What does that mean for the objectives of criminal justice discussed above?

Restraint

Under the *YCJA*, restraint is not a high-ranking objective. Restraint, particularly as custody, is to be used to protect the individual or the society in more extreme cases rather than in typical cases. Custodial sentences are to be reserved for the most serious of crimes and for situations where a range of other interventions has been unsuccessful.

Retribution

Retribution is not an objective of the *YCJA*. The underlying philosophy of the *YCJA* makes it clear that youth are not to be "punished" for what they have done wrong.

Specific/Individual Deterrence

The *YCJA* wishes to see young persons deterred from doing wrong, but it does not intend that deterrence to be produced by inflicting punishment on the youth so the youth will fear being the subject of such punishment in the future. That being said, the judges can impose sentences with the intent "to bring home to the young person what may happen if he contemplates further criminal activities" [*R. v. B.-S.(T.)* 2014 ONCJ CanLII at para 96].

General Deterrence

Due to the limits on the publication of information about specific young persons, the likelihood of general deterrence is reduced, assuming that such an effect was possible. The presence of police officers in schools, curfews, and the limited reporting that does go on, especially when the young person charged is known to peers, may make some contribution to general deterrence. The provisions of the *YCJA*, however, serve to reduce the likelihood that this will happen.

Symbolism

The symbolic functions of law are served by the community—including media—drawing attention to behaviour considered inappropriate.

Rehabilitation

Rehabilitation of young persons in conflict with the law is the cornerstone of the *YCJA*. Rehabilitation is seen in the broadest sense and the *YCJA* provides for broad and varied types of interventions being available and used at every step in the youth justice system, from pre-arrest to post-conviction. In this way, the *YCJA* expresses its heritage going back to the *Young Offenders Act* and its predecessor—the *Juvenile Delinquents*

Act. The emphasis is on trying to find those interventions that will address the needs of the young person and employing interventions that are less formal before applying the more formal ones.

Restitution

The *YCJA* is not, in the first place, focused on the victim so much as it is focused on the young person. The Act is mindful, however, of the need to protect victims from re-victimization and society from being at risk of further unlawful behaviour.

Focus on Reintegration and Restoration

The adult justice system and the youth justice system share some, but not all, of the same objectives. The principal differences are that the youth justice system deliberately avoids punishment and emphasizes rehabilitation and the restoration of social harmony. The *YCJA* has a major emphasis on the reintegration of young persons into the community. The Act is not prescriptive about how this reintegration is to take place, but it does require that a minimum of one-third of a sentence be served on probation. We see this period of partial restraint as necessary for there to be sufficient time for the process of reintegration to be realized. Except for the length of probation, the *YCJA* is non-specific about the stages or processes of reintegration. These are left to each jurisdiction to decide.

The emphasis on reintegration into the community raises the idea that reintegration is not something that young people can simply will. The process needs community involvement and commitment as well. The interest by the community is affected by the extent to which it too was victimized. Add to that the fact that the proximate victim is frequently a member of the same community. What you get is the intersection of at least three sets of interests: those of the offender, those of the victim, and those of the community. Restorative justice has its philosophical roots in the notion of restitution as restorative. It sees crime as an act that damages not only the victim and the community, but also the perpetrator. All three need to be restored so that social harmony may prevail.

RESTORATIVE JUSTICE IN CANADA

In Canada, the federal Parliament is responsible for enacting criminal law, while the administration of justice is the responsibility of provincial and territorial governments. The *Youth Criminal Justice Act* is federal legislation, but it is the responsibility of each jurisdiction to determine the manner in which they will carry out the administration of justice.

The *YCJA* calls for a variety of measures to be put in place that would make it possible to deal with some young persons in conflict with the law in a way that does not depend on the use of formal aspects of the youth criminal justice system. Among the types of measures that have been considered are those that we generally consider as involving restorative justice. The intent is not to replace the criminal justice system, but to expand options that are consistent with it. Especially, it looks to preventing further wrongdoing as its objective, not punishment. Restorative justice is also used in the adult system where punishment is not excluded.

Restorative justice is an approach to dealing with wrongs or injuries done. It considers that these wrongs or injuries affect not only the victim, but that they affect the community and the perpetrator as well. Restorative justice is not about finding the "right" punishment. It is about reparation: actions that attempt to repair the damage done to the victim, the community, and the perpetrator. The reparations may be *material* as in returning or paying for stolen or damaged property and they may also be symbolic as in acts or apologies that show a heartfelt sense of shame for the offending behaviour and an indication of why they will not repeat it.

In the sections that follow, we will outline the origins of restorative justice principles and the challenges associated with applying them in other than some traditional ways.

The idea that in order for justice to be done it ought to involve restitution is not new. Justice as an engine of restoration, for what has been damaged, is to be found in many societies as part of the cultural definitions and codes that date back thousands of years. According to Van Ness and Strong (2006: 7) the idea that offenders and their families should make restitution to victims and the community is an "ancient pattern":

> The Code of Hammurabi (c. 1700 B.C.E.) prescribed restitution for property offences, as did the Code of Lipit-Ishtar (1875 B.C.E.). Other Middle Eastern codes, such as the Sumerian Code of Ur-Nammu (c. 2050 B.C.E.) and the Code of Esnunna (c. 1700 B.C.E.), provided for restitution even in the case of violent offenses.... The Lex Salica (c. 496 C.E.) ...included restitution for crimes ranging from theft to homicide. The Laws of Ethelbert (c. 600 C.E.) ...contained detailed restitution schedules that distinguished the values, for example, of each finger and its nail. Each of these diverse cultures retained an expectation that offenders and their families should make amends to victims and their families—not simply to ensure that injured persons received restitution but also to restore community peace.

Restorative Justice: An Indigenous Tradition

In North America, Indigenous communities have practiced notions of restorative justice for some time. Mostly, these communities are small, fairly homogeneous, and characterized by extended kinship and clan groups. Many First Nations in Canada have populations of a few hundred persons. As a result, in most Indigenous communities everyone—or nearly everyone—is known to everyone else.

Healing circles carry out restorative justice where the victim, the offender, and the community come together to decide what and by what means each can have their dignity restored and made integral again. Justice, in this framework, is done when the victim, the offender, and the community are restored to the state of wholeness or integrity that prevailed before the offending behaviour.

The healing circle can only come together when the key participants are ready. The victim must be ready to face the offender and show how the harm that was inflicted hurt and otherwise affected that person. The offender must be ready to admit guilt for the act and be prepared to accept responsibility for the consequences of the act and the extent to which the victim suffered. The offender must be prepared to apologize to the victim and to the community for the actions that caused harm. The offender must also be willing to accept the decision of the community as to the appropriate manner of dealing with this behaviour. Representatives of the community are there to see to it that the victim is not further harmed, to receive the apology of the offender, to decide the appropriate way of dealing with the offender, and receive the repentant person back into the community so that three objectives may be reached.

1. The victim needs to feel restored in the sense that restitution has been made in fact or in symbol.
2. The offender needs to understand the severity of the act or actions and realize that not only did the victim suffer, but that the community was also victimized. The perpetrator must acknowledge that the offending behaviour was at odds with membership in the community and that the offender now wants to be restored to community membership.
3. The community needs to be restored to wholeness; this occurs when restitution to the victim takes place, when the offender's request to be re-admitted is accompanied with a promise of improved behaviour, and when the community itself pronounces on the appropriate disposition of the matter. The offender may have to do something for the victim or the victim's family to make them whole again. Some form of reparation for the community may also be involved.

Overall, there has been an increased adoption of restorative justice principles and practice over the last 10 years. For more information, you can research this topic at Correctional Service Canada, through the Government of Canada, which maintains a website on restorative justice programs, services, and initiatives throughout the country (http://www.csc-scc.gc.ca/restorative-justice/index-eng.shtml). *The Canadian Inventory of Restorative Justice Programs and Services* is intended to help victims, offenders, and the general public locate programs that teach, advocate, promote, conduct research, provide services, produce resources, and provide training related to restorative justice.

Restorative Justice and Youth in Conflict with the Law

Notions of restorative justice were applied in non-Indigenous communities even when the *Young Offenders Act* was in place. The *YCJA* has placed a greater emphasis on restorative justice as one means of dealing with violations by young persons without using the more formal apparatus of the youth justice system. Consistent with the *YCJA*, the emphasis is on addressing the misdeeds as early as possible and as close as possible to the community where the young person lives.

THE GENESIS OF RESTORATIVE JUSTICE FOR YOUTH IN CANADA

In this day and age, we can take the presence of restorative justice initiatives for granted—they are now mainstream in our approach to handling offenders, as opposed to unique. But that was not always the case. The Elmira Case discussed below was the beginning of the restorative justice approach. A police officer proposed to the judge that the young men be allowed to make personal apologies to the victims and work to earn money to pay compensation for damages. When this was proposed to the judge, there was no past precedent—previously decided case—that had used this approach to deal with young offenders. Community Justice Initiatives of Waterloo is known worldwide as starting the first restorative justice program.

"Elmira Case" Tells of Restorative Justice for Russ Kelly's 1974 Drunk Rampage

The reckless wrecking spree of a Mount Forest teenager is the subject of a new documentary, premiering at the Grand River Film Festival on Wednesday.

In 1974, 18-year-old Russ Kelly and a friend went on a drunken rampage in Elmira, slashing tires, smashing windows and even overturning a boat. By morning, 22 properties had been damaged at a cost exceeding $3,000 according to media reports at the time.

"We really messed up," said Kelly, now 59, in an interview on *The Morning Edition*. "We caused a lot of damage to a lot of innocent people."

> *"To see the anger in their eyes and the disgust on their face—I felt very much ashamed."—Russ Kelly*

No Jail Time

Kelly and his friend were arrested and questioned by the police the morning after the event, but instead of going to jail, the probation officer suggested a different punishment.

"He saw that there could be some therapeutic value in us meeting our victims," he said, so the two young men went door-to-door, apologizing to the people whose property they had destroyed.

"Honestly, it was very, very scary. It took every ounce of courage I had to stand on these people's property ... and meet them face to face," Kelly said. "To see the anger in their eyes and the disgust on their face—I felt very much ashamed."

Turning Point

"I probably would have ended up in jail again."—Russ Kelly

The experience was critical for Kelly, who said his life could have turned out much differently if he had been sent to jail at 18.

"I quite likely would have come out a hardened person—a hardened heart, chip on my shoulder, angry at society and everyone in it. I probably would have ended up in jail again."

Instead, Kelly went on to graduate from Conestoga College, has become an advocate for young offenders, and is now the subject of a new documentary, *The Elmira Case*, produced by Rosco Films.

Impact on Conflict Resolution

His story has also transformed the way conflict is resolved in more than 50 countries according to Community Justice Initiatives, a Kitchener, Ont. organization that partnered with Rosco Films to produce the documentary.

"It makes me very proud and honoured," Kelly said. "I made the right choice to do something that has turned into something very big that helps people to have closure and to heal from the effects of conflict and crime."

The documentary is available through https://cjiwr.com/order-online/the-elmira-case/

Source: "'Elmira Case' tells of restorative justice for Russ Kelly's 1974 drunk rampage." *CBC News*, November 2, 2015. Accessed March 15, 2018, at http://www.cbc.ca/news/canada/kitchener-waterloo/elmira-case-restorative-justice-russ-kelly-drunken-rampage-1.3300370.

Cases can come to these restorative justice programs in a variety of ways. Police officers occasionally make the referral as part of a decision to refer a young person who has come into conflict with the law. This is the decision to "refer to a program" rather than to charge the youth.

In other cases, when the police have laid a charge, the Crown may refer to a restorative justice program to divert the matter away from the more formal youth justice system. The Crown may also charge the young person and make the referral before court appearance as part of a plea bargain.

At the point at which the case reaches youth justice court, the judge can make the referral pre-trial or wait until a finding of guilt and then make the referral.

Differences exist among police services, Crown attorneys, and judges about what they consider to be the most appropriate times to make referrals to restorative justice programs. All these decisions occur within a context of the facts of the case that include but are not limited to the following:

- Type and severity of the crime
- Nature and extent of the injuries to the victim(s)
- History of criminal involvement of the young person
- Apparent willingness of the young person to admit guilt and make reparations

In broad strokes, restorative justice programs operate as follows:

1. A referral to the program occurs.
2. Restorative justice personnel interview the *young person* and those who support that person to achieve three objectives:
    (a) Ensure that the young person understands the restorative justice process and how it works.
    (b) Identify whether the young person is prepared to be accountable for the act committed, and is prepared to apologize and make amends.
    (c) Reach a judgment that the young person is ready for a restorative justice intervention and that it is likely to be beneficial to the victim, the community, and the young person.
3. Restorative justice personnel interview the *victim* and those who support that person to achieve the following objectives.
    (a) Ensure that the victim understands the restorative justice process and how it works.
    (b) Identify whether the victim is prepared to be in the same room with and interact with the perpetrator.
    (c) Reach a judgment that the victim and those who support that person are ready for a restorative justice intervention and that the intervention is likely to be beneficial to the victim, the offender, and the community.
4. The restorative justice personnel identify members of the community who would be appropriate to participate in the process. Ideally, these are respected members of the community who are known to the offender, the victim, and their supporters. In many urban settings, the "community representatives" are known to none of the other participants. It is their role, nonetheless, to express how crime damages the community, the victim, and the perpetrator. They express, symbolically, the pain of the community as a result of what was done as well as their view of the reparations that need to be made.
5. At a time and place suitable to all participants, the "conference" (sometimes it is called the "meeting" or the "encounter") takes place. A member of the restorative justice program team moderates it. The **moderator**, sometimes called "conference leader," begins the meeting by reminding everyone why they have come together and to what they have agreed. The moderator repeats ground rules and reminds all that a common goal exists, that is about reparation and moving forward. The past is not forgotten: it is an important part of the reason that the conference is taking place. The dominant view, however, needs to be toward the future.

The Conference Process
Usually it is the young person who speaks first and professes some degree of sorrow and offers an apology. If the tone or content is found shallow, the victim or a supporter of the victim will point it out. Occasionally, the supporters of the young person will urge greater disclosure and press for details.

The victim takes the opportunity to express the extent of the harm that was caused and how it has taken its toll in financial, emotional, and physical terms.

Representatives of the community address how violations of law interfere with the common good and the social health of the community. They may also point out how the incident has also damaged the young person and that there is now a rift between the young person and the community that must be fixed if the community is to be restored to wholeness. The community cannot be whole unless the victim and the offender have their proper places restored.

Discussion takes place about what it is that needs to be restored, how it should be done and who should do it. While all need to participate in the process of restoration, it is the young person who needs to commit to specific acts that are agreed to by the rest as appropriate for restoration of the victim, the community, and the young person. These actions can take a variety of forms. Frequently they involve apologies to the victim or others, sometimes they are oral, other times they are required to be written. When restitution is possible, in kind or in money, it is usually required. In addition, the conference leader may decide that the young person should provide some form of service to the victim, the victim's family, or the community.

After the Conference
Well-organized restorative justice programs follow-up with the victim, the offender, and their supporters to gauge their reactions to the conference and the process leading up to it to learn their level of satisfaction, whether it met their expectations, and whether they would recommend it to others or use it again themselves. They are usually asked whether they have suggestions about how the whole process could be improved.

The lack of systematic evaluations makes it impossible to say, at this time, whether these restorative justice interventions reduce rates of recidivism from what they would have been if the more formal youth justice apparatus had been used. Much of the existing evidence is anecdotal, but it does show a quite high level of satisfaction by victims, offenders, and community representatives.

Livingstone, Macdonald, and Carr (2013: 2) undertook a systematic review only to find that restorative justice process does not make a difference with respect to re-offending. The lack of good quality data continues to be problematic in reaching a definitive conclusion, even for this review. They summarized as follows:

> The purpose of this review was to look at whether young people who are part of a restorative justice conference are less likely to reoffend than those who go through normal court proceedings. Four randomized controlled trials were included in this review. Findings indicate that there was no difference between those who are part of restorative justice conferences and those in normal court proceedings in terms of the rate of reoffending after the intervention. There was also no difference between these two groups in terms of a change in their self-esteem or their satisfaction with the process. Results may indicate that victims who are part of a restorative conference are more satisfied than those who are part of court proceedings. The quality of the included studies was low. More high quality research using a design where participants are randomly allocated to an intervention or control group is needed.

IN THE NEWS

An Example of Restorative Justice in Action

Alberta youth comes forward, expresses "sincere remorse" after writing hate message in snow

A youth from Red Deer, Alberta, turned himself into police after having been caught on camera writing a hate message in the snow outside the Islamic Centre. Rather than press charges, the members of the Islamic Centre embraced the opportunity to talk to the young man and use this as a teaching moment to facilitate understanding.

The Red Deer RCMP worked with the youth, his family and the Red Deer Islamic Centre "to resolve the incident through restorative justice means, which includes a meeting between the youth and staff and the Islamic Centre," according to an RCMP news release. As noted by the RCMP officer Karyn Kay: "In our view, the best outcome for this file is to develop a positive change in understanding and in behaviour through relationships and education rather than pursuing a criminal charge."

Source: Emily Mertz, "Alberta youth comes forward, expresses 'sincere remorse' after writing hate message in snow," *Global News*, March 3, 2017. Accessed March 15, 2018 at

TEST YOUR KNOWLEDGE

Definitions

Define the following terms:

1. Restraint

_____

_____

_____

2. Retribution

_____

_____

_____

3. Specific deterrence

_____

_____

_____

4. General deterrence

_____

_____

_____

5. Symbolism

_____

_____

_____

6. Rehabilitation

_____

_____

_____

7. Restitution

_____

_____

_____

8. Victim impact statement

_____

_____

_____

9. Criminal Injuries Compensation Board

_____

_____

_____

10. Plea bargain

_____

_____

_____

11. Restorative justice initiatives

_____

_____

_____

12. Healing circles

_____

_____

_____

13. Moderator

_____

_____

_____

True/False

1.   T   F   The only objective of the criminal justice system is to find innocent people "not guilty."

2.   T   F   Restraint has the goal of protecting the community from further harm.

3.   T   F   Retribution is balanced.

4.   T   F   General deterrence depends on the vicarious experience of punishment.

5.   T   F   Even laws that are difficult to enforce can play a role in expressing where we stand, as a society, with respect to certain behaviours.

6.   T   F   In victim impact statements, victims get to tell the court the nature and length of punishment that the offender deserves.

7.   T   F   Typically in youth conferencing circles the community is represented.

8.   T   F   The notion of restorative justice was largely unknown until the *YCJA* came into effect.

9.   T   F   Restorative justice programs exist in large cities.

10.   T   F   The police can refer a young person to a restorative justice program.

Multiple Choice

1.   Capital punishment is the ultimate form of

   a.   rehabilitation
   b.   restraint
   c.   general deterrence
   d.   retribution

2.   One argument for retaining laws that are difficult to enforce is that they are

   a.   a specific deterrent
   b.   a form of restitution
   c.   symbolic
   d.   No such argument can be made for this situation.

3.   Primarily, restitution involves the notion of

   a.   making the victim whole again
   b.   returning cash and property to the victim
   c.   allowing the victim to be involved in the punishment of the offender
   d.   putting the case to "rest"

4.   The *Youth Criminal Justice Act* is focused primarily on

   a.   making the young offender function effectively in society
   b.   punishing the young offender
   c.   achieving balance between the offender and the victim
   d.   compensating the victim

5.   Restraint is

   a.   a primary goal of the *Youth Criminal Justice Act*
   b.   a concept used to limit how much a victim is compensated
   c.   the underlying principle of restorative justice
   d.   not a major focus of the *Youth Criminal Justice Act*

6. The manner in which restorative justice is to be implemented is

   a. clearly identified in the *Criminal Code of Canada*
   b. clearly identified in the *Youth Criminal Justice Act*
   c. clearly identified in the *Child and Family Services Act*
   d. left up to each provincial jurisdiction to determine

7. Restorative justice is intended to

   a. expand options that are consistent with the criminal justice system
   b. compensate the victim
   c. act as a form of general deterrence
   d. punish the young offender

8. For restorative justice to be effective, the offender must

   a. be ready to admit guilt for the act
   b. be prepared to accept responsibility for the consequences of the act
   c. acknowledge the extent to which the victim suffered
   d. all of the above

9. Restorative justice programs appear to be most effective in

   a. large, homogeneous communities
   b. Indigenous and First Nations communities only
   c. smaller, homogeneous communities
   d. communities with large proportions of young people

10. Restorative justice programs

   a. have been shown to be the most effective means of rehabilitating young offenders
   b. are the most cost-effective way of compensating victims and making them "whole" again
   c. usually initiated by victims wishing to receive compensation
   d. seem like a good idea but with some questions as to their overall effectiveness

Short Answer

1. Assume for a moment that the primary goals of the justice system are restraint, symbolism, rehabilitation, and restitution. What role do the police play in achieving those goals?

   _____

   _____

   _____

   _____

   _____

_____

_____

_____

2. To what degree are the police involved in implementing the goals of specific and general deterrence?

_____

_____

_____

_____

_____

_____

_____

3. Among the goals of restraint, retribution, specific deterrence, general deterrence, symbolism, rehabilitation, and restitution, which are incompatible with the goals of the _YCJA_ and why?

_____

_____

_____

_____

_____

_____

_____

4. What conditions relating to the offender have to exist in order for a restorative justice program to function?

_____

_____

_____

_____

_____

_____

_____

_____

5. Briefly outline what happens in a restorative justice program.

_____

_____

_____

_____

_____

_____

_____

_____

6. What is the role of the community in a restorative justice program?

_____

_____

_____

_____

_____

_____

_____

_____

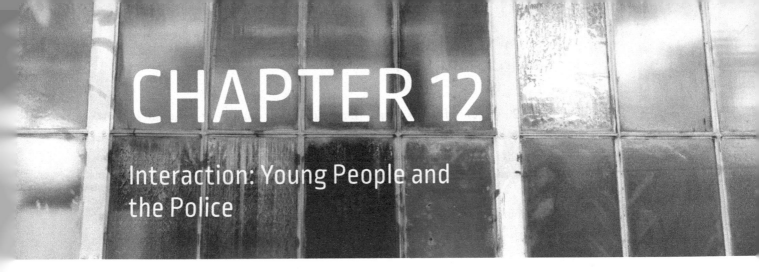

CHAPTER 12

Interaction: Young People and the Police

LEARNING OUTCOMES

Students who have mastered this chapter will have the ability to do the following:

- Discuss the complicated relationship between youthful offending and adult criminality.
- Explain the factors that appear to make a difference in the perception of the police by young people.
- Explain how race and ethnicity impacts policing and attitudes toward police.
- Explain the interaction of justice-involved youth and mental health.
- Identify things that the police can do in an effort to enhance their image in the community.
- Identify strategies that can be used in interaction with young people.
- Identify the responsibility of police officers when they perceive child endangerment occurring.
- Identify some common characteristics of victims of child abuse and child neglect.
- Identify some common characteristics of perpetrators of child abuse and child neglect.
- Explain the responsibilities and options available to the police in dealing with young people who are "out of control."
- Identify the indicators of gang presence.
- Explain the advantages of having a police service whose composition reflects that of the larger community.

YOUNG PEOPLE AND THE POLICE

Most adult criminals start their careers as young persons; most young persons who come into conflict with the law do not become adult criminals. In their classic study of delinquency in a birth cohort, for example, Wolfgang et al. (1987) discovered that only about 20 percent of those people they studied without a juvenile record became adult criminals, while almost half of those with chronic criminal records as young people became chronic adult offenders. This paradox underlies one of the biggest challenges facing the criminal justice system. The "key" to much adult crime, it seems, is to identify the chronic offenders and devise some successful strategy for getting them off the crime track. Unfortunately, it is often difficult to identify those who will become chronic offenders until they become chronic offenders. By that time, as much research suggests, it is very difficult to change their behaviour.

While those results might suggest a strong element of pessimism, we should not forget that most young people who come in contact with the authorities do not become chronic or hard-core offenders. It is the goal of the *Youth Criminal Justice Act (YCJA)* to handle both these categories. The lighter side of its philosophy is to recognize that the majority of young persons who come into conflict with the law need little, if any, intervention. Indeed, many argue that if we are too heavy handed with these youngsters, we may reinforce the very behaviour we wish to prevent. On the other hand, the *YCJA* recognizes that some young people pose a significant danger to themselves and to their communities and need serious intervention if they are to be rehabilitated and reintegrated into society.

The police officer is generally the first point of contact with the criminal justice system for both categories of young people. Because of this wide range of "clientele," the police officer must show great flexibility in responding to the problems posed by young persons. At the same time, the law places some restrictions on that flexibility.

In this chapter, we will provide some insights and advice that might make the task somewhat easier. The first part of the chapter reviews some of what we know about how young people view the police and why they react to them as they do. The second part of the chapter focuses on some strategies that might be useful in handling different types of young people who are "out of control."

ATTITUDES TOWARD THE POLICE

During the past 30 years, several studies have been conducted that shed some light on the views of young people toward the police. There has also been some research on the effectiveness of various efforts to improve the image of the police in the community, in general, and with young people, in particular. Overall, Canadian individuals with the following characteristics and/or lived experiences are more likely to have negative views of the police: "young people, visible minorities, males, those who have experienced criminal victimization, those dissatisfied with their safety and those who perceive their neighborhoods as being high in crime" (O'Connor, 2008: 590).

When we ask the question, what is the "attitude" of one or another group toward the police, we must recall what we mean by *attitude*. An **attitude** is an emotional predisposition to react in a particular way toward a particular stimulus. Toward a given stimulus (e.g., person of a particular race or person who does a particular kind of work), one may have a generally positive attitude or a generally negative attitude, but not both at the same time.

Existing research suggests that police officers and various symbols associated with police officers—for example, uniforms and squad cars—are for few people neutral stimuli. Rather, they tend to evoke in some sectors of the population negative sentiments, and, in other sectors of the population more positive sentiments. It is useful to know what it is that seems to generate more or less positive attitudes toward law enforcement officers and whether anything can be done to change those attitudes.

The major items that relate to attitudes toward the police are age, social class, race and ethnicity, misunderstanding, and adversarial contact. The principal findings that relate to each are discussed below.

Age

Public opinion polls in Canada and the United States show that young people have more negative attitudes toward the police than have older people. They are also less likely than adults to rate the performance of the police as satisfactory. Interestingly, younger children rate police work as more prestigious than do older children.

No one can say for sure what is the cause of less favourable attitudes toward the police as young people move through adolescence, but some perspectives appear quite reasonable.

- Adolescence is naturally a time of opposition to the *status quo* and a time of idealism and sympathy for the underdogs of society. The idealism and sympathy may be expressed as antagonism toward those in power and their representatives.
- There is a change in the perception of authority as children grow up. Younger children generally view authority as a positive personal characteristic; power is equated with personal goodness.
- Young people who come into contact with the police because of their having violated the law have less positive attitudes toward the police than those who have not had that type of contact.

Social Class

Social class or socioeconomic status (SES) refers to how factors, such as one's occupation and education, combine with wealth and income to position one relative to others in society. The relationship between social class and perception of the police is complicated, and no consistent trend has been found. In some research, lower income has been associated with more negative police perceptions, such that rising incomes have been associated with increased positive perception. Similarly, education has had inconsistent findings: some research has found that less educated people have more confidence in the police, while others have found the opposite—individuals with higher levels of education have more positive attitudes toward police; and still other research suggests that it is largely irrelevant (see O'Connor, 2008). Interestingly, married people tend to have more confidence in the police than unmarried people. Such a simple analysis misses important features that make a difference. Commonly, if one takes into account contacts with the police because of misbehaviour, much of the apparent relationship disappears. Across all social classes, the greater the contact with police because of official contacts involving arrest and citations for misbehaviour, the more negative are the attitudes toward the police.

The neighbourhood in which one grows up has an effect. Living in a neighbourhood that is low income, crime ridden, and contains broken windows, vandalism, and general disorder typically results in a young person having more contact with police and thereby generates stronger negative attitudes than in a young person who grows up in a neighbourhood without these characteristics and thereby experiences little police presence in their day-to-day life (Peirone, Maticka-Tyndale, Gbadebo & Kerr, 2017).

Young people who have been arrested, young people who self-report more rather than fewer acts of law-violating behaviour, and young people who define themselves as delinquents have much more negative attitudes toward the police than have young people who do not have those experiences. It is not surprising, therefore, that because members of the lower class have more official contact with the police, their attitudes tend to be more negative.

Race and Ethnicity

Concerns about race and the role it plays in the Canadian criminal justice system has risen to the fore, particularly with respect to how police treat racial and ethnic minorities. This has been at the forefront in the United States and Canada as concerns about the abuse of ethno-racialization as a part of policing, such as greater surveillance and policing of minority groups as compared to white individuals. Inappropriate police actions that have involved too-quick escalating enforcement tactics have been a concern in the deaths of black individuals—particularly black men. The public backlash against the deaths of Michael Brown in Ferguson, MO (2013), and Freddie Gray in Baltimore, MD (2015), has given rise to massive protests bringing attention to claims of racial profiling and police discrimination. Canada has had similar high profile cases: Dudley George, Lester Donaldson, Wade Lawson, and Sophia Cook (Owusu-Bempah & Wortley, 2014). The impact of social media has been revolutionary. The Black Lives Matter movement has risen from tragic incidents where African Americans and African Canadians have been killed at the hands of police in incidents that have been characterized by a quick escalation of increasing compliance demands by police who have been quick to use to the ultimate force—their guns—on individuals for which there has been little objective cause to substantiate that level of violence.

Henry and Tator (2005; as cited in Owusu-Bempah & Wortley, 2014: 284) offer these definitions of race and ethnicity:

Race is socially constructed category used to classify humankind according to common ancestry and reliant on differentiation by such physical characteristics as color of skin, hair texture, stature, and facial characteristics. The concept of race has no basis in biological reality and as such, has no meaning independent of its social definitions. But, as a social construction, race significantly affects the lives of people of color.

Ethnicity, on the other hand refers to the characteristics of a human group that shares a common heritage, culture, language, religion, and perhaps race.

Race and crime has long been a focus of research and commentary in the United States, but is a newer focus in Canada that has received relatively little attention, with suggestions that Canadians are uncomfortable discussing issues of racial difference and tend to focus on "culture" and "ethnicity" by counting "visible minorities" without distinguishing between the vast differences of people subsumed within this one category (Owusu-Bempah & Wortley, 2014).

The lack of careful statistical data collection has facilitated the ruse that racial bias is not an issue for the Canadian criminal justice system (Owusu-Bempah & Wortley, 2014). Canada has only started to consistently collect some data about race and crime over the last few decades (Reasons et al., 2016). The bottom-line conclusion is clear—race plays a role in the Canadian justice system (Reasons et al., 2016); and in Canada race is not only about black lives, but also the lives of its Indigenous peoples (Owusu-Bempah & Wortley, 2014).

One area of consistent data collection and reporting has been rates of incarceration, where minorities are over-represented in prison populations (Reasons et al., 2016). For instance, the adult Indigenous population is 4 percent of the Canadian population but accounts for 24 percent of custodial sentences (Reasons et al., 2016). While there is little research on black Canadians, survey data from Toronto on black Canadian youth has found them to be more involved with violence such as assaults (Wortley & Owusu-Bempah, 2011).

Lack of good data on this subject continues to thwart efforts to get a clear picture (Reasons et al., 2016); nevertheless, increased research in Canada has been undertaken. Statistics show that black Canadians and Indigenous individuals have relatively high rates of criminal involvement both as perpetrators and as victims (Owusu-Bempah & Wortley, 2014). And this also holds true for young minorities: black students in Toronto were significantly more likely to report multiple violent victimizations, including physical assaults, death threats, weapon-related threats, assault with a weapon, and sexual assault (as reported in the 2000 Toronto Youth Crime and Victimization Survey). Furthermore, black Canadians are also more likely to be the targets of hate crimes because of their race/ethnicity, religion, or sexual orientation.

Hayle, Wortley, and Tanner (2016) found that police are more likely to racially profile black youth who live at home as compared to white youth. Yet, black and white street youth were equally likely to be stopped and searched in Toronto. Earlier research on Toronto high school students found far higher rates of black students being stopped and questioned by police that could not be explained by criminal activity, gang membership, drug and alcohol use, or public leisure activities (Wortley & Tanner, 2005; in Owusu-Bempah & Wortley, 2014). Overall, these police practices contribute to black youth's hostility to police.

Therefore, not surprisingly, the research literature on race/ethnicity and attitudes toward the police has been largely consistent in concluding that race/ethnicity is the single most important factor in predicting attitudes toward the police (O'Connor, 2008). And those attitudes are largely negative—with black individuals reporting more negative views of police than white individuals and professing that police treat them unfairly and abuse their power.

Race is often compounded by other social characteristics—social class being a prime one. An *intersectional analysis* requires that individual's connection to the criminal justice system is a function of a complex dynamic that involves class, gender, as well as race/ethnicity.

When it comes to the attitudes of young people (13–18 years of age), race also has an inter-play with perceptions of police: black and Latino students were significantly less satisfied with the police than white students (Wu, Lake & Cao, 2015). As Wu and colleagues note, "the black-white dichotomy remains one of the most prominent features of public sentiments toward and perceptions of the police" (463). The concern is that attitudes formed during one's youth tend to remain and are difficult to change, particularly when they have been amplified and reinforced by peers.

As more recent efforts to collect data have been undertaken, a picture is emerging that is more clearly evident: police practices are not colour or ethnically blind. There is a bias in policing both in practice and underlying attitudes that influence how and what is done even when no crime has been committed. The following discussion on the practice of **carding** speaks to this issue.

WHEN POLICE ARE "POLICING" AND THERE ISN'T A CRIME TO INVESTIGATE: RACIAL PROFILING AND THE PRACTICE OF "CARDING"

Some youth will come under greater scrutiny of the police than others. As Peirone and colleagues summarize, "youth who spend more time in public spaces without adult supervision, who are out at night; who congregate on streets, in parks, or in alleys; or who frequent clubs have a greater likelihood and frequency of contact with police than youth not found in these locales" (Peirone, Maticka-Tyndale, Gbadebo & Kerr, 2017: 349). Police have long used the highly controversial practice of "carding"—a practice that has been formerly called "interventions" and "street checks." Currently, it is often referred as "community engagement." Generally, it refers to the police practice of stopping individuals and requesting identification and then collecting personal data about the individual for future reference by completing a "contact card."

This carding practice is permitted in accordance with Ontario Regulation 58/16 titled "Collection of Identifying Information in Certain Circumstances—Prohibition and Duties," part of the *Police Services Act*, R.S.O. 1990, c.P.15, as amended. It provides that the collection of identifying information may be done for the purpose of:

(a) inquiring into offences that have been or might be committed;

(b) inquiring into suspicious activities to detect offences; or

(c) gathering information for intelligence purposes [s. 1(1)]

The Regulations specifically note that this activity is *not* to be undertaken solely because the officer perceives the individual to belong to a racialized group unless there is an active investigation that makes that characteristic relevant [s. 5(1)]. Police typically seek the individual's name, age, skin colour, estimated height and weight, and names of friends and "associates." This information is entered into a database, which is then referred to when actual crimes are committed. While the practice is deemed to be racially neutral, the actual practice has been characterized as a type of racial profiling.

Racial profiling has emerged as important social issue in Canada. Black, Indigenous, South Asian, and Arab communities have raised concerns about police and airport security practices that target their groups solely on the basis of their race (Owusu-Bempah & Wortley, 2014). The *Toronto Star* newspaper sought access to the content of police contact cards that had been completed between 2003 and 2008. Of the 1.7 million cards, black individuals were the subject of 25 percent, yet only represented 8 percent of the Toronto population (Owusu-Bempah & Wortley, 2014). Similar findings have been reported for black youth living in Toronto, where they were disproportionately targeted for "stop-and-search practices" particularly when they were found in "white" neighbourhoods where they looked "out of place" (Meng, Giwa & Anucha, 2015). This level of greater surveillance results in two consequences: 1) black individuals are more likely to be caught when they are breaking the law as compared to white individuals doing the same activities; and 2) these practices continue to alienate black people from Canadian society, and further entrenches concerns about discrimination and racial injustice (Owusu-Bempah & Wortley, 2014: 304).

There are a number of concerns with human and Constitutional rights infringements for the following reasons:

1. This practice disproportionately is used with African-Canadians than white individuals.

2. The vast majority of these information requests result in no arrest or charges (in other words, there is no actual suspicion that a crime has been committed, but rather there is a group in a public place that attract police attention for simply being there).

3. Most individuals are unaware that they are *not* required to carry identification unless they are driving.

4. Even if they are carrying identification, most individuals are unaware that they are *not* required by law to produce such information [s. 6(1)(a)].

5. Psychologically, the situation of being surrounded by police invokes fear, particularly in young black youth who will feel compelled to comply with the request so as to not to escalate the situation and risk the ire of police.

Because of the intrusive nature of these requests, the Regulation stipulates that there must be training around conveying of rights and being mindful of bias:

Continued

11. (1) A chief of police shall ensure that every police officer on his or her police force who attempts to collect identifying information ... has successfully completed the training required under this section within the previous 36 months.

(2) The training ... shall include training on the following topics:

1. The right of an individual not to provide information to a police officer, the limitations on this right and how to ensure that this right is respected.

2. The right of an individual to discontinue an interaction with a police officer, the limitations on this right and how to avoid unlawfully psychologically detaining an individual.

3. Bias awareness, discrimination and racism and how to avoid bias, discrimination and racism when providing police services.

4. The rights that individuals have to access information about themselves that is in the custody, or under the control, of a police force.

5. The initiation of interactions with members of the public.

> Given what we hear in the media about Black Lives Matter and other negative interactions with police, do you think that the provisions in s. 11 are adequate to overcome racial bias and profiling?

THE SKIN WE'RE IN

You may want to watch this Canadian documentary by journalist Desmond Cole, directed by Charles Officer, on the practice of carding/racial profiling and how racism is at the root of the practice (premiered March 2017).

As summarized on the CBC website:

> This film marks a distinctly Canadian contribution to the "Black Lives Matter" movement which originated in the US, but which describes a set of systemic injustices and disadvantages faced by all black people living in white-dominated societies. Cole asserts that anti-black racism is so all-encompassing in Canada that black people and their allies, far from congratulating themselves that they do not live in America, should be following the American example and dismantling the structures that continue to hold them back.

http://www.cbc.ca/firsthand/episodes/the-skin-were-in

The following is a summary from the Ontario Human Rights Commission on "routine" traffic stops (a version of the "carding" practice), wherein black and other racial minorities who may be driving a luxury car, are driving in a "white" neighbourhood, or have racially diverse occupants (e.g., a black driver with a white female passenger) are pulled over and questioned about who they are and what they are doing.

ONTARIO HUMAN RIGHTS COMMISSION (OHRC) RESPONSE TO THE RACE DATA AND TRAFFIC STOPS IN OTTAWA REPORT

November 28, 2016

On October 24, 2016, researchers from York University released their analysis of race-based data collected by the Ottawa Police Service (OPS) on traffic stops. The OPS's Traffic Stop Race Data Collection Project (TSRDCP) arose as a result of a human rights complaint, in which a young Black man alleged that he experienced racial profiling by OPS officers.

The Ottawa Police Services Board (OPSB) and the Ontario Human Rights Commission (OHRC) reached a settlement in 2012. As part of the settlement, the OPS agreed that its officers would collect race-based data on traffic stops for two years beginning in 2013. The OPS fully complied with the settlement and even went beyond what was required in its data collection efforts, resulting in a comprehensive police data collection initiative.

The research findings that have arisen from the data collection are alarming and are consistent with racial profiling. They cannot and should not be easily explained away. The researchers found that Black and Middle Eastern people experienced disproportionately high incidences of traffic stops. Black drivers were stopped 2.3 times more than you would expect based on their driving population and Middle Eastern drivers were stopped 3.3 times more. Young male Black drivers (age 16–24) were stopped 8.3 times more than would be expected based on their driving population, while young male Middle Eastern drivers were stopped 12 times more.

Racial profiling is a particularly damaging form of racial discrimination. The OHRC defines racial profiling as any action undertaken for reasons of safety, security or public protection that relies on stereotypes about race, colour, ethnicity, ancestry, religion or place of origin rather than on reasonable suspicion, to single out an individual for greater scrutiny or different treatment.

Racial profiling undermines the relationship between police and racialized and Indigenous individuals, families and communities. It is important to note that racial profiling is not just based on officer bias, whether implicit or explicit. It is often found in systemic practices of policing such as officer deployment, intelligence gathering activities, and stopping people who are perceived to be "out of place" in the neighbourhood. These often appear as routine or "normal" policing activities.

The OPS and others have asserted that the researchers' findings do not "prove" racial profiling. However, the purpose of the study was to assess whether racialized or Indigenous people are over-represented in traffic stops, and to provide clear evidence the OPS could act on. The research was not designed to prove causation, nor could quantitative research on its own generally prove this. Given that other factors do not provide a conclusive non-discriminatory explanation for racialized people experiencing disproportionately high incidences of traffic stops, it is clear that the data is consistent with racial profiling.

The results from the OPS data collection project are situated within a context of historical police/community relations with racialized and Indigenous peoples in Ottawa and Canada generally. The findings are also similar to the results of other research conducted on police bias. These concerns and experiences, both in Ottawa and more broadly, reinforce that the over-representation of racialized people in traffic stops in the Ottawa data is consistent with racial profiling.

Continued

The results highlight the need for the OPS, other police services across Ontario and the government to put in place meaningful and effective measures to prevent and eliminate all forms of racial profiling. Elements of a broader strategy to address systemic racial profiling include providing leadership, reimagining models of community policing, providing training, and committing to monitoring and accountability measures.

Source: Ontario Human Rights Commission, "OHRC Response to the Race Data and Traffic Stops in Ottawa Report," November 28, 2016. This Executive summary was retrieved August 5, 2017 from http://www.ohrc.on.ca/en/book/export/html/19676. Follow this link, which includes the full report.

IN THE NEWS

Together the OHRC and the OFIFC Take Steps towards Reconciliation

LONDON—On July 8, 2017, the Ontario Human Rights Commission (OHRC) and the Ontario Federation of Indigenous Friendship Centres (OFIFC) signed an agreement with the ultimate goal of ending anti-Indigenous discrimination in Ontario. This agreement sets the stage for future collaboration with urban Indigenous communities that is based on trust, dignity, respect, and a shared commitment to reconciliation and substantive equality.

Under this agreement, the OFIFC and OHRC will work together to build the capacity and human rights knowledge of OFIFC and Friendship Centre staff, share information and data, engage with urban Indigenous people on policy development, and coordinate provincial advocacy in key areas such as health care, child welfare and criminal justice.

This agreement reflects the OHRC's commitment to engage with Indigenous leaders and communities on common issues and concerns. It will connect the OHRC with the nearly two-thirds of Indigenous people who live in urban areas and are protected from discrimination in housing, employment and services under the Ontario Human Rights Code. Friendship Centres are the primary service delivery agents for Indigenous people seeking culturally-sensitive and culturally-appropriate services in urban communities.

"This partnership is an important step in protecting and defending the human rights of Indigenous people in Ontario," said Susan Barberstock, President of the Ontario Federation of Indigenous Friendship Centres (OFIFC). "This agreement between our organizations will bring communities together to safeguard the human rights of Indigenous people."

Source: Ontario Human Rights Commission, "Together the OHRC and the OFIFC take steps towards reconciliation," Press Release, July 10, 2017. Retrieved from http://www.ohrc.on.ca/en/news_centre/together-ohrc-and-ofifc-take-steps-towards-reconciliation

Misunderstanding

It is not unusual that there is misunderstanding about the nature of police work by the public. Neither is it unusual for the police to misunderstand how the public perceives them. Perception of the police is shaped by the result of personal contacts with the police, but beyond that, many people do not understand the nature of police work or the environment in which police officers have to function. Stereotypes about the police are transmitted culturally from one generation to another. Experiences judged to be negative by some people are told to others and can shape the views of those who have not had the contact. Wrongdoing by individual police officers may be easily generalized to all members of the group.

Police are often viewed as "the bearers of bad news," since they present people with traffic tickets, arrest warrants, and the like. The fact that the police are only doing their duty—that is, the job they are assigned—is easily missed, and the charge is made that they "should have something better to do with their time, by catching real criminals, such as murderers and rapists."

It has been noted that some contacts between the police and the community go poorly because both sides have expectations that they will go badly. Whether it is a mutual expectation of violence or a mutual expectation of insolence, there is little opportunity for the interaction to go well or be perceived positively. This is, of course, the reason that some communities have worked hard to alter the perceptions of the community about the police and sensitize the police to the needs and concerns of the community.

Adversarial Contact

Not all contact with the police is adversarial, but it is adversarial contact that is associated with the more negative attitudes toward the police. People who seek and receive assistance from the police tend to have more favourable attitudes toward the police. They are the ones who are most apt to feel served and protected.

Few people the police arrest are likely to consider the contact as favourable; indeed, it is likely to be seen as adversarial. There are, however, many other circumstances where contact takes place that has an unfortunate element in it for a member of the public, but where the event does not have to be perceived as adversarial. While no one is happy about being cited for a traffic violation or being stopped at a roadside check for those who drink and drive, the *manner* in which persons are treated by the police can make the contact not seem adversarial. Tone of voice, politeness, and professional demeanour can create an atmosphere of mutual respect, and the contact need not foster a negative view of either the police or the citizen.

Enhancing the Image

Police services devote resources to making contacts with the community that will increase the likelihood of the police being perceived as those who serve and protect, for example, by addressing groups of seniors (who are among members of the public who already hold positive attitudes toward the police) about ways of increasing their personal safety and avoiding scams.

School visits by the police are used in many communities. They are part of the school's effort to "street proof " kids, and they are part of the police emphasis on humanizing the police officer to young people. Opportunities are taken to provide a perspective on the nature of police work and to encourage young people to see the police officer as, if not a friend, certainly a protector and someone who is not to be feared but who can be approached in times of need.

One initiative to bridge the gap between black youth and the police (Giwa, James, Anucha & Schwartz, 2014) involved bringing together 15 youths of colour with 9 police officers to have a 3.5 hour facilitated dialogue to discuss: 1) What goes wrong in the relationship between police and youth of colour, and why?; and 2) What would the police and youth of colour do differently in a relationship of trust?

Overall, the dialogue revealed that there was an absence of communication, lack of co-operation and understanding, and insensitivity in the way police and youth of colour approached one another. Both groups offered their suggestions.

The youth focused on "safety, respect, consideration and understanding":

> Take time to socialize; pull us over for a reason; be graceful; start every encounter with an open mind; treat everyone equally; be respectful—instead of "shut up" say "be quiet", be more personally present in the community; focus on prevention; solve more crimes; be conscious of your approach, have patience; be less guarded.

The police officers focused on maintaining the "safety of individuals and society, appreciation and understanding" by noting:

> Don't push the limits, be gracious; offer bottom-line respect; listen before you react; treat us fairly; be more cooperative; tell the truth; be less suspicious of us; do not be shy to come forward; cooperate more in investigations; present a respectable image; open discussions with us; see both sides; understand legal statutes; don't be afraid to socialize in groups with your peers; recognize that cops are human, and that our number one concern when being approached is officer safety. (Giwa et al., 2014: 227)

Studies produce contradictory results on the question of whether such programs make a difference in how the police are perceived. With the youngest children, the visits seem successful, but as these children become adolescents, the impact disappears.

Much police work is reactive, and the police depend on the co-operation of the community to be able to do what the community expects them to do. We can expect, therefore, that police services will continue to take steps to forge individual and collective alliances with the communities, their diverse groups, and individual citizens. In this sense, each police officer, besides having a wide range of other responsibilities, is also an ambassador who has a chance to make a difference in the amount of good will that prevails between the local police service and the citizenry.

DEALING WITH YOUNG PEOPLE

How we interact with others is determined by a combination of factors, including our personalities, our social roles, and the specific circumstances in which we find ourselves. Being a police officer, particularly an officer in uniform, pre-defines how an exchange is going to take place even before you speak to someone. This situation is not unique to being a police officer. People react to *what* we are as much as to *who* we are. Consequently, people have views of how they should behave when interacting with any professional groups, including members of the clergy, teachers, physicians, social workers and, of course, the police.

Most young people have ambivalent feelings when interacting with the police. On the one hand, their parents and teachers have told them that if they are lost or in trouble, the police are a source of assistance. On the other hand, the authority of the police causes many young people to approach them with a certain level of fear and trepidation. The uniform and the physical equipment carried by an officer—a gun, handcuffs, and, possibly, a nightstick—reinforce those feelings. Some children of immigrants to Canada come from cultures where the primary role of the police is repression, and their interaction with the "authorities" cannot have a positive outcome.

Officers should keep in mind that the uniform will shape their relationship with a young person before any personal interaction takes place. As with most things in life, this can have both positive and negative consequences. The uniform can sometimes be a hindrance when an officer is attempting to build interpersonal rapport. On the other hand, the uniform can help maintain a necessary amount of respect, authority, and interpersonal distance.

All officers have their own personality characteristics and their own ways of dealing with people. With time, each of us develops strategies that work for us. There are, in addition, some guidelines that are helpful, whatever the specific strategies we use when we interact with young people. We offer the following points:

- Be firm but fair. Avoid giving young people a reason for being suspicious of or hating the police more than they already do.
- Do not overreact to the defiant "punk-like" attitude of many young people. Be aware that much of the bravado and anti-establishment attitude expressed by many young people is put on for the benefit of their peers or to cover personal insecurities. Even more than adults, young people feel the need to "save face" in front of their friends. Speaking to them one-on-one is usually more helpful than talking to them in groups.
- Remember that adolescence can be an extremely emotionally volatile time for many young people. As Bart Simpson says, "Making an adolescent depressed is as easy as shooting fish in a barrel." Unfortunately, this emotional volatility can sometimes put both the young person and others around them in danger.
- Remain approachable and understanding. Remember, however, you are not one of their "buddies" and that you do represent authority. Young people

expect cops to be straight with them. Many young people justify their misbehaviour by taking an "everybody does it" attitude. "Everyone," for example, "is on the take" or "cuts corners," including the police. Do nothing to reinforce this view.

- Do sweat the small stuff. Intervene in minor events—even if you decide to do nothing further. It sends a message that you are aware of what is going on, and this can often prevent more significant events.
- Maintain a good relationship with youth workers, particularly street workers. They are invaluable resources for handling young people in crises. Cross-referencing information from street workers and young people can also be useful in identifying adults who prey on vulnerable young people, such as drug pushers, pimps, and pedophiles.
- Talk with young people. Information and "street awareness" are major assets in police work. While the basic problems of adolescence change little from one generation to the next, pop culture (music, interests, dress, street language) has a way of changing overnight. Some of these elements are simply expressions of normal rebellion and attempts to express "individuality." Others are signs of trouble, such as gang membership or drug use.

SPECIAL CIRCUMSTANCES

There is no need to comment on the fact that the primary role of the police is law enforcement. Yet, law enforcement takes up only a small portion of an individual officer's day. Treger (1981), for example, indicates that over 90 percent of police services are social service interventions and not strictly law enforcement interventions. Most of those interventions are of a minor sort, where an officer provides information or general assistance. There are, however, some grey areas that arise where the police are asked to intervene in problems that may not quite fit under the category of law enforcement. It is to some of those that we turn our attention.

Child Endangerment

While the primary focus of this text is on the young offender, there are many situations in policing where the police encounter a young person who is a victim. In some situations, the same legislation that requires the police to intervene when a young person offends also requires the police to intervene when the young person is a victim.

A typical situation relates to what is called **child endangerment**. According to Brown and colleagues (1990: 50), "Child endangerment is synonymous with child maltreatment, neglect, and physical, emotional, and child abuse. It is a generic term that also includes sexual molestation." Ironically, many children who are endangered eventually become young offenders. For example, a high proportion of young offenders are victims of dysfunctional families, where alcohol and drug abuse, violence, and parental conflict are common. These are many of the same factors that place a young person in immediate risk of being a victim. Brown et al. (1990: 53) report that studies of prison inmates indicate that up to 90 percent claim to have been abused as children.

The police are often called to intervene in domestic disputes. While spousal violence may be the precipitating element behind the call for service, child endangerment is often a secondary aspect of the call. Clear cases of child endangerment are usually easy to spot. Abused children will often display signs of physical assault, such as bruises on their backs and faces (eyes and cheeks). Normal, robust children typically have bruised knees, shins, elbows, and foreheads that result from falls and horseplay. Abused children's behaviour will often be atypical for the circumstances; for example, they may exhibit extreme shyness or cower when spoken to by an adult. In Ontario, officers have the option of intervening under the *Child, Youth and Family Services Act (CYFSA)* if they think that the child is in immediate danger. In situations that are less obvious, and where a case for abuse or neglect cannot be made, these can be handled by contacting the Children's Aid Society and asking for a follow-up.

Unfortunately, many cases of child endangerment are not easy to detect. Adults who abuse or neglect children will often go to great lengths to cover their activities. They also tend to threaten and intimidate their young victims so that it may be difficult to elicit co-operation from a young person. Sadly, the chances are that when the officer becomes aware of a problem of abuse or neglect, it will have been ongoing for a considerable time.

Child abuse and neglect seem to span most social and economic groups in society so targeting high-risk groups is difficult. Carson and Macmurray (1996: 116–17) identify some common characteristics of victims and perpetrators. Among victims, they note the following:

- As children get older, they are more likely to be victims of physical abuse, although younger children are more likely to require medical attention.
- Generally, children between the ages of 8 and 12 years are most vulnerable to sexual abuse.
- Overall, females are more likely to be victims of physical abuse than are males.
- Ethnicity has almost no relationship with sexual abuse.
- Sexual abuse victims tend to be more isolated from peers.
- Females who live *without* their natural mothers or fathers are more vulnerable, and mothers being employed outside the home is more characteristic of these families.
- Victims generally have poor relationships with their parents.
- Sexual abuse victims are particularly likely to have parents who do not get along well or are in conflict with each other.

Among the characteristics of perpetrators, they note the following:

- Parents are typically the perpetrators of child abuse, and younger parents are more likely to be involved than older ones.

- Mothers are more likely to be perpetrators of physical abuse than are fathers (since mothers typically spend more time with children).
- There are higher rates of abuse in families where the father is disabled or not currently employed.
- Perpetrators of child maltreatment tend to be socially isolated.
- Presence of a stepfather (or non-biologically related father) is more often related to sexual abuse.
- Most perpetrators of sexual abuse are related and/or known to the victim.
- Males are overwhelmingly responsible for sexual abuse.

The role of the police in less serious cases is complex. Clearly, the police officer cannot ignore situations of obvious neglect and abuse. Often, however, the intervention of a "disinterested" outsider can be successful in preventing future occurrences. Recognizing the situation and putting adults "on notice," particularly if no history of a problem exists, can serve the same purpose as intervening with young offenders without charging them.

While instances of child endangerment can evoke strong emotional responses, police officers responding to such calls should only serve as crisis mediators. The police have neither the mandate nor the resources to maintain the ongoing contact essential to change the causes of the behaviour. Thus, the individual officer's best response is to intervene, remove any child who is in *immediate* danger, document the situation, and act as a liaison with other agencies. As Brown et al. (1990: 59) point out,

> police officers should not attempt to assume dual roles: police and social worker. To attempt to assume dual roles is to minimize their effectiveness as police officers. They must know the boundaries of their roles …the police are charged by law to prevent crimes and to arrest criminals…. In contrast, social workers are guided by civil statutes …and view their responsibility as providing assistance to these families so that they can remain intact.

Officers must keep in mind, however, that persons in domestic crises often suffer from **secondary victimization**. This usually happens after the police or social service agents leave the scene. The offender retaliates for the victim either calling or being responsible for calling the police. This risk of secondary victimization is one reason some jurisdictions have set up mandatory charge policies. Under these policies, police officers lay charges on their own initiative and do not rely on the victim for a formal complaint. Even where the police subsequently drop charges, this process allows for a cooling-off period.

Although the implication in this discussion is that the perpetrator is an adult, this is not always the case. Sometimes, young persons (particularly older teens) may not be the victims but the causes of domestic abuse. Older teens may victimize younger siblings, their parents, or other vulnerable relatives.

Children Who Are Out of Control

Police officers generally deal with two categories of "problem" young people. The first category consists of those who have or appear to have clearly committed an offence under the *Criminal Code of Canada* or another statute. The second category consists of "youths identified as incorrigibles, runaways, habitual truants, involved in sexual and alcohol experimentation, and who refuse to obey the reasonable directives of parents, legal guardians, or custodians" (Brown et al. 1990: 93). Often, parents, teachers, and others responsible for this latter group turn to the police for help.

Domestic and other calls resulting from the non-criminal misbehaviour of young people are a nuisance to many officers, since they are not trained or mandated to deal with such problems. On the other hand, the problem of out-of-control youngsters is a major challenge for most people, and they are unsure of where to turn for help. As Brown et al. (1990: 98) tells us,

> a general view held of the police by the general public is that they are mental health practitioners and the police agency is a social service agency. This view probably results from the fact that the police operate 24 hours a day, seven days a week, and respond as quickly as possible to calls for services. These telephone calls requesting assistance are frequently viewed as emergencies. When faced with problems beyond their control, particularly in the area of mental health, families may first turn to the police for assistance.

Intervention is important in these cases because many of these young people are straddling the fence between becoming full-fledged offenders and basically "good kids" who are going through a rough time. If the intervention is not effective, there is a good chance the young persons may hurt either themselves or someone else, or the behaviour may escalate into outright criminality.

Out-of-control kids are difficult for police to deal with for a couple of reasons. They have often not committed a statutory offence, or, while their behaviour may be a problem, the particular act or offence they commit is one that warrants "no action" or some similar minor intervention under the *YCJA*. In this latter situation, police officers essentially have three options, depending upon the circumstances. They may (1) invoke a minor intervention, such as speaking to the young person and the youth's parents to see if they can resolve the immediate situation, (2) take action under the *CYFSA*, or (3) refer the parents, the young person, or both, to another agency.

While the police wear many hats, it is the case that police officers are *primarily* law enforcement officials and not social workers. It is the role of police in these situations to ensure that the young person does not pose any immediate harm to himself/herself, or to others. The longer-term responsibility for intervention resides with other professionals. Some police services make it easier for uniformed personnel by having "domestic intervention" specialists whose role is to deal with such situations. Uniformed police officers, however, cannot and should not take primary responsibility for solving these problems.

On the other hand, effective police practice involves follow-up. Sometimes, a phone call or in-person visit the next day to make sure that an appointment or a contact with a social service professional has been made can help. Out-of-control children can be immensely frustrating to parents and others who have to deal with them. Sometimes, that frustration can lead adults supervising those young people to lash out and commit acts of violence for which they can be charged. This creates the ironic situation where the person who is often responsible for the problem becomes the victim and the original "victims" become the offenders.

Police intervention in these situations is, at best, a Band-Aid approach. The objective of officers called to these occurrences is to defuse the situation by getting people to regain control of themselves or to restrain individuals so that they do not pose an immediate risk. The causes of out-of-control behaviour are complex and may range from dysfunctional child–parent relationships resulting from substance abuse and physical or psychological abuse, to normal adolescent boundary testing that has gone a little too far, to problems of raging hormones. These and other factors may be at play within the context of the young person having difficulties at school, being subjected to negative peer pressure, and having feelings of inadequacy and social marginality.

It is important that police officers know that this range of causes exists, not because they are responsible for sorting out those that apply in a given instance, but because they need to recognize the complexity of human behaviour and not rely on simplistic solutions.

YOUNG PEOPLE WITH MENTAL HEALTH ISSUES

Mental health issues are a serious concern and are more likely to be an issue for justice-involved youth than for adolescents more generally (Rawana, Gentile, Gangier, Davis & Moore, 2015). Police frequently come into contact with individuals who have psychiatric disorders and mental health issues, sometimes with tragic results—many fatal shootings by police involved a person with a mental health problem (Krameddine, DeMarco, Hassel, & Silverstone, 2013). The challenge for police is that they are often the first on the scene but because mental illness is invisible they will not fully understand the nature of the illness of the young person with whom they are dealing. In turn, individuals with mental illness are very distrustful of police, have negative attitudes, and are highly fearful that police will not listen or understand their needs. This can lead to escalation of the situation between the person and police as the police seek compliance and the person with the mental illness becomes increasingly agitated.

Many mental health illnesses have their onset in adolescence and young adulthood. Therefore, police may also be dealing with young people who have not yet been diagnosed. The most common mental health issues amongst justice-involved youth are conduct disorder, substance use disorder, oppositional defiant disorder (ODD), anxiety disorder, attention-deficit/hyperactivity disorder (ADHD), depression, and post-traumatic stress disorder (PTSD) (Colins et al., 2010, as cited in Rawana et al., 2015).

Rawana et al. (2015) outline the risk factors associated with an increased like-lihood that a youth in the justice system will also present with mental health issues: trauma and stressful/negative life events; parental incarceration and alcohol use; cognitive and educational difficulties; time spent in custody; and poor coping strategies to regulate emotions and distress. Indigenous youth have particular risk factors associated with historical traumas and are at higher risk for physical, sexual, and emotional abuse; suicide; school dropout; and violent behaviour and delinquency.

The following statistics are reported by the Canadian Mental Health Association outlining how mental health issues impact youth:

- It is estimated that 10–20 percent of Canadian youth are affected by a mental illness or disorder—the single most disabling group of disorders worldwide.
- Today, approximately 5 percent of male youth and 12 percent of female youth, age 12 to 19, have experienced a major depressive episode.
- The total number of 12- to 19-year-olds in Canada at risk for developing depression is a staggering 3.2 million.
- Once depression is recognized, help can make a difference for 80 percent of people who are affected, allowing them to get back to their regular activities.
- Mental illness is increasingly threatening the lives of our children; with Canada's youth suicide rate the third highest in the industrialized world.
- Suicide is among the leading causes of death in 15- to 24-year-old Canadians, second only to accidents; 4,000 people die prematurely each year by suicide.
- Schizophrenia is youth's greatest disabler as it strikes most often in the 16- to 30-year-age group, affecting an estimated one person in 100.
- Surpassed only by injuries, mental disorders in youth are ranked as the second highest hospital care expenditure in Canada.
- In Canada, only 1 out of 5 children who need mental health services receives them.

Police need special training to deal with individuals with mental illness, including verbal intervention strategies and techniques to keep situations from escalating (Krameddine et al., 2013). There need to be coordinated efforts with other first responders and connection to services, as adolescence also represents a time of significant brain development and changes that result in the brain's receptivity to positive influences. Rehabilitation strategies, as opposed to punitive measures, are necessary. Unlike adults, youth are not likely to seek out treatment services voluntarily, and even when engaged do not show much motivation to engage with the treatment process, thus requiring the need for specific efforts to increase opportunities for youth to succeed.

In Ontario, specialized mental health programs have been developed for justice-involved youth. *Mental health diversion* directs youth from the legal system into community-based programs to seek treatment with the goal of averting further criminal involvement. In addition, the Youth Mental Health Court Worker (YMHCW) program through the Ontario Court of Justice assigns a trained mental health worker within the court to provide support to the youth with mental health needs. There are also a growing number of mental health courts, some now specifically for youth, that have a focus much like the mental health diversion discussed above, but these courts are specifically tailored to be less adversarial and more supportive. These Community Youth Courts (CYC) are present in Ottawa, London, and Toronto and provide a high level of collaboration with community services to respond quickly and effectively to mental health and substance abuse. Overall, "the goals of the CYC are to improve access to community treatment services, reduce case processing time, improve well-being, reduce recidivism, and increase community safety" (Rawana et al., 2015: 273).

IN THE NEWS

"Where Do We Go from Here?"

What started as a sombre vigil for Pierre Coriolan, a 58-year-old black man who was fatally shot by Montreal police this week, quickly turned into a call for change in how officers respond when people of colour are in distress.

"There's no communication, there's no support, there's no care," said Venetta Gordon, an activist from Black Lives Matter Montreal.

Organized by Black Lives Matter, Montréal Noir and Hoodstock, the crowd swelled into the streets of Montreal early Sunday afternoon …

The demonstration comes just days after police were called to Coriolan's apartment around 7 p.m. last Tuesday. A neighbour said a man was destroying items and yelling in his home.

When officers arrived at the building, the man confronted them holding a screwdriver in each hand, according to a statement by Quebec's independent investigations bureau, known by its French acronym, BEI.

Police tried to subdue him with a stun gun and rubber bullets, but were unsuccessful. Officers then used their firearms, some time between 7:19 p.m. and 7:30 p.m., when paramedics arrived at the scene.

The fact that Coriolan was black raised immediate concern among activists earlier this week, who fear racial profiling affected how officers responded to a person of colour in distress.

The Sunday vigil to commemorate Coriolan's life, organized by groups advocating against racism and police brutality, also featured a list of demands.

Organizers are asking Montreal police to name the officer who shot Coriolan, as well as collect and publish data on police interventions involving racialized people.

They also want health and social services to better serve the black community and provide better mental health supports. They called for action on institutionalized racism, adding that police shouldn't be at the frontline when it comes to responding to people in mental distress.

"They can't de-escalate," said Montreal activist Robin Maynard.

Maynard said the use of a stun gun, plastic bullets and eventually firearms by police during the intervention "shows they don't value the lives of black people."

Source: "'Where do we go from here?': Fatal shooting by Montreal police raises hard questions." *CBC News*, June 28, 2017. Retrieved from http://www.cbc.ca/news/canada/montreal/montreal-police-shooting-mental-illness-1.4181469

It is important to note the intersection of race and the speculation around issues of mental illness in this tragic story. The organizers' demands focus on a non-police response team for individuals displaying mental health issues. Is this case about race? Mental health? How realistic is this request in the face of violent behaviour? What alternatives do you propose?

Dealing with Gangs

A report by Public Safety Canada (2007) on youths in gangs describes that they consist of young people who:

- self-identify as a group (e.g., have a group name),
- are generally perceived by others as a distinct group, and
- are involved in a significant number of delinquent incidents that produce consistent negative responses from the community and/or law enforcement agencies.

The Montreal Police Service's definition of youth gang also incorporate the anti-social and delinquent behaviours that are distinctive of youth gangs. It defines a youth gang as:

An organized group of adolescents and/or young adults who rely on group intimidation and violence, and commit criminal acts in order to gain power and recognition and/or control certain areas of unlawful activity.

Official police statistics on Canadian gangs are almost non-existent, but it has been argued that high rates of homicide and gun crime among African Canadians and Indigenous individuals in Canada is due to their over-representation in street gangs (Owusu-Bempah & Wortley, 2014: 295). Results from the *Canadian Policy Survey on Youth Gangs* in the early 2000s reported results from 264 police agencies from across the country. They identified 484 different youth gangs in Canada with a total of 6,760 gang members. The racial make-up of the gangs was also tied to geography: Asian and South Asian gangs dominate the West Coast, Indigenous gangs dominate the Prairie provinces and black gangs dominate Central and Eastern Canada. The majority of gang members are male (94 percent) and 48 percent are under age 18, with most between the ages of 16 and 18 years of age (39 percent). The largest proportion of youth gang members were African Canadian (25 percent) followed by Aboriginal (21 percent), and Caucasian (18 percent).

Gang behaviour is common in most large urban cities and even in many smaller centres. Even well-to-do suburban communities are not immune to gangs. For example, a recent phenomenon in some Canadian cities is "swarming." Groups of young people encircle (swarm) another young person or an adult in a shopping mall and often assault or rob the victim. At its worst, swarming is a very dangerous activity and, at best, it is a nasty form of harassment. Overall, however, gangs are more prominent amongst groups where there is large social inequality and disadvantage.

Traditional gang behaviour can include gang "rumbles," selling drugs, extortion, and running protection rackets. Gangs can be a significant problem in schools when they "shake down" other kids for their phones and money. Adults sometimes use young gang members to distribute drugs in the belief that since their distributers fall under youth legislation, the consequences will be minimal if those young people are caught. Gangs can also be distribution networks for illegal weapons. Violent gang behaviour in many American cities has resulted in numerous deaths of gang members and many bystander shootings. While gang problems in Canada are not as prevalent as in the United States, many groups of Canadian kids pattern themselves after gangs found in Los Angeles, Chicago, or New York.

Typically, males make up gangs; few females are core members of gangs, and there are few all-girl gangs. Gang members vary considerably in their level of attachment to the gang as a unit and to other individuals in the gang. Some gangs are very short-lived, while others have a permanence and a neighbourhood reputation that passes down from one generation to the next. It is this variability that can make working with gangs difficult. It is also the case that a substantial gang mythology has grown over time, based on the experiences of a few inner city gangs in the United States and Hollywood's myth-making machine. Most gangs do not have the direction and coherence that either the gangs or the mass media would like you to believe.

Gangs often do not have an all-dominant leader and a clearly defined command structure. Membership is often in considerable flux with many people drifting in and out over time. Different individuals may take on leadership roles depending on what the gang is doing. On the other hand, some gangs revolve around one or two core members and simply disappear when those members are arrested, grow up, or move away.

This does not mean, however, that gangs are not a problem in some areas. Even if they are not engaged in serious crimes, neighbourhood gangs often pose a problem for local businesses and residents. Gang members who "hang" or "chill" in the front of stores or in shopping malls can intimidate customers and reduce a merchant's business. On neighbourhood streets, they can be a serious nuisance to both adults and other young people who live there. Gangs are also responsible for a considerable amount of vandalism. While it is the occasional serious, violent act that gains attention from the media, most crime-related gang behaviour involves petty offences, often fuelled by alcohol or drugs.

Young people find criminal gangs attractive for the same reasons they find membership in other social groupings attractive. Gang membership offers identity, companionship, peer acceptance, status, and a source of entertainment. Being a gang member may also mean access to illicit goods and services, such as drugs, alcohol, and pornography, as well as stolen or bootlegged property.

IN THE NEWS

Gangs and Their "Turf"

Two months before Jordan Manners was shot dead in his school, the young men accused of his murder went to a local community group for help.

They didn't get it because they live in Canada's toughest neighbourhood, a place where guns are abundant and gang turf determines who can go where. One of the accused, a 17-year-old who dropped out in March and whose girlfriend gave birth a week before Jordan's death, said he had always struggled academically but wanted a program that could help him stabilize his life and finish high school.

...

The sad irony is that such a program already exists in Jane-Finch. But it's on the south side of Finch Avenue, which might as well be in another country.

The two accused are from the areas north of Finch that were targeted by police in this week's raids against the Driftwood Crips. The Crips have a sworn enemy in the Bloods, who live in the housing projects on Finch's south side, and they ceremoniously avoid each other's territory.

...

Most of those I spoke with live in the enormous Palisades apartment complex that sits at the corner of Jane Street and Finch Avenue. They are between 15 and 21 years old and consider themselves Bloods, an identity borrowed from the gang wars of Los Angeles.

On the Internet, they pass themselves off as hardcore gangsters. They want to look tough, and dress in baggy gangsta-style clothes, but few are deeply involved in criminal activity. The gang is a collective identity that provides a sense of security in a tough environment.

...

In their planning sessions, community workers refer solemnly to "boundary issues" that impede program delivery. When the police hold consultations with youth, they have meetings in each distinct area to prevent rival gangs from mingling.

It's as though the kids have redrawn the neighbourhood map and forced the adults to adapt. As a result, the teens from Palisades, who often complain of having nothing to do, don't use the well-equipped community centre that's a block away in Crips territory.

Source: Joe Friesen, "Where boundary issues turn deadly," *The Globe and Mail,* June 16, 2007, p. A16.

The first task of police officers in dealing with gang behaviour is determining whether serious gang activity exists in their community. Because of the ages of the people involved, most gangs have school connections. Kenney and colleagues (1989: 321) provide seven indicators or signs that might be useful for identifying gang presence in schools:

1. Graffiti, the first indicator of gang activity at school, contains numbers, names, secret codes, and messages
2. Identifiable clothing, wearing of colours, hats or baseball caps, flags, insignias, bandanas
3. Hand signals among students
4. Specific slang
5. Street nicknames
6. Presence in school of sophisticated weaponry
7. Information on gang activity from fellow students

Not all gangs, however, are criminal gangs. It is part of human nature to form groups, and most of those groups—whether we call them gangs or clubs—are not part of the crime problem. The key to good police work is intelligence. For gangs, intelligence not only involves identifying gangs but going to the next step of deciding whether these gangs are a problem. In some circumstances, victims provide this information; in others, informants provide it.

Gangs are often grouped by ethnicity or neighbourhood, although not always. Most often, we become aware of gangs from lower-income areas, but "middle-class" gangs are not unheard of. Many Canadian gangs pattern themselves after American gangs they see in the movies or on TV or read about in the media (for example, in some recent cases of gang shootings in Toronto, the kids modelled themselves after the Bloods and the Crips, gangs that started in California).

Ethnic gangs have always been an element of the streetscape and have paralleled successive waves of immigration. Yesterday's newspapers carried stories of Irish or Italian gangs; today's papers carry stories of Black or East Asian gangs. The fact that gangs often group by ethnicity should not be surprising. Immigrants often cluster in certain neighbourhoods until they move up the socioeconomic ladder and integrate into the broader cultural matrix. Meanwhile, young people who live in those areas share common bonds defined by language, race, and customs that set them apart from the rest of their peers. They also share similar hassles in dealing with parents who are "still living in the old country."

Once gangs spring up in an ethnic community, calls will appear for police services to hire more officers from those communities. Invariably, there will be a time lag between the appearance of the problem and when officers can be recruited. Twenty-five years ago, Toronto had a "shortage" of officers of Italian, Greek, or Portuguese origin; today, the shortage is of those of East Indian, black, Chinese, and Middle Eastern ancestries.

Clearly, there are advantages of having officers who reflect the social mix of their community. In the case of ethnicity, language and cultural barriers can be formidable impediments to effective police work. Young people, those who are in trouble and those who are not, *may* find it easier to interact with a constable who is from a similar cultural background. On the other hand, simply being a co-ethnic does not necessarily make the job of policing easier. Indeed, it can make it more difficult at times. Young people will sometimes view co-ethnic officers as "sell-outs," representatives of their parents' generation, or persons who they expect will give them "a break."

The key to successfully interacting with young people from ethnic communities is the same as interacting with a young person from any other group. Maintain a fair, honest, and professional demeanour while being sensitive to the problems that are faced by the children of immigrants.

Dealing with major gang situations is not something for an individual officer. An effective response to gang problems usually involves a coordinated effort of the police service, schools, community groups, and other social agencies. Individual police officers are invaluable sources of information on gang membership and local practices. Uniformed officers may also be assigned to work as police/school liaison personnel in crime prevention programs.

IN THE NEWS

How Gangs Are Changing: Toronto Gangs Smaller, Looser—But Packing More Heat

Toronto's organized crime is anything but. The city's gangs are smaller, their members more loosely organized than they were 20 years ago.

They're also more lethal: The number of homicides classified as "gang-related" has risen since the 1990s. Last Saturday's shooting at the Eaton Centre—while officially not gang-related in Toronto police lexicon—thrust into the limelight the sort of violence normally hidden in the city's most blighted neighbourhoods.

The changes are driven by a combination of successful police crackdowns and deeper despair in the city's poorest, increasingly isolated areas.

Toronto's biggest gangs, some of them with ties to international organized crime, have been largely decimated by police raids—or driven underground. While the idea of sporting gang "colours" was big years ago, it is no longer: It doesn't pay to advertise. But it's become much easier to get your hands on a gun.

Street crime was "the thing to do" in the Jane-Finch area where Andrew Bacchus grew up in the 1990s. But when he was younger, he says, you didn't see 14-year-olds with firearms. "Guys would duke it out in the parking lot, or a knife may get pulled," he said. "The odd guy might have a gun…. But today, guns are a bigger problem than any gang. There's just too many damn guns out there."

Continued

Toronto's "gang-related" deaths peaked in 2003 at 35, and have since ranged between 14 and 30 a year. In 2010, the last year for which statistics were available, Toronto had the fourth-highest rate of gang-related homicides per capita of any major Canadian city, after Winnipeg, Vancouver and Montreal.

People who study Toronto's street violence argue the issue isn't about gang membership: The definition of organized crime becomes fuzzy when it refers to teenagers who aren't so much organized as banded together in mutual desperation.

"You can't compare youth groups to bikers. Bikers have clubs. Bikers have locations. Bikers have import and export," said Segun Akinsanya, who twice landed in jail as a teen and now acts as a mentor. "For these kids, there's nothing else. If you want to classify it, call it opportunists without any opportunities."

For the vast majority of the population, Toronto is a safer city than it's been in decades. But it helps if you live in the right part of town. Poorer neighbourhoods are more isolated and harder to police.

"The design of some of these neighbourhoods, they're restrictive to vehicle traffic," said Chris White, superintendent in charge of Toronto Police's organized crime enforcement. "So it makes it more difficult to police it in the normal policing aspect."

Youth unemployment is high for people with university degrees. If you haven't graduated from high school and have the wrong address on your résumé, finding a job becomes nearly impossible. "The quality of life of our truly disadvantaged has actually deteriorated further over the last decade, and it looks like it might further deteriorate," says University of Toronto criminologist Scot Wortley. "If we see an entrenchment of these types of communities, we would probably also see an increase in gang recruitment."

Victor Beausoleil has lost track of the number of friends who've been gunned down—at a subway station, in a barber shop, on the street. At least 20, he figures. Mr. Beausoleil grew up in Toronto's east end, bouncing between one community and another. He knows the feeling of needing somewhere to belong, to feel accepted and empowered and to make more money than he could otherwise imagine. And he knows it isn't easy to extricate oneself.

"But you can only get so many collect calls from friends in Don [Jail]. You can only go to so many funerals," he said.

Mr. Bacchus has been working with street youth since he decided, at 22, he was tired of going to jail. The uproar over such high-profile shootings as last week's in the Eaton Centre drives him nuts.

"In the last four or five years I've attended 14, 15 funerals. And not once have I seen a politician from any level of government come out and make a statement," he said. "Incidents of gun violence happen in inner-city communities all the time. It's a shame that we don't rally the same way as when it happens on Yonge Street."

Source: A.M. Paperny, "Toronto gangs smaller, looser–but packing more heat." *Globe and Mail*, June 11, 2012. https://www.theglobeandmail.com/news/toronto/toronto-gangs-smaller-looser-but-packing-more-heat/article4243872/

THE LINK BETWEEN YOUNG MEN WHO JOIN GANGS AND YOUNG MEN WHO JOIN TERROR CELLS

Jamil Jivani is a young Canadian lawyer, community organizer and professor currently writing a book called *Why Young Men?* about the parallels between troubled young men who participate in local tragedies like shootings, and troubled young men whose acts of violence seize international attention. After the Paris attacks, he spent three months in Molenbeek, the Brussels neighbourhood where many of the attackers grew up, talking to people about common solutions to the challenges facing young men in Molenbeek and young men in his own community. Jivani is also a community organizer in the Jane and Finch neighbourhood in Toronto where he grew up, and the founder of the Policing Literacy Initiative. In the CBC interview listed below, He spoke to Michael Enright about why it's so easy for gangs and ISIS leaders to recruit young men, the parallels between police carding and stop-and-frisk policies in North America and police responses to terrorism in Europe, and how to empower young men to think differently about their masculinity.

http://www.cbc.ca/radio/thesundayedition/american-hypocrisy-on-russian-hacking-why-young-men-an-over-the-phone-book-club-bach-and-anti-semitism-1.3919404/the-link-between-young-men-who-join-gangs-and-young-men-who-join-terror-cells-1.3919406

Source: CBC Radio, "The link between young men who join gangs and young men who join terror cells," *The Sunday Edition*, August 6, 2017.

BULLYING AND CYBERBULLYING: THE IMPACT OF SOCIAL MEDIA

"Bullying" has often been seen as one of those inevitable components of growing up. Generations of children have bullied and have been the victims of bullies. Depending upon the time and circumstances, concerned adults have intervened to varying degrees, but the phenomenon has not often elicited much formal concern. Fortunately, that attitude of benign neglect by our social institutions has started to change and the extent and seriousness of bullying, particularly in schools, are increasingly drawing our attention. The potential consequences of bullying came to the forefront of public attention when several school shootings in the United States during the 1990s were linked to bullying. Increasingly, the police are called into schools to help deal with the situations and to become part of an overall community response.

While **bullying** is a very real problem, it is not a unique legal concept although the Province of Ontario has formally included the concept in its *Safe School Act, 2000*. Ross (1998) identifies two categories of bullying: direct and indirect. *Direct bullying* consists of such behaviours as shoving, throwing things, taking things, choking, punching and kicking, beatings, and stabbing. *Indirect bullying* consists of name-calling, taunting, spreading rumours, gossiping, threats of withdrawing friendship, the silent treatment, and exclusion from the group.

Most of the typical behaviours that we associate with direct bullying have counterparts within the *Criminal Code*. For example acts of uttering threats [*CCC* 264.1], assault [*CCC* 265, 267, 268, and 269], extortion [*CCC* 346], and robbery [*CCC* 343] are explicitly prohibited. Despite these formal prohibitions, much bullying falls outside the direct scope of traditional policing responsibilities. Many bullies are less than 11 years of age. Many behaviours associated with bullying are also sufficiently minor or indirect that the application of the *Criminal Code* appears excessive to all involved except, perhaps, for the victim. Still, evidence is accumulating that shows that young bullies often grow up to become adult bullies. The behaviour is contagious and, particularly among adolescents and older youth, specific acts can be very serious both in their expression and their consequences.

Our understanding of the underlying causes, dynamics, and what works to stop bullying is evolving. Despite this, one thing is clear: adult intervention is effective in reducing the behaviour. As a very visible symbol of authority, the presence of a police officer in a school or public area can act as a deterrent. Even informal intervention by a police officer can serve to deter the bully and comfort the victim. Where officers become aware of this type of behaviour by younger children, an appropriate response is to inform school officials, social service agencies, and the respective child's parents. We should note, however, that some research suggests that bullying behaviour among children results from the child mimicking their parent's behaviour. Abusive parents often produce abusive offspring. Where older youth are involved and the behaviour is clearly of a serious or repetitive nature, charges may be appropriate.

As indicated, the police are increasingly called upon as partners to deal with problems such as gang behaviour and schoolyard bullying. In some jurisdictions, specific officers are attached to particular schools. Sometimes, officers are called upon to take a formal role in addressing such topics as bullying. Because of this, some police organizations and individual officers have provided "toolkits" for others in the profession to use. Among the better sources currently available in Canada are the Centre for Youth Crime Prevention found at http://www.deal.org, where the RCMP have provided some material, and also at http://www.prevnet.ca.

How Social Media Is Transforming Youth Crime

IN THE NEWS

Youth, Aggression, and Social Media a Combustible Mix

Expert says the problem is deeper than kids being stupid on the Internet.

High school fights are as old as high schools themselves, but filming them expressly for social media is relatively new, and worrying. York police say it's a trend that has been spreading quickly. Toronto police say they've never seen anything like it.

Two recent fights at GTA schools are the latest in a recent string of social media incidents involving young people that have left many wondering what exactly is going on with such a supposedly digitally savvy population.

"You say to a young person who's done something really stupid, 'What were you thinking?' And they answer, 'No, I wasn't really thinking,'" said York University professor Debra Pepler. The psychology expert studies bullying, aggression and violence in youth. She says the problem is deeper than kids being stupid on the Internet.

Many youth, especially teenagers, have struggled to fully understand the consequences of their actions, Pepler says, because of the way their brains are developing. "Their brains are reorganizing and their thinking processes aren't as strong as they were even when they were a bit younger," she said. "There's also a lot of research about reinforcing deviance in young people," she says, "That they really encourage each other if they have anti-social values." Add to that the immediacy and reach of social media, and you have a very combustible mix, Pepler said.

Neighbours who saw the street fight in York Region near Cardinal Carter two weeks ago say carloads of teens were showing up in a coordinated manner, all ready to see—and film—a fight. At its height there were upwards of 50 students in the street, many wielding cell phones, neighbours said.

The same behaviour happened near Sir Wilfrid Laurier Collegiate in Scarborough in November after students there filmed two of their classmates getting jumped and badly beaten.

Students there call their fight-video trend Friday Night Fights. Three students were charged with assault causing bodily harm following the November attacks.

The second video of the Cardinal Carter fight, showing the 52-year-old father being severely beaten by a group of teens, has since appeared on the popular fight video site WorldStarHipHop, where it has been viewed 1.4 million times.

The student who shared the York Region fight publicly said she did so because people need to understand that these are not isolated incidents. She goes to a different school but said fights at her high school now often have their own designated videographer. "There was this one kid; everyone would say 'he needs to be here for this fight. He's the video guy,'" she said. "That's how intense these things get now; they're literally assigning kids to take videos of fights at schools. That's ridiculous."

York Regional Police spokesman Const. Andy Pattenden said officers on his force are seeing similar incidents more often. "In the case of the fights, the more disturbing trend for police is that you see all these people around with their cell phones out filming it, posting it to social media, yet no one calls police about it," Pattenden said.

"Anyone of those people with a phone could have called 911. We could have arrived, intervened and broken up the fight, and done what's necessary to stop it from happening."

Neighbours who saw the Cardinal Carter street fight say they did call police, but that response time was slow.

Pattenden said many York officers were busy dealing with a weapons call at a different school while the Cardinal Carter fight was happening.

Continued

High school can seem like such a blur, and for youth who are still forming their identities, the temptation to be the one with the viral video can outweigh almost all logical thought, she said.

"Identity forms in a social context," Pepler said. "If you are wanting to enhance your identity and be seen, although it's completely the wrong thing to do, some young people think that they're going to get a lot of attention from this, and they often do."

Research shows that groups of youth can easily reinforce delinquent behaviour among each other, Pepler explained, and when that group can instantly include pretty much everyone on the Internet, the consequences can be unpredictable.

Students say the videos of the fight and beating near Cardinal Carter Catholic originally started circulating in private channels as text messages and Snapchats.

The fight took place on a Friday, but it wasn't until one student posted them publicly on the following Monday that they gained widespread media and police attention.

The distinction between public and private channels is an important one. The student who first shared the video to Twitter suspects that whoever filmed it never intended for it to get out publicly, much less for it to remain online forever.

"I believe the one person who took the video assumed it was going to be private," she said. "They sent it to a few people. Those people who saw it went 'oh my god, I have to show these other people,'" and it spiraled out from there.

The Star is not revealing the student's name to protect her identity. After she posted the video publicly, she received a wave of online backlash urging her to take it down.

Toronto District School Board spokesperson Ryan Bird said his board has no specific policy regarding social media.

"If you're saying or doing something inappropriate in person or you're doing it online, it's still inappropriate," he said.

The York Catholic board has what it calls "digital citizenship" embedded in its curriculum, said spokesperson Sonia Gallo in an emailed statement.

Students are taught about "what is a credible source, to communicate and respond appropriately while maintaining a positive presence online, to safely participate in an online environment and protect and respect the privacy of self and others," the statement said.

Ontario's province-wide curriculum also requires instruction on cyberbullying that begins in Grade 2, and includes a week every fall where bullying prevention is the main focus.

But Pepler says none of this goes far enough in part because the technology changes so fast that parents and schools are being left behind.

"If we were actually going to support young people in learning how to use this and how to think about it, we'd be working on digital citizenship in kindergarten," she said.

"We ourselves aren't very informed about this," Pepler said. "And so it really requires a lot of collaborative work getting young people to inform us and to integrate it into the curriculum."

Source: J. Winter, "Youth, aggression and social media a combustible mix." *The Star,* December 20, 2016. Retrieved August 6, 2017 from https://www.thestar.com/news/gta/2016/12/20/youth-aggression-and-social-media-a-combustible-mix.html

Cyberbullying

With the advent of technology and social media, a new form of bullying has emerged that is known as **cyberbullying**. Along with providing a vehicle for such criminal activity as distributing child pornography, online fraud, illicit gambling, and opportunities for identity theft, the Internet also provides an opportunity for individuals to bully without having to appear in person and it is most likely to involve teens and young adults—as both victims and perpetrators. Canadian data indicate that one in three high school students have been victims of bullying and one in ten have reported experiencing cyberbullying (Stanbrook, 2014).

According to the RCMP (2017) website, cyberbullying

> **involves the use of communication technologies** such as the Internet, social networking sites, websites, email, text messaging and instant messaging to repeatedly intimidate or harass others. Cyberbullying includes:
>
> - Sending mean or threatening emails or text/instant messages.
> - Posting embarrassing photos of someone online.
> - Creating a website to make fun of others.
> - Pretending to be someone by using their name.
> - Tricking someone into revealing personal or embarrassing information and sending it to others.

> Cyberbullying affects victims in different ways than traditional bullying. It can follow a victim everywhere 24 hours a day, 7 days a week, from school, to the mall and all the way into the comfort of their home usually safe from traditional forms of bullying.

The effects can have a serious negative impact on the victim because

> the ...social connectivity facilitated by the Internet can lend cyberbullying a similar increase in the scale of its participation and impact: taunts, threats, embarrassing personal information and intimate images can now easily be spread instantly, globally and permanently. And cyberbullying may be crueler because it is performed with a menacing anonymity not mitigated by empathy that might otherwise be evoked when bullies have to look their victims in the face. (Stanbrook, 2014: 483)

The consequences for victims are serious including depression, low self-esteem, behavioural problems, substance abuse, and increasingly suicide, particularly for girls. The Canadian cases of teens Rehtaeh Parsons and Amanda Todd and their suicides have brought much publicity to the serious implications for young people who are the victims of cyberbullying.

Cybercrime is often difficult to address because of the anonymity afforded by the Internet. Servers may be located off-shore or perpetrators may use anonymous proxy servers to load or forward their material. In 2015, new federal legislation was passed into law to address cyberbullying.

CANADA'S CYBERBULLYING LAW

On December 9, 2014, Bill C-13, An Act to amend the *Criminal Code,* the *Canada Evidence Act,* the *Competition Act* and the *Mutual Legal Assistance in Criminal Matters Act,* also known as the *Protecting Canadians from Online Crime Act,* received Royal Assent. The Act, sometimes colloquially referred to as "Canada's cyberbullying law," came into force on March 9, 2015.

The Act provides for two main amendments to the *Criminal Code*:

1. A new offence of non-consensual distribution of intimate images (referred to as the cyberbullying section), making it an offence to knowingly publish an intimate image of a person, knowing that he or she did not provide consent or being reckless regarding the person's lack of consent.

2. New investigative powers (preservation demands, preservation orders, and production orders) that allow law enforcement officers to collect electronic evidence relating to individuals that are the subject of an investigation.

There are multiple challenges in responding to cyberbullying. First, there are questions of jurisdiction. Most cyberbullying happens off school grounds, thereby leaving schools with little or no jurisdiction to respond to such instances (Broll & Huey, 2015). Second, there are questions of competence. Schools, much like the police, may not have the technological acumen to respond to cybercrime. Third, there is the question of what is "mean behaviour" versus criminal activity—as one police officer interviewed by Broll and Huey expressed: "Just being mean to somebody isn't a police matter, right? So, I mean, if somebody says, 'Well, I don't like you and you're a jerk,' or they criticize them, or they're just generally mean to them … that is bullying. Once it reaches a certain point, then it becomes a criminal matter and it's a police matter" (2015: 163). This officer expressed dismay when he recounted being contacted by a mother who wanted him to do something because a young person had called her daughter an inappropriate name on Facebook. He expressed frustration that the law would be invoked for such trivial matters, rather than more serious criminal harassment or threats.

Police have an important role to play in educating youth about what constitutes cyberbullying and the legal consequences for perpetrators and the social-emotional consequences for victims. Also teaching parents is effective, since they often feel at a disadvantage over the current technology and social media site trends compared to their children. Officers have talked about the need to educate youth on "safe technology use and health relationships" (Broll & Huey, 2015: 167). At the forefront is teaching young people that the same rules of social etiquette apply online as they do in person.

IN THE NEWS

Bullying and Technology

Ontario introduced a new legislation Tuesday to add cyberbullying to the list of offences for which a student can be suspended or expelled from school.

Premier Dalton McGuinty said, "bullying is bullying …whether you do it online by way of the latest technology or you're doing it in person or over the old fashioned telephone, it still causes pain and suffering."

Changes to the province's *Safe Schools Act* were introduced to stop students from posting comments, pictures, or videos attacking another student or teacher on popular online sites such as YouTube.

This is the first time either physical or online bullying will be formally prohibited in provincial schools.

"It's unacceptable, and I'm proud of the fact our *Safe Schools Act* will in fact broaden the ambit of offences and take into account bullying and cyberbullying," said McGuinty.

Education Minister Kathleen Wynne noted one recent incident where students at a suburban Toronto high school posted derogatory comments about the vice-principal on the popular website Facebook.com, and felt their right to free speech was being trampled when they were suspended.

"Bullying is not currently listed as an infraction, and it's about time that we recognized the seriousness of these behaviours," she said.

Source: "Cyber-bullying law introduced in Ontario," *CityNews*, April 16, 2007. http://www.citynews.ca/news/news_9878.aspx.

TEST YOUR KNOWLEDGE

Definitions

Define the following terms:

1. Attitude

   _____

   _____

   _____

2. Carding

_____

_____

_____

3. Child endangerment

_____

_____

_____

4. Secondary victimization

_____

_____

_____

5. Bullying

_____

_____

_____

6. Cyberbullying

_____

_____

_____

True/False

1. T   F   Most adult criminals start their careers as young offenders.

2. T   F   Most young persons do not become adult criminals.

3. T   F   Once young persons in conflict with the law come into contact with the authorities they are bound to be chronic offenders.

4. T   F   Among young people, positive attitudes toward the police tend to decrease over time.

5. T   F   An attitude is an emotional predisposition.

6. T   F   The best advice for a police officer is to not talk to young people they encounter, unless they have something official to say to them.

7. T   F   Victims of child endangerment often become young offenders.

8. T   F   Police officers are not only law enforcement officers but social workers as well.

9. T   F   Gang behaviour is found only in the largest cities of Canada.

10. T   F   There are some clues as to whether gang behaviour exists in a community.

Multiple Choice

1. Which of the following is true about the attitude of young people toward the police?
    a. attitudes are more positive as young people move through adolescence
    b. attitudes are more positive among younger kids
    c. attitudes are remarkably stable over time
    d. attitudes are little affected by personal experience

2. Which of the following is related to young people's attitude toward the police?
    a. having been arrested
    b. self-definition as delinquent
    c. self-reported law-violating behaviour
    d. all of the above

3. Which of the following are more likely to think of police work as having prestige?
    a. younger children
    b. young offenders
    c. older children
    d. they are all about the same

4. Which of the following types of contact with the police is least likely to generate a positive image of the police?

    a. making a 911 call
    b. being arrested
    c. asking the police for directions
    d. reporting a robbery

5. Which of the following appears to play some role in determining people's attitude toward the police?

    a. culture
    b. age
    c. experience
    d. all of the above

6. Many young people have feelings when interacting with the police that can best be described as

    a. enthusiastic
    b. pitiful
    c. ambivalent
    d. joyful

7. What is the role of the police uniform in influencing the relationship with a young person?

    a. it can be positive
    b. it can be negative
    c. both of the above
    d. it has no effect

8. Which of the following is probably *not* good advice to give a police officer on how to deal with young people?

    a. be firm but fair
    b. don't let them beat you to the punch
    c. sweat the small stuff
    d. talk with kids

9. Which of the following is a form of child endangerment?

    a. neglect
    b. emotional abuse
    c. sexual molestation
    d. all of the above

10. Which of the following is least likely to be true of victims of child abuse and neglect?

    a. children between 8 and 12 years old are most vulnerable to sexual abuse
    b. sexual abuse victims have a dense web of peer relationships

    c. victims have poor relationships with their parents

    d. victims of sexual abuse have parents who do not get along well

Short Answer

1. Identify five symbols associated with police work.

_____

_____

_____

_____

_____

_____

_____

_____

2. Assess the following statement: "All kids want to grow up to be cops."

_____

_____

_____

_____

_____

_____

_____

_____

3. Why is it that lower socioeconomic parts of the population tend to have less favourable attitudes toward the police?

_____

_____

_____

_____

_____

_____

_____

4. Identify three possible sources of negative stereotypes about the police.

   _____

   _____

   _____

   _____

   _____

   _____

   _____

   _____

5. What sorts of attitudes, if they are held by a police officer, are unlikely to be helpful in dealing with young persons?

   _____

   _____

   _____

   _____

   _____

   _____

   _____

   _____

6. Identify four things that an individual police officer could do in an attempt to improve the image of the police in her or his community:

   _____

   _____

   _____

   _____

   _____

   _____

   _____

   _____

7. A police officer walks up to a youngster on the street. Identify three things that might influence the exchange that takes place next.

_____

_____

_____

_____

_____

_____

_____

8. The text identifies seven guidelines with respect to interaction with younger people. As far as you are concerned, what are the three most important ones, and why did you select each of these?

_____

_____

_____

_____

_____

_____

_____

9. Explain the fundamental truth in the following statement: "Policing young people involves a lot of social work, but the police officer should not become a social worker."

_____

_____

_____

_____

_____

_____

_____

10. You are a police officer who goes to a home as a result of a domestic dispute in progress. You observe a house in physical disarray, quarrelling parents who have been drinking, and a young child (about three years old) who is dirty, thin, and scarred. Identify five things that you would do.

_____

_____

_____

_____

_____

_____

_____

_____

11. What does it mean to say that good police work with respect to gangs involves "intelligence"?

_____

_____

_____

_____

_____

_____

_____

12. Discuss the association between young persons with mental health issues and youth criminal justice involvement.

_____

_____

_____

_____

_____

_____

_____

13. Race and ethnicity have been raised as a key area that needs addressing in the area of policing practices. Outline and discuss the issues.

_____

_____

_____

_____

_____

_____

_____

_____

Appendix

[text is also available at http://laws.justice.gc.ca/eng/acts/Y-1.5/FullText.html]

YOUTH CRIMINAL JUSTICE ACT

S.C. 2002, c. 1

Assented to 2002-02-19

An Act in respect of criminal justice for young persons and to amend and repeal other Acts

PREAMBLE

WHEREAS members of society share a responsibility to address the developmental challenges and the needs of young persons and to guide them into adulthood;

WHEREAS communities, families, parents and others concerned with the development of young persons should, through multi-disciplinary approaches, take reasonable steps to prevent youth crime by addressing its underlying causes, to respond to the needs of young persons, and to provide guidance and support to those at risk of committing crimes;

WHEREAS information about youth justice, youth crime and the effectiveness of measures taken to address youth crime should be publicly available;

WHEREAS Canada is a party to the United Nations Convention on the Rights of the Child and recognizes that young persons have rights and freedoms, including those stated in the *Canadian Charter of Rights and Freedoms* and the *Canadian Bill of Rights,* and have special guarantees of their rights and freedoms;

AND WHEREAS Canadian society should have a youth criminal justice system that commands respect, takes into account the interests of victims, fosters responsibility and ensures accountability through meaningful consequences and effective rehabilitation and reintegration, and that reserves its most serious intervention for the most serious crimes and reduces the over-reliance on incarceration for non-violent young persons;

NOW, THEREFORE, Her Majesty, by and with the advice and consent of the Senate and House of Commons of Canada, enacts as follows:

SHORT TITLE

Short title

1. This Act may be cited as the *Youth Criminal Justice Act.*

INTERPRETATION

Definitions

2 (1) The definitions in this subsection apply in this Act.

adult means a person who is neither a young person nor a child. (*adulte*)

adult sentence, in the case of a young person who is found guilty of an offence, means any sentence that could be imposed on an adult who has been convicted of the same offence. (*peine applicable aux adultes*)

Attorney General means the Attorney General as defined in section 2 of the *Criminal Code,* read as if the reference in that definition to "proceedings" were a reference to "proceedings or extrajudicial measures", and includes an agent or delegate of the Attorney General. (*procurer général*)

child means a person who is or, in the absence of evidence to the contrary, appears to be less than twelve years old. (*enfant*)

conference means a group of persons who are convened to give advice in accordance with section 19. (*groupe consultatif*)

confirmed delivery service means certified or registered mail or any other method of service that provides proof of delivery. (*service de messagerie*)

custodial portion with respect to a youth sentence imposed on a young person under paragraph 42(2)(n), (o), (q) or (r), means the period of time, or the portion of the young person's youth sentence, that must be served in custody before he or she begins to serve the remainder under supervision in the community subject to conditions under paragraph 42(2)(n) or under conditional supervision under paragraph 42(2)(o), (q) or (r). (*période de garde*)

disclosure means the communication of information other than by way of publication. (*communication*)

extrajudicial measures means measures other than judicial proceedings under this Act used to deal with a young person alleged to have committed an offence and includes extrajudicial sanctions. (*mesures extrajudiciaires*)

extrajudicial sanction means a sanction that is part of a program referred to in section 10. (*sanction extrajudiciaire*)

offence means an offence created by an Act of Parliament or by any regulation, rule, order, by-law or ordinance made under an Act of Parliament other than a law of Legislature of Yukon, of the Northwest Territories or for Nunavut. (*infraction*)

parent includes, in respect of a young person, any person who is under a legal duty to provide for the young person or any person who has, in law or in fact, the custody or control of the young person, but does not include a person who has the custody or control of the young person by reason only of proceedings under this Act. (*père ou mère ou père et mère*)

pre-sentence report means a report on the personal and family history and present environment of a young person made in accordance with section 40. (*rapport prédécisionnel*)

presumptive offence [Repealed, 2012, c. 1, s. 167]

provincial director means a person, a group or class of persons or a body appointed or designated by or under an Act of the legislature of a province or by the lieutenant governor in council of a province or his or her delegate to perform in that province, either generally or in a specific case, any of the duties or functions of a provincial director under this Act. (*directeur provincial ou directeur*)

publication means the communication of information by making it known or accessible to the general public through any means, including print, radio or television broadcast, telecommunication or electronic means. (*publication*)

record includes any thing containing information, regardless of its physical form or characteristics, including microform, sound recording, videotape, machine-readable record, and any copy of any of those things, that is created or kept for the purposes of this Act or for the investigation of an offence that is or could be prosecuted under this Act. (*dossier*)

review board means a review board referred to in subsection 87(2). (*commission d'examen*)

serious offence means an indictable offence under an Act of Parliament for which the maximum punishment is imprisonment for five years or more. (*infraction grave*)

serious violent offence means an offence under one of the following provisions of the *Criminal Code*:

(a) section 231 or 235 (first degree murder or second degree murder);

(b) section 239 (attempt to commit murder);

(c) section 232, 234 or 236 (manslaughter); or

(d) section 273 (aggravated sexual assault). (*infraction grave avec violence*)

Violent offence means

(a) an offence committed by a young person that includes as an element the causing of bodily harm;

(b) an attempt or a threat to commit an offence referred to in a paragraph (a); or

(c) an offence in the commission of which a young person endangers the life or safety of another person by creating a substantial likelihood of causing bodily harm. (*infraction avec violence*)

young person means a person who is or, in the absence of evidence to the contrary, appears to be twelve years old or older, but less than eighteen years old and, if the context requires, includes any person who is charged under this Act with having committed an offence while he or she was a young person or who is found guilty of an offence under this Act. (*adolescent*)

youth custody facility means a facility designated under subsection 85(2) for the placement of young persons and, if so designated, includes a facility for the secure restraint of young persons, a community residential centre, a group home, a child care institution and a forest or wilderness camp. (*lieu de garde*)

youth justice court means a youth justice court referred to in section 13. (*tribunal pour adolescents*)

youth justice court judge means a youth justice court judge referred to in section 13. (*juge du tribunal pour adolescents*)

youth sentence means a sentence imposed under section 42, 51 or 59 or any of sections 94 to 96 and includes a confirmation or a variation of that sentence. (*peine spécifique*)

youth worker means any person appointed or designated, whether by title of youth worker or probation officer or by any other title, by or under an Act of the legislature of a province or by the lieutenant governor in council of a province or his or her delegate to perform in that province, either generally or in a specific case, any of the duties or functions of a youth worker under this Act. (*délégué à la jeunesse*)

Words and expressions

(2) Unless otherwise provided, words and expressions used in this Act have the same meaning as in the *Criminal Code*.

Descriptive cross-references

(3) If, in any provision of this Act, a reference to another provision of this Act or a provision of any other Act is followed by words in parentheses that are or purport to be descriptive of the subject-matter of the provision referred to, those words form no part of the provision in which they occur but are inserted for convenience of reference only.

2002, c. 1, s. 2, c. 7, s. 274; 2012, c. 1, s. 167; 2014, c. 2, s. 52.

DECLARATION OF PRINCIPLE

Policy for Canada with respect to young persons

3 (1) The following principles apply in this Act:

(a) the youth criminal justice system is intended to protect the public by

(i) holding young persons accountable through measurers that are proportionate to the seriousness of the offence and the degree of responsibility of the young person

(ii) promoting the rehabilitation and reintegration of young persons who have committed offences, and

(iii) supporting the prevention of crime by referring young persons to programs or agencies in the community to address the circumstances underlying their offending behaviour

(b) the criminal justice system for young persons must be separate from that of adults, must be based on the principle of diminished moral blameworthiness or culpability and must emphasize the following:

(i) rehabilitation and reintegration,

(ii) fair and proportionate accountability that is consistent with the greater dependency of young persons and their reduced level of maturity,

(iii) enhanced procedural protection to ensure that young persons are treated fairly and that their rights, including their right to privacy, are protected,

(iv) timely intervention that reinforces the link between the offending behaviour and its consequences, and

(v) the promptness and speed with which persons responsible for enforcing this Act must act, given young persons' perception of time;

(c) within the limits of fair and proportionate accountability, the measures taken against young persons who commit offences should

(i) reinforce respect for societal values,

(ii) encourage the repair of harm done to victims and the community,

(iii) be meaningful for the individual young person given his or her needs and level of development and, where appropriate, involve the parents, the extended family, the community and social or other agencies in the young person's rehabilitation and reintegration, and

(iv) respect gender, ethnic, cultural and linguistic differences and respond to the needs of aboriginal young persons and of young persons with special requirements; and

(d) special considerations apply in respect of proceedings against young persons and, in particular,

(i) young persons have rights and freedoms in their own right, such as a right to be heard in the course of and to participate in the processes, other than the decision to prosecute, that lead to decisions that affect them, and young persons have special guarantees of their rights and freedoms,

(ii) victims should be treated with courtesy, compassion and respect for their dignity and privacy and should suffer the minimum degree of inconvenience as a result of their involvement with the youth criminal justice system,

(iii) victims should be provided with information about the proceedings and given an opportunity to participate and be heard, and

(iv) parents should be informed of measures or proceedings involving their children and encouraged to support them in addressing their offending behaviour.

Act to be liberally construed

(2) This Act shall be liberally construed so as to ensure that young persons are dealt with in accordance with the principles set out in subsection (1).

2002, c. 1, s. 3; 2012, c. 1, s. 168.

PART 1

EXTRAJUDICIAL MEASURES

Principles and Objectives

Declaration of Principles

4 The following principles apply in this Part in addition to the principles set out in section 3:

(a) extrajudicial measures are often the most appropriate and effective way to address youth crime;

(b) extrajudicial measures allow for effective and timely interventions focused on correcting offending behaviour;

(c) extrajudicial measures are presumed to be adequate to hold a young person accountable for his or her offending behaviour if the young person has committed a non-violent offence and has not previously been found guilty of an offence; and

(d) extrajudicial measures should be used if they are adequate to hold a young person accountable for his or her offending behaviour and, if the use of extrajudicial measures is consistent with the principles set out in this section, nothing in this Act precludes their use in respect of a young person who

(i) has previously been dealt with by the use of extrajudicial measures, or

(ii) has previously been found guilty of an offence.

Objectives

5 Extrajudicial measures should be designed to

(a) provide an effective and timely response to offending behaviour outside the bounds of judicial measures;

(b) encourage young persons to acknowledge and repair the harm caused to the victim and the community;

(c) encourage families of young persons—including extended families where appropriate—and the community to become involved in the design and implementation of those measures;

(d) provide an opportunity for victims to participate in decisions related to the measures selected and to receive reparation; and

(e) respect the rights and freedoms of young persons and be proportionate to the seriousness of the offence.

Warnings, Cautions and Referrals

Warnings, cautions and referrals

6 (1) A police officer shall, before starting judicial proceedings or taking any other measures under this Act against a young person alleged to have committed an offence, consider whether it would be sufficient, having regard to the principles set out in section 4, to take no further action, warn the young person, administer a caution, if a program has been established under section 7, or, with the consent of the young person, refer the young person to a program or agency in the community that may assist the young person not to commit offences.

Saving

(2) The failure of a police officer to consider the options set out in subsection (1) does not invalidate any subsequent charges against the young person for the offence.

Police cautions

7 The Attorney General, or any other minister designated by the lieutenant governor of a province, may establish a program authorizing the police to administer cautions to young persons instead of starting judicial proceedings under this Act.

Crown cautions

8 The Attorney General may establish a program authorizing prosecutors to administer cautions to young persons instead of starting or continuing judicial proceedings under this Act.

Evidence of measures is inadmissable

9 Evidence that a young person has received a warning, caution or referral mentioned in section 6, 7 or 8 or that a police officer has taken no further action in respect of an offence, and evidence of the offence, is inadmissible for the purpose of proving prior offending behaviour in any proceedings before a youth justice court in respect of the young person.

Extrajudicial Sanctions

Extrajudicial sanctions

10 (1) An extrajudicial sanction may be used to deal with a young person alleged to have committed an offence only if the young person cannot be adequately dealt with by a warning, caution or referral mentioned in section 6, 7 or 8 because of the seriousness of the offence, the nature and number of previous offences committed by the young person or any other aggravating circumstances.

Conditions

(2) An extrajudicial sanction may be used only if

(a) it is part of a program of sanctions that may be authorized by the Attorney General or authorized by a person, or a member of a class of persons, designated by the lieutenant governor in council of the province;

(b) the person who is considering whether to use the extrajudicial sanction is satisfied that it would be appropriate, having regard to the needs of the young person and the interests of society;

(c) the young person, having been informed of the extrajudicial sanction, fully and freely consents to be subject to it;

(d) the young person has, before consenting to be subject to the extrajudicial sanction, been advised of his or her right to be represented by counsel and been given a reasonable opportunity to consult with counsel;

(e) the young person accepts responsibility for the act or omission that forms the basis of the offence that he or she is alleged to have committed;

(f) there is, in the opinion of the Attorney General, sufficient evidence to proceed with the prosecution of the offence; and

(g) the prosecution of the offence is not in any way barred at law.

Restriction on use

(3) An extrajudicial sanction may not be used in respect of a young person who

(a) denies participation or involvement in the commission of the offence; or

(b) expresses the wish to have the charge dealt with by a youth justice court.

Admissions not admissible in evidence

(4) Any admission, confession or statement accepting responsibility for a given act or omission that is made by a young person as a condition of being dealt with by extrajudicial measures is inadmissible in evidence against any young person in civil or criminal proceedings.

No bar to judicial proceedings

(5) The use of an extrajudicial sanction in respect of a young person alleged to have committed an offence is not a bar to judicial proceedings under this Act, but if a charge is laid against the young person in respect of the offence,

(a) the youth justice court shall dismiss the charge if it is satisfied on a balance of probabilities that the young person has totally complied with the terms and conditions of the extrajudicial sanction; and

(b) the youth justice court may dismiss the charge if it is satisfied on a balance of probabilities that the young person has partially complied with the terms and conditions of the extrajudicial sanction and if, in the opinion of the court, prosecution of the charge would be unfair having regard to the circumstances and the young person's performance with respect to the extrajudicial sanction.

Laying of information, etc.

(6) Subject to subsection (5) and section 24 (private prosecutions only with consent of Attorney General), nothing in this section shall be construed as preventing any person from laying an information or indictment, obtaining the issue or confirmation of any process or proceeding with the prosecution of any offence in accordance with law.

Notice to parent

11 If a young person is dealt with by an extrajudicial sanction, the person who administers the program under which the sanction is used shall inform a parent of the young person of the sanction.

Victim's right to information

12 If a young person is dealt with by an extrajudicial sanction, a police officer, the Attorney General, the provincial director or any organization established by a province to provide assistance to victims shall, on request, inform the victim of the identity of the young person and how the offence has been dealt with.

PART 2

ORGANIZATION OF YOUTH CRIMINAL JUSTICE SYSTEM

Youth Justice Court

Designation of youth justice court

13 (1) A youth justice court is any court that may be established or designated by or under an Act of the legislature of a province, or designated by the Governor in Council or the lieutenant governor in council of a province, as a youth justice court for the purposes of this Act, and a youth justice court judge is a person who may be appointed or designated as a judge of the youth justice court or a judge sitting in a court established or designated as a youth justice court.

Deemed youth justice court

(2) When a young person elects to be tried by a judge without a jury, the judge shall be a judge as defined in section 552 of the *Criminal Code,* or if it is an offence set out in section 469 of that Act, the judge shall be a judge of the superior court of criminal jurisdiction in the province in which the election is made. In either case, the judge is deemed to be a youth justice court judge and the court is deemed to be a youth justice court for the purpose of the proceeding.

Deemed youth justice court

(3) When a young person elects or is deemed to have elected to be tried by a court composed of a judge and jury, the superior court of criminal jurisdiction in the province in which the election is made or deemed to have been made is deemed to be a youth justice court for the purpose of the proceeding, and the superior court judge is deemed to be a youth justice court judge.

Court of record

(4) A youth justice court is a court of record.

Exclusive jurisdiction of youth justice court

14 (1) Despite any other Act of Parliament but subject to the *Contraventions Act* and the *National Defence Act,* a youth justice court has exclusive jurisdiction in respect of any offence alleged to have been committed by a person while he or she was a young person, and that person shall be dealt with as provided in this Act.

Orders

(2) A youth justice court has jurisdiction to make orders against a young person under sections 83.3 (recognizance - terrorist activity), 810 (recognizance — fear of injury or damage), 810.01 (recognizance — fear of certain offences), 810.011 (recognizance - fear of terrorism

offence), 810.02 (recognizance – fear of forced marriage or marriage under age of 16 years) and 810.2 (recognizance – fear of serious personal injury offence) of the *Criminal Code*. If the young person fails or refuses to enter into a recognizance referred to in any of those sections, the court may impose any one of the sanctions set out in subsection 42(2) (youth sentences) except that, in the case of an order under paragraph 42(2)(n) (custody and supervision order), it shall not exceed 30 days.

Prosecution prohibited

(3) Unless the Attorney General and the young person agree, no extrajudicial measures shall be taken or judicial proceedings commenced under this Act in respect of an offence after the end of the time limit set out in any other Act of Parliament or any regulation made under it for the institution of proceedings in respect of that offence.

Continuation of proceedings

(4) Extrajudicial measures taken or judicial proceedings commenced under this Act against a young person may be continued under this Act after the person attains the age of eighteen years.

Young persons over the age of eighteen years

(5) This Act applies to persons eighteen years old or older who are alleged to have committed an offence while a young person.

Powers of youth justice court judge

(6) For the purpose of carrying out the provisions of this Act, a youth justice court judge is a justice and a provincial court judge and has the jurisdiction and powers of a summary conviction court under the *Criminal Code*.

Powers of a judge of a superior court

(7) A judge of a superior court of criminal jurisdiction, when deemed to be a youth justice court judge for the purpose of a proceeding, retains the jurisdiction and powers of a superior court of criminal jurisdiction.

2002, c.1, s. 14; 2015, c. 20, ss. 32, 36, c. 29, s. 14.

Contempt against youth justice court

15 (1) Every youth justice court has the same power, jurisdiction and authority to deal with and impose punishment for contempt against the court as may be exercised by the superior court of criminal jurisdiction of the province in which the court is situated.

Jurisdiction of youth justice court

(2) A youth justice court has jurisdiction in respect of every contempt of court committed by a young person against the youth justice court whether or not committed in the face of the court, and every contempt of court committed by a young person against any other court otherwise than in the face of that court.

Concurrent jurisdiction of youth justice court

(3) A youth justice court has jurisdiction in respect of every contempt of court committed by a young person against any other court in the face of that court and every contempt of court committed by an adult against the youth justice court in the face of the youth justice court, but nothing in this subsection affects the power, jurisdiction or authority of any other court to deal with or impose punishment for contempt of court.

Youth sentence – contempt

(4) When a youth justice court or any other court finds a young person guilty of contempt of court, it may impose as a youth sentence any one of the sanctions set out in subsection 42(2) (youth sentences), or any number of them that are not inconsistent with each other, but no other sentence.

Section 708 of *Criminal Code* applies in respect of adults

(5) Section 708 (contempt) of the *Criminal Code* applies in respect of proceedings under this section in youth justice court against adults, with any modifications that the circumstances require.

Status of offender uncertain

16 When a person is alleged to have committed an offence during a period that includes the date on which the person attains the age of eighteen years, the youth justice court has jurisdiction in respect of the offence and shall, after putting the person to their election under section 67 (adult sentence) if applicable, and on finding the person guilty of the offence,

(a) if it has been proven that the offence was committed before the person attained the age of eighteen years, impose a sentence under this Act;

(b) if it has been proven that the offence was committed after the person attained the age of eighteen years, impose any sentence that could be imposed under the *Criminal Code* or any other Act of Parliament on an adult who has been convicted of the same offence; and

(c) if it has not been proven that the offence was committed after the person attained the age of eighteen years, impose a sentence under this Act.

Youth justice court may make rules

17 (1) The youth justice court for a province may, subject to the approval of the lieutenant governor in council of the province, establish rules of court not inconsistent with this Act or any other Act of Parliament or with any regulations made under section 155 regulating proceedings within the jurisdiction of the youth justice court.

Rules of court

(2) Rules under subsection (1) may be made

(a) generally to regulate the duties of the officers of the youth justice court and any other matter considered expedient to attain the ends of justice and carry into effect the provisions of this Act;

(b) subject to any regulations made under paragraph 155(b), to regulate the practice and procedure in the youth justice court; and

(c) to prescribe forms to be used in the youth justice court if they are not otherwise provided for by or under this Act.

Publication of rules

(3) Rules of court that are made under the authority of this section shall be published in the appropriate provincial gazette.

Youth Justice Committees

Youth justice committees

18 (1) The Attorney General of Canada or a province or any other minister that the lieutenant governor in council of the province may designate may establish one or more committees of citizens, to be known as youth justice committees, to assist in any aspect of the administration of this Act or in any programs or services for young persons.

Role of committee

(2) The functions of a youth justice committee may include the following:

(a) in the case of a young person alleged to have committed an offence,

    (i) giving advice on the appropriate extrajudicial measure to be used in respect of the young person,

    (ii) supporting any victim of the alleged offence by soliciting his or her concerns and facilitating the reconciliation of the victim and the young person,

    (iii) ensuring that community support is available to the young person by arranging for the use of services from within the community, and enlisting members of the community to provide short-term mentoring and supervision, and

    (iv) when the young person is also being dealt with by a child protection agency or a community group, helping to coordinate the interaction of the agency or group with the youth criminal justice system;

(b) advising the federal and provincial governments on whether the provisions of this Act that grant rights to young persons, or provide for the protection of young persons, are being complied with;

(c) advising the federal and provincial governments on policies and procedures related to the youth criminal justice system;

(d) providing information to the public in respect of this Act and the youth criminal justice system;

(e) acting as a conference; and

(f) any other functions assigned by the person who establishes the committee.

Conferences

Conferences may be convened

19 (1) A youth justice court judge, the provincial director, a police officer, a justice of the peace, a prosecutor or a youth worker may convene or cause to be convened a conference for the purpose of making a decision required to be made under this Act.

Mandate of a conference

(2) The mandate of a conference may be, among other things, to give advice on appropriate extrajudicial measures, conditions for judicial interim release, sentences, including the review of sentences, and reintegration plans.

Rules for conferences

(3) The Attorney General or any other minister designated by the lieutenant governor in council of a province may establish rules for the convening and conducting of conferences other than conferences convened or caused to be convened by a youth justice court judge or a justice of the peace.

Rules to apply

(4) In provinces where rules are established under subsection (3), the conferences to which those rules apply must be convened and conducted in accordance with those rules.

Justices of the Peace

Certain proceedings may be taken before justices

20 (1) Any proceeding that may be carried out before a justice under the *Criminal Code*, other than a plea, a trial or an adjudication, may be carried out before a justice in respect of an offence alleged to have been committed by a young person, and any process that may be issued by a justice under the *Criminal Code* may be issued by a justice in respect of an offence alleged to have been committed by a young person.

Orders under section 810 of *Criminal Code*

(2) A justice has jurisdiction to make an order under section 810 (recognizance—fear of injury or damage) of the *Criminal Code* in respect of a young person. If the young person fails or refuses to enter into a recognizance referred to in that section, the justice shall refer the matter to a youth justice court.

Clerks of the Court

Powers of clerks

21 In addition to any powers conferred on a clerk of a court by the *Criminal Code*, a clerk of the youth justice court may exercise the powers ordinarily exercised by a clerk of a court, and, in particular, may

    (a) administer oaths or solemn affirmations in all matters relating to the business of the youth justice court; and

    (b) in the absence of a youth justice court judge, exercise all the powers of a youth justice court judge relating to adjournment.

Provincial Directors

Powers, duties and functions of provincial directors

22 The provincial director may authorize any person to exercise the powers or perform the duties or functions of the provincial director under this Act, in which case the powers, duties or functions are deemed to have been exercised or performed by the provincial director.

PART 3

JUDICIAL MEASURES

Consent to Prosecute

Pre-charge screening

23 (1) The Attorney General may establish a program of pre-charge screening that sets out the circumstances in which the consent of the Attorney General must be obtained before a young person is charged with an offence.

Pre-charge screening program

(2) Any program of pre-charge screening of young persons that is established under an Act of the legislature of a province or by a directive of a provincial government, and that is in place before the coming into force of this section, is deemed to be a program of pre-charge screening for the purposes of subsection (1).

Private prosecutions

24 No prosecutions may be conducted by a prosecutor other than the Attorney General without the consent of the Attorney General.

Right to Counsel

Right to counsel

25 (1) A young person has the right to retain and instruct counsel without delay, and to exercise that right personally, at any stage of proceedings against the young person and before and during any consideration of whether, instead of starting or continuing judicial proceedings against the young person under this Act, to use an extrajudicial sanction to deal with the young person.

Arresting officer to advise young person of right to counsel

(2) Every young person who is arrested or detained shall, on being arrested or detained, be advised without delay by the arresting officer or the officer in charge, as the case may be, of the right to retain and instruct counsel, and be given an opportunity to obtain counsel.

Justice, youth justice court or review board to advise young person of right to counsel

(3) When a young person is not represented by counsel

(a) at a hearing at which it will be determined whether to release the young person or detain the young person in custody prior to sentencing,

(b) at a hearing held under section 71 (hearing—adult sentences),

(c) at trial,

(d) at any proceedings held under subsection 98(3) (continuation of custody), 103(1) (review by youth justice court), 104(1) (continuation of custody), 105(1) (conditional supervision) or 109(1) (review of decision),

(e) at a review of a youth sentence held before a youth justice court under this Act, or

(f) at a review of the level of custody under section 87,

The justice or youth justice court before which the hearing, trial or review is held, or the review board before which the review is held, shall advise the young person of the right to retain and instruct counsel and shall give the young person a reasonable opportunity to obtain counsel.

Trial, hearing or review before youth justice court or review board

(4) When a young person at trial or at a hearing or review referred to in subsection (3) wishes to obtain counsel but is unable to do so, the youth justice court before which the hearing, trial or review is held or the review board before which the review is held

(a) shall, if there is a legal aid program or an assistance program available in the province where the hearing, trial or review is held, refer the young person to that program for the appointment of counsel; or

(b) if no legal aid program or assistance program is available or the young person is unable to obtain counsel through the program, may, and on the request of the young person shall, direct that the young person be represented by counsel.

Appointment of counsel

(5) When a direction is made under paragraph (4)(b) in respect of a young person, the Attorney General shall appoint counsel, or cause counsel to be appointed, to represent the young person.

Release hearing before justice

(6) When a young person, at a hearing referred to in paragraph (3)(a) that is held before a justice who is not a youth justice court judge, wishes to obtain counsel but is unable to do so, the justice shall

(a) if there is a legal aid program or an assistance program available in the province where the hearing is held,

(i) refer the young person to that program for the appointment of counsel, or

(ii) refer the matter to a youth justice court to be dealt with in accordance with paragraph (4)(a) or (b); or

(b) if no legal aid program or assistance program is available or the young person is unable to obtain counsel through the program, refer the matter without delay to a youth justice court to be dealt with in accordance with paragraph (4)(b).

Young person may be assisted by adult

(7) When a young person is not represented by counsel at trial or at a hearing or review referred to in subsection (3), the justice before whom or the youth justice court or review board before which the proceedings are held may, on the request of the young person, allow the young person to be assisted by an adult whom the justice, court or review board considers to be suitable.

Counsel independent of parents

(8) If it appears to a youth justice court judge or a justice that the interests of a young person and the interests of a parent are in conflict or that it would be in the best interests of the young person to be represented by his or her own counsel, the judge or justice shall ensure that the young person is represented by counsel independent of the parent.

Statement of right to counsel

(9) A statement that a young person has the right to be represented by counsel shall be included in

(a) any appearance notice or summons issued to the young person;

(b) any warrant to arrest the young person;

(c) any promise to appear given by the young person;

(d) any undertaking or recognizance entered into before an officer in charge by the young person;

(e) any notice given to the young person in relation to any proceedings held under subsection 98(3) (continuation of custody), 103(1) (review by youth justice court), 104(1) (continuation of custody), 105(1) (conditional supervision) or 109(1) (review of decision); or

(f) any notice of a review of a youth sentence given to the young person.

Recovery of costs of counsel

(10) Nothing in this Act prevents the lieutenant governor in council of a province or his or her delegate from establishing a program to authorize the recovery of the costs of a young person's counsel from the young person or the parents of the young person. The costs may be recovered only after the proceedings are completed and the time allowed for the taking of an appeal has expired or, if an appeal is taken, all proceedings in respect of the appeal have been completed.

Exception for persons over the age of twenty

(11) Subsections (4) to (9) do not apply to a person who is alleged to have committed an offence while a young person, if the person has attained the age of twenty years at the time of his or her first appearance before a youth justice court in respect of the offence; however, this does not restrict any rights that a person has under the law applicable to adults.

Notices to Parents

Notice in case of arrest or detention

26 (1) Subject to subsection (4), if a young person is arrested and detained in custody pending his or her appearance in court, the officer in charge at the time the young person is detained shall, as soon as possible, give or cause to be given to a parent of the young person, orally or in writing, notice of the arrest stating the place of detention and the reason for the arrest.

Notice in other cases

(2) Subject to subsection (4), if a summons or an appearance notice is issued in respect of a young person, the person who issued the summons or appearance notice, or, if a young person is released on giving a promise to appear or entering into an undertaking or recognizance, the officer in charge, shall, as soon as possible, give or cause to be given to a parent of the young person notice in writing of the summons, appearance notice, promise to appear, undertaking or recognizance.

Notice to parent in case of ticket

(3) Subject to subsection (4), a person who serves a ticket under the *Contraventions Act* on a young person, other than a ticket served for a contravention relating to parking a vehicle, shall, as soon as possible, give or cause to be given notice in writing of the ticket to a parent of the young person.

Notice to relative or other adult

(4) If the whereabouts of the parents of a young person are not known or it appears that no parent is available, a notice under this section may be given to an adult relative of the young person who is known to the young person and is likely to assist the young person or, if no such adult relative is available, to any other adult who is known to the young person and is likely to assist the young person and who the person giving the notice considers appropriate.

Notice on direction of youth justice court judge or justice

(5) If doubt exists as to the person to whom a notice under this section should be given, a youth justice court judge or, if a youth justice court judge is, having regard to the circumstances, not reasonably available, a justice may give directions as to the person to whom the notice should be given, and a notice given in accordance with those directions is sufficient notice for the purposes of this section.

Contents of notice

(6) Any notice under this section shall, in addition to any other requirements under this section, include

(a) the name of the young person in respect of whom it is given;

(b) the charge against the young person and, except in the case of a notice of a ticket served under the *Contraventions Act*, the time and place of appearance; and

(c) a statement that the young person has the right to be represented by counsel.

Notice of ticket under *Contraventions Act*

(7) A notice under subsection (3) shall include a copy of the ticket.

Service of notice

(8) Subject to subsections (10) and (11), a notice under this section that is given in writing may be served personally or be sent by confirmed delivery service.

Proceedings not invalid

(9) Subject to subsections (10) and (11), failure to give a notice in accordance with this section does not affect the validity of proceedings under this Act.

Exception

(10) Failure to give a notice under subsection (2) in accordance with this section in any case renders invalid any subsequent proceedings under this Act relating to the case unless

(a) a parent of the young person attends court with the young person; or

(b) a youth justice court judge or a justice before whom proceedings are held against the young person

(i) adjourns the proceedings and orders that the notice be given in the manner and to the persons that the judge or justice directs, or

(ii) dispenses with the notice if the judge or justice is of the opinion that, having regard to the circumstances, the notice may be dispensed with.

Where notice is not served

(11) Where there has been a failure to give a notice under subsection (1) or (3) in accordance with this section and none of the persons to whom the notice may be given attends court with the young person, a youth justice court judge or a justice before whom proceedings are held against the young person may

(a) adjourn the proceedings and order that the notice be given in the manner and to the persons that the judge or justice directs; or

(b) dispense with the notice if the judge or justice is of the opinion that, having regard to the circumstances, the notice may be dispensed with.

Exception for persons over the age of twenty

(12) This section does not apply to a person who is alleged to have committed an offence while a young person, if the person has attained the age of twenty years at the time of his or her first appearance before a youth justice court in respect of the offence.

Order requiring attendance of parent

27 (1) If a parent does not attend proceedings held before a youth justice court in respect of a young person, the court may, if in its opinion the presence of the parent is necessary or in the best interests of the young person, by order in writing require the parent to attend at any stage of the proceedings.

No order in ticket proceedings

(2) Subsection (1) does not apply in proceedings commenced by filing a ticket under the *Contraventions Act*.

Service of order

(3) A copy of the order shall be served by a peace officer or by a person designated by a youth justice court by delivering it personally to the parent to whom it is directed, unless the youth justice court authorizes service by confirmed delivery service.

Failure to attend

(4) A parent who is ordered to attend a youth justice court under subsection (1) and who fails without reasonable excuse, the proof of which lies on the parent, to comply with the order

(a) is guilty of contempt of court;

(b) may be dealt with summarily by the court; and

(c) is liable to the punishment provided for in the *Criminal Code* for a summary conviction offence.

Warrant to arrest parent

(5) If a parent who is ordered to attend a youth justice court under subsection (1) does not attend when required by the order or fails to remain in attendance as required and it is proved that a copy of the order was served on the parent, a youth justice court may issue a warrant to compel the attendance of the parent.

Detention Before Sentencing

Application of Part XVI of *Criminal Code*

28 Except to the extent that they are inconsistent with or excluded by this Act, the provisions of Part XVI (compelling appearance of an accused and interim release) of the *Criminal Code* apply to the detention and release of young persons under this Act.

Detention as social measure prohibited

29 (1) A youth justice court judge or a justice shall not detain a young person in custody prior to being sentenced as a substitute for appropriate child protection, mental health or other social measures.

Justification for detention in custody

(2) A youth justice court judge or a justice may order that a young person be detained in custody only if

(a) the young person has been charged with

(i) a serious offence, or

(ii) an offence other than a serious offence, if they have a history that indicates a pattern of either outstanding charges or findings of guilt;

(b) the judge or justice is satisfied, on a balance of probabilities,

(i) that there is a substantial likelihood that, before being dealt with according to law, the young person will not appear in court when required by law to do so,

(ii) that detention is necessary for the protection or safety of the public, including any victim of or witness to the offence, having regard to all the circumstances, including a substantial likelihood that the young person will, if released from custody, commit a serious offence, or

(iii) in the case where the young person has been charged with a serious offence and detention is not justified under subparagraph (i) or (ii), that there are exceptional circumstances that warrant detention is necessary to maintain confidence in the administration of justice, having regard to the principles set out in section 3 and to all the circumstances, including

(A) the apparent strength of the prosecution's case,

(B) the gravity of the offence,

(C) the circumstances surrounding the commission of the offence, including whether a firearm was used, and

(D) the fact that the young person is liable on being found guilty, for a potentially lengthy custodial sentence; and

(c) the judge or justice is satisfied, on a balance of probabilities, that no condition or combination of conditions of release would, depending on the justification on which the judge or justice relies under paragraph (b),

(i) reduce, to a level below substantial, the likelihood that the young person would not appear in court when required by law to do so,

(ii) offer adequate protection to the public from the risk that the young person might otherwise present, or

(iii) maintain confidence in the administration of justice.

Onus

(3) The onus of satisfying the youth justice court judge or the justice as to matters referred to in subsection (2) is on the Attorney General.

2002, c. 1, s. 29; 2012, c. 1, s. 169.

Designated place of temporary detention

30 (1) Subject to subsection (7), a young person who is arrested and detained prior to being sentenced, or who is detained in accordance with a warrant issued under subsection 59(6) (compelling appearance for review of sentence), shall be detained in any place of temporary detention that may be designated by the lieutenant governor in council of the province or his or her delegate or in a place within a class of places so designated.

Exception

(2) A young person who is detained in a place of temporary detention under subsection (1) may, in the course of being transferred from that place to the court or from the court to that place, be held under the supervision and control of a peace officer.

Detention separate from adults

(3) A young person referred to in subsection (1) shall be held separate and apart from any adult who is detained or held in custody unless a youth justice court judge or a justice is satisfied that, having regard to the best interests of the young person,

(a) the young person cannot, having regard to his or her own safety or the safety of others, be detained in a place of detention for young persons; or

(b) no place of detention for young persons is available within a reasonable distance.

Transfer to adult facility

(4) When a young person is detained under subsection (1), the youth justice court may, on application of the provincial director made at any time after the young person attains the age of eighteen years, after giving the young person an opportunity to be heard, authorize the provincial director to direct, despite subsection (3), that the young person be temporarily detained in a provincial correctional facility for adults, if the court considers it to be in the best interests of the young person or in the public interest.

When young person is twenty years old or older

(5) When a young person is twenty years old or older at the time his or her temporary detention under subsection (1) begins, the young person shall, despite subsection (3), be temporarily detained in a provincial correctional facility for adults.

Transfer by provincial director

(6) A young person who is detained in custody under subsection (1) may, during the period of detention, be transferred by the provincial director from one place of temporary detention to another.

Exception relating to temporary detention

(7) Subsections (1) and (3) do not apply in respect of any temporary restraint of a young person under the supervision and control of a peace officer after arrest, but a young person who is so restrained shall be transferred to a place of temporary detention referred to in subsection (1) as soon as is practicable, and in no case later than the first reasonable opportunity after the appearance of the young person before a youth justice court judge or a justice under section 503 of the *Criminal Code*.

Authorization of provincial authority for detention

(8) In any province for which the lieutenant governor in council has designated a person or a group of persons whose authorization is required, either in all circumstances or in circumstances specified by the lieutenant governor in council, before a young person who has been arrested may be detained in accordance with this section, no young person shall be so detained unless the authorization is obtained.

Determination by provincial authority of place of detention

(9) In any province for which the lieutenant governor in council has designated a person or a group of persons who may determine the place where a young person who has been arrested may be detained in accordance with this section, no young person may be so detained in a place other than the one so determined.

Placement of young person in care of responsible person

31 (1) A young person who has been arrested may be placed in the care of a responsible person instead of being detained in custody if a youth justice court or a justice is satisfied that

(a) the young person would, but for this subsection, be detained in custody under section 515 (judicial interim release) of the *Criminal Code*;

(b) the person is willing and able to take care of and exercise control over the young person; and

(c) the young person is willing to be placed in the care of that person.

Inquiry as to availability of a responsible person

(2) If a young person would, in the absence of a responsible person, be detained in custody, the youth justice court or the justice shall inquire as to the availability of a responsible person and whether the young person is willing to be placed in that person's care.

Condition of placement

(3) A young person shall not be placed in the care of a person under subsection (1) unless

(a) that person undertakes in writing to take care of and to be responsible for the attendance of the young person in court when required and to comply with any other conditions that the youth justice court judge or the justice may specify; and

(b) the young person undertakes in writing to comply with the arrangement and to comply with any other conditions that the youth justice court judge or the justice may specify.

Removing young person from care

(4) A young person, a person in whose care a young person has been placed or any other person may, by application in writing to a youth justice court judge or a justice, apply for an order under subsection (5) if

(a) the person in whose care the young person has been placed is no longer willing or able to take care of or exercise control over the young person; or

(b) it is, for any other reason, no longer appropriate that the young person remain in the care of the person with whom he or she has been placed.

Order

(5) When a youth justice court judge or a justice is satisfied that a young person should not remain in the custody of the person in whose care he or she was placed under subsection (1), the judge or justice shall

(a) make an order relieving the person and the young person of the obligations undertaken under subsection (3); and

(b) issue a warrant for the arrest of the young person.

Effect of arrest

(6) If a young person is arrested in accordance with a warrant issued under paragraph (5)(b), the young person shall be taken before a youth justice court judge or a justice without delay and dealt with under this section and sections 28 to 30.

Appearance

Appearance before judge or justice

32 (1) A young person against whom an information or indictment is laid must first appear before a youth justice court judge or a justice, and the judge or justice shall

(a) cause the information or indictment to be read to the young person;

(b) if the young person is not represented by counsel, inform the young person of the right to retain and instruct counsel; and

(c) if notified under subsection 64(2) (intention to seek adult sentence) or if section 16 (status of accused uncertain) applies, inform the young person that the youth justice court might, if the young person is found guilty, order that an adult sentence be imposed; and

(d) [Repealed, 2012, c. 1, s. 170]

Waiver

(2) A young person may waive the requirements of subsection (1) if the young person is represented by counsel and counsel advises the court that the young person has been informed of that provision.

Young person not represented by counsel

(3) When a young person is not represented by counsel, the youth justice court, before accepting a plea, shall

(a) satisfy itself that the young person understands the charge;

(b) if the young person is liable to an adult sentence, explain to the young person the consequences of being liable to an adult sentence and the procedure by which the young person may apply for an order that a youth sentence be imposed; and

(c) explain that the young person may plead guilty or not guilty to the charge or, if subsection 67(1) (election of court for trial — adult sentence) or (3) (election of court for trial in Nunavut — adult sentence) applies, explain that the young person may elect to be tried by a youth justice court judge without a jury and without having a preliminary inquiry, or to have a preliminary inquiry and be tried by a judge without a jury, or to have a preliminary inquiry and be tried by a court composed of a judge and jury and, in either of the latter two cases, a preliminary inquiry will only be conducted if requested by the young person or the prosecutor.

If youth justice court not satisfied

(4) If the youth justice court is not satisfied that a young person understands the charge, the court shall, unless the young person must be put to his or her election under subsection 67(1) (election of court for trial—adult sentence) or, with respect to Nunavut, subsection 67(3) (election of court for trial in Nunavut— adult sentence), enter a plea of not guilty on behalf of the young person and proceed with the trial in accordance with subsection 36(2) (young person pleads not guilty).

If youth justice court not satisfied

(5) If the youth justice court is not satisfied that a young person understands the matters set out in subsection (3), the court shall direct that the young person be represented by counsel.

2002, c. 1, s. 32, c. 13, s. 91; 2012, c. 1, s. 170.

Release from or Detention in Custody

Application for release from or detention in custody

33 (1) If an order is made under section 515 (judicial interim release) of the *Criminal Code* in respect of a young person by a justice who is not a youth justice court judge, an application may, at any time after the order is made, be made to a youth justice court for the release from or detention in custody of the young person, as the case may be, and the youth justice court shall hear the matter as an original application.

Notice to prosecutor

(2) An application under subsection (1) for release from custody shall not be heard unless the young person has given the prosecutor at least two clear days notice in writing of the application.

Notice to young person

(3) An application under subsection (1) for detention in custody shall not be heard unless the prosecutor has given the young person at least two clear days notice in writing of the application.

Waiver of notice

(4) The requirement for notice under subsection (2) or (3) may be waived by the prosecutor or by the young person or his or her counsel, as the case may be.

Application for review under section 520 or 521 of *Criminal Code*

(5) An application under section 520 or 521 of the *Criminal Code* for a review of an order made in respect of a young person by a youth justice court judge who is a judge of a superior court shall be made to a judge of the court of appeal.

Nunavut

(6) Despite subsection (5), an application under section 520 or 521 of the *Criminal Code* for a review of an order made in respect of a young person by a youth justice court judge who is a judge of the Nunavut Court of Justice shall be made to a judge of that court.

No review

(7) No application may be made under section 520 or 521 of the *Criminal Code* for a review of an order made in respect of a young person by a justice who is not a youth justice court judge.

Interim release by youth justice court judge only

(8) If a young person against whom proceedings have been taken under this Act is charged with an offence referred to in section 522 of the *Criminal Code*, a youth justice court judge, but no other court, judge or justice, may release the young person from custody under that section.

Review by court of appeal

(9) A decision made by a youth justice court judge under subsection (8) may be reviewed in accordance with section 680 of the *Criminal Code* and that section applies, with any modifications that the circumstances require, to any decision so made.

Medical and Psychological Reports

Medical or psychological assessment

34 (1) A youth justice court may, at any stage of proceedings against a young person, by order require that the young person be assessed by a qualified person who is required to report the results in writing to the court,

(a) with the consent of the young person and the prosecutor; or

(b) on its own motion or on application of the young person or the prosecutor, if the court believes a medical, psychological or psychiatric report in respect of the young person is necessary for a purpose mentioned in paragraphs (2)(a) to (g) and

(i) the court has reasonable grounds to believe that the young person may be suffering from a physical or mental illness or disorder, a psychological disorder, an emotional disturbance, a learning disability or a mental disability,

(ii) the young person's history indicates a pattern of repeated findings of guilt under this Act or the *Young Offenders Act,* chapter Y-1 of the Revised Statutes of Canada, 1985, or

(iii) the young person is alleged to have committed a serious violent offence.

Purpose of assessment

(2) A youth justice court may make an order under subsection (1) in respect of a young person for the purpose of

(a) considering an application under section 33 (release from or detention in custody);

(b) making its decision on an application heard under section 71 (hearing—adult sentences);

(c) making or reviewing a youth sentence;

(d) considering an application under subsection 104(1) (continuation of custody);

(e) setting conditions under subsection 105(1) (conditional supervision);

(f) making an order under subsection 109(2) (conditional supervision); or

(g) authorizing disclosure under subsection 127(1) (information about a young person).

Custody for assessment

(3) Subject to subsections (4) and (6), for the purpose of an assessment under this section, a youth justice court may remand a young person to any custody that it directs for a period not exceeding thirty days.

Presumption against custodial remand

(4) A young person shall not be remanded in custody in accordance with an order made under subsection (1) unless

(a) the youth justice court is satisfied that

(i) on the evidence custody is necessary to conduct an assessment of the young person, or

(ii) on the evidence of a qualified person detention of the young person in custody is desirable to conduct the assessment of the young person, and the young person consents to custody; or

(b) the young person is required to be detained in custody in respect of any other matter or by virtue of any provision of the *Criminal Code*.

Report of qualified person in writing

(5) For the purposes of paragraph (4)(a), if the prosecutor and the young person agree, evidence of a qualified person may be received in the form of a report in writing.

Application to vary assessment order if circumstances change

(6) A youth justice court may, at any time while an order made under subsection (1) is in force, on cause being shown, vary the terms and conditions specified in the order in any manner that the court considers appropriate in the circumstances.

Disclosure of report

(7) When a youth justice court receives a report made in respect of a young person under subsection (1),

(a) the court shall, subject to subsection (9), cause a copy of the report to be given to

(i) the young person,

(ii) any parent of the young person who is in attendance at the proceedings against the young person,

(iii) any counsel representing the young person, and

(iv) the prosecutor; and

(b) the court may cause a copy of the report to be given to

(i) a parent of the young person who is not in attendance at the proceedings if the parent is, in the opinion of the court, taking an active interest in the proceedings, or

(ii) despite subsection 119(6) (restrictions respecting access to certain records), the provincial director, or the director of the provincial correctional facility for adults or the penitentiary at which the young person is serving a youth sentence, if, in the opinion of the court, withholding the report would jeopardize the safety of any person.

Cross-examination

(8) When a report is made in respect of a young person under subsection (1), the young person, his or her counsel or the adult assisting the young person under subsection 25(7) and the prosecutor shall, subject to subsection (9), on application to the youth justice court, be given an opportunity to cross-examine the person who made the report.

Non-disclosure in certain cases

(9) A youth justice court shall withhold all or part of a report made in respect of a young person under subsection (1) from a private prosecutor, if disclosure of the report or part, in the opinion of the court, is not necessary for the prosecution of the case and might be prejudicial to the young person.

Non-disclosure in certain cases

(10) A youth justice court shall withhold all or part of a report made in respect of a young person under subsection (1) from the young person, the young person's parents or a private prosecutor if the court is satisfied, on the basis of the report or evidence given in the absence of the young person, parents or private prosecutor by the person who made the report, that disclosure of the report or part would seriously impair the treatment or recovery of the young person, or would be likely to endanger the life or safety of, or result in serious psychological harm to, another person.

Exception – interests of justice

(11) Despite subsection (10), the youth justice court may release all or part of the report to the young person, the young person's parents or the private prosecutor if the court is of the opinion that the interests of justice make disclosure essential.

Report to be part of record

(12) A report made under subsection (1) forms part of the record of the case in respect of which it was requested.

Disclosure by qualified person

(13) Despite any other provision of this Act, a qualified person who is of the opinion that a young person held in detention or committed to custody is likely to endanger his or her own life or safety or to endanger the life of, or cause bodily harm to, another person may immediately so advise any person who has the care and custody of the young person whether or not the same information is contained in a report made under subsection (1).

Definition of "qualified person"

(14) In this section, "qualified person" means a person duly qualified by provincial law to practice medicine or psychiatry or to carry out psychological examinations or assessments, as the circumstances require, or, if no such law exists, a person who is, in the opinion of the youth justice court, so qualified, and includes a person or a member of a class of persons designated by the lieutenant governor in council of a province or his or her delegate.

Referral to Child Welfare Agency

Referral to child welfare agency

35 In addition to any order that it is authorized to make, a youth justice court may, at any stage of proceedings against a young person, refer the young person to a child welfare agency for assessment to determine whether the young person is in need of child welfare services.

Adjudication

When young person pleads guilty

36 (1) If a young person pleads guilty to an offence charged against the young person and the youth justice court is satisfied that the facts support the charge, the court shall find the young person guilty of the offence.

When young person pleads not guilty

(2) If a young person charged with an offence pleads not guilty to the offence or pleads guilty but the youth justice court is not satisfied that the facts support the charge, the court shall proceed with the trial and shall, after considering the matter, find the young person guilty or not guilty or make an order dismissing the charge, as the case may be.

Appeals

Appeals

37 (1) An appeal in respect of an indictable offence or an offence that the Attorney General elects to proceed with as an indictable offence lies under this Act in accordance with Part XXI (appeals—indictable offences) of the *Criminal Code,* which Part applies with any modifications that the circumstances require.

Appeals for contempt of court

(2) A finding of guilt under section 15 for contempt of court or a sentence imposed in respect of the finding may be appealed as if the finding were a conviction or the sentence were a sentence in a prosecution by indictment.

Appeal

(3) Section 10 of the *Criminal Code* applies if a person is convicted of contempt of court under subsection 27(4) (failure of parent to attend court).

Appeals heard together

(4) An order under subsection 72(1) or (1.1) (adult or youth sentence), 75(3) (ban on publication) or 76(1) (placement when subject to adult sentence), 75 (2) (lifting of ban on publication) or 76 (1) (placement when subject to adult sentence) may be appealed as part of the sentence and, unless the court to which the appeal is taken otherwise orders, if more than one of these is appealed they must be part of the same appeal proceeding.

Appeals for summary conviction offences

(5) An appeal in respect of an offence punishable on summary conviction or an offence that the Attorney General elects to proceed with as an offence punishable on summary conviction lies under this Act in accordance with Part XXVII (summary conviction offences) of the *Criminal Code,* which Part applies with any modifications that the circumstances require.

Appeals where offences are tried jointly

(6) An appeal in respect of one or more indictable offences and one or more summary conviction offences that are tried jointly or in respect of which youth sentences are jointly imposed lies under this Act in accordance with Part XXI (appeals – indictable offences) of the *Criminal Code,* which Part applies with any modifications that the circumstances require.

Deemed election

(7) For the purpose of appeals under this Act, if no election is made in respect of an offence that may be prosecuted by indictment or proceeded with by way of summary conviction, the Attorney General is deemed to have elected to proceed with the offence as an offence punishable on summary conviction.

If the youth justice court is a superior court

(8) In any province where the youth justice court is a superior court, an appeal under subsection (5) shall be made to the court of appeal of the province.

Nunavut

(9) Despite subsection (8), if the Nunavut Court of Justice is acting as a youth justice court, an appeal under subsection (5) shall be made to a judge of the Nunavut Court of Appeal, and an appeal of that judge's decision shall be made to the Nunavut Court of Appeal in accordance with section 839 of the *Criminal Code.*

Appeal to the Supreme Court of Canada

(10) No appeal lies under subsection (1) from a judgment of the court of appeal in respect of a finding of guilt or an order dismissing an information or indictment to the Supreme Court of Canada unless leave to appeal is granted by the Supreme Court of Canada.

No appeal from youth sentence on review

(11) No appeal lies from a youth sentence under section 59 or any of sections 94 to 96.

2002, c. 1, s. 37; 2012, c. 1, s. 171.

PART 4

SENTENCING

Purpose and Principles

Purpose

38 (1) The purpose of sentencing under section 42 (youth sentences) is to hold a young person accountable for an offence through the imposition of just sanctions that have meaningful consequences for the young person and that promote his or her rehabilitation and reintegration into society, thereby contributing to the long-term protection of the public.

Sentencing principles

(2) A youth justice court that imposes a youth sentence on a young person shall determine the sentence in accordance with the principles set out in section 3 and the following principles:

(a) the sentence must not result in a punishment that is greater than the punishment that would be appropriate for an adult who has been convicted of the same offence committed in similar circumstances;

(b) the sentence must be similar to the sentences imposed in the region on similar young persons found guilty of the same offence committed in similar circumstances;

(c) the sentence must be proportionate to the seriousness of the offence and the degree of responsibility of the young person for that offence;

(d) all available sanctions other than custody that are reasonable in the circumstances should be considered for all young persons, with particular attention to the circumstances of aboriginal young persons;

(e) subject to paragraph (c), the sentence must

(i) be the least restrictive sentence that is capable of achieving the purpose set out in subsection (1),

(ii) be the one that is most likely to rehabilitate the young person and reintegrate him or her into society, and

(iii) promote a sense of responsibility in the young person, and an acknowledgement of the harm done to victims and the community; and

(f) subject to paragraph (c), the sentence may have the following objectives:

(i) to denounce the unlawful conduct, and

(ii) to deter the young person from committing offences.

Factors to be considered

(3) In determining a youth sentence, the youth justice court shall take into account

(a) the degree of participation by the young person in the commission of the offence;

(b) the harm done to victims and whether it was intentional or reasonably foreseeable;

(c) any reparation made by the young person to the victim or the community;

(d) the time spent in detention by the young person as a result of the offence;

(e) the previous findings of guilt of the young person; and

(f) any other aggravating and mitigating circumstances related to the young person or the offence that are relevant to the purpose and principles set out in this section.

2002, c. 1, s. 38; 2012, c. 1, s. 172.

Committal to custody

39 (1) A youth justice court shall not commit a young person to custody under section 42 (youth sentences) unless

(a) the young person has committed a violent offence;

(b) the young person has failed to comply with non-custodial sentences;

(c) the young person has committed an indictable offence for which an adult would be liable to imprisonment for a term of more than two years and has a history that indicates a pattern of either extrajudicial sanctions or of findings of guilt or of both under this Act or the *Young Offenders Act*, chapter Y-1 of the Revised Statutes of Canada, 1985; or

(d) in exceptional cases where the young person has committed an indictable offence, the aggravating circumstances of the offence are such that the imposition of a non-custodial sentence would be inconsistent with the purpose and principles set out in section 38.

Alternatives to custody

(2) If any of paragraphs (1)(a) to (c) apply, a youth justice court shall not impose a custodial sentence under section 42 (youth sentences) unless the court has considered all alternatives to custody raised at the sentencing hearing that are reasonable in the circumstances, and determined that there is not a reasonable alternative, or combination of alternatives, that is in accordance with the purpose and principles set out in section 38.

Factors to be considered

(3) In determining whether there is a reasonable alternative to custody, a youth justice court shall consider submissions relating to

(a) the alternatives to custody that are available;

(b) the likelihood that the young person will comply with a non-custodial sentence, taking into account his or her compliance with previous non-custodial sentences; and

(c) the alternatives to custody that have been used in respect of young persons for similar offences committed in similar circumstances.

Imposition of same sentence

(4) The previous imposition of a particular non-custodial sentence on a young person does not preclude a youth justice court from imposing the same or any other non-custodial sentence for another offence.

Custody as social measure prohibited

(5) A youth justice court shall not use custody as a substitute for appropriate child protection, mental health or other social measures.

Pre-sentence report

(6) Before imposing a custodial sentence under section 42 (youth sentences), a youth justice court shall consider a pre-sentence report and any sentencing proposal made by the young person or his or her counsel.

Report dispensed with

(7) A youth justice court may, with the consent of the prosecutor and the young person or his or her counsel, dispense with a pre-sentence report if the court is satisfied that the report is not necessary.

Length of custody

(8) In determining the length of a youth sentence that includes a custodial portion, a youth justice court shall be guided by the purpose and principles set out in section 38, and shall not take into consideration the fact that the supervision portion of the sentence may not be served in custody and that the sentence may be reviewed by the court under section 94.

Reasons

(9) If a youth justice court imposes a youth sentence that includes a custodial portion, the court shall state the reasons why it has determined that a non-custodial sentence is not adequate to achieve the purpose set out in subsection 38(1), including, if applicable, the reasons why the case is an exceptional case under paragraph (1)(d).

2002, c. 1, s. 39; 2012, c. 1, s. 173.

Pre-sentence Report

Pre-sentence report

40 (1) Before imposing sentence on a young person found guilty of an offence, a youth justice court

(a) shall, if it is required under this Act to consider a pre-sentence report before making an order or a sentence in respect of a young person, and

(b) may, if it considers it advisable,

require the provincial director to cause to be prepared a pre-sentence report in respect of the young person and to submit the report to the court.

Contents of report

(2) A pre-sentence report made in respect of a young person shall, subject to subsection (3), be in writing and shall include the following, to the extent that it is relevant to the purpose and principles of sentencing set out in section 38 and to the restrictions on custody set out in section 39:

(a) the results of an interview with the young person and, if reasonably possible, the parents of the young person and, if appropriate and reasonably possible, members of the young person's extended family;

(b) the results of an interview with the victim in the case, if applicable and reasonably possible;

(c) the recommendations resulting from any conference referred to in section 41;

(d) any information that is applicable to the case, including

(i) the age, maturity, character, behaviour and attitude of the young person and his or her willingness to make amends,

(ii) any plans put forward by the young person to change his or her conduct or to participate in activities or undertake measures to improve himself or herself,

(iii) subject to subsection 119(2) (period of access to records), the history of previous findings of delinquency under the *Juvenile Delinquents Act,* chapter J-3 of the Revised Statutes of Canada, 1970, or previous findings of guilt for offences under the *Young Offenders Act,* chapter Y-1 of the Revised Statutes of Canada, 1985, or under this or any other Act of Parliament or any regulation made under it, the history of community or other services rendered to the young person with respect to those findings and the response of the young person to previous sentences or dispositions and to services rendered to him or her,

(iv) subject to subsection 119(2) (period of access to records), the history of alternative measures under the *Young Offenders Act,* chapter Y-1 of the Revised Statutes of Canada, 1985, or extrajudicial sanctions used to deal with the young person and the response of the young person to those measures or sanctions,

(v) the availability and appropriateness of community services and facilities for young persons and the willingness of the young person to avail himself or herself of those services or facilities,

(vi) the relationship between the young person and the young person's parents and the degree of control and influence of the parents over the young person and, if appropriate and reasonably possible, the relationship between the young person and the young person's extended family and the degree of control and influence of the young person's extended family over the young person, and

(vii) the school attendance and performance record and the employment record of the young person;

(e) any information that may assist the court in determining under subsection 39(2) whether there is an alternative to custody; and

(f) any information that the provincial director considers relevant, including any recommendation that the provincial director considers appropriate.

Oral report with leave

(3) If a pre-sentence report cannot reasonably be committed to writing, it may, with leave of the youth justice court, be submitted orally in court.

Report forms part of record

(4) A pre-sentence report shall form part of the record of the case in respect of which it was requested.

Copies of pre-sentence report

(5) If a pre-sentence report made in respect of a young person is submitted to a youth justice court in writing, the court

(a) shall, subject to subsection (7), cause a copy of the report to be given to

(i) the young person,

(ii) any parent of the young person who is in attendance at the proceedings against the young person,

(iii) any counsel representing the young person, and

(iv) the prosecutor; and

(b) may cause a copy of the report to be given to a parent of the young person who is not in attendance at the proceedings if the parent is, in the opinion of the court, taking an active interest in the proceedings.

Cross-examination

(6) If a pre-sentence report made in respect of a young person is submitted to a youth justice court, the young person, his or her counsel or the adult assisting the young person under subsection 25(7) and the prosecutor shall, subject to subsection (7), on application to the court, be given the opportunity to cross-examine the person who made the report.

Report may be withheld from private prosecutor

(7) If a pre-sentence report made in respect of a young person is submitted to a youth justice court, the court may, when the prosecutor is a private prosecutor and disclosure of all or part of the report to the prosecutor might, in the opinion of the court, be prejudicial to the young person and is not, in the opinion of the court, necessary for the prosecution of the case against the young person,

(a) withhold the report or part from the prosecutor, if the report is submitted in writing; or

(b) exclude the prosecutor from the court during the submission of the report or part, if the report is submitted orally in court.

Report disclosed to other persons

(8) If a pre-sentence report made in respect of a young person is submitted to a youth justice court, the court

(a) shall, on request, cause a copy or a transcript of the report to be supplied to

(i) any court that is dealing with matters relating to the young person, and

(ii) any youth worker to whom the young person's case has been assigned; and

(b) may, on request, cause a copy or a transcript of all or part of the report to be supplied to any person not otherwise authorized under this section to receive a copy or a transcript of the report if, in the opinion of the court, the person has a valid interest in the proceedings.

Disclosure by the provincial director

(9) A provincial director who submits a pre-sentence report made in respect of a young person to a youth justice court may make all or part of the report available to any person in whose custody or under whose supervision the young person is placed or to any other person who is directly assisting in the care or treatment of the young person.

Inadmissibility of statements

(10) No statement made by a young person in the course of the preparation of a pre-sentence report in respect of the young person is admissible in evidence against any young person in civil or criminal proceedings except those under section 42 (youth sentences), 59 (review of non-custodial sentence) or 71 (hearing— adult sentences) or any of sections 94 to 96 (reviews and other proceedings related to custodial sentences).

Youth Sentences

Recommendation of conference

41 When a youth justice court finds a young person guilty of an offence, the court may convene or cause to be convened a conference under section 19 for recommendations to the court on an appropriate youth sentence.

Considerations as to youth sentence

42 (1) A youth justice court shall, before imposing a youth sentence, consider any recommendations submitted under section 41, any pre-sentence report, any representations made by the parties to the proceedings or their counsel or agents and by the parents of the young person, and any other relevant information before the court.

Youth sentence

(2) When a youth justice court finds a young person guilty of an offence and is imposing a youth sentence, the court shall, subject to this section, impose any one of the following sanctions or any number of them that are not inconsistent with each other and, if the offence is first degree murder or second degree murder within the meaning of section 231 of the *Criminal Code,* the court shall impose a sanction set out in paragraph (q) or subparagraph (r)(ii) or (iii) and may impose any other of the sanctions set out in this subsection that the court considers appropriate:

(a) reprimand the young person;

(b) by order direct that the young person be discharged absolutely, if the court considers it to be in the best interests of the young person and not contrary to the public interest;

(c) by order direct that the young person be discharged on any conditions that the court considers appropriate and may require the young person to report to and be supervised by the provincial director;

(d) impose on the young person a fine not exceeding $1,000 to be paid at the time and on the terms that the court may fix;

(e) order the young person to pay to any other person at the times and on the terms that the court may fix an amount by way of compensation for loss of or damage to property or for loss of income or support, or an amount for, in the Province of Quebec, pre-trial pecuniary loss or, in any other province, special damages, for personal injury arising from the commission of the offence if the value is readily ascertainable, but no order shall be made for other damages in the Province of Quebec or for general damages in any other province;

(f) order the young person to make restitution to any other person of any property obtained by the young person as a result of the commission of the offence within the time that the court may fix, if the property is owned by the other person or was, at the time of the offence, in his or her lawful possession;

(g) if property obtained as a result of the commission of the offence has been sold to an innocent purchaser, where restitution of the property to its owner or any other person has been made or ordered, order the young person to pay the purchaser, at the time and on the terms that the court may fix, an amount not exceeding the amount paid by the purchaser for the property;

(h) subject to section 54, order the young person to compensate any person in kind or by way of personal services at the time and on the terms that the court may fix for any loss, damage or injury suffered by that person in respect of which an order may be made under paragraph (e) or (g);

(i) subject to section 54, order the young person to perform a community service at the time and on the terms that the court may fix, and to report to and be supervised by the provincial director or a person designated by the youth justice court;

(j) subject to section 51 (mandatory prohibition order), make

any order of prohibition, seizure or forfeiture that may be imposed under any Act of Parliament or any regulation made under it if an accused is found guilty or convicted of that offence, other than an order under section 161 of the *Criminal Code;*

(k) place the young person on probation in accordance with sections 55 and 56 (conditions and other matters related to probation orders) for a specified period not exceeding two years;

(l) subject to subsection (3) (agreement of provincial director), order the young person into an intensive support and supervision program approved by the provincial director;

(m) subject to subsection (3) (agreement of provincial director) and section 54, order the young person to attend a non-residential program approved by the provincial director, at the times and on the terms that the court may fix, for a maximum of two hundred and forty hours, over a period not exceeding six months;

(n) make a custody and supervision order with respect to the young person, ordering that a period be served in custody and that a second period — which is one half as long as the first — be served, subject to sections 97 (conditions to be included) and 98 (continuation of custody), under supervision in the community subject to conditions, the total of the periods not to exceed two years from the date of the coming into force of the order or, if the young person is found guilty of an offence for which the punishment provided by the *Criminal Code* or any other Act of Parliament is imprisonment for life, three years from the date of coming into force of the order;

(o) in the case of an offence set out in section 239 (attempt to commit murder), 232, 234 or 236 (manslaughter) or 273 (aggravated sexual assault) of the *Criminal Code,* make a custody and supervision order in respect of the young person for a specified period not exceeding three years from the date of committal that orders the young person to be committed into a continuous period of custody for the first portion of the sentence and, subject to subsection 104(1) (continuation of custody), to serve the remainder of the sentence under conditional supervision in the community in accordance with section 105;

(p) subject to subsection (5), make a deferred custody and supervision order that is for a specified period not exceeding six months, subject to the conditions set out in subsection 105(2), and to any conditions set out in subsection 105(3) that the court considers appropriate;

(q) order the young person to serve a sentence not to exceed

(i) in the case of first degree murder, ten years comprised of

(A) a committal to custody, to be served continuously, for a period that must not, subject to subsection 104(1) (continuation of custody), exceed six years from the date of committal, and

(B) a placement under conditional supervision to be served in the community in accordance with section 105, and

(ii) in the case of second degree murder, seven years comprised of

(A) a committal to custody, to be served continuously, for a period that must not, subject to subsection 104(1) (continuation of custody), exceed four years from the date of committal, and

(B) a placement under conditional supervision to be served in the community in accordance with section 105;

(r) subject to subsection (7), make an intensive rehabilitative custody and supervision order in respect of the young person

(i) that is for a specified period that must not exceed

(A) two years from the date of committal, or

(B) if the young person is found guilty of an offence for which the punishment provided by the *Criminal Code* or any other Act of Parliament is imprisonment for life, three years from the date of committal,

and that orders the young person to be committed into a continuous period of intensive rehabilitative custody for the first portion of the sentence and, subject to subsection 104(1) (continuation of custody), to serve the remainder under conditional supervision in the community in accordance with section 105,

(ii) that is for a specified period that must not exceed, in the case of first degree murder, ten years from the date of committal, comprising

(A) a committal to intensive rehabilitative custody, to be served continuously, for a period that must not exceed six years from the date of committal, and

(B) subject to subsection 104(1) (continuation of custody), a placement under conditional supervision to be served in the community in accordance with section 105, and

(iii) that is for a specified period that must not exceed, in the case of second degree murder, seven years from the date of committal, comprising

(A) a committal to intensive rehabilitative custody, to be served continuously, for a period that must not exceed four years from the date of committal, and

(B) subject to subsection 104(1) (continuation of custody), a placement under conditional supervision to be served in the community in accordance with section 105; and

(s) impose on the young person any other reasonable and ancillary conditions that the court considers advisable and in the best interests of the young person and the public.

Agreement of provincial director

(3) A youth justice court may make an order under paragraph (2) (l) or (m) only if the provincial director has determined that a program to enforce the order is available.

Youth justice court statement

(4) When the youth justice court makes a custody and supervision order with respect to a young person under paragraph (2)(n), the court shall state the following with respect to that order:

You are ordered to serve (*state the number of days or months to be served*) in custody, to be followed by (*state one-half of the number of days or months stated above*) to be served under supervision in the community subject to conditions.

If you breach any of the conditions while you are under supervision in the community, you may be brought back into custody and required to serve the rest of the second period in custody as well.

You should also be aware that, under other provisions of the *Youth Criminal Justice Act*, a court could require you to serve the second period in custody as well.

The periods in custody and under supervision in the community may be changed if you are or become subject to another sentence.

Deferred custody and supervision order

(5) The court may make a deferred custody and supervision order under paragraph (2)(p) if

(a) the young person is found guilty of an offence other than one in the commission of which a young person causes or attempts to cause serious bodily harm; and

(b) it is consistent with the purpose and principles set out in section 38 and the restrictions on custody set out in section 39.

Application of sections 106 to 109

(6) Sections 106 to 109 (suspension of conditional supervision) apply to a breach of a deferred custody and supervision order made under paragraph (2)(p) as if the breach were a breach of an order for conditional supervision made under subsection 105(1) and, for the purposes of sections 106 to 109, supervision under a deferred custody and supervision order is deemed to be conditional supervision.

Intensive rehabilitative custody and supervision order

(7) A youth justice court may make an intensive rehabilitative custody and supervision order under paragraph (2)(r) in respect of a young person only if

(a) either

(i) the young person has been found guilty of a serious violent offence, or

(ii) the young person has been found guilty of an offence, in the commission of which the young person caused or attempted to cause serious bodily harm and for which an adult is liable to imprisonment for a term of more than two years, and the young person had previously been found guilty at least twice of such an offence;

(b) the young person is suffering from a mental illness or disorder, a psychological disorder or an emotional disturbance;

(c) a plan of treatment and intensive supervision has been developed for the young person, and there are reasonable grounds to believe that the plan might reduce the risk of the young person repeating the offence or committing a serious violent offence; and

(d) the provincial director has determined that an intensive rehabilitative custody and supervision program is available and that the young person's participation in the program is appropriate.

Safeguard of rights

(8) Nothing in this section abrogates or derogates from the rights of a young person regarding consent to physical or mental health treatment or care.

(9) and **(10)** [Repealed, 2012, c. 1, s. 174]

Inconsistency

(11) An order may not be made under paragraphs (2)(k) to (m) in respect of an offence for which a conditional discharge has been granted under paragraph (2)(c).

Coming into force of youth sentence

(12) A youth sentence or any part of it comes into force on the date on which it is imposed or on any later date that the youth justice court specifies.

Consecutive youth sentences

(13) Subject to subsections (15) and (16), a youth justice court that sentences a young person may direct that a sentence imposed on the young person under paragraph (2)(n), (o), (q) or (r) be served consecutively if the young person

(a) is sentenced while under sentence for an offence under any of those paragraphs; or

(b) is found guilty of more than one offence under any of those paragraphs.

Duration of youth sentence for a single offence

(14) No youth sentence, other than an order made under paragraph (2)(j), (n), (o), (q) or (r), shall continue in force for more than two years. If the youth sentence comprises more than one sanction imposed at the same time in respect of the same offence, the combined duration of the sanctions shall not exceed two years, unless the sentence includes a sanction under paragraph (2)(j), (n), (o), (q) or (r) that exceeds two years.

Duration of youth sentence for different offences

(15) Subject to subsection (16), if more than one youth sentence is imposed under this section in respect of a young person with respect to different offences, the continuous combined duration of those youth sentences shall not exceed three years, except if one of the offences is first degree murder or second degree murder within the meaning of section 231 of the *Criminal Code*, in which case the continuous combined duration of those youth sentences shall not exceed ten years in the case of first degree murder, or seven years in the case of second degree murder.

Duration of youth sentences made at different times

(16) If a youth sentence is imposed in respect of an offence committed by a young person after the commencement of, but before the completion of, any youth sentences imposed on the young person,

(a) the duration of the sentence imposed in respect of the subsequent offence shall be determined in accordance with subsections (14) and (15);

(b) the sentence may be served consecutively to the sentences imposed in respect of the previous offences; and

(c) the combined duration of all the sentences may exceed three years and, if the offence is, or one of the previous offences was,

(i) first degree murder within the meaning of section 231 of the *Criminal Code*, the continuous combined duration of the youth sentences may exceed ten years, or

(ii) second degree murder within the meaning of section 231 of the *Criminal Code*, the continuous combined duration of the youth sentences may exceed seven years.

Sentence continues when adult

(17) Subject to sections 89, 92 and 93 (provisions related to placement in adult facilities) of this Act and section 743.5 (transfer of jurisdiction) of the *Criminal Code*, a youth sentence imposed on a young person continues in effect in accordance with its terms after the young person becomes an adult.

2002, c. 1, s. 42; 2012, c. 1, s. 174.

–Additional youth sentences

43 Subject to subsection 42(15) (duration of youth sentences), if a young person who is subject to a custodial sentence imposed under paragraph 42(2)(n), (o), (q) or (r) that has not expired receives an additional youth sentence under one of those paragraphs, the young person is, for the purposes of the *Corrections and Conditional Release Act*, the *Criminal Code*, the *Prisons and Reformatories Act* and this Act, deemed to have been sentenced to one youth sentence commencing at the beginning of the first of those youth sentences to be served and ending on the expiry of the last of them to be served.

Custodial portion if additional youth sentence

44 Subject to subsection 42(15) (duration of youth sentences) and section 46 (exception when youth sentence in respect of earlier offence), if an additional youth sentence under paragraph 42(2)(n), (o), (q) or (r) is imposed on a young person on whom a youth sentence had already been imposed under one of those paragraphs that has not expired and the expiry date of the youth sentence that includes the additional youth sentence, as determined in accordance with section 43, is later than the expiry date of the youth sentence that the young person was serving before the additional youth sentence was imposed, the custodial portion of the young person's youth sentence is, from the date the additional sentence is imposed, the total of

(a) the unexpired portion of the custodial portion of the youth sentence before the additional youth sentence was imposed, and

(b) the relevant period set out in subparagraph (i), (ii) or (iii):

(i) if the additional youth sentence is imposed under paragraph 42(2)(n), the period that is two thirds of the period that constitutes the difference between the expiry of the youth sentence as determined in accordance with section 43 and the expiry of the youth sentence that the young person was serving before the additional youth sentence was imposed,

(ii) if the additional youth sentence is a concurrent youth sentence imposed under paragraph 42(2) (o), (q) or (r), the custodial portion of the youth sentence imposed under that paragraph that extends beyond the expiry date of the custodial portion of the sentence being served before the imposition of the additional sentence, or

(iii) if the additional youth sentence is a consecutive youth sentence imposed under paragraph 42(2) (o), (q) or (r), the custodial portion of the additional youth sentence imposed under that paragraph.

Supervision when additional youth sentence extends the period in custody

45 (1) If a young person has begun to serve a portion of a youth sentence in the community subject to conditions under paragraph 42(2)(n) or under conditional supervision under paragraph 42(2)(o), (q) or (r) at the time an additional youth sentence is imposed under one of those paragraphs, and, as a result of the application of section 44, the custodial portion of the young person's youth sentence ends on a day that is later than the day on which the young person received the additional youth sentence, the serving of a portion of the youth sentence under supervision in the community subject to conditions or under conditional supervision shall become inoperative and the young person shall be committed to custody under paragraph 102(1)(b) or 106(b) until the end of the extended portion of the youth sentence to be served in custody.

Supervision when additional youth sentence does not extend the period in custody

(2) If a youth sentence has been imposed under paragraph 42(2) (n), (o), (q) or (r) on a young person who is under supervision in the community subject to conditions under paragraph 42(2)(n) or under conditional supervision under paragraph 42(2)(o), (q) or (r), and the additional youth sentence would not modify the expiry date of the youth sentence that the young person was serving at the time the additional youth sentence was imposed, the young person may be remanded to the youth custody facility that the provincial director con-

siders appropriate. The provincial director shall review the case and, no later than forty-eight hours after the remand of the young person, shall either refer the case to the youth justice court for a review under section 103 or 109 or release the young person to continue the supervision in the community or the conditional supervision.

Supervision when youth sentence additional to supervision

(3) If a youth sentence has been imposed under paragraph 42(2)(n), (o), (q) or (r) on a young person who is under conditional supervision under paragraph 94(19)(b) or subsection 96(5), the young person shall be remanded to the youth custody facility that the provincial director considers appropriate. The provincial director shall review the case and, no later than forty-eight hours after the remand of the young person, shall either refer the case to the youth justice court for a review under section 103 or 109 or release the young person to continue the conditional supervision.

Exception when youth sentence in respect of earlier offence

46 The total of the custodial portions of a young person's youth sentences shall not exceed six years calculated from the beginning of the youth sentence that is determined in accordance with section 43 if

(a) a youth sentence is imposed under paragraph 42(2)(n), (o), (q) or (r) on the young person already serving a youth sentence under one of those paragraphs; and

(b) the later youth sentence imposed is in respect of an offence committed before the commencement of the earlier youth sentence.

Committal to custody deemed continuous

47 (1) Subject to subsections (2) and (3), a young person who is sentenced under paragraph 42(2)(n) is deemed to be committed to continuous custody for the custodial portion of the sentence.

Intermittent custody

(2) If the sentence does not exceed ninety days, the youth justice court may order that the custodial portion of the sentence be served intermittently if it is consistent with the purpose and principles set out in section 38.

Availability of place of intermittent custody

(3) Before making an order of committal to intermittent custody, the youth justice court shall require the prosecutor to make available to the court for its consideration a report of the provincial director as to the availability of a youth custody facility in which an order of intermittent custody can be enforced and, if the report discloses that no such youth custody facility is available, the court shall not make the order.

Reasons for the sentence

48 When a youth justice court imposes a youth sentence, it shall state its reasons for the sentence in the record of the case and shall, on request, give or cause to be given a copy of the sentence and the reasons for the sentence to

(a) the young person, the young person's counsel, a parent of the young person, the provincial director and the prosecutor; and

(b) in the case of a committal to custody under paragraph 42(2)(n), (o), (q) or (r), the review board.

Warrant of committal

49 (1) When a young person is committed to custody, the youth justice court shall issue or cause to be issued a warrant of committal.

Custody during transfer

(2) A young person who is committed to custody may, in the course of being transferred from custody to the court or from the court to custody, be held under the supervision and control of a peace officer or in any place of temporary detention referred to in subsection 30(1) that the provincial director may specify.

Subsection 30(3) applies

(3) Subsection 30(3) (detention separate from adults) applies, with any modifications that the circumstances require, in respect of a person held in a place of temporary detention under subsection (2).

Application of Part XXIII of *Criminal Code*

50 (1) Subject to section 74 (application of *Criminal Code* to adult sentences), Part XXIII (sentencing) of the *Criminal Code* does not apply in respect of proceedings under this Act except for paragraph 718.2(e) (sentencing principle for aboriginal offenders), sections 722 (victim impact statements), 722.1 (copy of statement) and 722.2 (inquiry by court), subsection 730(2) (court process continues in force) and sections 748 (pardons and remissions), 748.1 (remission by the Governor in Council) and 749 (royal prerogative) of that Act, which provisions apply with any modifications that the circumstances require.

Section 787 of *Criminal Code* does not apply

(2) Section 787 (general penalty) of the *Criminal Code* does not apply in respect of proceedings under this Act.

Mandatory prohibition order

51 (1) Despite section 42 (youth sentences), when a young person is found guilty of an offence referred to in any of paragraphs 109(1)(a) to (d) of the *Criminal Code*, the youth justice court shall, in addition to imposing a sentence under section 42 (youth sentences), make an order prohibiting the young person from possessing any firearm, cross-bow, prohibited weapon, restricted weapon, prohibited device, ammunition, prohibited ammunition or explosive substance during the period specified in the order as determined in accordance with subsection (2).

Duration of prohibition order

(2) An order made under subsection (1) begins on the day on which the order is made and ends not earlier than two years after the young person has completed the custodial portion of the sentence or, if the young person is not subject to custody, after the time the young person is found guilty of the offence.

Discretionary prohibition order

(3) Despite section 42 (youth sentences), where a young person is found guilty of an offence referred to in paragraph 110(1)(a) or (b) of the *Criminal Code*, the youth justice court shall, in addition to imposing a sentence under section 42 (youth sentences), consider whether it is desirable, in the interests of the safety of the young person or of any other person, to make an order prohibiting the young person from possessing any firearm, cross-bow, prohibited weapon, restricted weapon, prohibited device, ammunition, prohibited ammunition or explosive substance, or all such things, and where the court decides that it is so desirable, the court shall so order.

Duration of prohibition order

(4) An order made under subsection (3) against a young person begins on the day on which the order is made and ends not later than two years after the young person has completed the custodial portion of the sentence or, if the young person is not subject to custody, after the time the young person is found guilty of the offence.

Reasons for the prohibition order

(5) When a youth justice court makes an order under this section, it shall state its reasons for making the order in the record of the case and shall give or cause to be given a copy of the order and, on request, a transcript or copy of the reasons to the young person against whom the order was made, the counsel and a parent of the young person and the provincial director.

Reasons

(6) When the youth justice court does not make an order under subsection (3), or when the youth justice court does make such an order but does not prohibit the possession of everything referred to in that subsection, the youth justice court shall include in the record a statement of the youth justice court's reasons.

Application of *Criminal Code*

(7) Sections 113 to 117 (firearm prohibition orders) of the *Criminal Code* apply in respect of any order made under this section.

Report

(8) Before making an order referred to in section 113 (lifting firearms order) of the *Criminal Code* in respect of a young person, the youth justice court may require the provincial director to cause to be prepared, and to submit to the youth justice court, a report on the young person.

Review of order made under section 51

52 (1) A youth justice court may, on application, review an order made under section 51 at any time after the end of the period set out in subsection 119(2) (period of access to records) that applies to the record of the offence that resulted in the order being made.

Grounds

(2) In conducting a review under this section, the youth justice court shall take into account

(a) the nature and circumstances of the offence in respect of which the order was made; and

(b) the safety of the young person and of other persons.

Decision of review

(3) When a youth justice court conducts a review under this section, it may, after giving the young person, a parent of the young person, the Attorney General and the provincial director an opportunity to be heard,

(a) confirm the order;

(b) revoke the order; or

(c) vary the order as it considers appropriate in the circumstances of the case.

New order not to be more onerous

(4) No variation of an order made under paragraph (3)(c) may be more onerous than the order being reviewed.

Application of provisions

(5) Subsections 59(3) to (5) apply, with any modifications that the circumstances require, in respect of a review under this section.

Funding for victims

53 (1) The lieutenant governor in council of a province may order that, in respect of any fine imposed in the province under paragraph 42(2)(d), a percentage of the fine as fixed by the lieutenant governor in council be used to provide such assistance to victims of offences as the lieutenant governor in council may direct from time to time.

Victim fine surcharge

(2) If the lieutenant governor in council of a province has not made an order under subsection (1), a youth justice court that imposes a fine on a young person under paragraph 42(2)(d) may, in addition to any other punishment imposed on the young person, order the young person to pay a victim fine surcharge in an amount not exceeding fifteen per cent of the fine. The surcharge shall be used to provide such assistance to victims of offences as the lieutenant governor in council of the province in which the surcharge is imposed may direct from time to time.

Where a fine or other payment is ordered

54 (1) The youth justice court shall, in imposing a fine under paragraph 42(2)(d) or in making an order under paragraph 42(2)(e) or (g), have regard to the present and future means of the young person to pay.

Discharge of fine or surcharge

(2) A young person on whom a fine is imposed under paragraph 42(2)(d), including any percentage of a fine imposed under subsection 53(1), or on whom a victim fine surcharge is imposed under subsection 53(2), may discharge the fine or surcharge in whole or in part by earning credits for work performed in a program established for that purpose

(a) by the lieutenant governor in council of the province in which the fine or surcharge was imposed; or

(b) by the lieutenant governor in council of the province in which the young person resides, if an appropriate agreement is in effect between the government of that province and the government of the province in which the fine or surcharge was imposed.

Rates, crediting and other matters

(3) A program referred to in subsection (2) shall determine the rate at which credits are earned and may provide for the manner of crediting any amounts earned against the fine or surcharge and any other matters necessary for or incidental to carrying out the program.

Representations respecting orders under paragraphs 42(2) (e) to (h)

(4) In considering whether to make an order under any of paragraphs 42(2)(e) to (h), the youth justice court may consider any representations made by the person who would be compensated or to whom restitution or payment would be made.

Notice of orders under paragraphs 42(2)(e) to (h)

(5) If the youth justice court makes an order under any of paragraphs 42(2)(e) to (h), it shall cause notice of the terms of the order to be given to the person who is to be compensated or to whom restitution or payment is to be made.

Consent of person to be compensated

(6) No order may be made under paragraph 42(2)(h) unless the youth justice court has secured the consent of the person to be compensated.

Orders under paragraph 42(2)(h), (i) or (m)

(7) No order may be made under paragraph 42(2)(h), (i) or (m) unless the youth justice court is satisfied that

(a) the young person against whom the order is made is a suitable candidate for such an order; and

(b) the order does not interfere with the normal hours of work or education of the young person.

Duration of order for service

(8) No order may be made under paragraph 42(2)(h) or (i) to perform personal or community services unless those services can be completed in two hundred and forty hours or less and within twelve months after the date of the order.

Community service order

(9) No order may be made under paragraph 42(2)(i) unless

(a) the community service to be performed is part of a program that is approved by the provincial director; or

(b) the youth justice court is satisfied that the person or organization for whom the community service is to be performed has agreed to its performance.

Application for further time to complete youth sentence

(10) A youth justice court may, on application by or on behalf of the young person in respect of whom a youth sentence has been imposed under any of paragraphs 42(2)(d) to (i), allow further time for the completion of the sentence subject to any regulations made under paragraph 155(b) and to any rules made by the youth justice court under subsection 17(1).

Conditions that must appear in orders

55 (1) The youth justice court shall prescribe, as conditions of an order made under paragraph 42(2)(k) or (l), that the young person

(a) keep the peace and be of good behaviour; and

(b) appear before the youth justice court when required by the court to do so.

Conditions that may appear in orders

(2) A youth justice court may prescribe, as conditions of an order made under paragraph 42(2)(k) or (l), that a young person do one or more of the following that the youth justice court considers appropriate in the circumstances:

(a) report to and be supervised by the provincial director or a person designated by the youth justice court;

(b) notify the clerk of the youth justice court, the provincial director or the youth worker assigned to the case of any change of address or any change in the young person's place of employment, education or training;

(c) remain within the territorial jurisdiction of one or more courts named in the order;

(d) make reasonable efforts to obtain and maintain suitable employment;

(e) attend school or any other place of learning, training or recreation that is appropriate, if the youth justice court is satisfied that a suitable program for the young person is available there;

(f) reside with a parent, or any other adult that the youth justice court considers appropriate, who is willing to provide for the care and maintenance of the young person;

(g) reside at a place that the provincial director may specify;

(h) comply with any other conditions set out in the order that the youth justice court considers appropriate, including conditions for securing the young person's good conduct and for preventing the young person from repeating the offence or committing other offences; and

(i) not own, possess or have the control of any weapon, ammunition, prohibited ammunition, prohibited device or explosive substance, except as authorized by the order.

Communication of order

56 (1) A youth justice court that makes an order under paragraph 42(2)(k) or (l) shall

(a) cause the order to be read by or to the young person bound by it;

(b) explain or cause to be explained to the young person the purpose and effect of the order, and confirm that the young person understands it; and

(c) cause a copy of the order to be given to the young person, and to any parent of the young person who is in attendance at the sentencing hearing.

Copy of order to parent

(2) A youth justice court that makes an order under paragraph 42(2)(k) or (l) may cause a copy to be given to a parent of the young person who is not in attendance at the proceedings if the parent is, in the opinion of the court, taking an active interest in the proceedings.

Endorsement of order by young person

(3) After the order has been read and explained under subsection (1), the young person shall endorse on the order an acknowledgement that the young person has received a copy of the order and had its purpose and effect explained.

Validity of order

(4) The failure of a young person to endorse the order or of a parent to receive a copy of the order does not affect the validity of the order.

Commencement of order

(5) An order made under paragraph 42(2)(k) or (l) comes into force

(a) on the date on which it is made; or

(b) if a young person receives a sentence that includes a period of continuous custody and supervision, at the end of the period of supervision.

Effect of order in case of custody

(6) If a young person is subject to a sentence that includes both a period of continuous custody and supervision and an order made under paragraph 42(2)(k) or (l), and the court orders under subsection 42(12) a delay in the start of the period of custody, the court may divide the period that the order made under paragraph 42(2)(k) or (l) is in effect, with the first portion to have effect from the date on which it is made until the start of the period of custody, and the remainder to take effect at the end of the period of supervision.

Notice to appear

(7) A young person may be given notice either orally or in writing to appear before the youth justice court under paragraph 55(1)(b).

Warrant in default of appearance

(8) If service of a notice in writing is proved and the young person fails to attend court in accordance with the notice, a youth justice court may issue a warrant to compel the appearance of the young person.

Transfer of youth sentence

57 (1) When a youth sentence has been imposed under any of paragraphs 42(2)(d) to (i), (k), (l) or (s) in respect of a young person and the young person or a parent with whom the young person resides is or becomes a resident of a territorial division outside the jurisdiction of the youth justice court that imposed the youth sentence, whether in the same or in another province, a youth justice court judge in the territorial division in which the youth sentence was imposed may, on the application of the Attorney General or on the application of the young person or the young person's parent, with the consent of the

Attorney General, transfer to a youth justice court in another territorial division the youth sentence and any portion of the record of the case that is appropriate. All subsequent proceedings relating to the case shall then be carried out and enforced by that court.

No transfer outside province before appeal completed

(2) No youth sentence may be transferred from one province to another under this section until the time for an appeal against the youth sentence or the finding on which the youth sentence was based has expired or until all proceedings in respect of any such appeal have been completed.

Transfer to a province when person is adult

(3) When an application is made under subsection (1) to transfer the youth sentence of a young person to a province in which the young person is an adult, a youth justice court judge may, with the consent of the Attorney General, transfer the youth sentence and the record of the case to the youth justice court in the province to which the transfer is sought, and the youth justice court to which the case is transferred shall have full jurisdiction in respect of the youth sentence as if that court had imposed the youth sentence. The person shall be further dealt with in accordance with this Act.

Interprovincial arrangements

58 (1) When a youth sentence has been imposed under any of paragraphs 42(2)(k) to (r) in respect of a young person, the youth sentence in one province may be dealt with in any other province in accordance with any agreement that may have been made between those provinces.

Youth justice court retains jurisdiction

(2) Subject to subsection (3), when a youth sentence imposed in respect of a young person is dealt with under this section in a province other than that in which the youth sentence was imposed, the youth justice court of the province in which the youth sentence was imposed retains, for all purposes of this Act, exclusive jurisdiction over the young person as if the youth sentence were dealt with within that province, and any warrant or process issued in respect of the young person may be executed or served in any place in Canada outside the province where the youth sentence was imposed as if it were executed or served in that province.

Waiver of jurisdiction

(3) When a youth sentence imposed in respect of a young person is dealt with under this section in a province other than the one in which the youth sentence was imposed, the youth justice court of the province in which the youth sentence was imposed may, with the consent in writing of the Attorney General of that province and the young person, waive its jurisdiction, for the purpose of any proceeding under this Act, to the youth justice court of the province in which the youth sentence is dealt with, in which case the youth justice court in the province in which the youth sentence is dealt with shall have full jurisdiction in respect of the youth sentence as if that court had imposed the youth sentence.

Review of youth sentences not involving custody

59 (1) When a youth justice court has imposed a youth sentence in respect of a young person, other than a youth sentence under paragraph 42(2)(n), (o), (q) or (r), the youth justice court shall, on the application of the young person, the young person's parent, the Attorney General or the provincial director, made at any time after six months after the date of the youth sentence or, with leave of a youth justice court judge, at any earlier time, review the youth sentence if the court is satisfied that there are grounds for a review under subsection (2).

Grounds for review

(2) A review of a youth sentence may be made under this section

(a) on the ground that the circumstances that led to the youth sentence have changed materially;

(b) on the ground that the young person in respect of whom the review is to be made is unable to comply with or is experiencing serious difficulty in complying with the terms of the youth sentence;

(c) on the ground that the young person in respect of whom the review is to be made has contravened a condition of an order made under paragraph 42(2)(k) or (l) without reasonable excuse;

(d) on the ground that the terms of the youth sentence are adversely affecting the opportunities available to the young person to obtain services, education or employment; or

(e) on any other ground that the youth justice court considers appropriate.

Progress report

(3) The youth justice court may, before reviewing under this section a youth sentence imposed in respect of a young person, require the provincial director to cause to be prepared, and to submit to the youth justice court, a progress report on the performance of the young person since the youth sentence took effect.

Subsections 94(10) to (12) apply

(4) Subsections 94(10) to (12) apply, with any modifications that the circumstances require, in respect of any progress report required under subsection (3).

Subsections 94(7) and (14) to (18) apply

(5) Subsections 94(7) and (14) to (18) apply, with any modifications that the circumstances require, in respect of reviews made under this section and any notice required under subsection 94(14) shall also be given to the provincial director.

Compelling appearance of young person

(6) The youth justice court may, by summons or warrant, compel a young person in respect of whom a review is to be made under this section to appear before the youth justice court for the purposes of the review.

Decision of the youth justice court after review

(7) When a youth justice court reviews under this section a youth sentence imposed in respect of a young person, it may, after giving the young person, a parent of the young person, the Attorney General and the provincial director an opportunity to be heard,

(a) confirm the youth sentence;

(b) terminate the youth sentence and discharge the young person from any further obligation of the youth sentence; or

(c) vary the youth sentence or impose any new youth sentence under section 42, other than a committal to custody, for any period of time, not exceeding the remainder of the period of the earlier youth sentence, that the court considers appropriate in the circumstances of the case.

New youth sentence not to be more onerous

(8) Subject to subsection (9), when a youth sentence imposed in respect of a young person is reviewed under this section, no youth sentence imposed under subsection (7) shall, without the consent of the young person, be more onerous than the remainder of the youth sentence reviewed.

Exception

(9) A youth justice court may under this section extend the time within which a youth sentence imposed under paragraphs 42(2)(d) to (i) is to be complied with by a young person if the court is satisfied that the young person requires more time to comply with the youth sentence, but in no case shall the extension be for a period of time that expires more than twelve months after the date the youth sentence would otherwise have expired.

Provisions applicable to youth sentences on review

60 This Part and Part 5 (custody and supervision) apply with any modifications that the circumstances require to orders made in respect of reviews of youth sentences under sections 59 and 94 to 96.

Adult Sentence and Election

61 [Repealed, 2012, c. 1, s. 175]

62 [Repealed, 2012, c. 1, s. 175]

63 [Repealed, 2012, c. 1, s. 175]

Application by Attorney General

64 (1) The Attorney General may, before evidence is called as to sentence or, if no evidence is called, before submissions are made as to sentence, make an application to the youth justice court for an order that a young person is liable to an adult sentence if the young person is or has been found guilty of an offence for which an adult is liable to imprisonment for a term of more than two years, and that was committed after the young person attained the age of 14 years.

Obligation

(1.1) The Attorney General must consider whether it would be appropriate to make an application under subsection (1) if the offence is a serious violent offence and was committed after the young person attained the age of 14 years. If, in those circumstances, the Attorney General decides not to make an application, the Attorney General shall advise the youth justice court before the young person enters a plea with leave of the court before the commencement of the trial.

Order fixing age

(1.2) The lieutenant governor council of a province may by order fix an age greater than 14 years but not greater than 16 years for the purpose of subsection (1.1).

Notice of intention to seek adult sentence

(2) If the Attorney General intends to seek an adult sentence for an offence by making an application under subsection (1), the Attorney General shall, before the young person enters a plea or with leave of the youth justice court before the commencement of the trial, give notice to the young person and the youth justice court of the intention to seek an adult sentence.

Included offences

(3) A notice of intention to seek an adult sentence given in respect of an offence is notice in respect of any included offence of which the young person is found guilty for which an adult is liable to imprisonment for a term of more than two years.

(4) and (5) [Repealed, 2012, c. 1, s. 176]

2002, c. 1 s. 64; 2012, c. 1, s. 176.

65 [Repealed, 2012, c. 1, s. 177]

66 [Repealed, 2012, c. 1, s. 177]

Election - adult sentence

67 (1) The youth justice court shall, before a young person enters a plea, put the young person to his or her election in the words set out in subsection (2) if

(a) [Repealed, 2012, c. 1, s. 178]

(b) the Attorney General has given notice under subsection 64(2) of the intention to seek an adult sentence for an offence committed after the young person has attained the age of fourteen years;

(c) the young person is charged with having committed first or second degree murder within the meaning of section 231 of the *Criminal Code* before the young person has attained the age of fourteen years; or

(d) the person to whom section 16 (status of accused uncertain) applies is charged with having, after attaining the age of fourteen years, committed an offence for which an adult would be entitled to an election under section 536 of the *Criminal Code*, or over which a superior court of criminal jurisdiction would have exclusive jurisdiction under section 469 of that Act.

Wording of election

(2) The youth justice court shall put the young person to his or her election in the following words:

You have the option to elect to be tried by a youth justice court judge without a jury and without having had a preliminary inquiry; or you may elect to be tried by a judge without a jury; or you may elect to be tried by a court composed of a judge and jury. If you do not elect now, you are deemed to have elected to be tried by a court composed of a judge and jury. If you elect to be tried by a judge without a jury or by a court composed of a judge and jury or if you are deemed to have elected to be tried by a court composed of a judge and jury, you will have a preliminary inquiry only if you or the prosecutor requests one. How do you elect to be tried?

Election - Nunavut

(3) In respect of proceedings in Nunavut, the youth justice court shall, before a young person enters a plea, put the young person to his or her election in the words set out in subsection (4) if

(a) [Repealed, 2012, c. 1, s. 178]

(b) the Attorney General has given notice under subsection 64(2) of the intention to seek an adult sentence for an offence committed after the young person has attained the age of fourteen years;

(c) the young person is charged with having committed first or second degree murder within the meaning of section 231 of the *Criminal Code* before the young person has attained the age of fourteen years; or

(d) the person to whom section 16 (status of accused uncertain) applies is charged with having, after attaining the age of fourteen years, committed an offence for which an adult would be entitled to an election under section 536.1 of the *Criminal Code*.

Wording of election

(4) The youth justice court shall put the young person to his or her election in the following words:

You have the option to elect to be tried by a judge of the Nunavut Court of Justice alone, acting as a youth justice court without a jury and without a preliminary inquiry; or you may elect to be tried by a judge of the Nunavut Court of Justice, acting as a youth justice court without a jury; or you may elect to be tried by a judge of the Nunavut Court of Justice, acting as a youth justice court with a jury. If you elect to be tried by a judge without a jury or by a judge, acting as a youth justice court, with a jury or if you are deemed to have elected to be tried by a judge, acting as a youth justice court, with a jury, you will have a preliminary inquiry only if you or the prosecutor requests one. How do you elect to be tried?

Mode of trial where co-accused are young persons

(5) When two or more young persons who are charged with the same offence, who are jointly charged in the same information or indictment or in respect of whom the Attorney General seeks joinder of counts that are set out in separate informations or indictments are put to their election, then, unless all of them elect or re-elect or are deemed to have elected, as the case may be, the same mode of trial, the youth justice court judge

    (a) may decline to record any election, re-election or deemed election for trial by a youth justice court judge without a jury, a judge without a jury or, in Nunavut, a judge of the Nunavut Court Justice without a jury; and

    (b) if the judge declines to do so, shall hold a preliminary inquiry, if requested to do so by one of the parties, unless a preliminary inquiry has been held prior to the election, re-election or deemed election.

Attorney General may require trial by jury

(6) The Attorney General may, even if a young person elects under subsection (1) or (3) to be tried by a youth justice court judge without a jury or a judge without a jury, require the young person to be tried by a court composed of a judge and jury.

Preliminary inquiry

(7) When a young person elects to be tried by a judge without a jury, or elects or is deemed to have elected to be tried by a court composed of a judge and jury, the youth justice court referred to in subsection 13(1) shall, on the request of the young person or the prosecutor made at that time or within the period fixed by rules of court made under section 17 or 155 or, if there are no such rules, by the youth justice court judge, conduct a preliminary inquiry and if, on its conclusion, the young person is ordered to stand trial, the proceedings shall be conducted

    (a) before a judge without a jury or a court composed of a judge and jury, as the case may be; or

    (b) in Nunavut, before a judge of the Nunavut Court of Justice acting as a youth justice court, with or without a jury, as the case may be.

Preliminary inquiry if two or more accused

(7.1) If two or more young persons are jointly charged in an information and one or more of them make a request for a preliminary inquiry under subsection (7), a preliminary inquiry must be held with respect to all of them.

When no request for preliminary inquiry

(7.2) If no request for a preliminary inquiry is made under subsection (7), the youth justice court shall fix the date for the trial or the date on which the young person must appear in the trial court to have the date fixed.

Preliminary inquiry provisions of *Criminal Code*

(8) The preliminary inquiry shall be conducted in accordance with the provisions of Part XVIII (procedure on preliminary inquiry) of the *Criminal Code*, except to the extent that they are inconsistent with this Act.

Parts XIX and XX of *Criminal Code*

(9) Proceedings under this Act before a judge without a jury or a court composed of a judge and jury or, in Nunavut, a judge of the Nunavut Court of Justice acting as a youth justice court, with or without a jury, as the case may be, shall be conducted in accordance with the provisions of Parts XIX (indictable offences— trial without jury) and XX (procedure in jury trials and general provisions) of the *Criminal Code*, with any modifications that the circumstances require, except that

    (a) the provisions of this Act respecting the protection of privacy of young persons prevail over the provisions of the *Criminal Code;* and

    (b) the young person is entitled to be represented in court by counsel if the young person is removed from court in accordance with subsection 650(2) of the *Criminal Code.*

2002, c. 1, s. 67, c. 13, s. 91; 2012, c. 1, s. 178.

68 [Repealed, 2012, c. 1, s. 179]

69 (1) [Repealed, 2012, c. 1, s. 180]

Included offences

(2) If the Attorney General has given notice under subsection 64(2) of the intention to seek an adult sentence and the young person is found guilty of an included offence for which an adult is liable to imprisonment for a term of more than two years, committed after he or she has attained the age of 14 years, the Attorney General may make an application under subsection 64(1) (application for adult sentence).

2002, c. 1, s. 69; 2012, c. 1, s. 180.

70 [Repealed, 2012, c. 1, s. 181]

Hearing — adult sentences

71 The youth justice court shall, at the commencement of the sentencing hearing, hold a hearing in respect of an application under subsection 64(1) (application for adult sentence), unless the court has received notice that the application is not opposed. Both parties and the parents of the young person shall be given an opportunity to be heard at the hearing.

2002, c. 1, s. 71; 2012, c. 1, s. 182.

Order of adult sentence

72 (1) The youth justice court shall order that an adult sentence be imposed if it is satisfied that

    (a) the presumption of diminished moral blameworthiness or culpability of the young person is rebutted; and

    (b) a youth sentence imposed in accordance with the purpose and principles set out in subparagraph 3(1)(b)(ii) and section 38 would not be of sufficient length to hold the young person accountable for his or her offending behaviour.

Order of youth sentence

(1.1) If the youth justice court is not satisfied that an order should be made under subsection (1), it shall order that the young person is not liable to an adult sentence and that a youth sentence must be imposed.

Onus

(2) The onus of satisfying the youth justice court as to the matters referred to in subsection (1) on the Attorney General.

Pre-sentence report

(3) In making an order under subsection (1) or (1.1), the youth justice court shall consider the pre-sentence report.

Court to state reasons

(4) When the youth justice court makes an order under this section, it shall state the reasons for its decision.

Appeal

(5) For the purposes of an appeal in accordance with section 37, an order under subsection (1) or (1.1) is part of the sentence.

2002, c. 1, s. 72; 2012, c. 1, s. 183.

Court must impose adult sentence

73 (1) When the youth justice court makes an order under subsection 72(1) in respect of a young person, the court shall, on finding of guilt, impose an adult sentence on the young person.

Court must impose youth sentence

(2) When the youth justice court makes an order under subsection 72(1.1) in respect of a young person, the court shall, on a finding of guilt, impose a youth sentence on the young person.

2002, c. 1, s. 73; 2012, c. 1, s. 184.

Application of Parts XXIII and XXIV of *Criminal Code*

74 (1) Parts XXIII (sentencing) and XXIV (dangerous and long-term offenders) of the *Criminal Code* apply to a young person in respect of whom the youth justice court has ordered that an adult sentence be imposed.

Finding of guilt becomes a conviction

(2) A finding of guilt for an offence in respect of which an adult sentence is imposed becomes a conviction once the time allowed for the taking of an appeal has expired or, if an appeal is taken, all proceedings in respect of the appeal have been completed and the appeal court has upheld an adult sentence.

Interpretation

(3) This section does not affect the time of commencement of an adult sentence under subsection 719(1) of the *Criminal Code.*

Decision regarding lifting of publication ban

75 (1) When the youth justice court imposes a youth sentence on a young person who has been found guilty of a violent offence, the court shall decide whether it is appropriate to make an order lifting the ban on publication of information that would identify the young person as having been dealt with under this Act as referred to in subsection 110(1).

Order

(2) A youth justice court may order a lifting ban on publication if the court determines, taking into account the purpose and principles set out in sections 3 and 38, that the young person poses a significant risk of committing another violent offence and the lifting of the ban is necessary to protect the public against that risk.

Onus

(3) The onus of satisfying the youth justice court as to the appropriateness of lifting the ban is on the Attorney General.

Appeals

(4) For the purposes of an appeal in accordance with section 37, an order under subsection (2) is part of the sentence.

2002, c. 1, s. 75; 2012, c. 1, s. 185.

Placement when subject to adult sentence

76 (1) Subject to subsections (2) and (9) and sections 79 and 80 and despite anything else in this Act or any other Act of Parliament, when a young person who is subject to an adult sentence in respect of an offence is sentenced to a term of imprisonment for the offence, the youth justice court shall order that the young person serve any portion of the imprisonment in

(a) a youth custody facility separate and apart from any adult who is detained or held in custody;

(b) a provincial correctional facility for adults; or

(c) if the sentence is for two years or more, a penitentiary.

Young person under the age of 18

(2) No young person who is under the age of 18 years is to serve any portion of the imprisonment in a provincial correctional facility for adults or a penitentiary.

Opportunity to be heard

(3) Before making an order under subsection (1), the youth justice court shall give the young person, a parent of the young person, the Attorney General, the provincial director and representatives of the provincial and federal correctional systems an opportunity to be heard.

Report necessary

(4) Before making an order under subsection (1), the youth justice court shall require that a report be prepared for the purpose of assisting the court.

Appeals

(5) For the purposes of an appeal in accordance with section 37, an order under subsection (1) is part of the sentence.

Review

(6) On application, the youth justice court shall review the placement of a young person under this section and, if satisfied that the circumstances that resulted in the initial order have changed materially, and after having given the young person, a parent of the young person, the Attorney General, the provincial director and the representatives of the provincial and federal correctional systems an opportunity to be heard, the court may order that the young person be placed in

(a) a youth custody facility separate and apart from any adult who is detained or held in custody;

(b) a provincial correctional facility for adults; or

(c) if the sentence is for two years or more, a penitentiary.

Who may make application

(7) An application referred to in this section may be made by the young person, one of the young person's parents, the provincial director, representatives of the provincial and federal correctional systems and the Attorney General, after the time for all appeals has expired.

Notice

(8) When an application referred to in this section is made, the applicant shall cause a notice of the application to be given to the other persons referred to in subsection (7).

Limit – age twenty

(9) No young person shall remain in a youth custody facility under this section after the young person attains the age of twenty years, unless the youth justice court that makes the order under subsection (1) or reviews the placement under subsection (6) is satisfied that remaining in the youth custody facility would be in the best interests of the young person and would not jeopardize the safety of others.

> 2002, c. 1, s. 76; 2012, c. 1, s. 186.

Obligation to inform – parole

77 (1) When a young person is ordered to serve a portion of a sentence in a youth custody facility under paragraph 76(1)(a) (placement when subject to adult sentence), the provincial director shall inform the appropriate parole board.

Applicability of *Corrections and Conditional Release Act*

(2) For greater certainty, Part II of the *Corrections and Conditional Release Act* applies, subject to section 78, with respect to a young person who is the subject of an order under subsection 76(1) (placement when subject to adult sentence).

Appropriate parole board

(3) The appropriate parole board for the purposes of this section is

(a) if subsection 112(1) of the *Corrections and Conditional Release Act* would apply with respect to the young person but for the fact that the young person was ordered into a youth custody facility, the parole board mentioned in that subsection; and

(b) in any other case, the Parole Board of Canada.

> 2002, c. 1, s. 77; 2012, c. 1, s. 160.

Release entitlement

78 (1) For greater certainty, section 6 of the *Prisons and Reformatories Act* applies to a young person who is ordered to serve a portion of a sentence in a youth custody facility under paragraph 76(1)(a) (placement when subject to adult sentence) only if section 743.1 (rules respecting sentences of two or more years) of the *Criminal Code* would direct that the young person serve the sentence in a prison.

Release entitlement

(2) For greater certainty, section 127 of the *Corrections and Conditional Release Act* applies to a young person who is ordered to serve a portion of a sentence in a youth custody facility under paragraph 76(1)(a) (placement when subject to adult sentence) only if section 743.1 (rules respecting sentences of two or more years) of the *Criminal Code* would direct that the young person serve the sentence in a penitentiary.

If person convicted under another Act

79 If a person who is serving all or a portion of a sentence in a youth custody facility under paragraph 76(1)(a) (placement when subject to adult sentence) is sentenced to a term of imprisonment under an Act of Parliament other than this Act, the remainder of the portion of the sentence being served in the youth custody facility shall be served in a provincial correctional facility for adults or a penitentiary, in accordance with section 743.1 (rules respecting sentences of two or more years) of the *Criminal Code*.

If person who is serving a sentence under another Act is sentenced to an adult sentence

80 If a person who has been serving a sentence of imprisonment under an Act of Parliament other than this Act is sentenced to an adult sentence of imprisonment under this Act, the sentences shall be served in a provincial correctional facility for adults or a penitentiary, in accordance with section 743.1 (rules respecting sentences of two or more years) of the *Criminal Code*.

Procedure for application or notice

81 An application or a notice to the court under section 63, 64, 65 or 76 must be made or given orally, in the presence of the other party, or in writing with a copy served personally on the other party.

> 2002, c. 1, s. 81; 2012, c. 1, s. 187.

Effect of Termination of Youth Sentence

Effect of absolute discharge or termination of youth sentence

82 (1) Subject to section 12 (examination as to previous convictions) of the *Canada Evidence Act*, if a young person is found guilty of an offence, and a youth justice court directs under paragraph 42(2)(b) that the young person be discharged absolutely, or the youth sentence, or any disposition made under the *Young Offenders Act*, chapter Y-1 of the Revised Statutes of Canada, 1985, has ceased to have effect, other than an order under section 51 (mandatory prohibition order) of this Act or section 20.1 (mandatory prohibition order) of the *Young Offenders Act*, the young person is deemed not to have been found guilty or convicted of the offence except that

(a) the young person may plead *autrefois convict* in respect of any subsequent charge relating to the offence;

(b) a youth justice court may consider the finding of guilt in considering an application under subsection 64(1) (application for adult sentence);

(c) any court or justice may consider the finding of guilt in considering an application for judicial interim release or in considering what sentence to impose for any offence; and

(d) the Parole Board of Canada or any provincial parole board may consider the finding of guilt in considering an application for conditional release or for a record suspension under the *Criminal Records Act*.

Disqualifications removed

(2) For greater certainty and without restricting the generality of subsection (1), an absolute discharge under paragraph 42(2)(b) or the termination of the youth sentence or disposition in respect of an offence for which a young person is found guilty removes any disqualification in respect of the offence to which the young person is subject under any Act of Parliament by reason of a finding of guilt.

Applications for employment

(3) No application form for or relating to the following shall contain any question that by its terms requires the applicant to disclose that he or she has been charged with or found guilty of an offence in respect of which he or she has, under this Act or the *Young Offenders Act*, chapter Y-1 of the Revised Statutes of Canada, 1985, been discharged absolutely, or has completed the youth sentence under this Act or the disposition under the *Young Offenders Act*:

(a) employment in any department, as defined in section 2 of the *Financial Administration Act*;

(b) employment by any Crown corporation, as defined in section 83 of the *Financial Administration Act*;

(c) enrolment in the Canadian Forces; or

(d) employment on or in connection with the operation of any work, undertaking or business that is within the legislative authority of Parliament.

Finding of guilt not a previous conviction

(4) A finding of guilt under this Act is not a previous conviction for the purposes of any offence under any Act of Parliament for which a greater punishment is prescribed by reason of previous convictions, except for

(a) [Repealed, 2012, c. 1, s. 188]

(b) the purpose of determining the adult sentence to be imposed.

2002, c. 1, s. 82; 2012, c. 1, ss. 156, 160, 188.

PART 5

CUSTODY AND SUPERVISION

Purpose

83 (1) The purpose of the youth custody and supervision system is to contribute to the protection of society by

(a) carrying out sentences imposed by courts through the safe, fair and humane custody and supervision of young persons; and

(b) assisting young persons to be rehabilitated and reintegrated into the community as law-abiding citizens, by providing effective programs to young persons in custody and while under supervision in the community.

Principles to be used

(2) In addition to the principles set out in section 3, the following principles are to be used in achieving that purpose:

(a) that the least restrictive measures consistent with the protection of the public, of personnel working with young persons and of young persons be used;

(b) that young persons sentenced to custody retain the rights of other young persons, except the rights that are necessarily removed or restricted as a consequence of a sentence under this Act or another Act of Parliament;

(c) that the youth custody and supervision system facilitate the involvement of the families of young persons and members of the public;

(d) that custody and supervision decisions be made in a forthright, fair and timely manner, and that young persons have access to an effective review procedure; and

(e) that placements of young persons where they are treated as adults not disadvantage them with respect to their eligibility for and conditions of release.

Young person to be held apart from adults

84 Subject to subsection 30(3) (pre-trial detention), paragraphs 76(1)(b) and (c) (placement in adult facilities with adult sentence) and sections 89 to 93 (placement in adult facilities with youth sentence), a young person who is committed to custody shall be held separate and apart from any adult who is detained or held in custody.

Levels of custody

85 (1) In the youth custody and supervision system in each province there must be at least two levels of custody for young persons distinguished by the degree of restraint of the young persons in them.

Designation of youth custody facilities

(2) Every youth custody facility in a province that contains one or more levels of custody shall be designated by

(a) in the case of a youth custody facility with only one level of custody, being the level of custody with the least degree of

restraint of the young persons in it, the lieutenant governor in council or his or her delegate; and

(b) in any other case, the lieutenant governor in council.

Provincial director to specify custody level – committal to custody

(3) The provincial director shall, when a young person is committed to custody under paragraph 42(2)(n), (o), (q) or (r) or an order is made under subsection 98(3), paragraph 103(2)(b), subsection 104(1) or paragraph 109(2)(b), determine the level of custody appropriate for the young person, after having taken into account the factors set out in subsection (5).

Provincial director to specify custody level – transfer

(4) The provincial director may determine a different level of custody for the young person when the provincial director is satisfied that the needs of the young person and the interests of society would be better served by doing so, after having taken into account the factors set out in subsection (5).

Factors

(5) The factors referred to in subsections (3) and (4) are

(a) that the appropriate level of custody for the young person is the one that is the least restrictive to the young person, having regard to

(i) the seriousness of the offence in respect of which the young person was committed to custody and the circumstances in which that offence was committed,

(ii) the needs and circumstances of the young person, including proximity to family, school, employment and support services,

(iii) the safety of other young persons in custody, and

(iv) the interests of society;

(b) that the level of custody should allow for the best possible match of programs to the young person's needs and behaviour, having regard to the findings of any assessment in respect of the young person; and

(c) the likelihood of escape.

Placement and transfer at appropriate level

(6) After the provincial director has determined the appropriate level of custody for the young person under subsection (3) or (4), the young person shall be placed in the youth custody facility that contains that level of custody specified by the provincial director.

Notice

(7) The provincial director shall cause a notice in writing of a determination under subsection (3) or (4) to be given to the young person and a parent of the young person and set out in that notice the reasons for it.

Procedural safeguards

86 (1) The lieutenant governor in council of a province shall ensure that procedures are in place to ensure that the due process rights of the young person are protected with respect to a determination made under subsection 85(3) or (4), including that the young person be

(a) provided with any relevant information to which the provincial director has access in making the determination, subject to subsection (2);

(b) given the opportunity to be heard; and

(c) informed of any right to a review under section 87.

Withholding of information

(2) Where the provincial director has reasonable grounds to believe that providing the information referred to in paragraph (1)(a) would jeopardize the safety of any person or the security of a facility, he or she may authorize the withholding from the young person of as much information as is strictly necessary in order to protect such safety or security.

Review

87 (1) A young person may apply for a review under this section of a determination

(a) under subsection 85(3) that would place the young person in a facility at a level of custody that has more than a minimal degree of restraint; or

(b) under subsection 85(4) that would transfer a young person to a facility at a level of custody with a higher degree of restraint or increase the degree of restraint of the young person in the facility.

Procedural safeguards

(2) The lieutenant governor in council of a province shall ensure that procedures are in place for the review under subsection (1), including that

(a) the review board that conducts the review be independent;

(b) the young person be provided with any relevant information to which the review board has access, subject to subsection (3); and

(c) the young person be given the opportunity to be heard.

Withholding of information

(3) Where the review board has reasonable grounds to believe that providing the information referred to in paragraph (2)(b) would jeopardize the safety of any person or the security of a facility, it may authorize the withholding from the young person of as much information as is strictly necessary in order to protect such safety or security.

Factors

(4) The review board shall take into account the factors referred to in subsection 85(5) in reviewing a determination.

Decision is final

(5) A decision of the review board under this section in respect of a particular determination is final.

Functions to be exercised by youth justice court

88 The lieutenant governor in council of a province may order that the power to make determinations of the level of custody for young persons and to review those determinations be exercised in accordance with the *Young Offenders Act,* chapter Y-1 of the Revised Statutes of Canada, 1985. The following provisions of that Act apply, with any modifications that the circumstances require, to the exercise of those powers:

(a) the definitions "review board" and "progress report" in subsection 2(1);

(b) section 11;

(c) sections 24.1 to 24.3; and

(d) sections 28 to 31.

Exception if young person is twenty years old or older

89 (1) When a young person is twenty years old or older at the time the youth sentence is imposed on him or her under paragraph

42(2)(n), (o), (q) or (r), the young person shall, despite section 85, be committed to a provincial correctional facility for adults to serve the youth sentence.

If serving youth sentence in a provincial correctional facility

(2) If a young person is serving a youth sentence in a provincial correctional facility for adults pursuant to subsection (1), the youth justice court may, on application of the provincial director at any time after the young person begins to serve a portion of the youth sentence in a provincial correctional facility for adults, after giving the young person, the provincial director and representatives of the provincial and federal correctional systems an opportunity to be heard, authorize the provincial director to direct that the young person serve the remainder of the youth sentence in a penitentiary if the court considers it to be in the best interests of the young person or in the public interest and if, at the time of the application, that remainder is two years or more.

Provisions to apply

(3) If a young person is serving a youth sentence in a provincial correctional facility for adults or a penitentiary under subsection (1) or (2), the *Prisons and Reformatories Act* and the *Corrections and Conditional Release Act,* and any other statute, regulation or rule applicable in respect of prisoners or offenders within the meaning of those Acts, statutes, regulations and rules, apply in respect of the young person except to the extent that they conflict with Part 6 (publication, records and information) of this Act, which Part continues to apply to the young person.

Youth worker

90 (1) When a youth sentence is imposed committing a young person to custody, the provincial director of the province in which the young person received the youth sentence and was placed in custody shall, without delay, designate a youth worker to work with the young person to plan for his or her reintegration into the community, including the preparation and implementation of a reintegration plan that sets out the most effective programs for the young person in order to maximize his or her chances for reintegration into the community.

Role of youth worker when young person in the community

(2) When a portion of a young person's youth sentence is served in the community in accordance with section 97 or 105, the youth worker shall supervise the young person, continue to provide support to the young person and assist the young person to respect the conditions to which he or she is subject, and help the young person in the implementation of the reintegration plan.   ·

Reintegration leave

91 (1) The provincial director of a province may, subject to any terms or conditions that he or she considers desirable, authorize, for a young person committed to a youth custody facility in the province further to an order under paragraph 76(1)(a) (placement when subject to adult sentence) or a youth sentence imposed under paragraph 42(2)(n), (o), (q) or (r),

(a) a reintegration leave from the youth custody facility for a period not exceeding thirty days if, in the opinion of the provincial director, it is necessary or desirable that the young person be absent, with or without escort, for medical, compassionate or humanitarian reasons or for the purpose of rehabilitating the young person or reintegrating the young person into the community; or

(b) that the young person be released from the youth custody facility on the days and during the hours that the provincial director specifies in order that the young person may

(i) attend school or any other educational or training institution,

(ii) obtain or continue employment or perform domestic or other duties required by the young person's family,

(iii) participate in a program specified by the provincial director that, in the provincial director's opinion, will enable the young person to better carry out employment or improve his or her education or training, or

(iv) attend an out-patient treatment program or other program that provides services that are suitable to addressing the young person's needs.

Renewal of reintegration leave

(2) A reintegration leave authorized under paragraph (1)(a) may be renewed by the provincial director for one or more thirty-day periods on reassessment of the case.

Revocation of authorization

(3) The provincial director of a province may, at any time, revoke an authorization made under subsection (1).

Arrest and return to custody

(4) If the provincial director revokes an authorization under subsection (3) or if a young person fails to comply with any term or condition of a reintegration leave or a release from custody under this section, the young person may be arrested without warrant and returned to custody.

Transfer to adult facility

92 (1) When a young person is committed to custody under paragraph 42(2)(n), (o), (q) or (r), the youth justice court may, on application of the provincial director made at any time after the young person attains the age of eighteen years, after giving the young person, the provincial director and representatives of the provincial correctional system an opportunity to be heard, authorize the provincial director to direct that the young person, subject to subsection (3), serve the remainder of the youth sentence in a provincial correctional facility for adults, if the court considers it to be in the best interests of the young person or in the public interest.

If serving youth sentence in a provincial correctional facility

(2) The youth justice court may authorize the provincial director to direct that a young person, subject to subsection (3), serve the remainder of a youth sentence in a penitentiary

(a) if the youth justice court considers it to be in the best interests of the young person or in the public interest;

(b) if the provincial director applies for the authorization at any time after the young person begins to serve a portion of a youth sentence in a provincial correctional facility for adults further to a direction made under subsection (1);

(c) if, at the time of the application, that remainder is two years or more; and

(d) so long as the youth justice court gives the young person, the provincial director and representatives of the provincial and federal correctional systems an opportunity to be heard.

Provisions to apply

(3) If the provincial director makes a direction under subsection (1) or (2), the *Prisons and Reformatories Act* and the *Corrections and Conditional Release Act,* and any other statute, regulation or rule applicable in respect of prisoners and offenders within the meaning of those Acts, statutes, regulations and rules, apply in respect of the young person except to the extent that they conflict with Part 6 (pub-

lication, records and information) of this Act, which Part continues to apply to the young person.

Placement when adult and youth sentences

(4) If a person is subject to more than one sentence, at least one of which is a youth sentence imposed under paragraph 42(2)(n), (o), (q) or (r) and at least one of which is a sentence referred to in either paragraph (b) or (c), he or she shall serve, in a provincial correctional facility for adults or a penitentiary in accordance with section 743.1 (rules respecting sentences of two or more years) of the *Criminal Code,* the following:

(a) the remainder of any youth sentence imposed under paragraph 42(2)(n), (o), (q) or (r);

(b) an adult sentence to which an order under paragraph 76(1)(b) or (c) (placement in adult facility) applies; and

(c) any sentence of imprisonment imposed otherwise than under this Act.

Youth sentence and adult sentence

(5) If a young person is committed to custody under a youth sentence under paragraph 42(2)(n), (o), (q) or (r) and is also already subject to an adult sentence to which an order under paragraph 76(1)(a) (placement when subject to adult sentence) applies, the young person may, in the discretion of the provincial director, serve the sentences, or any portion of the sentences, in a youth custody facility, in a provincial correctional facility for adults or, if the unexpired portion of the sentence is two years or more, in a penitentiary.

When young person reaches twenty years of age

93 (1) When a young person who is committed to custody under paragraph 42(2)(n), (o), (q) or (r) is in a youth custody facility when the young person attains the age of twenty years, the young person shall be transferred to a provincial correctional facility for adults to serve the remainder of the youth sentence, unless the provincial director orders that the young person continue to serve the youth sentence in a youth custody facility.

If serving youth sentence in a provincial correctional facility

(2) If a young person is serving a portion of a youth sentence in a provincial correctional facility for adults pursuant to a transfer under subsection (1), the youth justice court may, on application of the provincial director after the transfer, after giving the young person, the provincial director and representatives of the provincial and federal correctional systems an opportunity to be heard, authorize the provincial director to direct that the young person serve the remainder of the youth sentence in a penitentiary if the court considers it to be in the best interests of the young person or in the public interest and if, at the time of the application, that remainder is two years or more.

Provisions to apply

(3) If the provincial director makes the direction, the *Prisons and Reformatories Act* and the *Corrections and Conditional Release Act,* and any other statute, regulation or rule applicable in respect of prisoners and offenders within the meaning of those Acts, statutes, regulations and rules, apply in respect of the young person except to the extent that they conflict with Part 6 (publication, records and information) of this Act, which Part continues to apply to the young person.

Annual review

94 (1) When a young person is committed to custody pursuant to a youth sentence under paragraph 42(2)(n), (o), (q) or (r) for a period exceeding one year, the provincial director of the province in which the young person is held in custody shall cause the young person to be brought before the youth justice court without delay at the end of one year from the date of the most recent youth sentence imposed in respect of the offence—and at the end of every subsequent year from that date—and the youth justice court shall review the youth sentence.

Annual review

(2) When a young person is committed to custody pursuant to youth sentences imposed under paragraph 42(2)(n), (o), (q) or (r) in respect of more than one offence for a total period exceeding one year, the provincial director of the province in which the young person is held in custody shall cause the young person to be brought before the youth justice court without delay at the end of one year from the date of the earliest youth sentence imposed—and at the end of every subsequent year from that date—and the youth justice court shall review the youth sentences.

Optional review

(3) When a young person is committed to custody pursuant to a youth sentence imposed under paragraph 42(2)(n), (o), (q) or (r) in respect of an offence, the provincial director may, on the provincial director's own initiative, and shall, on the request of the young person, the young person's parent or the Attorney General, on any of the grounds set out in subsection (6), cause the young person to be brought before a youth justice court to review the youth sentence,

    (a) when the youth sentence is for a period not exceeding one year, once at any time after the expiry of the greater of

        (i) thirty days after the date of the youth sentence imposed under subsection 42(2) in respect of the offence, and

        (ii) one third of the period of the youth sentence imposed under subsection 42(2) in respect of the offence; and

    (b) when the youth sentence is for a period exceeding one year, at any time after six months after the date of the most recent youth sentence imposed in respect of the offence.

Time for optional review

(4) The young person may be brought before the youth justice court at any other time, with leave of the youth justice court judge.

Review

(5) If a youth justice court is satisfied that there are grounds for review under subsection (6), the court shall review the youth sentence.

Grounds for review

(6) A youth sentence imposed in respect of a young person may be reviewed under subsection (5)

    (a) on the ground that the young person has made sufficient progress to justify a change in the youth sentence;

    (b) on the ground that the circumstances that led to the youth sentence have changed materially;

    (c) on the ground that new services or programs are available that were not available at the time of the youth sentence;

    (d) on the ground that the opportunities for rehabilitation are now greater in the community; or

    (e) on any other ground that the youth justice court considers appropriate.

No review if appeal pending

(7) Despite any other provision of this section, no review of a youth sentence in respect of which an appeal has been taken shall be made under this section until all proceedings in respect of any such appeal have been completed.

Youth justice court may order appearance of young person for review

(8) When a provincial director is required under subsections (1) to (3) to cause a young person to be brought before the youth justice court and fails to do so, the youth justice court may, on application made by the young person, his or her parent or the Attorney General, or on its own motion, order the provincial director to cause the young person to be brought before the youth justice court.

Progress report

(9) The youth justice court shall, before reviewing under this section a youth sentence imposed in respect of a young person, require the provincial director to cause to be prepared, and to submit to the youth justice court, a progress report on the performance of the young person since the youth sentence took effect.

Additional information in progress report

(10) A person preparing a progress report in respect of a young person may include in the report any information relating to the personal and family history and present environment of the young person that he or she considers advisable.

Written or oral report

(11) A progress report shall be in writing unless it cannot reasonably be committed to writing, in which case it may, with leave of the youth justice court, be submitted orally in court.

Subsections 40(4) to (10) to apply

(12) Subsections 40(4) to (10) (procedures respecting presentence reports) apply, with any modifications that the circumstances require, in respect of progress reports.

Notice of review from provincial director

(13) When a youth sentence imposed in respect of a young person is to be reviewed under subsection (1) or (2), the provincial director shall cause any notice that may be directed by rules of court applicable to the youth justice court or, in the absence of such a direction, at least five clear days notice of the review to be given in writing to the young person, a parent of the young person and the Attorney General.

Notice of review from person requesting it

(14) When a review of a youth sentence imposed in respect of a young person is requested under subsection (3), the person requesting the review shall cause any notice that may be directed by rules of court applicable to the youth justice court or, in the absence of such a direction, at least five clear days notice of the review to be given in writing to the young person, a parent of the young person and the Attorney General.

Statement of right to counsel

(15) A notice given to a parent under subsection (13) or (14) shall include a statement that the young person whose youth sentence is to be reviewed has the right to be represented by counsel.

Service of notice

(16) A notice under subsection (13) or (14) may be served personally or may be sent by confirmed delivery service.

Notice may be waived

(17) Any of the persons entitled to notice under subsection (13) or (14) may waive the right to that notice.

If notice not given

(18) If notice under subsection (13) or (14) is not given in accordance with this section, the youth justice court may

(a) adjourn the proceedings and order that the notice be given in the manner and to the persons that it directs; or

(b) dispense with the notice if, in the opinion of the court, having regard to the circumstances, notice may be dispensed with.

Decision of the youth justice court after review

(19) When a youth justice court reviews under this section a youth sentence imposed in respect of a young person, it may, after giving the young person, a parent of the young person, the Attorney General and the provincial director an opportunity to be heard, having regard to the needs of the young person and the interests of society,

(a) confirm the youth sentence;

(b) release the young person from custody and place the young person under conditional supervision in accordance with the procedure set out in section 105, with any modifications that the circumstances require, for a period not exceeding the remainder of the youth sentence that the young person is then serving; or

(c) if the provincial director so recommends, convert a youth sentence under paragraph 42(2)(r) to a youth sentence under paragraph 42(2)(q) if the offence was murder or to a youth sentence under paragraph 42(2)(n) or (o), as the case may be, if the offence was an offence other than murder.

Orders are youth sentences

95 Orders under subsections 97(2) (conditions) and 98(3) (continuation of custody), paragraph 103(2)(b) (continuation of custody), subsections 104(1) (continuation of custody) and 105(1) (conditional supervision) and paragraph 109(2)(b) (continuation of suspension of conditional supervision) are deemed to be youth sentences for the purposes of section 94 (reviews).

Recommendation of provincial director for conditional supervision of young person

96 (1) When a young person is held in custody pursuant to a youth sentence under paragraph 42(2)(n), (o), (q) or (r), the provincial director may, if satisfied that the needs of the young person and the interests of society would be better served by doing so, make a recommendation to the youth justice court that the young person be released from custody and placed under conditional supervision.

Notice

(2) If the provincial director makes a recommendation, the provincial director shall cause a notice to be given in writing that includes the reasons for the recommendation and the conditions that the provincial director would recommend be set under section 105 to the young person, a parent of the young person and the Attorney General and give a copy of the notice to the youth justice court.

Application to court for review of recommendation

(3) If notice of a recommendation is made under subsection (2) with respect to a youth sentence imposed on a young person, the youth justice court shall, if an application for review is made by the young person, the young person's parent or the Attorney General within ten days after service of the notice, review the youth sentence without delay.

Subsections 94(7), (9) to (12) and (14) to (19) apply

(4) Subject to subsection (5), subsections 94(7) (no review of appeal pending), (9) to (12) (progress reports) and (14) to (19) (provisions respecting notice and decision of the youth justice court) apply, with any modifications that the circumstances require, in respect of reviews made under this section and any notice required under subsection 94(14) shall also be given to the provincial director.

If no application for review made under subsection (3)

(5) A youth justice court that receives a notice under subsection (2) shall, if no application for a review is made under subsection (3),

(a) order the release of the young person and place the young person under conditional supervision in accordance with section 105, having regard to the recommendations of the provincial director; or

(b) if the court considers it advisable, order that the young person not be released.

For greater certainty, an order under this subsection may be made without a hearing.

Notice when no release ordered

(6) When a youth justice court orders that the young person not be released under paragraph (5)(b), it shall cause a notice of its order to be given to the provincial director without delay.

Provincial director may request review

(7) When the provincial director is given a notice under subsection (6), he or she may request a review under this section.

When provincial director requests a review

(8) When the provincial director requests a review under subsection (7),

(a) the provincial director shall cause any notice that may be directed by rules of court applicable to the youth justice court or, in the absence of such a direction, at least five clear days notice of the review to be given in writing to the young person, a parent of the young person and the Attorney General; and

(b) the youth justice court shall review the youth sentence without delay after the notice required under paragraph (a) is given.

Conditions to be included in custody and supervision order

97 (1) Every youth sentence imposed under paragraph 42(2)(n) shall contain the following conditions, namely, that the young person, while serving the portion of the youth sentence under supervision in the community,

(a) keep the peace and be of good behaviour;

(b) report to the provincial director and then be under the supervision of the provincial director;

(c) inform the provincial director immediately on being arrested or questioned by the police;

(d) report to the police, or any named individual, as instructed by the provincial director;

(e) advise the provincial director of the young person's address of residence and report immediately to the provincial director any change

(i) in that address,

(ii) in the young person's normal occupation, including employment, vocational or educational training and volunteer work,

(iii) in the young person's family or financial situation, and

(iv) that may reasonably be expected to affect the young person's ability to comply with the conditions of the sentence; and

(f) not own, possess or have the control of any weapon, ammunition, prohibited ammunition, prohibited device or explosive substance, except as authorized in writing by the provincial director for the purposes of the young person participating in a program specified in the authorization.

Other conditions

(2) The provincial director may set additional conditions that support and address the needs of the young person, promote the reintegration of the young person into the community and offer adequate protection to the public from the risk that the young person might otherwise present. The provincial director shall, in setting the conditions, take into account the needs of the young person, the most effective programs for the young person in order to maximize his or her chances for reintegration into the community, the nature of the offence and the ability of the young person to comply with the conditions.

Communication of conditions

(3) The provincial director shall

(a) cause the conditions to be read by or to the young person bound by them;

(b) explain or cause to be explained to the young person the purpose and effect of the conditions, and confirm that the young person understands them; and

(c) cause a copy of the conditions to be given to the young person, and to a parent of the young person.

Provisions to apply

(4) Subsections 56(3) (endorsement of order by young person) and (4) (validity of order) apply, with any modifications that the circumstances require, in respect of conditions under this section.

Application for continuation of custody

98 (1) Within a reasonable time before the expiry of the custodial portion of a young person's youth sentence, the Attorney General or the provincial director may apply to the youth justice court for an order that the young person remain in custody for a period not exceeding the remainder of the youth sentence.

Continuation of custody

(2) If the hearing for an application under subsection (1) cannot be completed before the expiry of the custodial portion of the youth sentence, the court may order that the young person remain in custody pending the determination of the application if the court is satisfied that the application was made in a reasonable time, having regard to all the circumstances, and that there are compelling reasons for keeping the young person in custody.

Decision

(3) The youth justice court may, after giving both parties and a parent of the young person an opportunity to be heard, order that a young person remain in custody for a period not exceeding the remainder of the youth sentence, if it is satisfied that there are reasonable grounds to believe that

(a) the young person is likely to commit a serious violent offence before the expiry of the youth sentence he or she is then serving; and

(b) the conditions that would be imposed on the young person if he or she were to serve a portion of the youth sentence in the community would not be adequate to prevent the commission of the offence.

Factors

(4) For the purpose of determining an application under subsection (1), the youth justice court shall take into consideration any factor that is relevant to the case of the young person, including

(a) evidence of a pattern of persistent violent behaviour and, in particular,

(i) the number of offences committed by the young person that caused physical or psychological harm to any other person,

(ii) the young person's difficulties in controlling violent impulses to the point of endangering the safety of any other person,

(iii) the use of weapons in the commission of any offence,

(iv) explicit threats of violence,

(v) behaviour of a brutal nature associated with the commission of any offence, and

(vi) a substantial degree of indifference on the part of the young person as to the reasonably foreseeable consequences, to other persons, of the young person's behaviour;

(b) psychiatric or psychological evidence that a physical or mental illness or disorder of the young person is of such a nature that the young person is likely to commit, before the expiry of the youth sentence the young person is then serving, a serious violent offence;

(c) reliable information that satisfies the youth justice court that the young person is planning to commit, before the expiry of the youth sentence the young person is then serving, a serious violent offence;

(d) the availability of supervision programs in the community that would offer adequate protection to the public from the risk that the young person might otherwise present until the expiry of the youth sentence the young person is then serving;

(e) whether the young person is more likely to reoffend if he or she serves his or her youth sentence entirely in custody without the benefits of serving a portion of the youth sentence in the community under supervision; and

(f) evidence of a pattern of committing violent offences while he or she was serving a portion of a youth sentence in the community under supervision.

Report

99 (1) For the purpose of determining an application under section 98 (application for continuation of custody), the youth justice court shall require the provincial director to cause to be prepared, and to submit to the youth justice court, a report setting out any information of which the provincial director is aware with respect to the factors set out in subsection 98(4) that may be of assistance to the court.

Written or oral report

(2) A report referred to in subsection (1) shall be in writing unless it cannot reasonably be committed to writing, in which case it may, with leave of the youth justice court, be submitted orally in court.

Provisions apply

(3) Subsections 40(4) to (10) (procedures respecting presentence reports) apply, with any modifications that the circumstances require, in respect of a report referred to in subsection (1).

Notice of hearing

(4) When an application is made under section 98 (application for continuation of custody) in respect of a young person, the provincial

director shall cause to be given, to the young person and to a parent of the young person, at least five clear days notice of the hearing in writing.

Statement of right to counsel

(5) Any notice given to a parent under subsection (4) shall include a statement that the young person has the right to be represented by counsel.

Service of notice

(6) A notice under subsection (4) may be served personally or may be sent by confirmed delivery service.

When notice not given

(7) When notice under subsection (4) is not given in accordance with this section, the youth justice court may

(a) adjourn the hearing and order that the notice be given in any manner and to any person that it directs; or

(b) dispense with the giving of the notice if, in the opinion of the youth justice court, having regard to the circumstances, the giving of the notice may be dispensed with.

Reasons

100 When a youth justice court makes an order under subsection 98(3) (decision for continued custody), it shall state its reasons for the order in the record of the case and shall provide, or cause to be provided, to the young person in respect of whom the order was made, the counsel and a parent of the young person, the Attorney General and the provincial director

(a) a copy of the order; and

(b) on request, a transcript or copy of the reasons for the order.

Review of youth justice court decision

101 (1) An order made under subsection 98(3) (decision for continued custody) in respect of a young person, or the refusal to make such an order, shall, on application of the young person, the young person's counsel, the Attorney General or the provincial director made within thirty days after the decision of the youth justice court, be reviewed by the court of appeal, and that court may, in its discretion, confirm or reverse the decision of the youth justice court.

Extension of time to make application

(2) The court of appeal may, at any time, extend the time within which an application under subsection (1) may be made.

Notice of application

(3) A person who proposes to apply for a review under subsection (1) shall give notice of the application in the manner and within the period of time that may be directed by rules of court.

Breach of conditions

102 (1) If the provincial director has reasonable grounds to believe that a young person has breached or is about to breach a condition to which he or she is subject under section 97 (conditions to be included in custody and supervision orders), the provincial director may, in writing,

(a) permit the young person to continue to serve a portion of his or her youth sentence in the community, on the same or different conditions; or

(b) if satisfied that the breach is a serious one that increases the risk to public safety, order that the young person be remand-

ed to any youth custody facility that the provincial director considers appropriate until a review is conducted.

Provisions apply

(2) Sections 107 (apprehension) and 108 (review by provincial director) apply, with any modifications that the circumstances require, to an order under paragraph (1)(b).

Review by youth justice court

103 (1) When the case of a young person is referred to the youth justice court under section 108 (review by provincial director), the provincial director shall, without delay, cause the young person to be brought before the youth justice court, and the youth justice court shall, after giving the young person an opportunity to be heard,

(a) if the court is not satisfied on reasonable grounds that the young person has breached or was about to breach one of the conditions under which he or she was being supervised in the community, order that the young person continue to serve a portion of his or her youth sentence in the community, on the same or different conditions; or

(b) if the court is satisfied on reasonable grounds that the young person has breached or was about to breach one of the conditions under which he or she was being supervised in the community, make an order under subsection (2).

Order

(2) On completion of a review under subsection (1), the youth justice court

(a) shall order that the young person continue to serve the remainder of the youth sentence the young person is then serving in the community, and when the court does so, the court may vary the existing conditions or impose new conditions; or

(b) shall, despite paragraph 42(2)(n) (custody and supervision order), order that the young person remain in custody for a period that does not exceed the remainder of the youth sentence the young person is then serving, if the youth justice court is satisfied that the breach of the conditions was serious.

Provisions apply

(3) Subsections 109(4) to (8) apply, with any modifications that the circumstances require, in respect of a review under this section.

Continuation of custody

104 (1) When a young person on whom a youth sentence under paragraph 42(2)(o), (q) or (r) has been imposed is held in custody and an application is made to the youth justice court by the Attorney General, within a reasonable time before the expiry of the custodial portion of the youth sentence, the provincial director of the province in which the young person is held in custody shall cause the young person to be brought before the youth justice court and the youth justice court may, after giving both parties and a parent of the young person an opportunity to be heard and if it is satisfied that there are reasonable grounds to believe that the young person is likely to commit an offence causing the death of or serious harm to another person before the expiry of the youth sentence the young person is then serving, order that the young person remain in custody for a period not exceeding the remainder of the youth sentence.

Continuation of custody

(2) If the hearing of an application under subsection (1) cannot be completed before the expiry of the custodial portion of the youth sentence, the court may order that the young person remain in custody until the determination of the application if the court is satisfied that the application was made in a reasonable time, having regard to all the circumstances, and that there are compelling reasons for keeping the young person in custody.

Factors

(3) For the purpose of determining an application under subsection (1), the youth justice court shall take into consideration any factor that is relevant to the case of the young person, including

(a) evidence of a pattern of persistent violent behaviour and, in particular,

(i) the number of offences committed by the young person that caused physical or psychological harm to any other person,

(ii) the young person's difficulties in controlling violent impulses to the point of endangering the safety of any other person,

(iii) the use of weapons in the commission of any offence,

(iv) explicit threats of violence,

(v) behaviour of a brutal nature associated with the commission of any offence, and

(vi) a substantial degree of indifference on the part of the young person as to the reasonably foreseeable consequences, to other persons, of the young person's behaviour;

(b) psychiatric or psychological evidence that a physical or mental illness or disorder of the young person is of such a nature that the young person is likely to commit, before the expiry of the youth sentence the young person is then serving, an offence causing the death of or serious harm to another person;

(c) reliable information that satisfies the youth justice court that the young person is planning to commit, before the expiry of the youth sentence the young person is then serving, an offence causing the death of or serious harm to another person; and

(d) the availability of supervision programs in the community that would offer adequate protection to the public from the risk that the young person might otherwise present until the expiry of the youth sentence the young person is then serving.

Youth justice court to order appearance of young person

(4) If a provincial director fails to cause a young person to be brought before the youth justice court under subsection (1), the youth justice court shall order the provincial director to cause the young person to be brought before the youth justice court without delay.

Provisions to apply

(5) Sections 99 to 101 apply, with any modifications that the circumstances require, in respect of an order made, or the refusal to make an order, under this section.

If application denied

(6) If an application under this section is denied, the court may, with the consent of the young person, the Attorney General and the provincial director, proceed as though the young person had been brought before the court as required under subsection 105(1).

Conditional supervision

105 (1) The provincial director of the province in which a young person on whom a youth sentence under paragraph 42(2)(o), (q) or (r) has been imposed is held in custody or, if applicable, with respect to whom an order has been made under subsection 104(1) (continuation of custody), shall cause the young person to be brought before the youth justice court at least one month before the expiry of the custodi-al portion of the youth sentence. The court shall, after giving the young person an opportunity to be heard, by order, set the conditions of the young person's conditional supervision.

Conditions to be included in order

(2) The youth justice court shall include in the order under subsection (1) the following conditions, namely, that the young person

(a) keep the peace and be of good behaviour;

(b) appear before the youth justice court when required by the court to do so;

(c) report to the provincial director immediately on release, and then be under the supervision of the provincial director or a person designated by the youth justice court;

(d) inform the provincial director immediately on being arrested or questioned by the police;

(e) report to the police, or any named individual, as instructed by the provincial director;

(f) advise the provincial director of the young person's address of residence on release and after release report immediately to the clerk of the youth justice court or the provincial director any change

(i) in that address,

(ii) in the young person's normal occupation, including employment, vocational or educational training and volunteer work,

(iii) in the young person's family or financial situation, and

(iv) that may reasonably be expected to affect the young person's ability to comply with the conditions of the order;

(g) not own, possess or have the control of any weapon, ammunition, prohibited ammunition, prohibited device or explosive substance, except as authorized by the order; and

(h) comply with any reasonable instructions that the provincial director considers necessary in respect of any condition of the conditional supervision in order to prevent a breach of that condition or to protect society.

Other conditions

(3) In setting conditions for the purposes of subsection (1), the youth justice court may include in the order the following conditions, namely, that the young person

(a) on release, travel directly to the young person's place of residence, or to any other place that is noted in the order;

(b) make reasonable efforts to obtain and maintain suitable employment;

(c) attend school or any other place of learning, training or recreation that is appropriate, if the court is satisfied that a suitable program is available for the young person at such a place;

(d) reside with a parent, or any other adult that the court considers appropriate, who is willing to provide for the care and maintenance of the young person;

(e) reside in any place that the provincial director may specify;

(f) remain within the territorial jurisdiction of one or more courts named in the order;

(g) comply with conditions set out in the order that support and address the needs of the young person and promote the reintegration of the young person into the community; and

(h) comply with any other conditions set out in the order that the court considers appropriate, including conditions for securing the young person's good conduct and for preventing the young person from repeating the offence or committing other offences.

Temporary conditions

(4) When a provincial director is required under subsection (1) to cause a young person to be brought before the youth justice court but cannot do so for reasons beyond the young person's control, the provincial director shall so advise the youth justice court and the court shall, by order, set any temporary conditions for the young person's conditional supervision that are appropriate in the circumstances.

Conditions to be set at first opportunity

(5) When an order is made under subsection (4), the provincial director shall bring the young person before the youth justice court as soon after the order is made as the circumstances permit and the court shall then set the conditions of the young person's conditional supervision.

Report

(6) For the purpose of setting conditions under this section, the youth justice court shall require the provincial director to cause to be prepared, and to submit to the youth justice court, a report setting out any information that may be of assistance to the court.

Provisions apply

(7) Subsections 99(2) to (7) (provisions respecting reports and notice) and 104(4) (ordering appearance of young person) apply, with any modifications that the circumstances require, in respect of any proceedings held under subsection (1).

Provisions apply

(8) Subsections 56(1) to (4) (provisions respecting probation orders), (7) (notice to appear) and (8) (warrant in default) and section 101 (review of youth justice court decision) apply, with any modifications that the circumstances require, in respect of an order made under subsection (1).

Suspension of conditional supervision

106 If the provincial director has reasonable grounds to believe that a young person has breached or is about to breach a condition of an order made under subsection 105(1), the provincial director may, in writing,

   (a) suspend the conditional supervision; and

   (b) order that the young person be remanded to any youth custody facility that the provincial director considers appropriate until a review is conducted under section 108 and, if applicable, section 109.

Apprehension

107 (1) If the conditional supervision of a young person is suspended under section 106, the provincial director may issue a warrant in writing, authorizing the apprehension of the young person and, until the young person is apprehended, the young person is deemed not to be continuing to serve the youth sentence the young person is then serving.

Warrants

(2) A warrant issued under subsection (1) shall be executed by any peace officer to whom it is given at any place in Canada and has the same force and effect in all parts of Canada as if it had been originally issued or subsequently endorsed by a provincial court judge or other lawful authority having jurisdiction in the place where it is executed.

Peace officer may arrest

(3) If a peace officer believes on reasonable grounds that a warrant issued under subsection (1) is in force in respect of a young person, the peace officer may arrest the young person without the warrant at any place in Canada.

Requirement to bring before provincial director

(4) If a young person is arrested under subsection (3) and detained, the peace officer making the arrest shall cause the young person to be brought before the provincial director or a person designated by the provincial director

   (a) if the provincial director or the designated person is available within a period of twenty-four hours after the young person is arrested, without unreasonable delay and in any event within that period; and

   (b) if the provincial director or the designated person is not available within that period, as soon as possible.

Release or remand in custody

(5) If a young person is brought before the provincial director or a person designated by the provincial director under subsection (4), the provincial director or the designated person

   (a) if not satisfied that there are reasonable grounds to believe that the young person is the young person in respect of whom the warrant referred to in subsection (1) was issued, shall release the young person; or

   (b) if satisfied that there are reasonable grounds to believe that the young person is the young person in respect of whom the warrant referred to in subsection (1) was issued, may remand the young person in custody to await execution of the warrant, but if no warrant for the young person's arrest is executed within a period of forty-eight hours after the time the young person is remanded in custody, the person in whose custody the young person then is shall release the young person.

Review by provincial director

108 Without delay after the remand to custody of a young person whose conditional supervision has been suspended under section 106, or without delay after being informed of the arrest of such a young person, the provincial director shall review the case and, within forty-eight hours, cancel the suspension of the conditional supervision or refer the case to the youth justice court for a review under section 109.

Review by youth justice court

109 (1) If the case of a young person is referred to the youth justice court under section 108, the provincial director shall, without delay, cause the young person to be brought before the youth justice court, and the youth justice court shall, after giving the young person an opportunity to be heard,

   (a) if the court is not satisfied on reasonable grounds that the young person has breached or was about to breach a condition of the conditional supervision, cancel the suspension of the conditional supervision; or

   (b) if the court is satisfied on reasonable grounds that the young person has breached or was about to breach a condition of the conditional supervision, review the decision of the provincial director to suspend the conditional supervision and make an order under subsection (2).

Order

(2) On completion of a review under subsection (1), the youth justice court shall order

   (a) the cancellation of the suspension of the conditional supervision, and when the court does so, the court may vary the conditions of the conditional supervision or impose new conditions;

   (b) in a case other than a deferred custody and supervision order made under paragraph 42(2)(p), the continuation of the suspension of the conditional supervision for any period of time, not to exceed the remainder of the youth sentence the young person is then serving, that the court considers appropriate, and when the court does so, the court shall order that the young person remain in custody; or

(c) in the case of a deferred custody and supervision order made under paragraph 42(2)(p), that the young person serve the remainder of the order as if it were a custody and supervision order under paragraph 42(2)(n).

Custody and supervision order

(3) After a court has made a direction under paragraph (2)(c), the provisions of this Act applicable to orders under paragraph 42(2)(n) apply in respect of the deferred custody and supervision order.

Factors to be considered

(4) In making its decision under subsection (2), the court shall consider the length of time the young person has been subject to the order, whether the young person has previously contravened it, and the nature of the contravention, if any.

Reasons

(5) When a youth justice court makes an order under subsection (2), it shall state its reasons for the order in the record of the case and shall give, or cause to be given, to the young person in respect of whom the order was made, the counsel and a parent of the young person, the Attorney General and the provincial director,

(a) a copy of the order; and

(b) on request, a transcript or copy of the reasons for the order.

Report

(6) For the purposes of a review under subsection (1), the youth justice court shall require the provincial director to cause to be prepared, and to submit to the youth justice court, a report setting out any information of which the provincial director is aware that may be of assistance to the court.

Provisions apply

(7) Subsections 99(2) to (7) (provisions respecting reports and notice) and 105(6) (report for the purpose of setting conditions) apply, with any modifications that the circumstances require, in respect of a review under this section.

Provisions apply

(8) Section 101 (review of youth justice court decision) applies, with any modifications that the circumstances require, in respect of an order made under subsection (2).

PART 6

PUBLICATION, RECORDS AND INFORMATION

Protection of Privacy of Young Persons

Identity of offender not to be published

110 (1) Subject to this section, no person shall publish the name of a young person, or any other information related to a young person,

if it would identify the young person as a young person dealt with under this Act.

Limitation

(2) Subsection (1) does not apply

(a) in a case where the information relates to a young person who has received an adult sentence;

(b) in a case where the information relates to a young person who has received a youth sentence for a violent offence and the youth justice court has ordered a lifting of the publication ban under subsection 75(2); and

(c) in a case where the publication of information is made in the course of the administration of justice, if it is not the purpose of the publication to make the information known in the community.

Exception

(3) A young person referred to in subsection (1) may, after he or she attains the age of eighteen years, publish or cause to be published information that would identify him or her as having been dealt with under this Act or the *Young Offenders Act,* chapter Y-1 of the Revised Statutes of Canada, 1985, provided that he or she is not in custody pursuant to either Act at the time of the publication.

Ex parte application for leave to publish

(4) A youth justice court judge shall, on the *ex parte* application of a peace officer, make an order permitting any person to publish information that identifies a young person as having committed or allegedly committed an indictable offence, if the judge is satisfied that

(a) there is reason to believe that the young person is a danger to others; and

(b) publication of the information is necessary to assist in apprehending the young person.

Order ceases to have effect

(5) An order made under subsection (4) ceases to have effect five days after it is made.

Application for leave to publish

(6) The youth justice court may, on the application of a young person referred to in subsection (1), make an order permitting the young person to publish information that would identify him or her as having been dealt with under this Act or the *Young Offenders Act,* chapter Y-1 of the Revised Statutes of Canada, 1985, if the court is satisfied that the publication would not be contrary to the young person's best interests or the public interest.

2002, c. 1, s. 110; 2012, c. 1, s. 189.

Identity of victim or witness not to be published

111 (1) Subject to this section, no person shall publish the name of a child or young person, or any other information related to a child or a young person, if it would identify the child or young person as having been a victim of, or as having appeared as a witness in connection with, an offence committed or alleged to have been committed by a young person.

Exception

(2) Information that would serve to identify a child or young person referred to in subsection (1) as having been a victim or a witness may be published, or caused to be published, by

(a) that child or young person after he or she attains the age of eighteen years or before that age with the consent of his or her parents; or

(b) the parents of that child or young person if he or she is deceased.

Application for leave to publish

(3) The youth justice court may, on the application of a child or a young person referred to in subsection (1), make an order permitting the child or young person to publish information that would identify him or her as having been a victim or a witness if the court is satisfied that the publication would not be contrary to his or her best interests or the public interest.

Non-application

112 Once information is published under subsection 110(3) or (6) or 111(2) or (3), subsection 110(1) (identity of offender not to be published) or 111(1) (identity of victim or witness not to be published), as the case may be, no longer applies in respect of the information.

Fingerprints and Photographs

Identification of Criminals Act applies

113 (1) The *Identification of Criminals Act* applies in respect of young persons.

Limitation

(2) No fingerprint, palmprint or photograph or other measurement, process or operation referred to in the *Identification of Criminals Act* shall be taken of, or applied in respect of, a young person who is charged with having committed an offence except in the circumstances in which an adult may, under that Act, be subjected to the measurements, processes and operations.

Records That May Be Kept

Youth justice court, review board and other courts

114 A youth justice court, review board or any court dealing with matters arising out of proceedings under this Act may keep a record of any case that comes before it arising under this Act.

Police records

115 (1) A record relating to any offence alleged to have been committed by a young person, including the original or a copy of any fingerprints or photographs of the young person, may be kept by any police force responsible for or participating in the investigation of the offence.

Extrajudicial measures

(1.1) The police force shall keep a record of any extrajudicial measures that they use to deal with young persons.

Police records

(2) When a young person is charged with having committed an offence in respect of which an adult may be subjected to any measurement, process or operation referred to in the *Identification of Criminals Act,* the police force responsible for the investigation of the offence may provide a record relating to the offence to the Royal Canadian Mounted Police. If the young person is found guilty of the offence, the police force shall provide the record.

Records held by R.C.M.P.

(3) The Royal Canadian Mounted Police shall keep the records provided under subsection (2) in the central repository that the Commissioner of the Royal Canadian Mounted Police may, from time to time, designate for the purpose of keeping criminal history files or records of offenders or keeping records for the identification of offenders.

2002, c. 1, s. 115; 2012, c. 1, s. 190.

Government records

116 (1) A department or an agency of any government in Canada may keep records containing information obtained by the department or agency

(a) for the purposes of an investigation of an offence alleged to have been committed by a young person;

(b) for use in proceedings against a young person under this Act;

(c) for the purpose of administering a youth sentence or an order of the youth justice court;

(d) for the purpose of considering whether to use extrajudicial measures to deal with a young person; or

(e) as a result of the use of extrajudicial measures to deal with a young person.

Other records

(2) A person or organization may keep records containing information obtained by the person or organization

(a) as a result of the use of extrajudicial measures to deal with a young person; or

(b) for the purpose of administering or participating in the administration of a youth sentence.

Access to Records

Exception—adult sentence

117 Sections 118 to 129 do not apply to records kept in respect of an offence for which an adult sentence has been imposed once the time allowed for the taking of an appeal has expired or, if an appeal is taken, all proceedings in respect of the appeal have been completed and the appeal court has upheld an adult sentence. The record shall be dealt with as a record of an adult and, for the purposes of the *Criminal Records Act,* the finding of guilt in respect of the offence for which the record is kept is deemed to be a conviction.

No access unless authorized

118 (1) Except as authorized or required by this Act, no person shall be given access to a record kept under sections 114 to 116, and no information contained in it may be given to any person, where to do so would identify the young person to whom it relates as a young person dealt with under this Act.

Exception for employees

(2) No person who is employed in keeping or maintaining records referred to in subsection (1) is restricted from doing anything prohibited under subsection (1) with respect to any other person so employed.

Persons having access to records

119 (1) Subject to subsections (4) to (6), from the date that a record is created until the end of the applicable period set out in subsection (2), the following persons, on request, shall be given access to a record kept under section 114, and may be given access to a record kept under sections 115 and 116:

(a) the young person to whom the record relates;

(b) the young person's counsel, or any representative of that counsel;

(c) the Attorney General;

(d) the victim of the offence or alleged offence to which the record relates;

(e) the parents of the young person, during the course of any proceedings relating to the offence or alleged offence to which the record relates or during the term of any youth sentence made in respect of the offence;

(f) any adult assisting the young person under subsection 25(7), during the course of any proceedings relating to the offence or alleged offence to which the record relates or during the term of any youth sentence made in respect of the offence;

(g) any peace officer for

(i) law enforcement purposes, or

(ii) any purpose related to the administration of the case to which the record relates, during the course of proceedings against the young person or the term of the youth sentence;

(h) a judge, court or review board, for any purpose relating to proceedings against the young person, or proceedings against the person after he or she becomes an adult, in respect of offences committed or alleged to have been committed by that person;

(i) the provincial director, or the director of the provincial correctional facility for adults or the penitentiary at which the young person is serving a sentence;

(j) a person participating in a conference or in the administration of extrajudicial measures, if required for the administration of the case to which the record relates;

(k) a person acting as ombudsman, privacy commissioner or information commissioner, whatever his or her official designation might be, who in the course of his or her duties under an Act of Parliament or the legislature of a province is investigating a complaint to which the record relates;

(l) a coroner or a person acting as a child advocate, whatever his or her official designation might be, who is acting in the course of his or her duties under an Act of Parliament or the legislature of a province;

(m) a person acting under the *Firearms Act;*

(n) a member of a department or agency of a government in Canada, or of an organization that is an agent of, or under contract with, the department or agency, who is

(i) acting in the exercise of his or her duties under this Act,

(ii) engaged in the supervision or care of the young person, whether as a young person or an adult, or in an investigation related to the young person under an Act of the legislature of a province respecting child welfare,

(iii) considering an application for conditional release, or for a record suspension under the *Criminal Records Act*, made by the young person, whether as a young person or an adult,

(iv) administering a prohibition order made under an Act of Parliament or the legislature of a province, or

(v) administering a youth sentence, if the young person has been committed to custody and is serving the custody in a provincial correctional facility for adults or a penitentiary;

(o) a person, for the purpose of carrying out a criminal record check required by the Government of Canada or the government of a province or a municipality for purposes of employment or the performance of services, with or without remuneration;

(p) an employee or agent of the Government of Canada, for statistical purposes under the *Statistics Act;*

(q) an accused or his or her counsel who swears an affidavit to the effect that access to the record is necessary to make a full answer and defence;

(r) a person or a member of a class of persons designated by order of the Governor in Council, or the lieutenant governor in council of the appropriate province, for a purpose and to the extent specified in the order; and

(s) any person or member of a class of persons that a youth justice court judge considers has a valid interest in the record, to the extent directed by the judge, if the judge is satisfied that access to the record is

(i) desirable in the public interest for research or statistical purposes, or

(ii) desirable in the interest of the proper administration of justice.

Period of access

(2) The period of access referred to in subsection (1) is

(a) if an extrajudicial sanction is used to deal with the young person, the period ending two years after the young person consents to be subject to the sanction in accordance with paragraph 10(2)(c);

(b) if the young person is acquitted of the offence otherwise than by reason of a verdict of not criminally responsible on account of mental disorder, the period ending two months after the expiry of the time allowed for the taking of an appeal or, if an appeal is taken, the period ending three months after all proceedings in respect of the appeal have been completed;

(c) if the charge against the young person is dismissed for any reason other than acquittal, the charge is withdrawn, or the young person is found guilty of the offence and a reprimand is given, the period ending two months after the dismissal, withdrawal, or finding of guilt;

(d) if the charge against the young person is stayed, with no proceedings being taken against the young person for a period of one year, at the end of that period;

(e) if the young person is found guilty of the offence and the youth sentence is an absolute discharge, the period ending one year after the young person is found guilty;

(f) if the young person is found guilty of the offence and the youth sentence is a conditional discharge, the period ending three years after the young person is found guilty;

(g) subject to paragraphs (i) and (j) and subsection (9), if the young person is found guilty of the offence and it is a summary conviction offence, the period ending three years after the youth sentence imposed in respect of the offence has been completed;

(h) subject to paragraphs (i) and (j) and subsection (9), if the young person is found guilty of the offence and it is an indictable offence, the period ending five years after the youth sentence imposed in respect of the offence has been completed;

(i) subject to subsection (9), if, during the period calculated in accordance with paragraph (g) or (h), the young person is found guilty of an offence punishable on summary conviction committed when he or she was a young person, the latest of

(i) the period calculated in accordance with paragraph (g) or (h), as the case may be, and

(ii) the period ending three years after the youth sentence imposed for that offence has been completed; and

(j) subject to subsection (9), if, during the period calculated in accordance with paragraph (g) or (h), the young person is found guilty of an indictable offence committed when he or she was a young person, the period ending five years after the sentence imposed for that indictable offence has been completed.

Prohibition orders not included

(3) Prohibition orders made under an Act of Parliament or the legislature of a province, including any order made under section 51, shall not be taken into account in determining any period referred to in subsection (2).

Extrajudicial measures

(4) Access to a record kept under section 115 or 116 in respect of extrajudicial measures, other than extrajudicial sanctions, used in respect of a young person shall be given only to the following persons for the following purposes:

(a) a peace officer or the Attorney General, in order to make a decision whether to again use extrajudicial measures in respect of the young person;

(b) a person participating in a conference, in order to decide on the appropriate extrajudicial measure;

(c) a peace officer, the Attorney General or a person participating in a conference, if access is required for the administration of the case to which the record relates; and

(d) a peace officer for the purpose of investigating an offence.

Exception

(5) When a youth justice court has withheld all or part of a report from any person under subsection 34(9) or (10) (nondisclosure of medical or psychological report) or 40(7) (nondisclosure of pre-sentence report), that person shall not be given access under subsection (1) to that report or part.

Records of assessments or forensic DNA analysis

(6) Access to a report made under section 34 (medical and psychological reports) or a record of the results of forensic DNA analysis of a bodily substance taken from a young person in execution of a warrant issued under section 487.05 of the *Criminal Code* may be given only under paragraphs (1)(a) to (c), (e) to (h) and (q) and subparagraph (1)(s)(ii).

Introduction into evidence

(7) Nothing in paragraph (1)(h) or (q) authorizes the introduction into evidence of any part of a record that would not otherwise be admissible in evidence.

Disclosures for research or statistical purposes

(8) When access to a record is given to a person under paragraph (1)(p) or subparagraph (1)(s)(i), the person may subsequently disclose information contained in the record, but shall not disclose the information in any form that would reasonably be expected to identify the young person to whom it relates.

Application of usual rules

(9) If, during the period of access to a record under any of paragraphs (2)(g) to (j), the young person is convicted of an offence committed when he or she is an adult,

(a) section 82 (effect of absolute discharge or termination of youth sentence) does not apply to the young person in respect of the offence for which the record is kept under sections 114 to 116;

(b) this Part no longer applies to the record and the record shall be dealt with as a record of an adult; and

(c) for the purposes of the *Criminal Records Act,* the finding

of guilt in respect of the offence for which the record is kept is deemed to be a conviction.

Records of offences that result in a prohibition order

(10) Despite anything in this Act, when a young person is found guilty of an offence that results in a prohibition order being made, and the order is still in force at the end of the applicable period for which access to a record kept in respect of the order may be given under subsection (2),

(a) the record kept by the Royal Canadian Mounted Police pursuant to subsection 115(3) may be disclosed only to establish the existence of the order for purposes of law enforcement; and

(b) the record referred to in section 114 that is kept by the youth justice court may be disclosed only to establish the existence of the order in any offence involving a breach of the order.

2002, c. 1, s. 119; 2012, c. 1, ss. 157, 191(F).

Access to R.C.M.P. records

120 (1) The following persons may, during the period set out in subsection (3), be given access to a record kept under subsection 115(3) in respect of an offence set out in the schedule:

(a) the young person to whom the record relates;

(b) the young person's counsel, or any representative of that counsel;

(c) an employee or agent of the Government of Canada, for statistical purposes under the *Statistics Act;*

(d) any person or member of a class of persons that a youth justice court judge considers has a valid interest in the record, to the extent directed by the judge, if the judge is satisfied that access is desirable in the public interest for research or statistical purposes;

(e) the Attorney General or a peace officer, when the young person is or has been charged with another offence set out in the schedule or the same offence more than once, for the purpose of investigating any offence that the young person is suspected of having committed, or in respect of which the young person has been arrested or charged, whether as a young person or as an adult;

(f) the Attorney General or a peace officer to establish the existence of an order in any offence involving a breach of the order; and

(g) any person for the purposes of the *Firearms Act.*

Access for identification purposes

(2) During the period set out in subsection (3), access to the portion of a record kept under subsection 115(3) that contains the name, date of birth and last known address of the young person to whom the fingerprints belong, may be given to a person for identification purposes if a fingerprint identified as that of the young person is found during the investigation of an offence or during an attempt to identify a deceased person or a person suffering from amnesia.

Period of access

(3) For the purposes of subsections (1) and (2), the period of access to a record kept under subsection 115(3) in respect of an offence is the following:

(a) if the offence is an indictable offence, other than a presumptive offence, the period starting at the end of the applicable period set out in paragraphs 119(2)(h) to (j) and ending five years later; and

(b) if the offence is a serious violent offence for which the Attorney General has given notice under subsection 64(2) (intention to seek adult sentence), the period starting at the end of the applicable period set out in paragraphs 119(2)(h) to (j) and continuing indefinitely.

Subsequent offences as young person

(4) If a young person was found guilty of an offence set out in the schedule is, during the period of access to a record under subsection (3), found guilty of an additional offence set out in the schedule, committed when he or she was a young person, access to the record may be given to the following additional persons:

(a) a parent of the young person or any adult assisting the young person under subsection 25(7);

(b) a judge, court or review board, for a purpose relating to proceedings against the young person under this Act or any other Act of Parliament in respect of offences committed or alleged to have been committed by the young person, whether as a young person or as an adult; or

(c) a member of a department or agency of a government in Canada, or of an organization that is an agent of, or is under contract with, the department or agency, who is

(i) preparing a report in respect of the young person under this Act or for the purpose of assisting a court in sentencing the young person after the young person becomes an adult,

(ii) engaged in the supervision or care of the young person, whether as a young person or as an adult, or in the administration of a sentence in respect of the young person, whether as a young person or as an adult, or

(iii) considering an application for conditional release, or for a record suspension under the *Criminal Records Act*, made by the young person after the young person becomes an adult.

Disclosure for research or statistical purposes

(5) A person who is given access to a record under paragraph (1) (c) or (d) may subsequently disclose information contained in the record, but shall not disclose the information in any form that would reasonably be expected to identify the young person to whom it relates.

Subsequent offences as an adult

(6) If, during the period of access to a record under subsection (3), the young person is convicted of an additional offence set out in the schedule, committed when he or she was an adult,

(a) this Part no longer applies to the record and the record shall be dealt with as a record of an adult and may be included on the automated criminal conviction records retrieval system maintained by the Royal Canadian Mounted Police; and

(b) for the purposes of the *Criminal Records Act,* the finding of guilt in respect of the offence for which the record is kept is deemed to be a conviction.

2002, c. 1, s. 120; 2012, c. 1, ss. 158, 192.

Deemed election

121 For the purposes of sections 119 and 120, if no election is made in respect of an offence that may be prosecuted by indictment or proceeded with by way of summary conviction, the Attorney General is deemed to have elected to proceed with the offence as an offence punishable on summary conviction.

Disclosure of information and copies of record

122 A person who is required or authorized to be given access

to a record under section 119, 120, 123 or 124 may be given any information contained in the record and may be given a copy of any part of the record.

Where records may be made available

123 (1) A youth justice court judge may, on application by a person after the end of the applicable period set out in subsection 119(2), order that the person be given access to all or part of a record kept under sections 114 to 116 or that a copy of the record or part be given to that person,

(a) if the youth justice court judge is satisfied that

(i) the person has a valid and substantial interest in the record or part,

(ii) it is necessary for access to be given to the record or part in the interest of the proper administration of justice, and

(iii) disclosure of the record or part or the information in it is not prohibited under any other Act of Parliament or the legislature of a province; or

(b) if the youth court judge is satisfied that access to the record or part is desirable in the public interest for research or statistical purposes.

Restriction for paragraph (1)(a)

(2) Paragraph (1)(a) applies in respect of a record relating to a particular young person or to a record relating to a class of young persons only if the identity of young persons in the class at the time of the making of the application referred to in that paragraph cannot reasonably be ascertained and the disclosure of the record is necessary for the purpose of investigating any offence that a person is suspected on reasonable grounds of having committed against a young person while the young person is, or was, serving a sentence.

Notice

(3) Subject to subsection (4), an application for an order under paragraph (1)(a) in respect of a record shall not be heard unless the person who makes the application has given the young person to whom the record relates and the person or body that has possession of the record at least five days notice in writing of the application, and the young person and the person or body that has possession have had a reasonable opportunity to be heard.

Where notice not required

(4) A youth justice court judge may waive the requirement in subsection (3) to give notice to a young person when the judge is of the opinion that

(a) to insist on the giving of the notice would frustrate the application; or

(b) reasonable efforts have not been successful in finding the young person.

Use of record

(5) In any order under subsection (1), the youth justice court judge shall set out the purposes for which the record may be used.

Disclosure for research or statistical purposes

(6) When access to a record is given to any person under paragraph (1)(b), that person may subsequently disclose information contained in the record, but shall not disclose the information in any form that would reasonably be expected to identify the young person to whom it relates.

Access to record by young person

124 A young person to whom a record relates and his or her counsel may have access to the record at any time.

Disclosure of Information in a Record

Disclosure by peace officer during investigation

125 (1) A peace officer may disclose to any person any information in a record kept under section 114 (court records) or 115 (police records) that it is necessary to disclose in the conduct of the investigation of an offence.

Disclosure by Attorney General

(2) The Attorney General may, in the course of a proceeding under this Act or any other Act of Parliament, disclose the following information in a record kept under section 114 (court reports) or 115 (police records):

(a) to a person who is a co-accused with the young person in respect of the offence for which the record is kept, any information contained in the record; and

(b) to an accused in a proceeding, if the record is in respect of a witness in the proceeding, information that identifies the witness as a young person who has been dealt with under this Act.

Information that may be disclosed to a foreign state

(3) The Attorney General or a peace officer may disclose to the Minister of Justice of Canada information in a record that is kept under section 114 (court records) or 115 (police records) to the extent that it is necessary to deal with a request to or by a foreign state under the *Mutual Legal Assistance in Criminal Matters Act,* or for the purposes of any extradition matter under the *Extradition Act.* The Minister of Justice of Canada may disclose the information to the foreign state in respect of which the request was made, or to which the extradition matter relates, as the case may be.

Disclosure to insurance company

(4) A peace officer may disclose to an insurance company information in a record that is kept under section 114 (court records) or 115 (police records) for the purpose of investigating a claim arising out of an offence committed or alleged to have been committed by the young person to whom the record relates.

Preparation of reports

(5) The provincial director or a youth worker may disclose information contained in a record if the disclosure is necessary for procuring information that relates to the preparation of a report required by this Act.

Schools and others

(6) The provincial director, a youth worker, the Attorney General, a peace officer or any other person engaged in the provision of services to young persons may disclose to any professional or other person engaged in the supervision or care of a young person—including a representative of any school board or school or any other educational or training institution—any information contained in a record kept under sections 114 to 116 if the disclosure is necessary

(a) to ensure compliance by the young person with an authorization under section 91 or an order of the youth justice court;

(b) to ensure the safety of staff, students or other persons; or

(c) to facilitate the rehabilitation of the young person.

Information to be kept separate

(7) A person to whom information is disclosed under subsection (6) shall

(a) keep the information separate from any other record of the young person to whom the information relates;

(b) ensure that no other person has access to the information except if authorized under this Act, or if necessary for the purposes of subsection (6); and

(c) destroy their copy of the record when the information is no longer required for the purpose for which it was disclosed.

Time limit

(8) No information may be disclosed under this section after the end of the applicable period set out in subsection 119(2) (period of access to records).

Records in the custody, etc., of archivists

126 When records originally kept under sections 114 to 116 are under the custody or control of the Librarian and Archivist of Canada or the archivist for any province, that person may disclose any information contained in the records to any other person if

(a) a youth justice court judge is satisfied that the disclosure is desirable in the public interest for research or statistical purposes; and

(b) the person to whom the information is disclosed undertakes not to disclose the information in any form that could reasonably be expected to identify the young person to whom it relates.

2002, c. 1, s. 126; 2004, c. 11, s. 48.

Disclosure with court order

127 (1) The youth justice court may, on the application of the provincial director, the Attorney General or a peace officer, make an order permitting the applicant to disclose to the person or persons specified by the court any information about a young person that is specified, if the court is satisfied that the disclosure is necessary, having regard to the following circumstances:

(a) the young person has been found guilty of an offence involving serious personal injury;

(b) the young person poses a risk of serious harm to persons; and

(c) the disclosure of the information is relevant to the avoidance of that risk.

Opportunity to be heard

(2) Subject to subsection (3), before making an order under subsection (1), the youth justice court shall give the young person, a parent of the young person and the Attorney General an opportunity to be heard.

Ex parte application

(3) An application under subsection (1) may be made *ex parte* by the Attorney General where the youth justice court is satisfied that reasonable efforts have been made to locate the young person and that those efforts have not been successful.

Time limit

(4) No information may be disclosed under subsection (1) after the end of the applicable period set out in subsection 119(2) (period of access to records).

Disposition or Destruction of Records and Prohibition on Use and Disclosure

Effect of end of access periods

128 (1) Subject to sections 123, 124 and 126, after the end of the applicable period set out in section 119 or 120 no record kept under sections 114 to 116 may be used for any purpose that would identify the young person to whom the record relates as a young person dealt with under this Act or the *Young Offenders Act,* chapter Y-1 of the Revised Statutes of Canada, 1985.

Disposal of records

(2) Subject to paragraph 125(7)(c), any record kept under sections 114 to 116, other than a record kept under subsection 115(3), may, in the discretion of the person or body keeping the record, be destroyed or transmitted to the Librarian and Archivist of Canada or the archivist for any province, at any time before or after the end of the applicable period set out in section 119.

Disposal of R.C.M.P. records

(3) All records kept under subsection 115(3) shall be destroyed or, if the Librarian and Archivist of Canada requires it, transmitted to the Librarian and Archivist, at the end of the applicable period set out in section 119 or 120.

Purging CPIC

(4) The Commissioner of the Royal Canadian Mounted Police shall remove a record from the automated criminal conviction records retrieval system maintained by the Royal Canadian Mounted Police at the end of the applicable period referred to in section 119; however, information relating to a prohibition order made under an Act of Parliament or the legislature of a province shall be removed only at the end of the period for which the order is in force.

Exception

(5) Despite subsections (1), (2) and (4), an entry that is contained in a system maintained by the Royal Canadian Mounted Police to match crime scene information and that relates to an offence committed or alleged to have been committed by a young person shall be dealt with in the same manner as information that relates to an offence committed by an adult for which a record suspension ordered under the *Criminal Records Act* is in effect.

Authority to inspect

(6) The Librarian and Archivist of Canada may, at any time, inspect records kept under sections 114 to 116 that are under the control of a government institution as defined in section 2 of the *Library and Archives of Canada Act,* and the archivist for a province may at any time inspect any records kept under those sections that the archivist is authorized to inspect under any Act of the legislature of the province.

Definition of "destroy"

(7) For the purposes of subsections (2) and (3), "destroy", in respect of a record, means

(a) to shred, burn or otherwise physically destroy the record, in the case of a record other than a record in electronic form; and

(b) to delete, write over or otherwise render the record inaccessible, in the case of a record in electronic form.

2002, c. 1, s. 128; 2004, c. 11, s. 49; 2012, c. 1, s. 159.

No subsequent disclosure

129 No person who is given access to a record or to whom information is disclosed under this Act shall disclose that information to any other person unless the disclosure is authorized under this Act.

PART 7

GENERAL PROVISIONS

Disqualification of Judge

Disqualification of judge

130 (1) Subject to subsection (2), a youth justice court judge who, prior to an adjudication in respect of a young person charged with an offence, examines a pre-sentence report made in respect of the young person in connection with that offence or has, after a guilty plea or a finding of guilt, heard submissions as to sentence and then there has been a change of plea, shall not in any capacity conduct or continue the trial of the young person for the offence and shall transfer the case to another judge to be dealt with according to law.

Exception

(2) A youth justice court judge may, in the circumstances referred to in subsection (1), with the consent of the young person and the prosecutor, conduct or continue the trial of the young person if the judge is satisfied that he or she has not been predisposed by a guilty plea or finding of guilt, or by information contained in the pre-sentence report or submissions as to sentence.

Substitution of Judge

Powers of substitute youth justice court judge

131 (1) A youth justice court judge who acts in the place of another youth justice court judge under subsection 669.2(1) (continuation of proceedings) of the *Criminal Code* shall

(a) if an adjudication has been made, proceed to sentence the young person or make the order that, in the circumstances, is authorized by law; or

(b) if no adjudication has been made, recommence the trial as if no evidence had been taken.

Transcript of evidence already given

(2) A youth justice court judge who recommences a trial under paragraph (1)(b) may, if the parties consent, admit into evidence a transcript of any evidence already given in the case.

Exclusion from Hearing

Exclusion from hearing

132 (1) Subject to subsection (2), a court or justice before whom proceedings are carried out under this Act may exclude any person from all or part of the proceedings if the court or justice considers that the person's presence is unnecessary to the conduct of the proceedings and the court or justice is of the opinion that

(a) any evidence or information presented to the court or justice would be seriously injurious or seriously prejudicial to

(i) the young person who is being dealt with in the proceedings,

(ii) a child or young person who is a witness in the proceedings, or

(iii) a child or young person who is aggrieved by or the victim of the offence charged in the proceedings; or

(b) it would be in the interest of public morals, the maintenance of order or the proper administration of justice to exclude any or all members of the public from the court room.

Exception

(2) Subject to section 650 (accused to be present) of the *Criminal Code* and except if it is necessary for the purposes of subsection 34(9) (nondisclosure of medical or psychological report) of this Act, a court or justice may not, under subsection (1), exclude from proceedings under this Act

(a) the prosecutor;

(b) the young person who is being dealt with in the proceedings, the counsel or a parent of the young person or any adult assisting the young person under subsection 25(7);

(c) the provincial director or his or her agent; or

(d) the youth worker to whom the young person's case has been assigned.

Exclusion after adjudication or during review

(3) A youth justice court, after it has found a young person guilty of an offence, or a youth justice court or a review board, during a review, may, in its discretion, exclude from the court or from a hearing of the review board any person other than the following, when it is being presented with information the knowledge of which might, in its opinion, be seriously injurious or seriously prejudicial to the young person:

(a) the young person or his or her counsel;

(b) the provincial director or his or her agent;

(c) the youth worker to whom the young person's case has been assigned; and

(d) the Attorney General.

Exception

(4) The exception set out in paragraph (3)(a) is subject to subsection 34(9) (nondisclosure of medical or psychological report) of this Act and section 650 (accused to be present) of the *Criminal Code*.

Transfer of Charges

Transfer of charges

133 Despite subsections 478(1) and (3) of the *Criminal Code*, a young person charged with an offence that is alleged to have been committed in one province may, if the Attorney General of the province consents, appear before a youth justice court of any other province and

(a) if the young person pleads guilty to that offence and the youth justice court is satisfied that the facts support the charge, the court shall find the young person guilty of the offence alleged in the information or indictment; and

(b) if the young person pleads not guilty to that offence, or pleads guilty but the court is not satisfied that the facts support the charge, the young person shall, if he or she was detained in custody prior to the appearance, be returned to custody and dealt with according to law.

Forfeiture of Recognizances

Applications for forfeiture of recognizances

134 Applications for the forfeiture of recognizances of young persons shall be made to the youth justice court.

Proceedings in case of default

135 (1) When a recognizance binding a young person has been endorsed with a certificate under subsection 770(1) of the *Criminal Code*, a youth justice court judge shall

(a) on the request of the Attorney General, fix a time and place for the hearing of an application for the forfeiture of the recognizance; and

(b) after fixing a time and place for the hearing, cause to be sent by confirmed delivery service, not less than ten days before the time so fixed, to each principal and surety named in the recognizance, directed to his or her latest known address, a notice requiring him or her to appear at the time and place fixed by the judge to show cause why the recognizance should not be forfeited.

Order for forfeiture of recognizance

(2) When subsection (1) is complied with, the youth justice court judge may, after giving the parties an opportunity to be heard, in his or her discretion grant or refuse the application and make any order with respect to the forfeiture of the recognizance that he or she considers proper.

Judgment debtors of the Crown

(3) If, under subsection (2), a youth justice court judge orders forfeiture of a recognizance, the principal and his or her sureties become judgment debtors of the Crown, each in the amount that the judge orders him or her to pay.

Order may be filed

(4) An order made under subsection (2) may be filed with the clerk of the superior court or, in the province of Quebec, the prothonotary and, if an order is filed, the clerk or the prothonotary shall issue a writ of *fieri facias* in Form 34 set out in the *Criminal Code* and deliver it to the sheriff of each of the territorial divisions in which any of the principal and his or her sureties resides, carries on business or has property.

If a deposit has been made

(5) If a deposit has been made by a person against whom an order for forfeiture of a recognizance has been made, no writ of *fieri facias* shall issue, but the amount of the deposit shall be transferred by the person who has custody of it to the person who is entitled by law to receive it.

Subsections 770(2) and (4) of *Criminal Code* do not apply

(6) Subsections 770(2) (transmission of recognizance) and (4) (transmission of deposit) of the *Criminal Code* do not apply in respect of proceedings under this Act.

Sections 772 and 773 of *Criminal Code* apply

(7) Sections 772 (levy under writ) and 773 (committal when writ not satisfied) of the *Criminal Code* apply in respect of writs of *fieri facias* issued under this section as if they were issued under section 771 (proceedings in case of default) of that Act.

Offences and Punishment

Inducing a young person, etc.

136 (1) Every person who

(a) induces or assists a young person to leave unlawfully a place of custody or other place in which the young person has been placed in accordance with a youth sentence or a disposition imposed under the *Young Offenders Act,* chapter Y-1 of the Revised Statutes of Canada, 1985,

(b) unlawfully removes a young person from a place referred to in paragraph (a),

(c) knowingly harbours or conceals a young person who has unlawfully left a place referred to in paragraph (a),

(d) wilfully induces or assists a young person to breach or disobey a term or condition of a youth sentence or other order of the youth justice court, or a term or condition of a disposition or other order under the *Young Offenders Act,* chapter Y-1 of the Revised Statutes of Canada, 1985, or

(e) wilfully prevents or interferes with the performance by a young person of a term or condition of a youth sentence or other order of the youth justice court, or a term or condition of a disposition or other order under the *Young Offenders Act,* chapter Y-1 of the Revised Statutes of Canada, 1985,

is guilty of an indictable offence and liable to imprisonment for a term not exceeding two years or is guilty of an offence punishable on summary conviction.

Absolute jurisdiction of provincial court judge

(2) The jurisdiction of a provincial court judge to try an adult charged with an indictable offence under this section is absolute and does not depend on the consent of the accused.

Failure to comply with sentence or disposition

137 Every person who is subject to a youth sentence imposed under any of paragraphs 42(2)(c) to (m) or (s) of this Act, to a victim fine surcharge ordered under subsection 53(2) of this Act or to a disposition made under any of paragraphs 20(1)(a.1) to (g), (j) or (l) of the *Young Offenders Act,* chapter Y-1 of the Revised Statutes of Canada, 1985, and who wilfully fails or refuses to comply with that sentence, surcharge or disposition is guilty of an offence punishable on summary conviction.

Offences

138 (1) Every person who contravenes subsection 110(1) (identity of offender not to be published), 111(1) (identity of victim or witness not to be published), 118(1) (no access to records unless authorized) or 128(3) (disposal of R.C.M.P. records) or section 129 (no subsequent disclosure) of this Act, or subsection 38(1) (identity not to be published), (1.12) (no subsequent disclosure), (1.14) (no subsequent disclosure by school) or (1.15) (information to be kept separate), 45(2) (destruction of records) or 46(1) (prohibition against disclosure) of the *Young Offenders Act,* chapter Y-1 of the Revised Statutes of Canada, 1985,

(a) is guilty of an indictable offence and liable to imprisonment for a term not exceeding two years; or

(b) is guilty of an offence punishable on summary conviction.

Provincial court judge has absolute jurisdiction on indictment

(2) The jurisdiction of a provincial court judge to try an adult charged with an offence under paragraph (1)(a) is absolute and does not depend on the consent of the accused.

Offence and punishment

139 (1) Every person who wilfully fails to comply with section 30 (designated place of temporary detention), or with an undertaking entered into under subsection 31(3) (condition of placement),

(a) is guilty of an indictable offence and liable to imprisonment for a term not exceeding two years; or

(b) is guilty of an offence punishable on summary conviction.

Offence and punishment

(2) Every person who wilfully fails to comply with section 7 (designated place of temporary detention) of the *Young Offenders Act,* chapter Y-1 of the Revised Statutes of Canada, 1985, or with an undertaking entered into under subsection 7.1(2) (condition of placement) of that Act is guilty of an offence punishable on summary conviction.

Punishment

(3) Any person who uses or authorizes the use of an application form in contravention of subsection 82(3) (application for employment) is guilty of an offence punishable on summary conviction.

Application of Criminal Code

Application of *Criminal Code*

140 Except to the extent that it is inconsistent with or excluded by this Act, the provisions of the *Criminal Code* apply, with any modifications that the circumstances require, in respect of offences alleged to have been committed by young persons.

Sections of *Criminal Code* applicable

141 (1) Except to the extent that they are inconsistent with or excluded by this Act, section 16 (defence of mental disorder) and Part XX.1 (mental disorder) of the *Criminal Code* apply, with any modifications that the circumstances require, in respect of proceedings under this Act in relation to offences alleged to have been committed by young persons.

Notice and copies to counsel and parents

(2) For the purposes of subsection (1),

(a) wherever in Part XX.1 (mental disorder) of the *Criminal Code* a reference is made to a copy to be sent or otherwise given to an accused or a party to the proceedings, the reference shall be read as including a reference to a copy to be sent or otherwise given to

(i) any counsel representing the young person,

(ii) a parent of the young person who is in attendance at the proceedings against the young person, and

(iii) a parent of the young person not in attendance at the proceedings who is, in the opinion of the youth justice court or Review Board, taking an active interest in the proceedings; and

(b) wherever in Part XX.1 (mental disorder) of the *Criminal Code* a reference is made to notice to be given to an accused or a party to proceedings, the reference shall be read as including a reference to notice to be given to a parent of the young person and any counsel representing the young person.

Proceedings not invalid

(3) Subject to subsection (4), failure to give a notice referred to in paragraph (2)(b) to a parent of a young person does not affect the validity of proceedings under this Act.

Exception

(4) Failure to give a notice referred to in paragraph (2)(b) to a parent of a young person in any case renders invalid any subsequent proceedings under this Act relating to the case unless

>> **(a)** a parent of the young person attends at the court or Review Board with the young person; or

>> **(b)** a youth justice court judge or Review Board before whom proceedings are held against the young person

>>> **(i)** adjourns the proceedings and orders that the notice be given in the manner and to the persons that the judge or Review Board directs, or

>>> **(ii)** dispenses with the notice if the youth justice court or Review Board is of the opinion that, having regard to the circumstances, the notice may be dispensed with.

(5) [Repealed, 2005, c. 22, s. 63]

Considerations of court or Review Board making a disposition

(6) Before making or reviewing a disposition in respect of a young person under Part XX.1 (mental disorder) of the *Criminal Code*, a youth justice court or Review Board shall consider the age and special needs of the young person and any representations or submissions made by a parent of the young person.

(7) to **(9)** [Repealed, 2005, c. 22, s. 63]

Prima facie case to be made every year

(10) For the purpose of applying subsection 672.33(1) (fitness to stand trial) of the *Criminal Code* to proceedings under this Act in relation to an offence alleged to have been committed by a young person, wherever in that subsection a reference is made to two years, there shall be substituted a reference to one year.

Designation of hospitals for young persons

(11) A reference in Part XX.1 (mental disorder) of the *Criminal Code* to a hospital in a province shall be construed as a reference to a hospital designated by the Minister of Health for the province for the custody, treatment or assessment of young persons.

Definition of *Review Board*

(12) In this section, "Review Board" has the meaning assigned by section 672.1 of the *Criminal Code*.

2002, c. 1, s. 141; 2005, c. 22, s. 63.

Part XXVII and summary conviction trial provisions of *Criminal Code* to apply

142 (1) Subject to this section and except to the extent that they are inconsistent with this Act, the provisions of Part XXVII (summary conviction offences) of the *Criminal Code*, and any other provisions of that Act that apply in respect of summary conviction offences and relate to trial proceedings, apply to proceedings under this Act

>> **(a)** in respect of an order under section 810 (recognizance—fear of injury or damage), 810.01 (recognizance—fear of criminal organization offence) or 810.2 (recognizance—fear of serious personal injury offence) of that Act or an offence under section 811 (breach of recognizance) of that Act;

>> **(b)** in respect of a summary conviction offence; and

>> **(c)** in respect of an indictable offence as if it were defined in the enactment creating it as a summary conviction offence.

Indictable offences

(2) For greater certainty and despite subsection (1) or any other provision of this Act, an indictable offence committed by a young person is, for the purposes of this Act or any other Act of Parliament, an indictable offence.

Attendance of young person

(3) Section 650 of the *Criminal Code* applies in respect of proceedings under this Act, whether the proceedings relate to an indictable offence or an offence punishable on summary conviction.

Limitation period

(4) In proceedings under this Act, subsection 786(2) of the *Criminal Code* does not apply in respect of an indictable offence.

Costs

(5) Section 809 of the *Criminal Code* does not apply in respect of proceedings under this Act.

2002, c. 1, s. 142; 2015, c. 20, ss. 33, 36, c. 29, s. 15.

Procedure

Counts charged in information

143 Indictable offences and offences punishable on summary conviction may under this Act be charged in the same information or indictment and tried jointly.

Issue of subpoena

144 (1) If a person is required to attend to give evidence before a youth justice court, the subpoena directed to that person may be issued by a youth justice court judge, whether or not the person whose attendance is required is within the same province as the youth justice court.

Service of subpoena

(2) A subpoena issued by a youth justice court and directed to a person who is not within the same province as the youth justice court shall be served personally on the person to whom it is directed.

Warrant

145 A warrant issued by a youth justice court may be executed anywhere in Canada.

Evidence

General law on admissibility of statements to apply

146 (1) Subject to this section, the law relating to the admissibility of statements made by persons accused of committing offences applies in respect of young persons.

When statements are admissible

(2) No oral or written statement made by a young person who is less than eighteen years old, to a peace officer or to any other person who is, in law, a person in authority, on the arrest or detention of the young person or in circumstances where the peace officer or other person has reasonable grounds for believing that the young person has committed an offence is admissible against the young person unless

>> **(a)** the statement was voluntary;

>> **(b)** the person to whom the statement was made has, before the statement was made, clearly explained to the young person, in language appropriate to his or her age and understanding, that

(i) the young person is under no obligation to make a statement,

(ii) any statement made by the young person may be used as evidence in proceedings against him or her,

(iii) the young person has the right to consult counsel and a parent or other person in accordance with paragraph (c), and

(iv) any statement made by the young person is required to be made in the presence of counsel and any other person consulted in accordance with paragraph (c), if any, unless the young person desires otherwise;

(c) the young person has, before the statement was made, been given a reasonable opportunity to consult

(i) with counsel, and

(ii) with a parent or, in the absence of a parent, an adult relative or, in the absence of a parent and an adult relative, any other appropriate adult chosen by the young person, as long as that person is not a co-accused, or under investigation, in respect of the same offence; and

(d) if the young person consults a person in accordance with paragraph (c), the young person has been given a reasonable opportunity to make the statement in the presence of that person.

Exception in certain cases for oral statements

(3) The requirements set out in paragraphs (2)(b) to (d) do not apply in respect of oral statements if they are made spontaneously by the young person to a peace officer or other person in authority before that person has had a reasonable opportunity to comply with those requirements.

Waiver of right to consult

(4) A young person may waive the rights under paragraph (2)(c) or (d) but any such waiver

(a) must be recorded on video tape or audio tape; or

(b) must be in writing and contain a statement signed by the young person that he or she has been informed of the right being waived.

Waiver of right to consult

(5) When a waiver of rights under paragraph (2)(c) or (d) is not made in accordance with subsection (4) owing to a technical irregularity, the youth justice court may determine that the waiver is valid if it is satisfied that the young person was informed of his or her rights, and voluntarily waived them.

Admissibility of statements

(6) When there has been a technical irregularity in complying with paragraphs (2)(b) to (d), the youth justice court may admit into evidence a statement referred to in subsection (2), if satisfied that the admission of the statement would not bring into disrepute the principle that young persons are entitled to enhanced procedural protection to ensure that they are treated fairly and their rights are protected.

Statements made under duress are inadmissible

(7) A youth justice court judge may rule inadmissible in any proceedings under this Act a statement made by the young person in respect of whom the proceedings are taken if the young person satisfies the judge that the statement was made under duress imposed by any person who is not, in law, a person in authority.

Misrepresentation of age

(8) A youth justice court judge may in any proceedings under this Act rule admissible any statement or waiver by a young person if, at the time of the making of the statement or waiver,

(a) the young person held himself or herself to be eighteen years old or older;

(b) the person to whom the statement or waiver was made conducted reasonable inquiries as to the age of the young person and had reasonable grounds for believing that the young person was eighteen years old or older; and

(c) in all other circumstances the statement or waiver would otherwise be admissible.

Parent, etc., not a person in authority

(9) For the purpose of this section, a person consulted under paragraph (2)(c) is, in the absence of evidence to the contrary, deemed not to be a person in authority.

Statements not admissible against young person

147 (1) Subject to subsection (2), if a young person is assessed in accordance with an order made under subsection 34(1) (medical or psychological assessment), no statement or reference to a statement made by the young person during the course and for the purposes of the assessment to the person who conducts the assessment or to anyone acting under that person's direction is admissible in evidence, without the consent of the young person, in any proceeding before a court, tribunal, body or person with jurisdiction to compel the production of evidence.

Exceptions

(2) A statement referred to in subsection (1) is admissible in evidence for the purposes of

(a) making a decision on an application heard under section 71 (hearing — adult sentences);

(b) determining whether the young person is unfit to stand trial;

(c) determining whether the balance of the mind of the young person was disturbed at the time of commission of the alleged offence, if the young person is a female person charged with an offence arising out of the death of her newly-born child;

(d) making or reviewing a sentence in respect of the young person;

(e) determining whether the young person was, at the time of the commission of an alleged offence, suffering from automatism or a mental disorder so as to be exempt from criminal responsibility by virtue of subsection 16(1) of the *Criminal Code*, if the accused puts his or her mental capacity for criminal intent into issue, or if the prosecutor raises the issue after verdict;

(f) challenging the credibility of a young person in any proceeding if the testimony of the young person is inconsistent in a material particular with a statement referred to in subsection (1) that the young person made previously;

(g) establishing the perjury of a young person who is charged with perjury in respect of a statement made in any proceeding;

(h) deciding an application for an order under subsection 104(1) (continuation of custody);

(i) setting the conditions under subsection 105(1) (conditional supervision);

(j) conducting a review under subsection 109(1) (review of decision); or

(k) deciding an application for a disclosure order under subsection 127(1) (information about a young person).

Testimony of a parent

148 (1) In any proceedings under this Act, the testimony of a parent as to the age of a person of whom he or she is a parent is admissible as evidence of the age of that person.

Evidence of age by certificate or record

(2) In any proceedings under this Act,

(a) a birth or baptismal certificate or a copy of it purporting to be certified under the hand of the person in whose custody those records are held is evidence of the age of the person named in the certificate or copy; and

(b) an entry or record of an incorporated society that has had the control or care of the person alleged to have committed the offence in respect of which the proceedings are taken at or about the time the person came to Canada is evidence of the age of that person, if the entry or record was made before the time when the offence is alleged to have been committed.

Other evidence

(3) In the absence of any certificate, copy, entry or record mentioned in subsection (2), or in corroboration of that certificate, copy, entry or record, the youth justice court may receive and act on any other information relating to age that it considers reliable.

When age may be inferred

(4) In any proceedings under this Act, the youth justice court may draw inferences as to the age of a person from the person's appearance or from statements made by the person in direct examination or cross-examination.

Admissions

149 (1) A party to any proceedings under this Act may admit any relevant fact or matter for the purpose of dispensing with proof of it, including any fact or matter the admissibility of which depends on a ruling of law or of mixed law and fact.

Other party may adduce evidence

(2) Nothing in this section precludes a party to a proceeding from adducing evidence to prove a fact or matter admitted by another party.

Material evidence

150 Any evidence material to proceedings under this Act that would not but for this section be admissible in evidence may, with the consent of the parties to the proceedings and if the young person is represented by counsel, be given in such proceedings.

Evidence of a child or young person

151 The evidence of a child or a young person may be taken in proceedings under this Act only after the youth justice court judge or the justice in the proceedings has

(a) if the witness is a child, instructed the child as to the duty to speak the truth and the consequences of failing to do so; and

(b) if the witness is a young person and the judge or justice considers it necessary, instructed the young person as to the duty to speak the truth and the consequences of failing to do so.

Proof of service

152 (1) For the purposes of this Act, service of any document may be proved by oral evidence given under oath by, or by the affidavit or statutory declaration of, the person claiming to have personally served it or sent it by confirmed delivery service.

Proof of signature and official character unnecessary

(2) If proof of service of any document is offered by affidavit or statutory declaration, it is not necessary to prove the signature or official character of the person making or taking the affidavit or declaration, if the official character of that person appears on the face of the affidavit or declaration.

Seal not required

153 It is not necessary to the validity of any information, indictment, summons, warrant, minute, sentence, conviction, order or other process or document laid, issued, filed or entered in any proceedings under this Act that any seal be attached or affixed to it.

Forms, Regulations and Rules of Court

Forms

154 (1) The forms prescribed under section 155, varied to suit the case, or forms to the like effect, are valid and sufficient in the circumstances for which they are provided.

If forms not prescribed

(2) In any case for which forms are not prescribed under section 155, the forms set out in Part XXVIII of the *Criminal Code*, with any modifications that the circumstances require, or other appropriate forms, may be used.

Regulations

155 The Governor in Council may make regulations

(a) prescribing forms that may be used for the purposes of this Act;

(b) establishing uniform rules of court for youth justice courts across Canada, including rules regulating the practice and procedure to be followed by youth justice courts; and

(c) generally for carrying out the purposes and provisions of this Act.

Agreements with Provinces

Agreements with provinces

156 Any minister of the Crown may, with the approval of the Governor in Council, enter into an agreement with the government of any province providing for payments by Canada to the province in respect of costs incurred by the province or a municipality in the province for care of and services provided to young persons dealt with under this Act.

Programs

Community-based programs

157 The Attorney General of Canada or a minister designated by the lieutenant governor in council of a province may establish the following types of community-based programs:

(a) programs that are an alternative to judicial proceedings, such as victim-offender reconciliation programs, mediation programs and restitution programs;

(b) programs that are an alternative to detention before sentencing, such as bail supervision programs; and

(c) programs that are an alternative to custody, such as intensive support and supervision programs, and programs to carry out attendance orders.

PART 8

TRANSITIONAL PROVISIONS

Prohibition on proceedings

158 On and after the coming into force of this section, no proceedings may be commenced under the *Young Offenders Act,* chapter Y-1 of the Revised Statutes of Canada, 1985, in respect of an offence within the meaning of that Act, or under the *Juvenile Delinquents Act,* chapter J-3 of the Revised Statutes of Canada, 1970, in respect of a delinquency within the meaning of that Act.

Proceedings commenced under *Young Offenders Act*

159 (1) Subject to section 161, where, before the coming into force of this section, proceedings are commenced under the *Young Offenders Act,* chapter Y-1 of the Revised Statutes of Canada, 1985, in respect of an offence within the meaning of that Act alleged to have been committed by a person who was at the time of the offence a young person within the meaning of that Act, the proceedings and all related matters shall be dealt with in all respects as if this Act had not come into force.

Proceedings commenced under *Juvenile Delinquents Act*

(2) Subject to section 161, where, before the coming into force of this section, proceedings are commenced under the *Juvenile Delinquents Act,* chapter J-3 of the Revised Statutes of Canada, 1970, in respect of a delinquency within the meaning of that Act alleged to have been committed by a person who was at the time of the delinquency a child as defined in that Act, the proceedings and all related matters shall be dealt with under this Act as if the delinquency were an offence that occurred after the coming into force of this section.

160 [Repealed, 2012, c. 1, s. 193]

Applicable sentence

161 (1) A person referred to in section 159 who is found guilty of an offence or delinquency, other than a person convicted of an offence in ordinary court, as defined in subsection 2(1) of the *Young Offenders Act,* chapter Y-1 of the Revised Statutes of Canada, 1985, shall be sentenced under this Act, except that

(a) paragraph 110(2)(b) does not apply in respect of the offence or delinquency; and

(b) paragraph 42(2)(r) applies in respect of the offence or delinquency only if the young person consents to its application.

The provisions of this Act applicable to sentences imposed under section 42 apply in respect of the sentence.

Dispositions under paragraph 20(1)(k) or (k.1) of *Young Offenders Act*

(2) Where a young person is to be sentenced under this Act while subject to a disposition under paragraph 20(1)(k) or (k.1) of the *Young Offenders Act,* chapter Y-1 of the Revised Statutes of Canada, 1985, on the application of the Attorney General or the young person, a youth justice court shall, unless to do so would bring the administration of justice into disrepute, order that the remaining portion of the disposition made under that Act be dealt with, for all purposes under this Act or any other Act of Parliament, as if it had been a sentence imposed under paragraph 42(2)(n) or (q) of this Act, as the case may be.

Review of sentence

(3) For greater certainty, for the purpose of determining when the sentence is reviewed under section 94, the relevant date is the one on which the disposition came into force under the *Young Offenders Act,* chapter Y-1 of the Revised Statutes of Canada, 1985.

Commencement of proceedings

162 For the purposes of sections 158 and 159, proceedings are commenced by the laying of an information or indictment.

2002, c. 1, s. 162; 2012, c. 1, s. 194.

Application to delinquency and other offending behaviour

163 Sections 114 to 129 apply, with any modifications that the circumstances require, in respect of records relating to the offence of delinquency under the *Juvenile Delinquents Act,* chapter J-3 of the Revised Statutes of Canada, 1970, and in respect of records kept under sections 40 to 43 of the *Young Offenders Act,* chapter Y-1 of the Revised Statutes of Canada, 1985.

Agreements continue in force

164 Any agreement made under the *Young Offenders Act,* chapter Y-1 of the Revised Statutes of Canada, 1985, remains in force until it expires, unless it is amended or a new agreement is made under this Act.

Designation of youth justice court

165 (1) Any court established or designated as a youth court for the purposes of the *Young Offenders Act,* chapter Y-1 of the Revised Statutes of Canada, 1985, is deemed, as of the coming into force of this section, to have been established or designated as a youth justice court for the purposes of this Act.

Designation of youth justice court judges

(2) Any person appointed to be a judge of the youth court for the purposes of the *Young Offenders Act,* chapter Y-1 of the Revised Statutes of Canada, 1985, is deemed, as of the coming into force of this section, to have been appointed as a judge of the youth justice court for the purposes of this Act.

Designation of provincial directors and youth workers

(3) Any person, group or class of persons or body appointed or designated as a provincial director for the purposes of the *Young Offenders Act,* chapter Y-1 of the Revised Statutes of Canada, 1985, and any person appointed or designated as a youth worker for the purposes of that Act is deemed, as of the coming into force of this section, to have been appointed or designated as a provincial director or youth worker, as the case may be, for the purposes of this Act.

Designation of review boards and youth justice committees

(4) Any review board established or designated for the purposes of the *Young Offenders Act,* chapter Y-1 of the Revised Statutes of Canada, 1985, and any youth justice committee established for the purposes of that Act is deemed, as of the coming into force of this section, to have been established or designated as a review board or a youth justice committee, as the case may be, for the purposes of this Act.

Alternative measures continued as extrajudicial sanctions

(5) Any program of alternative measures authorized for the purposes of the *Young Offenders Act,* chapter Y-1 of the Revised Statutes of Canada, 1985, is deemed, as of the coming into force of this section, to be a program of extrajudicial sanctions authorized for the purposes of this Act.

Designation of places of temporary detention and youth custody

(6) Subject to subsection (7), any place that was designated as a place of temporary detention or open custody for the purposes of the *Young Offenders Act,* chapter Y-1 of the Revised Statutes of Canada, 1985, and any place or facility designated as a place of secure custody for the purposes of that Act is deemed, as of the coming into force of this section, to have been designated for the purposes of this Act as

(a) in the case of a place of temporary detention, a place of temporary detention; and

(b) in the case of a place of open custody or secure custody, a youth custody facility.

Exception

(7) If the lieutenant governor in council of a province makes an order under section 88 that the power to make determinations of the level of custody for young persons and to review those determinations be exercised in accordance with the *Young Offenders Act,* chapter Y-1 of the Revised Statutes of Canada, 1985, the designation of any place as a place of open custody or secure custody for the purposes of that Act remains in force for the purposes of section 88, subject to revocation or amendment of the designation.

Designation of other persons

(8) Any person designated as a clerk of the youth court for the purposes of the *Young Offenders Act,* chapter Y-1 of the Revised Statutes of Canada, 1985, or any person or group of persons who were designated under that Act to carry out specified functions and duties are deemed, as of the coming into force of this section, to have been designated as a clerk of the youth justice court, or to carry out the same functions and duties, as the case may be, under this Act.

PART 9

CONSEQUENTIAL AMENDMENTS, REPEAL AND COMING INTO FORCE

Consequential Amendments

166 to 198 [Amendments]

Repeal

199 [Repeal]

Coming into Force

Coming into force

*200. The provisions of this Act come into force on a day or days to be fixed by order of the Governor in Council.

*[Note: Act in force April 1, 2003, *see* SI/2002-91.]

SCHEDULE

(Subsections 120(1), (4) and (6))

1 An offence under any of the following provisions of the *Criminal Code:*

(a) paragraph 81(2)(a) (using explosives);

(b) subsection 85(1) (using firearm in commission of offence);

(c) section 151 (sexual interference);

(d) section 152 (invitation to sexual touching);

(e) section 153 (sexual exploitation);

(f) section 155 (incest);

(g) section 159 (anal intercourse);

(h) section 170 (parent or guardian procuring sexual activity by child);

(i) **and** (j) [Repealed, 2014, c. 25, s. 43]

(k) section 231 or 235 (first degree murder or second degree murder within the meaning of section 231);

(l) section 232, 234 or 236 (manslaughter);

(m) section 239 (attempt to commit murder);

(n) section 267 (assault with a weapon or causing bodily harm);

(o) section 268 (aggravated assault);

(p) section 269 (unlawfully causing bodily harm);

(q) section 271 (sexual assault);

(r) section 272 (sexual assault with a weapon, threats to a third party or causing bodily harm);

(s) section 273 (aggravated sexual assault);

(t) section 279 (kidnapping);

(t.1) section 279.011 (trafficking – person under 18 years);

(t.2) subsection 279.02(2) (material benefit – trafficking of person under 18 years);

(t.3) subsection 279.03(2) (withholding or destroying documents – trafficking of person under 18 years);

(t.4) subsection 286.1(2) (obtaining sexual services for consideration from person under 18 years);

(t.5) subsection 286.2(2) (material benefit from sexual services provided by person under 18 years);

(t.6) subsection 286.3(2) (procuring – person under 18 years);

(u) section 344 (robbery);

(v) section 433 (arson — disregard for human life);

(w) section 434.1 (arson — own property);

(x) section 436 (arson by negligence); and

(y) paragraph 465(1)(a) (conspiracy to commit murder).

1.1 An offence under one of the following provisions of the *Criminal Code,* as they read from time to time before the day on which this section comes into force:

(a) subsection 212(2) (living on the avails of prostitution of person under 18 years); and

(b) subsection 212(4) (prostitution of person under 18 years).

2 An offence under any of the following provisions of the *Criminal Code,* as they read immediately before July 1, 1990:

(a) section 433 (arson);

(b) section 434 (setting fire to other substance); and

(c) section 436 (setting fire by negligence).

3 An offence under any of the following provisions of the *Criminal Code,* chapter C-34 of the Revised Statutes of Canada, 1970, as they read immediately before January 4, 1983:

(a) section 144 (rape);

(b) section 145 (attempt to commit rape);

(c) section 149 (indecent assault on female);

(d) section 156 (indecent assault on male); and

(e) section 246 (assault with intent).

4 An offence under any of the following provisions of the *Controlled Drugs and Substances Act:*

(a) section 5 (trafficking);

(b) section 6 (importing and exporting); and

(c) section 7 (production of substance).

2002, c. 1, Sch; 2014, c. 25, s. 43.

RELATED PROVISIONS

—2012, c. 1, par. 163(c)

Pending applications – references in other legislation

163 A reference to an application for a record suspension in the following provisions, as enacted by this Part, is deemed also to be a reference to an application for a pardon that is not finally disposed of on the day on which this section comes into force:

(c) paragraph 82(1)(d) and subparagraphs 119(1)(n)(iii) and 120(4)(c)(iii) of the *Youth Criminal Justice Act*

—2012, c. 1, par. 165(f)

Pardons in effect – references in other legislation

165 A reference to a record suspension in the following provisions, as enacted by this Part, is deemed also to be a reference to a pardon that is granted or issued under the *Criminal Records Act:*

(f) subsection 128(5) of the *Youth Criminal Justice Act*.

—2012, c. 1, s. 195

Offences committed before this section in force

195 Any person who, before the coming into force of this section, while he or she was a young person, committed an offence in respect of which no proceedings were commenced before that coming into force shall be dealt with under the *Youth Criminal Justice Act* as amended by this Part as if the offence occurred after that coming into force, except that

(a) the definition *violent offence* in subsection 2(1) of the *Youth Criminal Justice Act*, as enacted by subsection 167(3), does not apply in respect of the offence;

(b) paragraph 3(1)(a) of that Act, as enacted by subsection 168(1), does not apply in respect of the offence;

(c) paragraph 38(2)(f) of that Act, as enacted by section 172, does not apply in respect of the offence;

(d) paragraph 39(1)(c) of that Act, as enacted by section 173, does not apply in respect of the offence;

(e) section 75 of that Act, as enacted by section 185, does not apply in respect of the offence.

—2014, c. 25, s. 45.1

Review

45.1(1) Within five years after this section comes into force, a comprehensive review of the provisions and operation of this Act shall be undertaken by such committee of the House of Commons as may be designated or established by the House for that purpose.

Report

(2) The committee referred to in subsection (1) shall, within a year after a review is undertaken pursuant to that subsection or within such further time as the House may authorize, submit a report on the review to the Speaker of the House, including a statement of any changes the committee recommends.

Glossary

Absolute discharge: A disposition under which the court releases a young person with no obligations or restrictions on his or her freedom.

Actus reus: The physical action of committing an offence (from Latin).

Adult sentence: A young person may only be subject to an adult sentence if the young person is found guilty of an offence that is one of a pattern of repeated serious violent offences or of an offence for which an adult would receive over two years in jail, the young person is 14 years or older, and the Crown has rebutted the presumption of diminished moral blameworthiness or culpability of the young person.

Age-appropriate explanation: The clear explanation of a young person's legal rights in a language appropriate to the person's age and understanding.

Age of culpability: The age at which one is deserving of blame in the commission of a crime or offence. In Canada, the minimum age is 12 years.

Alternative measures: Under the *Young Offenders Act*, non-judicial alternatives of dealing with young persons who are in conflict with the law in a manner that reduces continued formal processing in the criminal justice system.

Appearance notice: A peace officer may issue an appearance notice to a person for an offence listed under section 553 of the *Criminal Code*, a hybrid offence, or a summary conviction offence. At this stage, a person is not yet charged with an offence.

Apprehension: The act of a child protection worker bringing a child to a place of safety, without a warrant, if the worker believes on reasonable and probable grounds that a child is in need of protection and that taking the time for a hearing or obtaining a warrant would put the child at substantial risk.

Attitude: An emotional predisposition to react in a particular way toward a particular stimulus.

Bail: The conditions, usually financial, under which a person will be released with a promise to appear in court. Bail money may be forfeited if the defendant fails to appear.

Bail hearing: (See also *Show-cause hearing*) A judicial process where it is decided whether and under what circumstances a person charged with an offence will be released (e.g., conditions imposed or posting money).

Best interests of the child: A guiding principle of legislation like the *Child, Youth and Family Services Act* or the United Nations Convention on the Rights of the Child that stipulates that in all matters affecting children, decisions must be made that are deemed to best protect a child's physical, emotional, and psychological safety and well-being.

Bullying (direct and indirect): *Direct bullying* consists of such behaviours as shoving, throwing things, taking things, choking, punching and kicking, beating, and stabbing. *Indirect bullying* consists of name-calling, taunting, spreading rumours, gossiping, threats of withdrawing friendship, the silent treatment, and exclusion from the group.

***Canadian Charter of Rights and Freedoms*:** Introduced in 1982, the *Charter* protects all Canadians, including young people from arbitrary and excessive state intervention in their lives. The *Charter* guarantees, among other things, equality before the law, whatever one's social characteristics (such as age, gender, religious affiliation, or ethnicity), and the right to due process.

Carding: The police practice of stopping individuals and requesting identification and then collecting personal data about the individual for future reference by completing a "contact card."

Child endangerment: Child maltreatment, neglect, and physical, emotional, and child abuse, including sexual molestation.

Child in need of protection: A legal definition/determination that is made based on specified criteria and evidence and serves as the basis for a protection order in child welfare matters.

Clearance rate: Refers to the proportion of criminal incidents solved by the police, also known as crimes cleared.

Common law: The part of English law that is derived from custom and judicial precedent (cases) rather than statutes. It is often contrasted with *statutory law*. Canada's legal system is based on common law (except for the province of Quebec which is based on *civil law*).

Community service order (CSO): Part of a disposition involving service work within the community, often with a voluntary organization. A judge may require the young person to perform up to 240 hours of community service.

Compensation: This usually involves a monetary payment when the offender cannot make restitution or it is inappropriate in the circumstances. It can also involve "compensation in kind" by way of personal service.

Conditional discharge: A disposition that allows for the young person "to be discharged on any conditions as the court considers appropriate." A typical condition imposed by the court is that the offender remains at work, or returns to school and is supervised. Once the young person fulfills the conditions imposed, the sentence results in an absolute discharge.

Conditional supervision order: A disposition that allows young persons to serve part of their sentence in the community with a set of restrictions or "conditions" with which they must comply.

Conference: Pursuant to s. 19 [*YCJA*], a youth court judge as well as other officers of the court such as a police officer, Crown counsel, justice of the peace, or youth worker may request that a meeting be held to give advice and help make a decision on appropriate extrajudicial measures, conditions for judicial interim release, sentences, a review of sentences, and reintegration plans. These conferences can take the form of family group conferencing, youth justice committees, community accountability panels, sentencing circles, and inter-agency case conferences.

Crime rate: A measure based on the number of *Criminal Code* offences in an area reported to the police per 100,000 population in that area.

Crimes known to police: A count of all crimes that the police are aware of, whether solved (cleared) or not.

Criminal Code of Canada: A compilation of Canadian criminal statutes. The first *Criminal Code of Canada* was compiled in 1891, drawing together a diversity of common laws and existing statutes.

Criminal Injuries Compensation Board: A quasi-judicial tribunal, created and funded by the Government of Ontario. It receives formal requests for financial compensation from victims of crime for the pain, suffering, and cost of the injuries that they have sustained.

Crossover youth: A term coined to understand the patterns among children who have been involved in the child welfare system who also become involved in the youth justice system and vice versa.

Crown cautions: The *YCJA* makes provision for provinces to establish a program that authorizes prosecutors to administer cautions to young persons, rather than starting or continuing judicial proceedings. The *YCJA* does not explicitly give a name to such cautions, but it is implicit that they are Crown prosecutor cautions.

Custody and supervision: A period of incarceration plus a period of supervision. The supervision period is to be one-half as long as the custody. The notion is that the supervision part of the sentence will assist in the rehabilitation and reintegration into society of the young person. Conditional supervision orders are generally more restrictive than probation orders.

Cyberbullying: This consists of such things as sending threatening or harassing messages, creating defamatory websites, posting a surreptitiously acquired video to embarrass the victim, or spreading malicious rumours and innuendoes through online blogs.

Day release: A type of leave usually allowing the young offender to be absent from the institution during the day to perform some duty, such as work or school, and then return at night.

Deferred custody and supervision order (DCSO): Subsection 42(2)(p) of the *YCJA* permits a DCSO no longer than six months where the young person is found guilty of an offence that is *not* a serious violent offence.

Delinquent (delinquency): A term that is falling out of use but connotes a young person or that person's behaviour as showing or characterized by a tendency to commit (minor) crime. Delinquency was formerly a type of status offence such that a youth could be charged for behaviours for which adults would not be held criminally responsible (e.g., being truant or absent from school).

Diminished moral blameworthiness: Pursuant to the *YCJA*, the principle that young offenders have less responsibility for their actions due to their age and stage of development and are thus entitled to rehabilitation and reintegration, fair and proportionate accountability, and enhanced procedural protection to protect their rights.

Disclosure: The sharing of information among counsel concerning the facts of a case. The basic rules of disclosure that apply to adult cases also apply to those of young persons. In general, the Crown must disclose its case—including evidence and the names of potential witnesses—to the young person's counsel before the trial.

Due process: The principle that the government must respect all of the legal rights a person is entitled to under the law.

Duty to report: The responsibility of a person, including a person who performs professional or official duties with respect to children, who has reasonable grounds to "suspect" that a child meets any of the criteria for being a child in need of protection, that person shall "forthwith" report the suspicion and the information on which it is based to the Children's Aid Society.

Extrajudicial measures: Means "outside the court" and refers to less formal ways of dealing with young persons who are in conflict with the law in a manner that reduces continued formal processing in the criminal justice system.

Extrajudicial sanctions: These are Crown-initiated formal interventions administered to a young person who has been accused of an offence, but where the process is a non-court (extrajudicial) one.

Family reunification: A core principle of the *Child, Youth and Family Services Act*, which brings children into care with the goal to furnish parents with time and resources to improve their parenting so that children can be returned to their parents.

Fine: A financial penalty. The young person can be fined an amount no larger than would be required of an adult for a similar offence. The maximum fine under the *YCJA* is $1,000.

Forthwith: (In the context of a duty to report) Right away; without delay.

General deterrence (societal deterrence): An objective of the criminal justice system based on the idea that when other members of society are aware of the punishment of an offender, they will be less likely to commit that offence themselves.

Healing circles: An expression of restorative justice where the victim, the offender, and the community come together to decide what and by what means each can have their dignity restored and made integral again.

Higher degree of restraint: One of two levels of custody referred to in the *YCJA*. One level is the "least degree of restraint," the other level is referred to variously as "more than a minimal degree of restraint," "a higher degree of restraint," and "increase the degree of restraint." Ontario has decided to use the more well-known term *secure custody*.

Houses of refuge: An institutional response to the problem of juvenile crime that grew out of the juvenile sections of the English workhouses of the 16th and 17th centuries. Their principal features were that they kept youths separate from adults and focused on hard work and discipline.

Hybrid offences: Offences, such as some types of assault, that can be treated as either summary or indictable offences at the discretion of the Crown.

In care: According to the *Child, Youth and Family Services Act*, a child who is placed with a residential care provider (e.g., foster home, group home) after having been deemed to be a child in need of protection.

Indictable offences: Offences where the potential penalty is greater than either six months in jail or a fine of more than $2,000. More often, indictable offences carry sentences of two or more years' imprisonment (including life).

Intensive rehabilitative custody and supervision (IRCS) program: An exceptional order under paragraph 42(2)(r) and subsection 42(7) of the *YCJA*. Since 2003, this therapeutic sentencing option is available for youth suffering from a mental illness or disorder, psychological disorder, or an emotional disturbance and who are convicted of murder, attempted murder, manslaughter, and aggravated sexual assault.

Intensive support and supervision program (ISSP): This is a clinically focused, community-based program for young offenders. This sentencing option is used if the Provincial Director has determined that an alternative to custody is needed for young persons who are found guilty of a criminal offence and who are diagnosed with a mental health disorder or developmental delay, or both (dual diagnosis). Such programs are to address the needs of the young person and contribute to rehabilitation and reintegration without placing society at risk.

***Juvenile Delinquents Act (JDA)*:** The *JDA* (1908) was a law passed by the Parliament of Canada to better the response to juvenile crime. The act established procedures for handling juvenile offenders, including implementing that government assume control of juvenile offenders.

Least degree of restraint: One of two levels of custody referred to in the *YCJA*. This involves a minimal degree of restraint in contrast to other levels referred to variously as "more than a minimal degree of restraint," "a higher degree of restraint," and "increase the degree of restraint." Ontario has decided to use the more familiar term *open custody*.

Legal infant: English common law defined a person between the ages of 7 and 14 years as a legal infant; that is, a person with limited ability to form criminal intent.

***Mens rea*:** A guilty mind; a legal concept used to denote criminal intent (from Latin).

Moderator (conference leader): A member of the restorative justice program team who begins the meeting by reminding everyone why they have come together and the ground rules to which they have already agreed and reminds participants that their common goal is about reparation and moving forward.

Neglected minors: According to the *New York Family Court Act* of 1963, any minor "under 18 years of age . . . whose environment is injurious to his welfare or whose behaviour is injurious to his welfare or that of others."

Notification to a parent: When a police officer arrests and keeps a young person in custody, section 26 of the *YCJA* obliges the officer to notify the parent of the young person as soon as possible. The parent must be contacted and told, either orally or in writing, where the young person is detained and the reason for the arrest.

Official statistics on crime: Information on crime collected by official agencies, such as the police, the courts, and the corrections system.

Onus: Burden of responsibility or proof.

Open custody/detention: The removal of a young person from his or her home and placement in a group home for a fixed length of time.

Open temporary detention program: A facility in which restrictions less stringent than in a secure temporary detention program are imposed on the liberty of young persons.

Parens patriae: A Latin term meaning "parent of the country" used to denote the role of the state as guardians of underage and disabled persons. Under this doctrine, the jurisdiction of the Chancery Court could be invoked to intercede on behalf of children when their parents or guardians were neglecting or mistreating them.

Person in authority: Under the *YCJA,* an adult who is directly involved in the administration of justice or prosecution of offences. This would normally include probation officers and anyone who is a peace officer.

Persons in need of supervision (P.I.N.S.): The *New York Family Court Act* of 1963 created a separate category of youths appearing in front of the family court known as persons in need of supervision or P.I.N.S. This classification was an attempt to deal with "obnoxious" or "undesirable" youthful behaviour not strictly of a criminal nature.

Plea bargain: The Crown may use its judgment and agree to reduce charges if the offender agrees to enter a guilty plea to a lesser offence. This is a trade-off whereby the Crown and the accused's lawyer weigh the likelihood of conviction against the cost of conviction to the accused and the cost of prosecution to the community.

Police caution: A notice to a young person and his or her parents about the offence that has been alleged. This is just short of laying a charge, which would have led to judicial proceedings. This might take the form of a letter.

Police warning: An informal notice (admonitions) issued to a young person by a police officer. Warnings are a more serious intervention than "doing nothing further," but a less serious intervention than issuing a caution.

Positive correlation: A relationship between two variables in which both variables move in tandem. A positive correlation exists when one variable decreases as the other variable decreases, or one variable increases while the other increases.

Preliminary inquiry: For serious offences, the accused youth will also have to make a decision about whether to have a hearing called a preliminary inquiry—an opportunity for the Crown to present its case so that a determination can be made whether there is sufficient evidence to proceed to trial.

Pre-sentence assessment: Occasionally, a young person may be suffering from disturbances that are severe enough that the court should consider them when making a disposition. Section 34 of the *YCJA* indicates the conditions under which the court can order an assessment of the medical, psychological, or psychiatric condition of the young person. Those assessments should be based on a clinical evaluation of the emotional, cognitive, and social functioning of the young person along with the needs of that person, the individual and social risk posed, and the need for intervention.

Pre-sentence report: A report, usually prepared and written by a probation officer or "youth worker," to assist the youth court judge in the sentencing process. Pre-sentence reports contain information gathered from the young person, the young person's family, victims, and others who might have relevant information.

Presumptive offence: Prior to the *YCJA* 2012 amendments, there was a category of offence called a "presumptive offence." The Supreme Court ruled that this presumption was unconstitutional (*R. v. D.B.*, 2008 S.C.C. 25), and this concept was abolished in the 2012 amendments. Prior to this ruling, pursuant to s. 2(1) of the unamended *YCJA*, this was an offence that was committed by a person who had attained at least the age of 14 years and that fell into one of the following categories: first-degree or second-degree murder; attempt to commit murder; manslaughter; aggravated sexual assault; or a serious violent offence for which an adult was liable to imprisonment for more than two years, after having had at least two judicial determinations, at different proceedings, that the young person had committed a serious violent offence. The commission of one these serious crimes came with the presumption that an adult sentence would be imposed unless the Crown gave notice to seek a youth sentence or the youth could persuade the court that a youth sentence would hold the youth accountable.

Pre-trial detention: Refers to detaining an accused person in a criminal case before the trial has taken place, either because of failure to post bail or due to denial of release under a pre-trial detention statute.

Principle of proportionality: A basic legal principle wherein less serious offences should result in less severe consequences and more serious offences should result in more severe consequences; often stated as "the punishment should fit the crime."

Probation order: An order that the young person must "keep the peace and be of good behaviour" and must "appear before the youth justice court when required to do so." These usually may be for no longer than two years.

Prohibition: The forbidding by the youth justice court judge of a young person from owning something that they could otherwise legally possess if they had not been involved in the commission of the offence.

Promise to appear: Upon being issued an appearance notice, the accused is asked to sign a notice promising to appear before the court for trial on a specific date.

Proportion: The number of cases in a subgroup divided by the total number of cases in the whole group.

Provincial Director: A term found often in the *YCJA*; it applies to a fairly broad category of people. Generally, it refers to a person, a group or class of persons, or a body appointed by a province to perform a function under the *YCJA*. Those in charge of probation services as well as persons in charge of provincial correctional facilities, for example, are provincial directors.

Publication: The public release of information relating to the offence, hearing, adjudication, disposition, or appeal of a young person. There are strict limitations on what information can be released to the public.

Publication ban: The prohibition in subsection 110(1) of the *YCJA* is clear: "No person shall publish the name of a young person, or any other information related to a young person, if it would identify the young person as a young person dealt with under this *Act*."

Rate: A type of ratio with a large number—usually 1,000 or 100,000—as its fixed base. It is used to compare events that actually occurred with the potential number of events that could have occurred.

Ratio: The comparison of one portion of a population count with another, as in the number of women in a community in comparison with the number of men.

Reasonable grounds: (In the context of a duty to report) *CYFSA* section 125(6) stipulates that various professionals have a legally mandated obligation to immediately report suspicions of child abuse and/or neglect to the appropriate CAS where there are "reasonable grounds." The threshold of reasonable grounds does not require that the person conduct any type of investigation—suspicion is sufficient to invoke the duty to report.

Recognizance: A promise to do something, typically appear in court, that may be with or without the posting of surety. Where no bond is required, it is called personal recognizance.

Referral to a program: Referral to a service in the community that may assist the young person not to commit offences in the future. Such referrals are considered to be a more serious intervention than a caution, but stop short of starting judicial proceedings. Referrals require the consent of the young person.

Rehabilitation: An objective of the criminal justice system that involves a set of interventions to change a person so they will function as law-abiding members of society.

Re-integrative leave: At the discretion of the Provincial Director, a young person may be allowed to be absent from custody with or without an escort for no more than 30 days. It is used for medical, compassionate, or humanitarian reasons, or for the purpose of rehabilitation or reintegration into the community.

Reprimand: A statement by the youth justice court judge that indicates to the young person that some law has been violated. The statement may indicate the severity with which the offence could be dealt with and the reasons why, on this occasion and in these circumstances, the judge considers that the young person should have learned the appropriate lesson.

Responsible person: An adult who is willing and able to take care of, and exercise control over, the young person and under whose care the young person is willing to be placed.

Restitution: An objective of the criminal justice system that is about giving back (restoring) the victim to the original state or condition, before the crime that victimized them. When possible, it involves returning any property that may have been taken to its rightful owner.

Restorative justice initiatives: Opportunities created for the victim, the offender, and the community to come together so that the victim may indicate the nature, extent, and consequences of the harm received. Offenders have the opportunity to express sorrow, shame, or other emotions for the consequences of their behaviour. The community indicates how it too has been affected and helps to determine how the situation may best be dealt with in order that a resolution may be restorative for all parties.

Restraint: An objective of the criminal justice system where society is protected by incapacitating (e.g., house arrest, parole, incarceration) the individual from committing further crimes.

Retribution: An objective of the criminal justice system that means to give back to the perpetrator in equal measure what was done to or taken from the victim.

Reverse onus: This refers to the burden (or onus) being shifted from the Crown to the young person to show cause as to why release is justified.

Secondary caution: When an interview takes place, the police officer must advise the young person of his or her legal rights. It is also essential to give the young person what is known as a "secondary caution." This is to help ensure that the young person has not been pressured or coerced into giving a statement.

Secondary victimization: This usually happens after the police or social service agents leave the scene of an offence or complaint. The offender retaliates because the victim either called or was responsible for calling the police.

Secure custody/detention: The placement of a young person in a more restrictive (higher level of restraint), jail-type facility with bars and electronic surveillance to prevent leaving.

Secure temporary detention program: A facility in which restrictions are continuously imposed on the liberty of young persons by physical barriers, close staff supervision, and/or limited access to the community.

Self-report survey: A survey asking people how much crime they have committed.

Sentencing hearing: This hearing takes place after the issue of guilt has been decided. At this point, the court decides on the merits of an application of a youth sentence or of an adult sentence.

Serious offence: An indictable offence under an Act of Parliament for which the maximum punishment is imprisonment for five years or more.

Serious violent offence: An offence under the *Criminal Code* that includes first-degree murder or second-degree murder (section 231 or 235); attempt to commit murder (section 239); manslaughter (section 232, 234, or 236); or aggravated sexual assault (section 273).

Show-cause hearing: (See also *Bail hearing*) A judicial process where it is decided whether and under what circumstances a person charged with an offence will be released (e.g., conditions imposed or posting money).

Specific deterrence (individual deterrence): An objective of the criminal justice system based on the idea that there can be interventions, in the form of punishment or pain, that, if inflicted on the perpetrator, will make it less likely that the crime will again be committed by that person.

Status offence: An act that is considered to be an offence or crime that would not be an offence if committed by a person who was an adult.

Summary offences: Offences where the potential penalty is a fine of not more than $2,000 or imprisonment for six months, or both. When a youth is charged with a summary offence it means that the youth will be tried in a provincial court, with a judge alone (no jury option), proceeding without an indictment; and, as a "lesser" offence, the accused is not fingerprinted or photographed.

Surety: The posting of money or other collateral to ensure the accused person's appearance in court.

Symbolism: An objective of the criminal justice system based on the idea that the presence of laws and the fact that violators are processed serves an important indication of the mores (societal conventions and customs) of the society.

Temporary care agreement: Pursuant to the *Child, Youth and Family Services Act*, children can be brought into care with the consent of the parent(s).

Temporary detention: Normally refers to the period when the young person is in a detention centre before sentencing. Typically, this would occur if the young person has committed a very serious offence or has a history of non-appearance and had been denied bail as a consequence.

Temporary restraint: This occurs when the young person is in the custody of a police officer before a youth justice court judge can remand (order) the young person to a detention centre.

Truant: A student who stays away from school without leave or explanation.

Undertaking: A set of conditions (e.g., parental supervision, school attendance, or a curfew) that the youth must follow when released following being issued a notice of appearance.

Unfounded crime: An offence reported to the police that either did not take place or a behaviour that, upon investigation, does not constitute an illegal act.

Victim impact statement: A written presentation, prepared by a victim of crime, that describes, for the court and the offender, the depth and seriousness of their injury and how it has affected their life, relationships, health, finances, and trust in others.

Victimization survey: A survey asking people if they have been the victim of a crime.

Violent offence: An offence committed by a young person that includes as an element the causing of bodily harm; an attempt or a threat to cause bodily harm; or a young person endangers the life or safety of another person by creating a substantial likelihood of causing bodily harm while committing an offence.

Ward of the Crown: A child who has been found by the court to be in need of protection and is placed in the care of a Children's Aid Society. Once a child has been made a Crown ward, he or she is eligible for adoption, kinship care (live with relatives), customary care, legal custody by a family member, independent living situation, or a foster parent/family.

Warrant: Generally, an instrument that is issued by a magistrate, authorizing police to make an arrest, seize property, or conduct a search. Under the *Child, Youth and Family Services Act*, it is an order issued by a justice of the peace that authorizes a child protection worker to bring a child to a place of safety.

Young Offenders Act (YOA): The *Young Offenders Act* (*YOA*) was an Act of the Parliament of Canada, granted Royal Assent in 1982, that regulated the criminal prosecution of Canadian youths. The act was repealed in 2003 with the passing of the *Youth Criminal Justice Act* (*YCJA*).

Young person: Under the *YCJA*, someone "who is or, in the absence of evidence to the contrary, appears to be 12 years of age or more, but under 18 years of age." This also aligns with the definition of a young person in the *CYFSA*.

***Youth Criminal Justice Act* (*YCJA*):** The *YCJA* (2003) is the law that governs Canada's youth justice system. It applies to youth who are at least 12 but under 18 years old, who are alleged to have committed criminal offences.

Youth justice court: Under the *YCJA*, any court that deals with a young person.

References

Abramovitch, R., M.P. Badali, and M. Rohan. 1995. Young people's understanding and assertion of their rights to silence and legal counsel. *Canadian Journal of Criminology* 37: 1–18.

Abramovitch, R., K.L. Higgins-Biss, and S.R. Biss. 1993. Young persons' comprehension of waivers in criminal proceedings. *Canadian Journal of Criminology* 35: 309–22.

Allen, F.A. 1964. *The Borderland of Criminal Justice: Essays in Law and Criminology*. Chicago, IL: University of Chicago Press.

Avison, W.R., and P.C. Whitehead. 1997. *Evaluation of London Family Court Clinic's (YOA) Section 13 Assessments*. London, ON: London Family Court Clinic.

Avison, W.R., and P.C. Whitehead. 1998. *Evaluation of the London Family Court Clinic's Clinical Support Program*. London, ON: Ontario Ministry of Community and Social Services.

Bala, N. 1997. *Young Offenders Law*. Concord, ON: Irwin.

Bala, N. 2015. Changing professional culture and reducing use of courts and custody for youth: The *Youth Criminal Justice Act* and Bill C-10. *Saskatchewan Law Review* 78: 127–80.

Bala, N., R. De Filippis, and K. Hunter. 2013. Crossover youth: Improving Ontario's responses. *Association of Family & Conciliation Courts, Ontario Chapter*, 1–46. Retrieved from http://afccontario.ca/wp-content/uploads/2015/11/Bala-De-Filippis-Hunter-Crossover-Kids.pdf.

Bala, N., and D. Mahoney. 1995. *Responding to Criminal Behaviour of Children Under 12: An Analysis of Canadian Law and Practice*. Paper submitted to the House of Commons Committee on Justice and Legal Affairs for Phase II of Young Offenders Study, July 1995, available at http://qsilver.queensu.ca/ law/balalpapers/ crimbeh.htm.

Barnes, H.E. 1972. *The Story of Punishment*. Montclair, NJ: Patterson Smith.

Broll, R., and L. Huey. 2015. "Just being mean to somebody isn't a police matter": Police perspectives on policing cyberbullying. *Journal of School Violence* 14: 155–76.

Brown, J.A., P.C. Unsinger, and H.W. More. 1990. *Law Enforcement and Social Welfare: The Emergency Response*. Springfield, IL: C.C. Thomas.

Brown, P.C., H.L. Roediger, and M.A. McDaniel. 2014. *Make It Stick: The Science of Successful Learning*. Cambridge, MA: The Belknap Press of Harvard University Press.

Carr, G., and J. Ecker. 1996. Recommendation from the Task Force on Strict Discipline for Young Offenders. Toronto, ON: Ministry of the Solicitor General and Correctional Services.

Carrigan, D.O. 1998. *Juvenile Delinquency in Canada: A History*. Concord, ON: Irwin.

Carrington, P.J., J.V. Roberts, and S. Davis-Barron. 2011. The last chance sanction in youth court: Exploring the deferred custody and supervision order. *Canadian Criminal Law Review* 15: 299–336.

Carson, B.A., and B.K. Macmurray. 1996. Child abuse and neglect. In J.E. Hendricks and B. Byers, eds., *Crisis Intervention in Criminal Justice/Social Service*, 2nd ed. Springfield, IL: C.C. Thomas.

Chuang, E., and R. Wells. 2010. The role of interagency collaboration in facilitating receipt of behavioral health services for youth involved with child welfare and juvenile justice. *Child Youth Services Review* 32(12): 1814–22.

Edmison, A. 1977. Some aspects of nineteenth-century Canadian prisons. In W.T. McGrath, ed., *Crime and Its Treatment in Canada*. Toronto, ON: Macmillan.

Finlay, J. 2003. Crossover Kids: Care to Custody. A Report (draft paper). Office of Child and Family Service Advocacy.

Finlay, J. 2012. Keeping kids safe in custody. In A. Westhues and B. Wharf, eds., *Canadian Social Policy Issues and Perspectives*, 5th ed. (pp. 253–71). Waterloo: Wilfrid Laurier University Press.

Giwa, S., C.E. James, U. Anucha, and K. Schwartz. 2014. Community policing—a shared responsibility: A voice centred relational method analysis of a police/youth-of-color dialogue. *Journal of Ethnicity in Criminal Justice* 12: 218–45.

Government of Canada, Department of Justice. 1965. *Juvenile Delinquency in Canada*. Ottawa, ON: Government of Canada.

Hagan, J., and J. Leon. 1977. Rediscovering delinquency: Social history, political ideology and the sociology of law. *American Sociological Review* 42: 587–98.

Haight, W., L. Bidwell, W.S. Choi, and M. Cho. 2016. An evaluation of the Crossover Youth Practice Model (CYPM): Recidivism outcomes for maltreated youth involved in the juvenile justice system. *Children and Youth Services Review* 65: 78–85.

Hayle, S., S. Wortley, and J. Tanner. 2016. Race, street life, and policing: Implications for racial profiling. *Canadian Journal of Criminology and Criminal Justice* 58(3): 322–53.

Herz, D., P. Lee, L. Lutz, J. Tuell, S. Bilchik, E. Kelley, and R.F. Kennedy. 2012. *Addressing the Needs of Multi-system Youth: Strengthening the Connection between Child Welfare and Juvenile Justice*. Washington: Center for Juvenile Justice Reform.

Hobbes, T. 1996 (1651). *Leviathan*. Cambridge, UK: Cambridge University Press.

Hoskins, E., and M. Meilleur. 2012. *Ontario's Youth Action Plan*. Retrieved from http://www.children.gov.on.ca/htdocs/English/documents/youthandthelaw/youthactionplan/yap.pdf.

Hurley, A. 1905. Necessity for the lawyer in the juvenile court. *Proceedings of the National Conference of Charities and Correction* 32: 172.

Kenney, J.P., D.G. Pursuit, D.E. Fuller, et al. 1989. *Police Work with Juveniles and the Administration of Juvenile Justice*. Springfield, IL: C.C. Thomas.

Kieran, S. 1986. *The Family Matters: Two Centuries of Family Law and Life in Ontario*. Toronto, ON: Key Porter.

Krameddine, Y.I., D. DeMarco, R. Hassel, and P.H. Silverstone. 2013. A novel training program for police officers that improves interactions with mentally ill individuals and is cost-effective. *Frontiers in Psychiatry* 4: 1–10.

Kwok, S.M., R. Houwer, H. HeavyShield, R. Weatherstone, and D. Tam. 2017. Supporting Positive Outcomes for Youth Involved with the Law. Youth Research and Evaluation eXchange (YouthREX). Toronto, ON.

Leschied, A.W., D. Chiodo, P.C. Whitehead, and D. Hurley. 2006. The association of poverty with child welfare service and child and family clinical outcomes. *Community, Work & Family* 9(1): 29–46. https://doi.org/10.1080/13668800500420988.

Livingstone N., G. Macdonald, and N. Carr. 2013. Restorative justice conferencing for reducing recidivism in young offenders (aged 7 to 21). *Cochrane Database of Systematic Reviews* 2. DOI: 10.1002/14651858.CD008898.pub2.

Lutz, L., and M. Stewart. 2015. *The crossover youth practice model (CYPM).* (B. Shay, Ed.). Washington: Center for Juvenile Justice Reform (Georgetown University).

MacGill, H.G. 1925. *The Juvenile Court in Canada: Origins, Underlying Principles, Governing Legislation and Practice.* Ottawa, ON: Canadian Council on Child Welfare.

Malakieh, J. 2017. Youth correctional statistics in Canada, 2015/2016. *Juristat* (Catalogue no. 85-002-X). Ottawa, ON: Statistics Canada, Canadian Centre for Justice Statistics.

Maxim, P.S., and P.C. Whitehead. 1997. *Explaining Crime.* Boston, MA: Butterworths.

McCuish, E.C., J. Cale, and R.R. Corrado. 2017. Abuse experiences of family members, child maltreatment, and the development of sex offending among incarcerated adolescent males. *International Journal of Offender Therapy and Comparative Criminology* 61(2): 127–49.

Meng, Y., S. Giwa, and U. Anucha. 2015. Is there racial discrimination in police stop-and-searches of Black youth? A Toronto case study. *Canadian Journal of Family and Youth* 7(1): 115–48.

Mennel, R.M. 1973. *Thorns and Thistles.* Hanover, NH: University Press of New England.

Mewett, A.W., and M. Manning. 1978. *Criminal Law.* Toronto, ON: Butterworths.

Miladinovic, Z. 2016. Youth court statistics in Canada 2014/2015. *Juristat* (Catalogue no. 85-002-X). Ottawa, ON: Statistics Canada.

O'Connor, C.D. 2008. Citizen attitudes toward the police in Canada. *Policing: An International Journal of Police Strategies & Management* 31(4): 578–95.

Ontario Association of Children's Aid Societies (OACAS). n.d. Facts and figures. Retrieved from http://www.oacas.org/childrens-aid-child-protection/facts-and-figures/.

Ontario Ministry of Children and Youth Services. n.d. Youth leaving care. Available at http://www.children.gov.on.ca/htdocs/English/childrensaid/leavingcare.aspx.

Ontario Ministry of Children and Youth Services. 2015. Supporting effective transitions for Ontario youth. Toronto: ON.

Ontario Ministry of Children and Youth Services. 2017. Ontario strengthens legislation for child and youth services. Retrieved from http://www.children.gov.on.ca/htdocs/English/professionals/childwelfare/modern-legislation.aspx.

Owusu-Bempah, A., and S. Wortley. 2014. Race, crime, and criminal justice in Canada. In S.M. Bucerius and M. Tonry, eds. *The Oxford Handbook of Ethnicity, Crime, and Immigration* (pp. 281–320). Toronto, ON: Oxford University Press.

Peirone, A., E. Maticka-Tyndale, K. Gbadebo, and J. Kerr. 2017. The social environment of daily life and perceptions of police and/or court discrimination among African, Caribbean, and Black youth. *Canadian Journal of Criminology and Criminal Justice* 59(3): 346–72.

Platt, A. 1969. *The Child Savers.* Chicago, IL: University of Chicago Press.

Platt, P. 1991. *Police Guide to the Young Offenders Act.* Markham, ON: Butterworths.

Presidential Commission on Law Enforcement and Administration of Justice. 1967. *Task Force Report: Juvenile Delinquency and Youth Crime.* Washington, DC: U.S.G.P.O.

Public Safety Canada. 2007. *Youth Gangs in Canada: What do We Know?* Ottawa, ON: Government of Canada. Retrieved from https://www.publicsafety.gc.ca/cnt/rsrcs/pblctns/gngs-cnd/index-en.aspx.

Public Safety Canada. 2012. *A Statistical Snapshot of Youth at Risk and Youth Offending in Canada.* Ottawa, ON: National Crime Prevention Centre (NCPC).

Rawana, J., P. Gentile, K.R. Gangier, K. Davis, and T.E. Moore. 2015. Mental health issues and youth offending: Trends, theories, and treatments. In R. Carrado, A. Leschied, P. Lussier, and J. Whatley, eds., *Serious and Violent Young Offenders and Youth Criminal Justice: A Canadian Perspective* (pp. 251–90). Burnaby, BC: Simon Fraser Publications.

Reasons, C., S. Hassan, M. Ma, L. Monchalin, M. Bige, C. Paras, and S. Arora. 2016. Race and criminal justice in Canada. *International Journal of Criminal Justice Sciences* 11(2): 75–99.

Rendleman, D.K. 1971. *Parens Patriae:* From chancery to the juvenile court. In F.L. Faust, and P.J. Brantingham, eds., *Juvenile Justice Philosophy.* St. Paul, MN: West.

Residential Services Review Board. 2016. Because Young People Matter: Report of the Residential Services Review Panel. Ontario: Queen's Printer. Available at http://www.children.gov.on.ca/htdocs/English/professionals/childwelfare/residential/residential-review-panel-report/youthjustice.aspx.

Ross, P.N. 1998. *Arresting Violence: A Resource Guide for Schools and Their Communities.* Toronto: Ontario Public School Teachers' Federation.

Royal Canadian Mounted Police (RCMP). 2017. Bullying and Cyberbullying. Retrieved from http://www.rcmp-grc.gc.ca/cycp-cpcj/bull-inti/index-eng.htm.

Ryan, J.P., J.M. Marshall, D. Herz, and P.M. Hernandez. 2008. Juvenile delinquency in child welfare: Investigating group home effects. *Children and Youth Services Review* 30(9): 1088–99.

Sacco, V.F., and L.W. Kennedy. 1998. *The Criminal Event.* Scarborough, ON: ITP Nelson.

Salhany, R.E. 1997. *The Police Manual of Arrest, Seizure and Interrogation.* Scarborough, ON: Carswell.

Schwartz, D. 2013. Kingston Pen: 7 things to know about Canada's notorious prison: High-security prison closes after 178 years. CBC News. Retrieved March 3, 2018, from http://www.cbc.ca/news/canada/kingston-pen-7-things-to-know-about-canada-s-notorious-prison-1.1865605.

Scott, W.L. 1952. *The Juvenile Court in Law*, 4th ed. Ottawa, ON: Canadian Welfare Council.

Stanbrook, M.B. 2014. Stopping cyberbullying requires a combined societal effort. *Canadian Medical Association Journal* 186(7): 483.

Statistics Canada. 2012. Portrait of families and living arrangements in Canada. Ottawa, ON. Retrieved from http://www12.statcan.gc.ca/census-recensement/2011/as-sa/98-312-x/98-312-x2011001-eng.cfm

Statistics Canada (*Juristat*). 2012. Definitions. Available at https://www.statcan.gc.ca/pub/85-002-x/2012001/definitions-eng.htm.

Stewart, V.L. 1974. *The Development of Juvenile Justice in Canada*. Philadelphia, PA: Center for Studies in Criminology & Criminal Law, University of Pennsylvania.

Sutherland, E.H., and D.R. Cressey. 1974. *Criminology*, 6th ed. Philadelphia, PA: Lippincott.

Taylor, J. 2017. The ultimate goal is to reduce the number of children in care: Indigenous Affairs Minister. CBC News. Retrieved March 29, 2017, from http://www.cbc.ca/news/canada/manitoba/manitoba-carolyn-bennett-child-welfare-1.4042484.

Treger, H. 1981. Police–social work cooperation. *Journal of Contemporary Social Work* 62: 426–33.

Van Ness, D.W., and K.H. Strong, 2006. *Restoring Justice*. Cincinnati: Anderson.

Waite, E.E. 1921. How far can court procedure be socialized without impairing individual rights? *Journal of Criminal Law, Criminology and Police Science* 12: 339.

Whitehead, P.C., and W.R. Avison. 1998. *An Evaluation of the Impact of Changes in Funding on Section 13 Assessments under the Young Offenders Act*. London, ON: Ontario Ministry of Community and Social Services.

Whitehead, P.C., A. Leschied, D. Chiodo, and D. Hurley. 2004. Referrals and admissions to the Children's Aid Society: A test of four hypotheses. *Child and Youth Care Forum* 33: 425–440.

Wolfgang, M.E., T.P. Thornberry, and M.F. Robert. 1987. *From Boy to Man, from Delinquency to Crime*. Chicago, IL: University of Chicago Press.

Wortley, S., and A. Owusu-Bempah. 2011. The usual suspects: Police stop and search practices in Canada. *Policing & Society* 21(4): 395–407.

Wu, Y., R. Lake, and L. Cao. 2015. Race, social bonds, and juvenile attitudes toward the police. *Justice Quarterly* 32(3): 445–70.

Copyright Acknowledgements

Index